FORM AND REFORM IN EIGHTEENTH-CENTURY SPAIN
UTOPIAN NARRATIVES AND SOCIO-POLITICAL DEBATE

LEGENDA

LEGENDA is the Modern Humanities Research Association's book imprint for new research in the Humanities. Founded in 1995 by Malcolm Bowie and others within the University of Oxford, Legenda has always been a collaborative publishing enterprise, directly governed by scholars. The Modern Humanities Research Association (MHRA) joined this collaboration in 1998, became half-owner in 2004, in partnership with Maney Publishing and then Routledge, and has since 2016 been sole owner. Titles range from medieval texts to contemporary cinema and form a widely comparative view of the modern humanities, including works on Arabic, Catalan, English, French, German, Greek, Italian, Portuguese, Russian, Spanish, and Yiddish literature. Editorial boards and committees of more than 60 leading academic specialists work in collaboration with bodies such as the Society for French Studies, the British Comparative Literature Association and the Association of Hispanists of Great Britain & Ireland.

The MHRA encourages and promotes advanced study and research in the field of the modern humanities, especially modern European languages and literature, including English, and also cinema. It aims to break down the barriers between scholars working in different disciplines and to maintain the unity of humanistic scholarship. The Association fulfils this purpose through the publication of journals, bibliographies, monographs, critical editions, and the MHRA Style Guide, and by making grants in support of research. Membership is open to all who work in the Humanities, whether independent or in a University post, and the participation of younger colleagues entering the field is especially welcomed.

ALSO PUBLISHED BY THE ASSOCIATION

Critical Texts
Tudor and Stuart Translations • New Translations • European Translations
MHRA Library of Medieval Welsh Literature

MHRA Bibliographies
Publications of the Modern Humanities Research Association

The Annual Bibliography of English Language & Literature
Austrian Studies
Modern Language Review
Portuguese Studies
The Slavonic and East European Review
Working Papers in the Humanities
The Yearbook of English Studies

www.mhra.org.uk
www.legendabooks.com

STUDIES IN HISPANIC AND LUSOPHONE CULTURES

Studies in Hispanic and Lusophone Cultures are selected and edited by the Association of Hispanists of Great Britain & Ireland. The series seeks to publish the best new research in all areas of the literature, thought, history, culture, film, and languages of Spain, Spanish America, and the Portuguese-speaking world.

The Association of Hispanists of Great Britain & Ireland is a professional association which represents a very diverse discipline, in terms of both geographical coverage and objects of study. Its website showcases new work by members, and publicises jobs, conferences and grants in the field.

Editorial Committee
Chair: Professor Trevor Dadson (Queen Mary, University of London)
Professor Catherine Davies (University of Nottingham)
Professor Sally Faulkner (University of Exeter)
Professor Andrew Ginger (University of Bristol)
Professor James Mandrell (Brandeis University, USA)
Professor Hilary Owen (University of Manchester)
Professor Christopher Perriam (University of Manchester)
Professor Philip Swanson (University of Sheffield)

Managing Editor
Dr Graham Nelson
41 Wellington Square, Oxford OX1 2JF, UK

www.legendabooks.com/series/shlc

STUDIES IN HISPANIC AND LUSOPHONE CULTURES

1. *Unamuno's Theory of the Novel*, by C. A. Longhurst
2. *Pessoa's Geometry of the Abyss: Modernity and the* Book of Disquiet, by Paulo de Medeiros
3. *Artifice and Invention in the Spanish Golden Age*, edited by Stephen Boyd and Terence O'Reilly
4. *The Latin American Short Story at its Limits: Fragmentation, Hybridity and Intermediality*, by Lucy Bell
5. *Spanish New York Narratives 1898–1936: Modernisation, Otherness and Nation*, by David Miranda-Barreiro
6. *The Art of Ana Clavel: Ghosts, Urinals, Dolls, Shadows and Outlaw Desires*, by Jane Elizabeth Lavery
7. *Alejo Carpentier and the Musical Text*, by Katia Chornik
8. *Britain, Spain and the Treaty of Utrecht 1713-2013*, edited by Trevor J. Dadson and J. H. Elliott
9. *Books and Periodicals in Brazil 1768-1930: A Transatlantic Perspective*, edited by Ana Cláudia Suriani da Silva and Sandra Guardini Vasconcelos
10. *Lisbon Revisited: Urban Masculinities in Twentieth-Century Portuguese Fiction*, by Rhian Atkin
11. *Urban Space, Identity and Postmodernity in 1980s Spain: Rethinking the Movida*, by Maite Usoz de la Fuente
12. *Santería, Vodou and Resistance in Caribbean Literature: Daughters of the Spirits*, by Paul Humphrey
13. *Reprojecting the City: Urban Space and Dissident Sexualities in Recent Latin American Cinema*, by Benedict Hoff
14. *Rethinking Juan Rulfo's Creative World: Prose, Photography, Film*, edited by Dylan Brennan and Nuala Finnegan
15. *The Last Days of Humanism: A Reappraisal of Quevedo's Thought*, by Alfonso Rey
16. *Catalan Narrative 1875-2015*, edited by Jordi Larios and Montserrat Lunati
17. *Islamic Culture in Spain to 1614: Essays and Studies*, by L. P. Harvey
18. *Film Festivals: Cinema and Cultural Exchange*, by Mar Diestro-Dópido
19. *St Teresa of Avila: Her Writings and Life*, edited by Terence O'Reilly, Colin Thompson and Lesley Twomey
20. *(Un)veiling Bodies: A Trajectory of Chilean Post-Dictatorship Documentary*, by Elizabeth Ramírez Soto

Form and Reform in Eighteenth-Century Spain

Utopian Narratives and Socio-Political Debate

Carla Almanza-Gálvez

LEGENDA

Studies in Hispanic and Lusophone Cultures 33
Modern Humanities Research Association
2019

*Published by Legenda
an imprint of the Modern Humanities Research Association
Salisbury House, Station Road, Cambridge CB1 2LA*

*ISBN 978-1-78188-585-7 (HB)
ISBN 978-1-78188-586-4 (PB)*

*First published 2019
Paperback edition 2021*

All rights reserved. No part of this publication may be reproduced or disseminated or transmitted in any form or by any means, electronic, mechanical, photocopying, recording or otherwise, or stored in any retrieval system, or otherwise used in any manner whatsoever without written permission of the copyright owner, except in accordance with the provisions of the Copyright, Designs and Patents Act 1988, or under the terms of a licence permitting restricted copying issued in the UK by the Copyright Licensing Agency Ltd, Saffron House, 6–10 Kirby Street, London EC1N 8TS, England, or in the USA by the Copyright Clearance Center, 222 Rosewood Drive, Danvers MA 01923. Application for the written permission of the copyright owner to reproduce any part of this publication must be made by email to legenda@mhra.org.uk.

Disclaimer: Statements of fact and opinion contained in this book are those of the author and not of the editors or the Modern Humanities Research Association. The publisher makes no representation, express or implied, in respect of the accuracy of the material in this book and cannot accept any legal responsibility or liability for any errors or omissions that may be made.

Trademark notice: Product or corporate names may be trademarks or registered trademarks, and are used only for identification and explanation without intent to infringe.

© *Modern Humanities Research Association 2019*

Copy-Editor: Richard Correll

CONTENTS

	Acknowledgements	ix
	Introduction	1
PART I: THE LITERARY AND SOCIO-POLITICAL FOUNDATIONS OF SPANISH UTOPIANISM		
1	Utopian Fiction and the Morean Model	15
2	Colonial Utopianism and Eighteenth-Century Reformism	28
PART II: CHARACTERIZING THE SPANISH UTOPIAN TRADITION		
3	*Sinapia*: A Foundational Spanish Utopia	59
4	Social Satire and Utopia in the *Suplemento de los viajes de Enrique Wanton al país de las monas*	87
5	Utopianism in the *Monarquía de los Ayparchontes* and Related Periodical Texts of the 1780s	119
6	Anti-Enlightenment Perspectives in the *Monarquía columbina*	143
7	Between Utopia and Reform: The Educational and Socio-Economic Vision of the 'Cartas de Mariano a Antonio' in *El Evangelio en triunfo*	163
	Conclusion	189
	Bibliography	197
	Index	215

ACKNOWLEDGEMENTS

The doctoral thesis on which this book is based was awarded the 2017 Postgraduate Publication Prize of the Association of Hispanists of Great Britain and Ireland. I would like to express my gratitude to the AHGBI as well as to the Office for Cultural and Scientific Affairs of the Spanish Embassy in London and to my publisher Legenda (award partners both) for their generous recognition and support of the research presented here. In particular, I would like to thank Professor Trevor Dadson, General Editor of Legenda's 'Studies in Hispanic and Lusophone Cultures' series, for his enthusiastic consideration of my work, and Dr Graham Nelson, Managing Editor of Legenda, for his expert help and dedication. I would also like to record my appreciation to the University of Sheffield for having generously supported my doctoral research by granting me a three-year Faculty Scholarship, and to the Cátedra de Altos Estudios del Español at the University of Salamanca for a postdoctoral fellowship during which the work on this book was brought to completion. I am also thankful to my alma mater, the Pontifical Catholic University of Peru, and to Emory University and Boston University for having played an important role in the academic journey that has resulted in the present book.

Sincere thanks are due to my PhD supervisors for their guidance and critical input at every stage of the writing of my thesis. I am most grateful to Dr Geraldine Lawless for many fruitful early discussions about the overall shaping and presentation of each chapter. I am equally grateful to Dr Rhian Davies for offering invaluable advice at all stages in the doctoral process, and to Dr David McCallam for enthusiastically supervising my work during the revision phase, providing illuminating feedback and insightful comments. Many thanks as well to my viva examiners, Professor Philip Swanson and Dr Gabriel Sánchez Espinosa, for their useful suggestions and stimulating remarks. I would also like to acknowledge Legenda's anonymous reader for providing detailed and constructive observations that helped improve the manuscript. My profound gratitude equally goes to Richard Correll for his careful and laborious copy-editing of the book.

I am especially indebted to Professor Philip Deacon for having been a devoted mentor throughout my doctoral experience and for having shared his extensive knowledge of eighteenth-century Spanish culture with me. His genuine interest in every aspect of my research and his erudite criticism were a source of inspiration for my work. I would also like to thank Dr María José Rodríguez Sánchez de León for giving me the opportunity to further discuss my research and findings while at the University of Salamanca. Special thanks are extended to Dr Michael G. Kelly for his unfailing encouragement, practical advice, and constant motivation during the preparation of the manuscript.

Finally, my heartfelt appreciation goes to my parents, Saúl and Raquel, and to my sister, Jessica, for their unconditional support in the completion of this book.

December 2018

INTRODUCTION

The pursuit of utopia is understood as a desire to change an unsatisfactory order of things by proposing an alternative organizational system that can better an existing society. However, utopian desire goes beyond being a mere mental concept and first crystallized as a fictional narrative when the English humanist Thomas More wrote his foundational work *Utopia* in 1516. Building on the Morean model, a utopian tradition subsequently flourished in Europe, but compelling utopian fictions were not written in Spain until the late seventeenth and throughout the eighteenth centuries. This late manifestation of Spanish utopian writing can be seen to parallel the reformist spirit that characterized the political and cultural life of the Enlightenment era.

It is in this context that the present book aims to set out new analyses of the most outstanding utopian works of the long eighteenth century in Spain,[1] a neglected area of study when compared with the scholarly interest in utopian narratives elsewhere in Europe during the same period. What is more, recent academic research, principally in the last forty years, has brought to light new texts relating to the utopian tradition and found references to lost works, such as José de Cadalso's *Observaciones de un oficial holandés en el nuevamente descubierto reino de Feliztá* [*Observations of a Dutch Officer in the Newly Discovered Kingdom of Felicity*].[2] Scholarly surveys have also underscored the existence of utopian material in Spanish works belonging to other generic forms such as novels or in texts constituting narrative episodes published in contemporary periodicals.[3]

Seeking to contribute new perspectives to the existing field of utopian texts, this book will analyse five works that are illustrative of these heterogeneous forms of textual expression. The texts have been chosen, on the one hand, because of their literary import — that is to say, their relationship to a literary tradition of utopian writing in Spain as well as in the rest of Europe — and, on the other hand, because of their links to reformist socio-political writings designed to contribute to the debate in Spain about society, its structures, and practices. The five texts are also significant because of their variety and complexity, in that they highlight different features of the utopian tradition and display the experimental vision of their authors in setting their ideas within a utopian framework. The objective in grouping these writings together is to offer a fresh approach to the history of the Spanish utopian genre in the long eighteenth century, one that takes into account the ideological and stylistic interplay between the selected texts and explores how each of them establishes a dialogue with literary utopianism as a genre.

The works to be studied in detail, and in chronological sequence, are fictitious accounts of ideal societies and their corresponding social, political, economic, and religious institutions. The first is the *Descripción de la Sinapia, península en la tierra austral* [*Description of Sinapia, Peninsula in the Southern Land*],[4] one of the most recently discovered texts that, although undated, may justifiably be included within the framework of the long eighteenth century, as will be explained below. The second text is Gutierre Joaquín Vaca de Guzmán's *Suplemento de los viajes de Enrique Wanton al país de las monas* [*A Supplement to the Travels of Henry Wanton to the Country of the Monkeys*] (1778),[5] an extensive two-volume sequel composed by a Spanish author to an existing Italian work, and which can be read independently of the stimulus text. The third work to be analysed is what can appropriately be called the *Monarquía de los Ayparchontes* [*The Monarchy of the Ayparchontes*] (1784–85),[6] an anonymous utopian text that appeared in three instalments in the critical periodical *El Censor* [*The Censor*].[7] The fourth work in the corpus is Andrés Merino de Jesucristo's *Monarquía columbina* [*The Monarchy of Doves*] (pre-1787),[8] published posthumously and anonymously in the *Semanario Erudito* [*Erudite Weekly*],[9] but whose authorship was revealed by Pedro Álvarez de Miranda thanks to the discovery of another version of the text in a later periodical.[10] The fifth text to be examined is the utopian narrative interpolated in the fourth, concluding volume of Pablo de Olavide y Jáuregui's epistolary composition *El Evangelio en triunfo, o historia de un filósofo desengañado* [*The Triumph of the Gospel; or, The Story of a Disillusioned Philosopher*] (1797–98),[11] which has been re-edited as an autonomous work, but has not attracted detailed critical attention. Each of these five texts has a particular formal configuration, but they are all structured around the portrayal of an organized utopian space that serves to indirectly criticize the existing order while proposing or insinuating an improved version of it.

A number of writings often mentioned in surveys of eighteenth-century Spanish utopias will not be included in this book because they are novels, translations of foreign texts, or accounts of imaginary voyages in which the utopian component forms a minimal part of the narrative. However, their contribution to Spanish utopianism can be briefly commented on at this point. For example, Diego Ventura Rejón y Lucas's *Aventuras de Juan Luis: historia divertida que puede ser útil* [*The Adventures of Juan Luis: An Entertaining Story that Can Be Useful*] (1781) describes the experiences of the noble Juan Luis on a utopian island called Fortunaria, characterized by efficient systems of social justice and education enjoyed by its exemplary citizens.[12] Another frequently cited work is the utopian story of a rustic village known as Zenit, included in four issues (57–60) of the periodical *Correo de Madrid* [*The Madrid Post*] in 1787. The narration takes the form of a letter sent to the journal by a shipwrecked traveller who was stranded in the Arctic and encountered a primitive society that resembles an earthly paradise and contrasts with the civilized world the traveller returns to.[13] Three novels by Pedro Montengón also contain brief depictions of utopian spaces: Pennsylvania as a utopian Quaker paradise in the pedagogical novel *Eusebio* (1786–88), where the shipwrecked and orphaned six-year-old Eusebio is taken by a Quaker couple to their plantation near Philadelphia;[14] the utopian republic of Elime in *El Antenor* [*Antenor*] (1788), in which the protagonist, upon returning to his homeland and becoming king, intends to apply a series of economic and social reforms that echo those proposed by Olavide for the repopulation of the Sierra Morena, a subject that will be discussed in Chapter 7 of this book;[15] and finally, the idealized Spanish countryside in the pastoral novel *El Mirtilo, o los pastores trashumantes* [*Mirtilo; or, The Nomadic Shepherds*] (1795), in which Mirtilo, disappointed with court life, takes refuge in rural Andalusia.[16]

There are two additional Spanish texts that constitute important examples of lunar utopias, but both are adaptations of foreign works: Pedro Gatell i Carnicer's 'Aventura magna del Bachiller' ['The Great Adventure of the Bachelor'], published in *El Argonauta Español: Periódico Gaditano* [*The Spanish Argonaut: A Cadiz Newspaper*] (1790) and based on Cyrano de Bergerac's *Histoire comique des états et empires de la lune et du soleil* [*A Comical History of the States and Empires of the Moon and Sun*] (1662);[17] and Antonio Marqués y Espejo's *Viaje de un filósofo a Selenópolis, corte desconocida de los habitantes de la tierra* [*The Journey of a Philosopher to Selenopolis, A Court Unknown to the Inhabitants of the Earth*], published in 1804 as a translation of Daniel Villeneuve's *Le Voyageur philosophe dans un pays inconnu aux habitants de la terre* [*The Philosophical Traveller in a Land Unknown to the Inhabitants of the Earth*] (1761).[18] In both Spanish versions, the description of the social practices and institutions of the inhabitants of the moon serves to criticize the life and customs of Spanish society.

Academic Research on Spanish Utopian Texts

No book-length study on eighteenth-century Spanish utopias has yet appeared. In terms of existing criticism on utopian writings in Spain and the rhetorical and structural aspects of Spanish utopian narrative in that period, academic research is confined to journal articles, book chapters, surveys in histories of literature, or introductions to editions of the texts. There are, however, two Spanish theses on major eighteenth-century Spanish utopias that their authors have left unpublished.[19]

Concerning utopian writings in the long eighteenth century, some critics have studied the expression of the utopian imagination in relation to the Spanish Enlightenment, highlighting the interaction between the European utopian tradition and the specific circumstances of eighteenth-century Spain. An important work of this type is Francisco López Estrada's *Tomás Moro y España: sus relaciones hasta el siglo XVIII* [*Thomas More and Spain: Interactions until the Eighteenth Century*] (1980),[20] in which the author claims that, although More's thought continued to be influential in Spain, as shown by the eighteenth-century reprints of the Spanish translation of *Utopia* after its first Spanish edition in 1637, Hispanic utopian production responded to the need to project concrete socio-political concerns. From this perspective, López Estrada conceives of *Sinapia* as a work that is more important for its political than its literary significance because of what he considers its lack of imaginative power. In general, the author argues that there were no eighteenth-century Spanish utopias strictly speaking, but merely manifestations of utopian writing in didactic and moralistic novels or in the periodical press. Nevertheless, the discovery of unpublished, clearly autonomous utopian texts undermines López Estrada's argument, as this book will demonstrate.

In a more radical formulation, Jesús Torrecilla rejects the existence of a utopian mentality and utopian fiction in Spain in his book chapter 'El tiempo y los márgenes: utopía y conciencia de atraso' ['Time and Margins: Utopia and the Awareness of Backwardness'] (1996).[21] According to Torrecilla, the use of the nebulous concept of practical utopia — that is, the practical implementation of the abstract principles of a utopian plan — to define the peculiar characterization of Hispanic utopias in the sixteenth century only disguises the fact that the utopian spirit did not flourish in Spain as a coherent discourse during the Enlightenment period. The notion of a practical or empirical Spanish utopia was developed primarily by the Italian scholar Stelio Cro, whose viewpoint will be presented in detail later on.

A conclusion similar to Torrecilla's is reached by Ismael Piñera Tarque in 'Retórica de la ficción utópica: del género al texto en torno al siglo XVIII español' ['The Rhetoric of Utopian Fiction: From Genre to Text in Eighteenth-Century Spain'] (2003),[22] in which he advances the idea that the limited interest generated by utopian fiction in eighteenth-century Spain implies scepticism about a correlative development of the Spanish Enlightenment model. By contrast, a considerable number of critics argue for the presence of a utopian current in Enlightenment Spain, a position that is supported in the present book. A contribution in this respect is José Luis Calvo Carilla's chapter on Tomás de Iriarte's fables as microutopias of the pragmatic Enlightenment in his book *El sueño sostenible: estudios sobre la utopía literaria en España* [*The Sustainable Dream: Studies on Literary Utopia in Spain*] (2008),[23] even though the didactic intention of fables is satirical and literary rather than utopian. Calvo Carilla places eighteenth-century fables alongside less well-developed literary utopias and Olavide's utopian repopulation project, a topic that will be examined in the final chapter of this book.

Among the scholarly surveys of eighteenth-century Spanish utopian writings, there is a group of studies that will be discussed here in chronological order. The first is Monroe Hafter's article 'Toward a History of Spanish Imaginary Voyages' (1975).[24] Like other overviews of the subject, Hafter could only include the Spanish utopias that were known to exist at the time when he was writing — *Suplemento de los viajes de Enrique Wanton*, *Aventuras de Juan Luis*, the utopia of the Ayparchontes — in a more general list comprising the main imaginary travel accounts in Spain in the eighteenth century, such as the *Viaje de un filósofo a Selenópolis* and *El triunfo de las castañuelas, o mi viaje a Crotalópolis* [*The Triumph of the Castanets; or, My Voyage to Crotalopolis*].[25] Hafter claims that the writing of utopian voyages in Spain started in the 1780s and that this interest was motivated by the publication of Zaccaria Seriman's *Viaggi di Enrico Wanton* [*The Travels of Henry Wanton*] in 1749. He also stresses the difference between the exoticism that the depiction of remote peoples represented in earlier centuries and the function of social satire implied in the portrayal of non-European societies as a way of criticizing Spain's defects.

An equally substantial analysis is that of Paul-Jacques Guinard, who in his article 'Les Utopies en Espagne au XVIIIe siècle' ['Utopias in Spain in the Eighteenth

Century'] (1977)²⁶ offers synopses of six Spanish texts that he identifies as the only Spanish utopias produced in the second half of the eighteenth century: *Aventuras de Juan Luis*, the utopia of the Ayparchontes, *El Antenor*, *El Mirtilo*, *Eudamonopeia*, and *Sinapia*. Guinard posits that the utopian genre developed late in Spain because of the existence of the Inquisition. He highlights the discovery of Joaquín Traggia's *Eudamonopeia* (1796) by Annick Emieux, who provided him with her transcription of the manuscript.²⁷ In this text, Father Traggia relates the travels of the Greek hero Filaretes²⁸ on his way to Eudamonia,²⁹ a kind of Promised Land. Regarding the then recent discovery of the manuscript of *Sinapia*, Guinard suggests that the author might have been an Italian functionary of Carlos III because of certain linguistic features of the text, in particular the original spelling of Machiavelli.

A subsequent succinct evaluation of eighteenth-century Spanish utopian writings is José Luis Abellán's 'La utopía dieciochesca' ['Eighteenth-Century Utopias'] (1981).³⁰ Abellán's approach to the subject is based on the premise that Enlightenment thought is inherently utopian because of its desire for social change. Thus, after questionably claiming that Gaspar de Jovellanos was the perfect model of a Spanish enlightened thinker whose vision was imbued with a utopian spirit, the historian of ideas briefly reviews four utopian texts: the utopia of the Ayparchontes, *Sinapia*, *El Evangelio en triunfo*, and the *Monarquía columbina*. Interestingly, is examination of the texts reveals correspondences between Enlightenment and utopian discourses, especially in terms of the ideal coexistence of the state and Church in Spain. As he sees it, an illustrative example of the correlation between pragmatic Enlightenment projects and their utopian attributes is the narrativization of Olavide's *Plan de Nuevas Poblaciones* [Plan for New Settlements] to create a utopian programme in the fourth volume of *El Evangelio en triunfo*. Abellán ends by highlighting the then very recent publication of Pedro Álvarez de Miranda's edition of the *Monarquía columbina*, which undermines the idea of the concurrence of utopia and Enlightenment because the editor asserts that this text is an anti-Enlightenment utopia, an issue that will be explored in greater detail in Chapter 6 of this book.

Álvarez de Miranda is perhaps the critic who has contributed most overall to the study of imaginary voyages and utopias in eighteenth-century Spain. In his article 'Sobre utopías y viajes imaginarios en el siglo XVIII español' ['On Utopias and Imaginary Voyages in Eighteenth-Century Spain'] (1981),³¹ he adds to the list of Spanish utopias described by Hafter and Guinard in their respective articles and emphasizes the importance of the periodical press as a means of propagating the utopian genre in Spain. In addition to the account of the Ayparchontes in *El Censor*, Álvarez de Miranda draws attention to the utopian story included in letters 20 and 21 of *El Corresponsal del Censor* [*The Censor's Correspondent*] in 1787,³² and overlooked by Guinard in his survey. He also analyses a brief utopian account contained in 'Discurso 4' ['Essay 4'] of José Marchena's periodical *El Observador* [*The Observer*] of 1787 (the story is sometimes called 'Parábola sobre la religión y la política entre los selenitas' ['Parable on Religion and Politics among the Selenites']).³³ Álvarez de Miranda affirms that the proliferation of Spanish utopian writings in the 1780s took its inspiration from the invention of the hot-air balloon by the Montgolfier brothers in 1783. In a later and more detailed book chapter, 'Los libros de viajes y las utopías en el XVIII español' ['Travel Books and Utopias in Eighteenth-Century Spain'] (1995),[34] Álvarez de Miranda highlights the outcome and contributions of the colloquium *Las utopías en el mundo hispánico* [*Utopias in the Hispanic World*], held in Madrid in 1988, at which he revealed the identity of the author of the *Monarquía columbina*: Father Andrés Merino de Jesucristo. He also suggests that the manuscripts of other Spanish utopias may still survive, like that of the *Observaciones de un oficial holandés en el nuevamente descubierto reino de Feliztá* by José de Cadalso.[35] Álvarez de Miranda regards utopia as a narrative subgenre of imaginary travel writing; hence, he emphasizes the understanding of travel as an activity that promotes criticism, a central theme in Enlightenment thought.[36]

In 'Las utopías y el reformismo borbónico' ['Utopias and Bourbon Reformism'] (1996),[37] Salvador Bernabéu Albert briefly surveys the Spanish utopian writings listed by Hafter, Guinard, Abellán, and Álvarez de Miranda, without adding anything of note. However, he brings into focus the discovery made by Francisco Aguilar Piñal of the very brief utopian text *El mundo sin vicios* [*A World Free of Vices*], written by Cándido María Trigueros between 1780 and 1785.[38] He also emphasizes the utopian character of Olavide's colonization project in the Sierra Morena, calling it a 'concrete utopia' as opposed to an 'abstract' or 'literary' utopia, a concept that will be taken up later in this book.

An extensive and more valuable survey is offered by Elena de Lorenzo Álvarez in 'Literatura de viajes y utopías' ['Travel Literature and Utopias'] (2005).[39] She details the main characteristics of the aforementioned eighteenth-century Spanish utopias and highlights the fact that they appeared in very different formats: novels, short episodes within novels, or narratives published in instalments in periodicals. However, as she also indicates, each text adopted a critical attitude to contemporary Spanish society. Like Álvarez de Miranda, who describes the transition from the narrative of imaginary voyages to that of utopia in Spain, Lorenzo Álvarez subtly argues that an imaginary travel account turns into a utopia when travel ceases to be an end in itself and gives way to the description of the utopian society.

Based on the appendix to a thesis submitted at the University of Salamanca,[40] José Carlos Martínez García's 'Un catálogo de utopías de la Ilustración española' ['A Catalogue of Spanish Enlightenment Utopias'] (2006)[41] is one of the most complete inventories of editions of utopian writings of the Spanish Enlightenment. The list includes twenty texts published between 1769 and 1804, that is, between the year of publication of the first Spanish volume of the *Viajes de Enrique Wanton* and that of the *Viaje de un filósofo a Selenópolis*. The catalogue features all the utopias mentioned above, but does not include *Sinapia*, apparently because of the author's uncertainty over its date of composition. Martínez García underlines the diverse literary forms in which these utopian creations appeared, that is, as independent texts or as part of an extended narrative, even though the interpolated utopian episodes can be seen as independent from the main story. Moreover, he identifies the defence of Spanish Enlightenment ideals in these utopias, while attributing a reactionary, counter-Enlightenment purpose to some of them, especially those written by clerics.

Another recent survey is that of Jesús Cañas Murillo in 'Utopías y libros de viajes en el siglo XVIII español: un capítulo de historia literaria de la Ilustración' ['Utopias and Travel Books in Eighteenth-Century Spain: A Chapter of the Literary History of the Enlightenment'] (2007).⁴² Cañas Murillo summarizes the main points made by previous authors, stressing the invalidity of the idea that the realistic and rational disposition of eighteenth-century writing precluded the development of utopian fiction in Spain. He does not analyse the utopian texts that he cites, but provides a general description of the elements of the utopian society that the texts present. Cañas Murillo makes reference to three other undated Spanish utopias: the anonymous sixteenth-century *Omnibona* and two eighteenth-century manuscripts, namely the anonymous translation *El arte de cultivar la razón, o descripción del establecimiento de la colonia de Ponthiamas* [*The Art of Cultivating Reason; or, The Description of the Establishment of the Colony of Ponthiamas*] and the politician Melchor de Macanaz's *El deseado gobierno, buscado por el amor de Dios para el reino de España* [*The Desired Government, Sought by God's Love for the Kingdom of Spain*].⁴³

One final overview that is worth mentioning is Helmut Jacobs's 'Aspectos de la imagen utópica de España en la literatura española del siglo XVIII' ['Aspects of the Utopian Image of Spain in Eighteenth-Century Spanish Literature'] (2007).⁴⁴ The fundamental point made by Jacobs is that the discovery of eighteenth-century Spanish utopias has positively changed the underestimated image of the Spanish Enlightenment given that these utopian texts reveal the most innovative, subversive, and anticlerical tendencies of the period. In other words, it can be argued that Spanish utopias played an important role in the articulation of the reformist discourse of the Spanish Enlightenment. In addition to presenting the principal characteristics of *Sinapia*, *Suplemento de los viajes de Enrique Wanton*, *Aventuras de Juan Luis*, and *Monarquía columbina*, Jacobs outlines the utopian qualities of Cadalso's *Cartas marruecas* [*Moroccan Letters*] (1789), Macanaz's *El deseado gobierno*, and Merino de Jesucristo's *La mujer feliz, dependiente del mundo y de la fortuna* [*The Happy Woman, Dependent on the World and Fortune*] (1786).

The contributions and more debatable aspects of these general surveys of eighteenth-century Spanish utopian writings⁴⁵ will be returned to in the chapters of Part II of this book, where they will be complemented by the discussion of a number of academic studies focused specifically on the five utopian texts selected for detailed examination.

The Structure of the Present Book

Part I comprises two preliminary chapters that set out the main ideological, literary, and social features of the utopian genre in its Western and Spanish contexts before moving on to discuss the development of utopianism and reformism in eighteenth-century Spain. Part II examines the five selected texts, chronologically organized according to the likely order in which they were written, exploring specific narrative features relating to the utopian tradition and demonstrating their distinctiveness with regard to discussions of economic, political, religious, and social structures in contemporary Spain, while probing their reformist and idealizing tendencies.

Chapter 1 defines the theoretical framework that has informed discussion of the utopian genre as established by Thomas More's *Utopia*. In outlining the basic elements of the utopian model and its antecedents in other narrative traditions, special relevance is given to the relationship between utopianism and colonialism, an aspect to be applied to the Spanish context in the following chapter. Key notions pertaining to utopian discourse, such as insularity, civilization, and the possibility of a Christian utopia, are also addressed.

Chapter 2 presents the Hispanic aspects of an eighteenth-century utopian consciousness in relation to Spain. Acknowledging the magnitude of the colonizing experience in the New World as a germ of the Spanish utopian impulse and following Stelio Cro's insights on the subject, this chapter reviews the most significant practical utopian projects envisioned in the Spanish American colonies at around the time of the publication of More's text. The chapter also focuses on the ideas of seventeenth-century Spanish *arbitristas* [political economists] as precedents for the emergence of Enlightenment utopianism in Spain. It similarly examines the ideological context of eighteenth-century Spain, starting with the intellectual work of the *novatores* [innovators], and how it was conducive to the development of utopian fiction. The utopian consciousness of Enlightenment Spain was not only socio-political, as reflected in the role of the *proyectistas* [planners] and governmental reform plans, but also strongly religious because Christianity was considered a fundamental component of Spanish identity. The ideological thrust behind the social criticism of the Spanish Enlightenment would naturally seem fundamental to the promotion of utopian thinking in Spain at that historical moment.

Part II is dedicated to a detailed examination of the five chosen works. Chapter 3 studies the *Descripción de la Sinapia, península en la tierra austral*. Despite its anonymity and uncertain date of composition, the text embraces the distinctive features of eighteenth-century Spanish utopianism: the construction of an ideal society whose structure and institutions are guided by Christian principles in tune with an appropriate implementation of secular education. The chapter also considers the representation of *Sinapia* as the prototype of Spanish pragmatic utopianism on the basis of the similarities of its imagined socio-political model to the evangelical reform programme of the Jesuit *reducciones* [Indian mission settlements] in Paraguay.

Chapter 4 centres on Gutierre Vaca de Guzmán's *Suplemento de los viajes de Enrique Wanton al país de las monas* (1778). Vaca de Guzmán's Spanish continuation of Zaccaria Seriman's utopia written in Italian can be read as a criticism of the artificial and worthless customs of eighteenth-century Spanish society reflected in the derisive depiction of the kingdom of the monkeys. The satirical representation of civilized habits exposes an undesirable cosmopolitanism that hampers the development of a national identity.

Chapter 5 examines the anonymous story of the *Monarquía de los Ayparchontes*, published in the periodical *El Censor* in 1784–85. The first part of this chapter discusses the importance of *El Censor*, the most radical periodical of the time that either satirized or critically denounced various aspects of Spanish life and institutions, criticism that led to censorship and condemnation of some of its *discursos* [essays] by the Inquisition. The main targets of the text's attacks are the irrational hereditary privileges of the nobility and the contradictorily wealthy Church. However, in contrast with other Spanish utopias, the Ayparchontes belong to a highly civilized society in which the idyllic myth of the good savage has no place.

Chapter 6 studies Andrés Merino de Jesucristo's *Monarquía columbina* (pre-1787), an allegorical utopia that can be interpreted as a direct critique of eighteenth-century Spanish society. While the use of birds as inhabitants of the utopian space recalls Vaca de Guzmán's republic of monkeys and the use of animals in fables more generally, the overwhelming presence of religious components in the *Monarquía columbina* brings Merino's utopia closer to the concerns of *Sinapia*. Moreover, the symbolic significance of doves reaffirms the dichotomy of civilization and barbarism as a recurring theme in Spanish utopian writing. Nonetheless, the ending of the story, in which evil (or cruel civilization) triumphs over good (or nature), enables the *Monarquía columbina* to be properly considered an anti-Enlightenment utopia.

Finally, Chapter 7 analyses Pablo de Olavide y Jáuregui's utopian narrative in *El Evangelio en triunfo, o historia de un filósofo desengañado* (1797–98), a text that is as representative of Spanish utopianism as *Sinapia* because it brings together the most decisive factors in shaping the ideological and practical nature of the Spanish utopian model. Similar to the interaction between the societal system of the Jesuit *reducciones* and its recreation in the Sinapian nation, the utopian village designed by the philosopher in *El Evangelio en triunfo* matches the *Plan de Nuevas Poblaciones*, a government project implemented by Olavide in 1767, which entailed the repopulation and renewal of unproductive territories in the Sierra Morena region of Spain. Olavide's agrarian project is a rural utopia based on a rational Christianity. This text reconciles the civic and religious spheres while promoting the concept of good model citizens who are also Christians.

In the Conclusion, the various narrative and thematic features revealed in the analysis of the five works lead to an overview of the utopian genre in eighteenth-century Spain, as well as to a review of the correlation between the literary characteristics of the utopian model and the vision of social transformation that defines the expression of reformism during the Spanish Enlightenment.

The spelling, capitalization, and punctuation of quotations from pre-1900 sources have been modernized in the interests of clarity and uniformity. Translations in the text are my own unless otherwise stated.

Notes to the Introduction

1. By 'the long eighteenth century' is meant the period between approximately 1675 and 1808. The dates for the beginning and the end of the period correspond to both ideological and historical factors. The intellectual origins of the Spanish Enlightenment can be traced to the time of the philosophy of the *novatores* [innovators] (1675–1725), who contributed to the emergence of modern science in Spain. The Napoleonic invasion of Spain in 1808 led to the outbreak of the Spanish War of Independence and subsequently to the proclamation of the first Spanish Constitution by the Courts of Cadiz in 1812, which restructured the absolute monarchy into a constitutional one, marking the end of the Old Regime in Spain.
2. See José de Cadalso, *Escritos autobiográficos y epistolario*, ed. by Nigel Glendinning and Nicole Harrison (London: Tamesis, 1979).

3. Pedro Álvarez de Miranda, 'Sobre utopías y viajes imaginarios en el siglo XVIII español', in *Homenaje a Gonzalo Torrente Ballester*, ed. by Víctor García de la Concha (Salamanca: Biblioteca de la Caja de Ahorros y Monte de Piedad de Salamanca, 1981), pp. 351–82; Elena de Lorenzo Álvarez, 'Literatura de viajes y utopías', in *Literatura española del siglo XVIII*, ed. by Alberto Romero Ferrer and Joaquín Álvarez Barrientos (Madrid: Liceus, 2005), pp. 1–21, ebook.
4. *Descripción de la Sinapia, península en la tierra austral*, in *'Sinapia': una utopía española del Siglo de las Luces*, ed. by Miguel Avilés Fernández (Madrid: Editora Nacional, 1976), pp. 67–134.
5. [Gutierre] Joaquín [Vaca] de Guzmán y Manrique, *Suplemento, o sea tomo tercero [–cuarto y último] de los viajes de Enrique Wanton al país de las monas*, 2 vols (Madrid: Antonio de Sancha, 1778).
6. The text itself is untitled, with each of the three sections included in separate issues of the periodical. The society depicted is more than once referred to as a *monarquía*, and, therefore, the title of *Monarquía de los Ayparchontes* will be used in this book. In his edition of a selection of *El Censor*, Franciso Uzcanga Meinecke gives the *discursos* [essays] in question the title *Viaje a la tierra de los ayparchontes* [*A Voyage to the Land of the Ayparchontes*] as part of his edition's criteria (Francisco Uzcanga Meinecke, ed., *El Censor* (Barcelona: Crítica, 2005), pp. 51, 157, 205). Other critics have expressly incorporated the word *utopía* into the title without carefully considering what was in accord with the original author's concept of the text.
7. See *El Censor*, 8 vols (Madrid: n. pub., 1781–87; facsimile edition by José Miguel Caso González, Oviedo: Universidad de Oviedo, Instituto Feijoo de Estudios del Siglo XVIII, 1989), III [1784]: 'Discurso LXI', pp. 225–39, 'Discurso LXIII', pp. 257–70; IV [1785]: 'Discurso LXXV', pp. 131–50. The dates of composition of the three *discursos* were determined by Caso González in '*El Censor*, ¿periódico de Carlos III?', in *El Censor*, ed. by José Miguel Caso González (Oviedo: Universidad de Oviedo, Instituto Feijoo de Estudios del Siglo XVIII, 1989), pp. 776–99 (p. 786).
8. [Andrés Merino de Jesucristo], *Monarquía columbina*, in *'Tratado sobre la monarquía columbina': una utopía antiilustrada del siglo XVIII*, ed. by Pedro Álvarez de Miranda (Madrid: El Archipiélago, 1980), pp. 1–29.
9. [Andrés Merino de Jesucristo], *Tratado sobre la monarquía columbina*, in *Semanario Erudito, que comprende varias obras inéditas, críticas, morales, instructivas, políticas, históricas, satíricas y jocosas de nuestros mejores autores antiguos y modernos*, ed. by Antonio Valladares de Sotomayor, 34 vols (Madrid: Antonio Espinosa, 1787–91), XXX (1790), pp. 61–84.
10. Pedro Álvarez de Miranda, 'El Padre Andrés Merino, autor de la *Monarquía columbina*', in *Las utopías en el mundo hispánico: actas del coloquio celebrado en la Casa de Velázquez*, ed. by Jean-Pierre Étienvre (Madrid: Casa de Velázquez, Universidad Complutense, 1990), pp. 19–39.
11. Pablo de Olavide y Jáuregui, 'Cartas de Mariano a Antonio', in *Cartas de Mariano a Antonio: el programa ilustrado de 'El Evangelio en triunfo'*, ed. by Gérard Dufour (Aix-en-Provence: Université de Provence, 1988), pp. 37–229.
12. Diego Ventura Rejón y Lucas, *Aventuras de Juan Luis: historia divertida que puede ser útil* (Madrid: Joaquín Ibarra, 1781; facsimile edition, Murcia: Tres Fronteras, 2008).
13. *Correo de Madrid*, No. 57, 9 May 1787, pp. 241–44; No. 58, 12 May 1787, pp. 245–48; No. 59, 16 May 1787, pp. 249–52; No. 60, 19 May 1787, pp. 253–56.
14. Pedro Montengón, *Eusebio*, ed. by Fernando García Lara (Madrid: Cátedra, 1998).
15. Pedro Montengón, *El Antenor*, 2 vols (Madrid: Antonio de Sancha, 1788).
16. Pedro Montengón, *El Mirtilo, o los pastores trashumantes* (Madrid: Imprenta de Sancha, 1795).
17. Pedro Gatell i Carnicer, 'Aventura magna del Bachiller', No. 8, in *El Argonauta Español: Periódico Gaditano*, ed. by Marieta Cantos Casenave and María José Rodríguez Sánchez de León (Seville: Renacimiento, 2008), pp. 210–13.
18. [Antonio Marqués y Espejo], *Viaje de un filósofo a Selenópolis, corte desconocida de los habitantes de la tierra* (Madrid: Gómez Fuentenebro, 1804).
19. José Carlos Martínez García, 'Historia de la literatura utópica española: las utopías de la Ilustración' (unpublished *licenciatura* thesis, Universidad de Salamanca, 2004); Amable Fernández Sanz, 'Utopía y realidad en la Ilustración española: Pablo de Olavide y las "nuevas poblaciones"' (unpublished doctoral thesis, Universidad Complutense de Madrid, 1990).
20. Francisco López Estrada, *Tomás Moro y España: sus relaciones hasta el siglo XVIII* (Madrid: Universidad Complutense, 1980).

21. Jesús Torrecilla, 'El tiempo y los márgenes: utopía y conciencia de atraso', in Jesús Torrecilla, *El tiempo y los márgenes: Europa como utopía y como amenaza en la literatura española* (Chapel Hill: University of North Carolina, Department of Romance Languages, 1996), pp. 19–52.
22. Ismael Piñera Tarque, 'Retórica de la ficción utópica: del género al texto en torno al siglo XVIII español', *Cuadernos de Estudios del Siglo XVIII*, 12–13 (2003), 137–65.
23. José Luis Calvo Carilla, 'Las fábulas de Iriarte: microutopías de la razón pragmática', in José Luis Calvo Carilla, *El sueño sostenible: estudios sobre la utopía literaria en España* (Madrid: Marcial Pons, 2008), pp. 63–104.
24. Monroe Z. Hafter, 'Toward a History of Spanish Imaginary Voyages', *Eighteenth-Century Studies*, 8 (1975), 265–82.
25. A satirical text written by Juan Fernández de Rojas in 1792 and published under the pseudonym of Alejandro Moya. See Noel Fallows, *Satire and Invective in Enlightened Spain: 'Crotalogía, o ciencia de las castañuelas' by Juan Fernández de Rojas* (Newark, DL: Juan de la Cuesta, 2001).
26. Paul-Jacques Guinard, 'Les Utopies en Espagne au XVIIIe siècle', in *Recherches sur le roman historique en Europe, XVIIIe–XIXe siècles*, 2 vols (Paris: Les Belles Lettres, 1977–79), I, ed. by Michel Apel-Muller (1977), pp. 171–202.
27. Emieux discovered the manuscript of the *Eudamonopeia* in the library of the Royal Academy of History in Madrid and announced the preparation of an edition of the text in her 1991 article 'Un roman qui cherche sa forme: le manuscrit de l'*Eudamonopeia* du Père Joaquín Traggia', in *Mélanges offerts à Paul Guinard*, 2 vols (Paris: Éditions Hispaniques, 1990–91), II: *Hommage des dix-huitièmistes français*, ed. by Jean René Aymes and Annick Emieux (1991), pp. 97–108. However, the edition has so far not been published.
28. The name signifies 'love of virtue' in Greek.
29. Aristotle introduced the concept of *eudaimonia*, which means 'happiness' or 'well-being'. See Daniel M. Haybron, *Happiness: A Very Short Introduction* (Oxford: Oxford University Press, 2013), p. 82.
30. José Luis Abellán, *Historia crítica del pensamiento español*, 7 vols (Madrid: Espasa-Calpe, 1979–92), III: *Del Barroco a la Ilustración (siglos XVII y XVIII)* (1981), pp. 607–22.
31. Álvarez de Miranda, 'Sobre utopías y viajes imaginarios en el siglo XVIII español', pp. 351–82.
32. Manuel Rubín de Celis, *El Corresponsal del Censor*, ed. by Klaus-Dieter Ertler, Renate Hodab, and Inmaculada Urzainqui (Madrid: Iberoamericana; Frankfurt: Vervuert, 2009).
33. José Marchena, 'Discurso cuarto' [in *El Observador*], in José Marchena, *Obra española en prosa: historia, política, literatura*, ed. by Juan Francisco Fuentes (Madrid: Centro de Estudios Constitucionales, 1990), pp. 67–72.
34. Pedro Álvarez de Miranda, 'Los libros de viajes y las utopías en el XVIII español', in *Historia de la literatura española*, ed. by Víctor García de la Concha, 4 vols (Madrid: Espasa-Calpe, 1995–98), VII: *Siglo XVIII (II)*, ed. by Guillermo Carnero (1995), pp. 682–706.
35. The manuscript was given by Cadalso to the Count of Aranda (Cadalso, *Escritos autobiográficos y epistolario*, p. 13).
36. Utopian texts were constantly produced at the same time as exploration accounts during the Enlightenment. However, more than operating in parallel, the overlap of both discourses can be understood as a desire of geographical utopias to imitate the narratives of explorers and conquerors. It is by virtue of this aspect that utopias usually turn into imaginary voyages. The most popular imaginary travel book in Spain was François Fénelon's *Les Aventures de Télémaque* [*The Adventures of Telemachus*] (1699).
37. Salvador Bernabéu Albert, 'Las utopías y el reformismo borbónico', in *El reformismo borbónico: una visión interdisciplinar*, ed. by Agustín Guimerá (Madrid: Alianza, 1996), pp. 247–63.
38. Francisco Aguilar Piñal, 'La anti-utopía dieciochesca de Trigueros', in *Las utopías en el mundo hispánico*, ed. by Étienvre, pp. 65–72. Trigueros's utopian text is included in a collection of his tales and short novels entitled *Mis pasatiempos: almacén de fruslerías agradables* [*My Pastimes: Stock of Pleasant Trifles*], which was published posthumously in 1804.
39. Lorenzo Álvarez, 'Literatura de viajes y utopías'.
40. See note 19 above.
41. José Carlos Martínez García, 'Un catálogo de utopías de la Ilustración española', *Cuadernos de Ilustración y Romanticismo*, 14 (2006), 257–69.

42. Jesús Cañas Murillo, 'Utopías y libros de viajes en el siglo XVIII español: un capítulo de historia literaria de la Ilustración', in *Aufklärung: estudios sobre la Ilustración española dedicados a Hans-Joachim Lope*, ed. by Jesús Cañas Murillo and José Roso Díaz (Cáceres: Universidad de Extremadura, 2007), pp. 71–88.
43. *Omnibona* and *El deseado gobierno* are studied by Miguel Avilés in 'Otros cuatro relatos utópicos en la España moderna: las utopías de J. Maldonado, *Omnibona* y *El Deseado Gobierno*', in *Las utopías en el mundo hispánico*, ed. by Étienvre, pp. 109–28. The manuscript of the former is held at the Royal Academy of History, while copies of that of the latter are in the National Library of Spain (dated 1777) and the Huesca Public Library (dated 1855); a 1728 copy of *El deseado gobierno* is mentioned in the *Semanario Pintoresco Español* [*Spanish Picturesque Weekly*] (*Semanario Pintoresco Español. Lectura de las familias. Enciclopedia popular*, 22 vols (Madrid: Oficinas y Establecimiento Tipográfico del Semanario Pintoresco, 1836–57), XVIII (1853), p. 50). The manuscript of *El arte de cultivar la razón* was discovered by Pilar Nieva de la Paz in the National Library of Spain. The text is apparently a translation of a French travel account written by Pierre Poivre in 1768. See Pilar Nieva de la Paz, '*El arte de cultivar la razón o descripción del establecimiento de la colonia de Ponthiamas*: un texto utópico traducido del francés en el siglo XVIII', in *Las utopías en el mundo hispánico*, ed. by Étienvre, pp. 79–94.
44. Helmut C. Jacobs, 'Aspectos de la imagen utópica de España en la literatura española del siglo XVIII', in *Una de las dos Españas: representaciones de un conflicto identitario en la historia y en las literaturas hispánicas. Estudios reunidos en homenaje a Manfred Tietz*, ed. by Gero Arnscheidt and Pere Joan i Tous (Madrid: Iberoamericana; Frankfurt am Main: Vervuert, 2007), pp. 619–33.
45. A brief consideration of major Spanish utopian texts can be found in Giovanni Stiffoni, 'Considerazioni su di una possibile storia dell'utopia nella Spagna del Sei-Settecento', in *Un 'hombre de bien': saggi di lingue e letterature iberiche in onore di Rinaldo Froldi*, ed. by Patrizia Garelli and Giovanni Marchetti, 2 vols (Alessandria: Edizioni dell'Orso, 2004), II, pp. 577–87.

PART I

The Literary and Socio-Political Foundations of Spanish Utopianism

CHAPTER 1

Utopian Fiction and the Morean Model

Utopia can be conceived of as an ideological engagement with an evolving socio-political model responsive to specific historical circumstances. Parallel to this perspective, the literary dimension of utopia centres on its conception as a narrative artefact belonging to a flexible generic mode. By taking as starting point the structural characteristics of Thomas More's *Utopia* and tracing a brief historical outline of utopian thought, the present chapter will establish the elements of the prevailing tradition relevant to the configuration of utopian fiction and discourse in eighteenth-century Spain. In order to assess the extent to which Spanish utopian texts borrow from, allude to, and develop ideas, structural features, and literary characteristics deriving from More's work, it is necessary to set out some of the key defining components contained in the fictional account given by the traveller Raphael Hythloday in Book II of *Utopia*, as they shaped the literary genre that gave rise to the rich tradition of European utopian writing.

Principles of the Utopian Genre

The basic notion of utopia derives from the etymological significance of the neologism coined by Thomas More in his 1516 text written in Latin.[1] Understood as both 'no place' (*outopia*) and 'good place' (*eutopia*),[2] utopia is an ambiguous term that has led some scholars to approach the topic from the point of view of the unrealistic or impossible character of an ideal society. The concept has been explored before and since in a wide range of discursive contexts such as classical mythology, Platonism, imaginary geopolitical experiments, fantastic voyages, and science fiction. Due to its conventional ascription to a fantastic or chimerical realm, utopian texts are often seen as vain speculation and, at worst, as dangerous dreams that threaten the stability of the existing social order. The impulse to create utopias was present in cultural history before More invented a term to express such a tendency. Thus, in ancient history, there were several myths or narrative traditions in which a primitive form of the utopian component was the means of conveying the idealistic image of a better time or a better world. The main antecedents include Plato's *Republic*, the idea of a Golden Age, Virgil's Arcadia, and the earthly paradise.[3]

More's *Utopia* was directly influenced by the *Republic*, although Plato's work proves to be more of a portrayal of the principles of the ideal state than the application of those principles to concrete institutions and lifestyles. In a more nostalgic vein, diverse versions of the myth of the Golden Age can be found in all societies and each one refers to a time in which humanity lived in a state of happiness and in harmony with nature.[4] This primordial era was characterized by simplicity and frugality; therefore, human needs were easily fulfilled by an abundant nature. In accordance with this belief in the virtues of nature, the tradition of Arcadia — a region in the Peloponnese typified by a rural life of rustic pleasures that prompted the literary pastoral until the end of the eighteenth century — was rooted in the belief that human nature is good. Such a preconception of primitive innocence and purity was discussed by Michel de Montaigne in his essay 'Des cannibales' ['Of Cannibals'] (1580),[5] and it was the premise of Étienne-Gabriel Morelly's later utopian text *Naufrage des îles flottantes, ou Basiliade du célèbre Pilpai* [*The Shipwreck of the Floating Islands; or, The Basiliade of the celebrated Pilpai*] (1753),[6] in which Arcadianism is exhibited in the absolute governance of nature over the Floating Islanders, who are safe from the mistakes of civilization caused by man's efforts to prescribe rules that only pervert nature.[7] Moving away somewhat from the perception of the Golden Age as an idyllic period in the past, the myth of a Christian paradise projects the recovery of the lost Garden of Eden into the future. The discovery of the New World renewed the faith in this legend since Christopher Columbus thought that he had found the earthly paradise when he first encountered the new continent and its peoples.[8]

There are other traditions that reveal a utopian inclination, but in a highly satirical way, such as the medieval legend of the Land of Cockaigne (poor man's paradise), the Feast of Fools, and the Roman Saturnalia. All of them temporarily provide the poor and oppressed with power over their superiors for a day or a week, although this unrealistic inversion of social and political roles develops in a land dominated by extravagance and excess: nobody works and everything is free.[9] The formal relations between utopia and satire have always been present ever since Aristophanes and are evident in the writings of the Anglo-Irish author Jonathan Swift, More's great follower.[10] A utopian vision inevitably involves a satirical look at a given society and results from a negative assessment of its current conditions. As Robert Elliott underlines,

> Satire and utopia are not really separable, the one a critique of the real world in the name of something better, the other a hopeful construct of a world that might be. The hope feeds the criticism, the criticism the hope.[11]

In contrast with a life based on a lack of moderation, work and austerity are essential components of utopian societies. The description of this and other main features of the utopian state and its way of life is normally embedded in a conventional narrative structure that exhibits the defining formal traits of utopian fiction as a literary genre as follows. A traveller arrives in the utopian country, typically an island, after an imaginary voyage, which is located in settings such as the New World, the hypothetical continent of *Terra Australis Incognita* [the Unknown Southern Land], or the moon. The visitor gives a detailed account of the political and social institutions of the utopian society, usually accompanied by a native of the country who acts as his guide and provides explanations of what they see. This narration turns out to be the future report that the traveller will write upon the return to his homeland in order to make known what he saw during his visit to the utopian place.[12] The account specifies the common ideal attributes of the archetypal utopian community, which customarily follow the model established by More. The structure of the story — drawing on More's *Utopia* — encompasses elements such as a patriarchal family system, an agrarian economy, the abolition of private property, a simple legislative system, an elaborate social hierarchy, a topographical organization of the city according to the division of labour, scientific and technological discoveries, and a dominant position for religion. In spite of counting on a complex political organization, the fundamental unit of utopian society is the patriarchal family, which provides the economic basis for agricultural production. However, a significant limitation of the traditional utopia, to modern eyes, is the marginalization of the feminine by the superimposition of a masculine order that can be observed in the forms of social organization that utopian fiction depicts.

A basic condition of the utopian space is its insularity, that is, its deliberate separation from the outside world justified by the aim of protecting its own values and institutions. Utopus founded Utopia after conquering the country of Abraxa and turned it into an island by excavating a channel that would isolate the conquered territory from the mainland. The island comprised forty-four city-states, which were the equivalents of England's forty-three counties plus London,[13] renamed Amaurotum, or 'Darkling City', an allusion to foggy London.[14] Each of the cities was an economic unit and had the same administrative, spatial, and cultural structure. It is important to make it clear that Utopia is the result of a process of conquest and colonization, not the discovery of a paradisiacal place as is implicitly the case in some narrative traditions that share the idealistic worldview of utopian discourse. Dominic Baker-Smith equates the imposing character of Utopia's creation with its artificial essence:

> The first thing to note about the Utopian commonwealth is its artificiality; it is not the fortuitous survival of some aboriginal golden age, such as the early discoverers were inclined to suppose [*sic*] American Indians, but a deliberate creation, set apart from the rest of the world by the daunting channel which the conqueror Utopus dug in order to isolate his subject state from surrounding territory.[15]

The primary objective of Utopus's intervention in Abraxa is to civilize its rustic people and made them culturally superior to all other peoples. In contrast with the sense of tyranny implied in the initial act of subjugation, the political system in Utopia is a combination of democracy and monarchy, a political model that might have been inspired by Sparta's governmental system.[16] In Utopia, the governor is an elected monarch, the syphogrants represent families in the senate, and the tranibors constitute an intellectual elite without privileges of any kind. Families are the basic social unit of Utopian cities: a syphogrant is elected annually by thirty households, and a tranibor is set to rule over ten syphogrants with their families. The syphogrants constitute the lowest rank in the government structure and inculcate the citizens with the habit of obedience to authority, which guarantees the stability of economy and society. A city has six thousand households, each comprising between ten and sixteen adults, a figure increased to forty in rural households, and each household is ruled by its oldest member.

The main occupation of the inhabitants is agriculture, a subject in which all citizens are instructed from childhood, 'partly in the schools, where they learn theory, partly through field trips to nearby farms, which make something like a game of practical instruction'.[17] They work six hours a day and are expected to dedicate the rest of their time to some other occupation, especially intellectual activities, chosen according to personal preference. The opportunity for self-cultivation through public lectures in the dawn hours is perhaps the most innovative attribute of the Utopian system.[18] The Utopians spend one hour in recreation after supper, 'in their gardens during the summer, or during winter in the common halls where they have their meals. There they either play music or amuse themselves with conversation'.[19] It should be emphasized that the Utopians are very attached to their gardens. The fact that this is the principal source of pleasure for the citizens indicates the importance that More gives to nature in the formation of the Utopian state. Virtue is actually dependent on nature: 'They [the Utopians] define virtue as living according to nature; and God, they say, created us to that end'.[20] Nature is ultimately the instrument to achieve happiness, and virtue is the vehicle for a joyous life.

Another fundamental aspect of the social system in Utopia is the absence of money and private property. Nothing is privately owned, and the population lives unconcerned about the provision of food and other worldly goods:

> [H]ere, where everything belongs to everybody, no one need fear that, so long as the public warehouses are filled, anyone will ever lack for anything for his own use. For the distribution of goods is not niggardly; no one is poor there, there are no beggars, and though no one owns anything, everyone is rich.[21]

In turn, the non-existence of private property results in the absence of power, greed, corruption, and crime. Although More expresses his concerns about the impracticability of eradicating the institution of private property, he longs for the implementation of such a change.

In terms of intellectual development, the Utopians learn the different disciplines that constitute knowledge in their native language. In the field of the arts, they master the art of printing and the manufacture of paper. In the area of scientific research, the islanders stand out for their observation of the natural world, in particular for their study of astronomy and meteorology. They are also interested in moral philosophy, especially in the argument that happiness depends on good and decent pleasure: '[T]hey say, nature herself prescribes for us a joyous life, in other words, pleasure, as the goal of all our actions'.[22] Pleasure is the ultimate end of life, and the most pleasurable experience is the virtuous life. According to Quentin Skinner, virtue represents the true view of nobility for the citizens of Utopia, as opposed to a false view based on wealth and privileges.[23]

Since virtue is the guiding principle of their lives, the Utopians' behaviour is impeccable, and, as a result, they have very few laws to regulate their behaviour. Lawyers are not allowed in the commonwealth because they are seen as dishonest:

> The chief fault they find with other nations is that even their infinite volumes of laws and interpretations are not adequate. They think it completely unjust to bind people by a set of laws that are too many to be read or too obscure for anyone to understand. As for lawyers, [...] they exclude them entirely. They think it practical for each man to plead his own case [...]. This makes for less confusion and readier access to the truth. [...] [I]n Utopia everyone is a legal expert.[24]

The citizens themselves are consequently in charge of applying corrective measures: 'Husbands chastise their wives and parents their children, unless the offence is so serious that public punishment is called for'.[25] Slavery is contemplated as a means of punishment for crimes and offences. Utopian criminals are kept chained and continually at work. Besides these slaves, there is also a category consisting of people from other countries who voluntarily choose to be slaves. Premarital sexual intercourse is severely punished, while adultery is condemned with punishment comprising the strictest form of slavery. The death penalty is imposed on rebellious slaves, but for slaves who show sincere repentance, their slavery may be either lightened or remitted.

As to religious beliefs, the Utopians follow a variety of creeds and practices. Some of them worship heavenly bodies, while others venerate an unknown supreme being, to whom the creation and the providential government of the world are due. Utopia is predominantly a heathen society:

> [T]he vast majority, and those by far the wiser ones, [...] believe in a single divinity, unknown, eternal, infinite, inexplicable, beyond the grasp of the human mind, and diffused throughout the universe, not physically, but in influence. Him they call their parent.[26]

More importantly, the Utopians see in religion and reason two complementary forces that contribute to the idea of happiness:

> [T]hey never discuss happiness without joining to the rational arguments of philosophy certain principles drawn from religion. Without these religious principles, they think that reason by itself is weak and defective in its efforts to investigate true happiness. [...] Though these are [...] religious principles, they think that reason leads us to believe and accept them.[27]

Religious tolerance is key to maintaining civil order in Utopia, and if someone is too vehement in expressing their religious preference, they are punished with exile or enslavement. The adherence to religion does not contradict the scientific investigation of nature because all the manifestations of religion tend to the worship of divine nature.[28] The Utopians' mentality is ultimately based on their faith in virtue and reason.

These central components of More's Utopian society were adapted by eighteenth-century Spanish utopian writers to provoke questioning of Spain's institutions and political system, as will be seen in Part II of this book. Although all of the traditional elements of the utopian model are present in Spanish literary utopias, their development is significantly determined by the importance of the colonizing enterprise in the founding of the utopian state and by the pragmatic dimension of the utopian imagination.

Utopianism and Colonialism[29]

The composition of More's *Utopia* was inspired by the letters in which Christopher Columbus and Amerigo Vespucci described the discovery of new worlds and peoples.[30] The new American continent and other then unknown territories functioned as utopian scenarios in which the association of colonization with civilization played an important ideological role in justifying the act of conquest itself. Nicole Pohl argues that eighteenth-century utopias were primarily ethnological utopias that speculated on models of progressive socialization, perfectibility, reason, and reform.[31] Such narratives were natural histories of civil society that

> served to demarcate Western achievements in science and technology, the arts and culture, in short, civilization. This conjectural historiography not only reinforced the superiority of the 'Old World' but justified and naturalized the extensive appropriation and colonization of the 'New World'.[32]

In addition to these texts, Pohl observes the presence of non-utopian historiographies in which historical pessimism created utopias that idealized the 'state of nature' and promised the regeneration of society in order to take it back to its original state of innocence. Consequently, the New World became the projection of utopian hopes and desires: 'These utopias promoted domestic, self-sufficient economies of production, based on Native American economies, accompanied by the abolition of private property and money within the utopian society'.[33]

In *Utopia*, Raphael Hythloday, a Portuguese gentleman, joined Vespucci in his last three voyages, but did not return with him in the final one because of his eagerness to travel the world, which gave him the opportunity to arrive in Utopia. Hythloday recounts the establishment of the utopian state through a process of conquest and colonization: the land of Abraxa was conquered by Utopus, who 'gave it his name, and who brought its rude, uncouth inhabitants to such a high level of culture and humanity that they now surpass almost every other people'.[34] Utopus immediately subdued the natives and put them to work on the excavation of a channel with the aim of converting the land into an island, but he also set his own soldiers to the task in order to prevent the natives from thinking that labour should be considered an act of humiliation.

King Utopus's gesture can be interpreted as the recognition of otherness, but contrary to Fátima Vieira's assertion that 'More used the emerging awareness of otherness to legitimize the invention of other spaces, with other people and different forms of organization',[35] the discovery of the Other serves to reinforce the traditional Western values that are reconfigured in a new space. As Chris Ferns points out,

> Where an indigenous population exists, its function is to be moulded in the image of a King Utopus; neighbouring races are portrayed either as enemies to be destroyed, or else as eager to be governed by the superior wisdom of the Utopians.[36]

The utopian encounter with the Other not only brings about the confrontation between civilization and barbarism, but also entails a sense of xenophobia resulting from the geographical insularity of the utopian space. However, as Raymond Trousson rightly infers, the utopian insularity is basically a mental state because the image of the island acts as a metaphorical representation of the need to protect the utopian community from the corruption of the external world.[37] Thus, any xenophobic reaction against cultural interaction with other communities should be understood as a way of preserving the state of perfection of the utopian country. As Ferns concludes, the arrival of foreign visitors is a sign that the utopian space is not unreachable after all:

> Although utopia's isolation is clearly designed to protect it from contamination by the squalor and disorder of the real world, it can never be *so* isolated as to be inaccessible to the privileged individual who will eventually return to bear witness to the superiority of the utopian way.[38]

According to More's text, the lands were proportionally assigned to the cities, and nobody had the desire to extend their territory because they saw themselves as tenants rather than owners of their possessions. However, if the population rose above the fixed quotas, colonies were established in unoccupied spaces of the mainland as a way of expanding the utopian lifestyle. In terms of training in farming, twenty Utopians from each rural household returned to the city every year after having spent two years in the country learning agricultural activities; the same number of citizens would come from the city to replace those leaving the fields. Their faith in agriculture relates to their conviction that happiness can only be reached by living according to nature and the pragmatic dictates of reason.

As can be seen, utopian thought has been associated with social control and colonialism from the outset. More's *Utopia* has been regarded as a theory of colonization of new worlds[39] with the purpose of turning them into productive and profitable lands. In this respect, the desire to forge an ideal republic resorts to the reorganization of already occupied territories, which, in some measure, implies the imposition of an existing system on a new one, as well as a kind of authoritarian spirit in utopian discourse. With regard to this matter, Fredric Jameson stresses the importance of understanding utopian writing as a type of praxis, rather than as a specific mode of representation:

> [A] praxis which has less to do with the construction and perfection of someone's 'idea' of a 'perfect society' than it does with a concrete set of mental operations to be performed on a determinate type of raw material given in advance, which is contemporary society itself.[40]

However, as colonies embody utopian dreams in themselves, they tend to be the experimental space in which to enforce the changes originally devised for dominant societies.[41] As Lyman Sargent claims, colonies have always been designed to serve the interests of the colonizing country, not to fulfil the needs of the colonies. Moreover, since the dreams of the colonizers clash with the expectations of the colonized, the utopian enterprise ends up being a dystopia for indigenous peoples.[42] Utopian writers, similar to explorers or conquerors, can be pictured as speculative colonizers or political idealists who try to find solutions to the social and political problems of European countries. This relationship between colonialism and utopianism is particularly present in the configuration of Spanish utopian narrative. Utopian colonialism not only brings up the debate about the imposition of civilization on supposedly uncivilized cultures, but also permits one to conceive of utopian texts as a parallel or unofficial project to Spain's reform agenda. The convergence and divergence of the ideals of the Enlightenment with those of utopianism will similarly have a particular relevance.

The Empirical and Human-Centred Utopia

The difference between theoretical and practical utopia is constantly discussed in the field of utopian studies and constitutes a major topic in the representation of Spanish utopias. Although the practice of utopia has commonly been assessed in the light of a socialist concept of utopia,[43] there are earlier examples of the practical impact of utopia. The most significant case was the programme of organized science that Francis Bacon included in his unfinished *New Atlantis* (1627).[44] Solomon's House, a scientific organization of collaborative research, has been seen as the inspiration for the creation of the Royal Society in London in 1662. The premise of Bacon's scientific utopia was that 'science would revolutionize life and realize utopian aspirations'.[45] Similarly, James Harrington's *The Commonwealth of Oceana* (1656) was extremely influential in the American and French revolutionary experiences of the eighteenth century; there was even a proposal that the American state of Massachusetts should be renamed Oceana.[46] This ambivalence concerning the conception of utopia can be understood as an aspect corresponding to what Ruth Levitas identifies as the function of utopia, that is, the realization of utopia through some kind of specific action.[47]

Among the various conceptual categorizations that the problematic nature of utopia has given rise to, the one that is most commented on is Lewis Mumford's differentiation between utopias of escape and utopias of reconstruction. Whereas the former type does not intend to change reality and provides only a temporary escape from it, the latter seeks to transform the world according to one's own desires: 'In one we build impossible castles in the air; in the other we consult a surveyor and an architect and a mason and proceed to build a house which meets our essential needs'.[48] Ultimately, the perception of utopia as a notion torn between the comforting relief of fantasy and the projective or practical impulse underlying man's dream of a better world is raised in Raphael Hythloday's speech about the credibility of his account of what he saw in Utopia: 'What if I told them [the English councillors] the kind of thing that Plato imagines in his republic, or that the Utopians actually practise in theirs?'[49] What distances the commonwealth of Utopia from the merely hypothetical republic imagined by Plato is the fact that the utopian model has been effectively put into practice. This duality of utopia as an empirical realization of a fantastic project is especially relevant to the Spanish utopian tradition. However, as explained above, the imaginary republic, principally the one invented by More, is not necessarily created from scratch, but over the foundations of an existing society.

According to Trousson, a utopian is a theorizer who creates an abstract world in an attempt to override an actual world that he judges undesirable and defective. As opposed to a reformer whose concrete actions seek to have an impact on reality, the utopian thinker, for Trousson, is a sceptical, idealistic figure who does not intend to effect historical changes because he does not have the power to implement them.[50] However, one might take issue with this view and argue that it is possible for a utopian thinker to influence other people to take some kind of action to change the existing order of things. Furthermore, the position of the utopian writer confronting the established order of society can also be understood in the context of the confrontation between the notion of ideology as the official discourse of the ruling class and the concept of utopia as the discourse of social minorities, as maintained by Karl Mannheim:

> Utopias [...] are not ideologies in the measure and in so far as they succeed through counteractivity in transforming the existing historical reality into one more in accord with their own conceptions. [...] It is clear that those social strata which represent the prevailing social and intellectual order will experience as reality that structure of relationships of which they are the bearers, while the groups driven into opposition to the present order will be oriented towards the first stirrings of the social order for which they are striving and which is being realized through them.[51]

With regard to the utopian writer's creativity, Raymond Ruyer alleges that certain messianic myths entail the utopian construction of spiritual worlds in the same way that the utopian thinker devises his ideal city.[52] Despite the fact that the majority of utopian writers since Plato have endowed their utopian spaces with religious infrastructures and that three of the most important utopias — *Utopia*, *Christianopolis* (1619),[53] *La Città del Sole* [*The City of the Sun*] (1623)[54] — were written by priests — Thomas More, Johann Valentin Andreae, Tommaso Campanella — utopia is often a secular construct that is located in the earthly world.[55] In this sense, as Ruyer explains, religion is anti-utopian because it does not propose an alternative reality on an empirical basis, but advocates the fusion of the existing world with a transcendental and immanent reality; in other words, utopia is located not in this world, but in the afterlife.[56] Yet, contrary to the religious sense of a superior life, as Darko Suvin and Fátima Vieira emphasize in their respective surveys of utopian writing, utopia is primarily human-centred, a product of human endeavour that is meant for human beings and not dependent on divine intervention.[57] Thus, utopia may not be timeless, as a supernatural understanding of the concept implies, but intrinsically historical and determined by its relationship with the circumstances in which it is produced and disseminated. However, unlike the objectivity of historians' perceptions, utopian visions are grounded in a combination of fact and fiction, although this characteristic does not constrain utopia to being an escapist dream. Moreover, even though the imagined place is usually an opposite or inverted image of the one that needs to be changed, utopias transcend the criticism of the present situation and put forward innovative ideas that could be adopted in the future and bring about substantive changes.[58]

In spite of their Christian beliefs, the authors of utopian texts, such as More, Bacon, and Campanella, envisioned better societies whose reference point was the historical reality of the social systems that they were trying to improve. Their imaginary countries were the result of faith in human reason, not in the idea of an eternal life postulated by Christianity's claims. Rather than a Christian theological view of the world, their ideology reveals a secularizing, humanistic component to their thought because they endorse attitudes such as those involving tolerance, virtue, and reason, which have sometimes been considered opposed to Christian theology or Christian ways of thought. In fact, More's Utopians, Bacon's citizens of Bensalem, and Campanella's Solarians are all pagans and rely on their human ability to achieve a better state of things. As Krishan Kumar points out, '[T]hey [the Christian practitioners of utopia] were more concerned with the City of Man than the City of God',[59] alluding to St Augustine's *The City of God* (AD 426), a work that can hardly be treated as a utopia because St Augustine visualizes the ideal city in the afterlife. What he created can instead be seen as an anti-utopia or alotopia.[60]

However, it is important to note that the historical circumstances from which the image of the utopian space unfolds are not supposed to be explicitly reflected in a space that is ahistorical by definition, as in the implicit correspondence between Utopia and England. Since utopia is fundamentally a spatial conception devoid of a specific historical setting, the preservation of the ideal society tends to be associated with a sense of stability for which change becomes a threat to perfection. In any case, as Bronisław Baczko observes, the historical time of both the narrator and the reader is tacitly represented in a negative way because its omission or the unawareness of its existence by the inhabitants of the utopian place is the precondition for the successful establishment of a better society: 'Les Utopiens ont réussi à échapper à cette histoire et c'est pourquoi ils n'ont pas connu nos maux, nos vices, nos injustices' [The Utopians have succeeded in escaping from this history, and that is why they have not known our ills, our vices, our injustices].[61] The interaction between the real world and its fictional counterpart is not reciprocal: while utopian residents do not need to know the reader's historical situation because it is not a determining factor of their history, readers must understand the imaginary history — if one is described — of the imaginary country in order to judge their own social reality by contrast.

Darko Suvin underscores the comprehensive construction of an alternative location that is radically different from the author's socio-political environment. The invention of such an alternative world generates a mechanism of estrangement that subverts the unconscious internalization of social institutions.[62] Elaborating on Suvin's interpretation of utopia as an estranged world, Tom Moylan posits the notion of a critical utopia, that is, a text that presents the utopian society in a more critical light than traditional utopias do: '[T]he critical utopia [...] breaks with previous utopias by presenting in much greater, almost balanced, detail both the utopian society and the original society against which the utopia is pitted as a revolutionary alternative'.[63] Nevertheless, the image of utopia as an alternative social model produced different variations in the eighteenth century. The majority of the literary utopias of that period interacted with Enlightenment concerns about reason, reform, and progress. In this context, utopian writers conceived of alternative possibilities as arguments against absolutism, the role of the aristocracy, and the position of the Catholic Church, especially in the French case.[64]

Ruth Levitas and J. C. Davis cast doubt on the necessary condition of fictionality that utopia should exhibit in order to be treated as such.[65] Descriptions of good societies do not necessarily take the form of literary fictions, especially in the context of political writing. When there is an attempt to translate theoretical fictions into experimental facts, such as political programmes that become militant or designed for action, utopias cease to exist.[66] This feature was inherent in the transition from the Platonic utopia to the literary utopia of the seventeenth and eighteenth centuries when the fictional aspect of utopianism became strengthened, possibly in response to the realistic nature of political writing that began to prevail in the period. Apart from marking the dividing line between reformism and utopianism, the aspiration to actualize a utopian vision reaffirms the fact that utopia is anchored in a real society, giving prominence to the meaning of utopia as somewhere good over the sense of it being nowhere.

Notes to Chapter 1

1. The full title is *Libellus vere aureus, nec minus salutaris quam festivus, de optimo reipublicae statu, deque nova insula Utopia* [*A Truly Golden Little Book, No Less Beneficial Than Entertaining, of the Best State of a Republic, and of the New Island Utopia*].
2. The neologism is based on the Greek prefix *ou* ('no' or 'not') and the Greek word *topos* ('place' or 'where'). However, in addition to the meaning of nowhere, More derived the neologism *eutopia* from the first to refer to a good (*eu*) or happy place. This new meaning appears in a six-verse poem published at the end of the first edition of *Utopia*. According to Raymond Trousson, the pun lies in the ambiguous English pronunciation of the prefixes *u* and *eu* (Raymond Trousson, *Voyages aux pays de nulle part: histoire littéraire de la pensée utopique* (Brussels: Éditions de l'Université de Bruxelles, 1999), p. 9).
3. For a study of early modern utopia as a conglomeration of subgenres that contributed to nascent European imperialism, see Nina Chordas, *Forms in Early Modern Utopia: The Ethnography of Perfection* (Farnham, UK, and Burlington, VT: Ashgate, 2010).
4. An important literary concept to mention in this respect is that of the *locus amoenus* [pleasant place], formulated by Ernst Robert Curtius as an idealized place similar to the earthly paradise. See Ernst Robert Curtius, *European Literature and the Latin Middle Ages*, trans. by Willard R. Trask (New York: Pantheon Books, 1953), pp. 197–99.
5. Michel de Montaigne, 'Des cannibales', in Michel de Montaigne, *Essais*, ed. by Albert Thibaudet (Paris: Gallimard, 1950), pp. 239–53.
6. Morelly, Étienne-Gabriel, *Naufrage des îles flottantes, ou Basiliade du célèbre Pilpai*, 2 vols (Messine: n. pub., 1753).
7. Paul Bloomfield, *Imaginary Worlds; or, The Evolution of Utopia* (London: Hamish Hamilton, 1932), pp. 114–15.
8. Krishan Kumar, *Utopianism* (Minneapolis: University of Minnesota Press, 1991), pp. 4–5.
9. Lyman Tower Sargent, *Utopianism: A Very Short Introduction* (Oxford: Oxford University Press, 2010), pp. 12–13.

10. Christine Rees, *Utopian Imagination and Eighteenth-Century Fiction* (London and New York: Longman, 1996), p. 123.
11. Robert C. Elliott, *The Shape of Utopia: Studies in a Literary Genre* (Chicago, IL, and London: University of Chicago Press, 1970), p. 24.
12. Paul Arthur notices that, in opposition to the tyrannical image of the colonizer, the fictional traveller is frequently portrayed as a peacekeeper who may try to impose European values by invitation rather than by force: 'The traveller usually arrives powerless in the new world but slowly begins to exert an influence. If the antipodean inhabitants are persuaded by the traveller's arguments in support of the value of European culture, he is often given the role of negotiator or instigator of change' (Paul Longley Arthur, *Virtual Voyages: Travel Writing and the Antipodes, 1605–1837* (London: Anthem, 2011), p. 6).
13. Dominic Baker-Smith, *More's 'Utopia'* (London: HarperCollins Academic, 1991), p. 151.
14. See Thomas More, *Utopia*, ed. and trans. by Edward Surtz (New Haven, CT: Yale University Press, 1964), p. 61, note 8.
15. Baker-Smith, *More's 'Utopia'*, p. 151.
16. Ibid., p. 156.
17. Thomas More, *Utopia*, ed. by George M. Logan and trans. by Robert M. Adams (Cambridge: Cambridge University Press, 2006), pp. 48–49.
18. Dominic Baker-Smith, 'Reading *Utopia*', in *The Cambridge Companion to Thomas More*, ed. by George M. Logan (Cambridge: Cambridge University Press, 2011), pp. 141–67 (p. 151).
19. More, *Utopia*, ed. by Logan and trans. by Adams, p. 50.
20. Ibid., p. 67.
21. Ibid., p. 103.
22. Ibid., p. 68.
23. Quentin Skinner, *Visions of Politics*, 3 vols (Cambridge: Cambridge University Press, 2002), II: *Renaissance Virtues*, p. 234.
24. More, *Utopia*, ed. by Logan and trans. by Adams, p. 82.
25. Ibid., p. 81.
26. Ibid., p. 93.
27. Ibid., p. 66.
28. Ibid., pp. 93, 94, 97.
29. The term 'utopianism' was coined by the literary historian Alexandre Cioranescu (1911–1999) to refer to a current of thought, distinguishing it from utopia as a literary genre (Trousson, p. 12).
30. Fátima Vieira, 'The Concept of Utopia', in *The Cambridge Companion to Utopian Literature*, ed. by Gregory Claeys (Cambridge: Cambridge University Press, 2010), pp. 3–27 (p. 4).
31. Nicole Pohl, 'Utopianism after More: The Renaissance and Enlightenment', in *The Cambridge Companion to Utopian Literature*, ed. by Gregory Claeys (Cambridge: Cambridge University Press, 2010), pp. 51–78 (p. 63).
32. Ibid.
33. Ibid., p. 64.
34. More, *Utopia*, ed. by Logan and trans. by Adams, p. 42.
35. Vieira, p. 4.
36. Chris Ferns, *Narrating Utopia: Ideology, Gender, Form in Utopian Literature* (Liverpool: Liverpool University Press, 1999), p. 49.
37. Trousson, pp. 15–16.
38. Ferns, pp. 2–3.
39. Arthur, p. 10.
40. Fredric Jameson, 'Of Islands and Trenches: Naturalization and the Production of Utopian Discourse', *Diacritics*, 7 (1977), 2–21 (p. 6).
41. Sargent, *Utopianism*, p. 50.
42. Lyman Tower Sargent, 'Colonial and Postcolonial Utopias', in *The Cambridge Companion to Utopian Literature*, ed. by Gregory Claeys (Cambridge: Cambridge University Press, 2010), pp. 200–22 (p. 204).

43. Utopian socialism flourished in Europe in the nineteenth century; its main representatives were the Frenchmen Henri de Saint-Simon and Charles Fourier, and the Welshman Robert Owen. For a selection of texts by Spanish utopian socialists, see Antonio Elorza, *El fourierismo en España* (Madrid: Ediciones de la Revista de Trabajo, 1975).
44. Francis Bacon, *New Atlantis*, in *Three Early Modern Utopias: Thomas More, 'Utopia'; Francis Bacon, 'New Atlantis'; Henry Neville, 'The Isle of Pines'*, ed. by Susan Bruce (Oxford: Oxford University Press, 1999), pp. 149–86.
45. Krishan Kumar, *Utopia and Anti-Utopia in Modern Times* (Oxford: Basil Blackwell, 1987), p. 31.
46. Kumar, *Utopianism*, pp. 68–69.
47. In attempting to differentiate the essential attributes of utopian writing, Levitas distinguishes the form of utopia from what she defines as the content (the portrayal of a good society) and the function (the concrete goals) of utopia. The form refers to the definition of utopia as a literary genre, which involves the detailed fictional depiction of an alternative society (Ruth Levitas, *The Concept of Utopia* (London: Philip Allan, 1990), pp. 4–5).
48. Lewis Mumford, *The Story of Utopias: Ideal Commonwealths and Social Myths* (London: Harrap, 1923), p. 15.
49. More, *Utopia*, ed. by Logan and trans. by Adams, pp. 35–36.
50. Trousson, p. 13.
51. Karl Mannheim, *Ideology and Utopia: An Introduction to the Sociology of Knowledge* (London: Routledge and Kegan Paul, 1936), p. 176.
52. Raymond Ruyer, *L'Utopie et les utopies* (Paris: Presses Universitaires de France, 1950), p. 30.
53. Johann Valentin Andreae, *Christianopolis: An Ideal State of the Seventeenth Century* (Oxford: Oxford University Press, 1916).
54. Tommaso Campanella, *La Città del Sole: dialogo poetico / The City of the Sun: A Poetical Dialogue*, trans. by Daniel J. Donno (Berkeley: University of California Press, 1981).
55. In describing utopia as a secular variety of social thought, Krishan Kumar inevitably argues that 'One reason why it is difficult to find utopia in non-Western societies is that they have mostly been dominated by religious systems of thought' (Kumar, *Utopianism*, p. 35).
56. Ruyer, p. 31.
57. Darko Suvin, *Defined by a Hollow: Essays on Utopia, Science Fiction and Political Epistemology* (Bern and Oxford: Peter Lang, 2010), p. 23; Vieira, p. 7.
58. Vieira, p. 8.
59. Kumar, *Utopianism*, p. 35.
60. Vieira, p. 6. Alotopia is the presentation of a fictional world as if it was the only possible real world. See Umberto Eco, 'Los mundos de la ciencia ficción', in Umberto Eco, *De los espejos y otros ensayos* (Barcelona: Lumen, 1988), pp. 185–92 (p. 186).
61. Bronisław Baczko, *Lumières de l'utopie* (Paris: Payot, 1978), p. 156.
62. Suvin, pp. 21, 30.
63. Tom Moylan, *Demand the Impossible: Science Fiction and the Utopian Imagination* (London and New York: Methuen, 1986), p. 44.
64. Pohl, p. 63.
65. J. C. Davis, *Utopia and the Ideal Society: A Study of English Utopian Writing, 1516–1700* (Cambridge: Cambridge University Press, 1981), pp. 15–16; Levitas, p. 5.
66. Judith Shklar, 'The Political Theory of Utopia: From Melancholy to Nostalgia', in *Utopias and Utopian Thought*, ed. by Frank E. Manuel (London: Souvenir Press, 1973), pp. 101–15 (pp. 106–07).

CHAPTER 2

Colonial Utopianism and Eighteenth-Century Reformism

Spanish history has been significantly marked by a spirit of discovery and expansion as a result of the encounter with the New World in 1492 and the subsequent new era of scientific investigation that began in the late seventeenth century. The vision of exploration and innovation promoted by the Spanish Crown not only responded to a thirst for knowledge in all fields, equally pursued by other dominant European nations, but also contributed to the development of utopian thought in Spain. In this way, Spanish utopianism would find in social experimentation in Spanish America a significant antecedent of its principles and practices. In addition to the transatlantic experience, the reformist vision of a group of intellectuals in seventeenth-century Spain was a strong precedent that laid the foundation for the flourishing of a Spanish utopian mentality. Relevant aspects of these attitudes will be explored below.

The present chapter also aims to outline the historical process of reformist writing in Spain and to show how progressive thought in the eighteenth century provided a stimulus for setting out plans for change within the new spirit of the Enlightenment. A curious feature that became significantly notable in eighteenth-century Spain was the recovery of past reformist writings. Works from the seventeenth century that remained in manuscript were printed for the first time as they perhaps no longer seemed threateningly radical. Censorship revealed a greater tolerance for alternative points of view to the orthodox in the eighteenth century, especially in the second half.[1]

Experimental Utopia in the New World

The utopian character of the Spanish American colonies derived from the opportunity that they offered to create a better society in a then unknown territory, where the supposed innocence of its inhabitants and the apparently pristine nature of its environment seemed to promise well-being and material abundance. For the Spanish historian José Antonio Maravall, Spain sees in newly discovered America the opportunity to carry out its dream-like aspirations of imperial domination. The New World represented the untouched place where Spanish inventive and transformative power could be put into practice, and its unknown inhabitants were treated as a blank slate for implementing an entire system of thinking. This non-violent act of indoctrination was unthinkable in the European context because of the resistance put up by its peoples.[2] Similarly, José Luis Abellán has written extensively on the act of imagining the New World as the most rudimentary expression of Spanish utopian thought. The vision of the colonial territory as a potential space in which the principles of religion, justice, and happiness could be better achieved corresponds to a phenomenon of 'inverted' Western values, explained by Abellán as follows:

> [E]n América se invierten los valores y las relaciones del Antiguo Continente: lo que en el uno es malo en el otro es bueno, y viceversa. Así se valora positivamente el Nuevo Mundo frente al Viejo; aquél es el mundo del futuro, del porvenir, de la abundancia y de la fertilidad, mientras éste es habitáculo de un pretérito que pesa excesivamente sobre sus espaldas, un mundo de pobreza, escasez y esterilidad.[3]
>
> [In America the values and relationships of the Old Continent are inverted: what in the one is bad in the other is good, and vice versa. This is how the New World is positively valued in relation to the Old; the former is the world of the future, of what is to come, of abundance and fertility, while the latter is the space of a past that weighs heavily on people's backs, a world of poverty, scarcity, and sterility.]

As a result, it was the imagined conception of America and its inherent condition as a 'good place' that gave the continent its status as a utopia, even though the identification of utopia with a specific place in the southern hemisphere undermines one standard feature of utopia itself, which is meant to refer to a 'no place'.[4] It is also noteworthy that the discovery of the New World was stigmatized by Columbus's messianic consciousness of his mission as a discoverer: 'Columbus always insisted that his "execution of the affair of the Indies" was a fulfilment of prophecies in Isaiah and not a matter of mere reason, mathematics, and maps'.[5] Columbus was convinced that he had arrived in the earthly paradise because the characteristics of the place he had discovered fitted the description of it given by theologians. The account of his third voyage contains his speculations concerning the location of the mythical land:

> [C]reo que si yo pasara por debajo de la línea equinoccial, [...] hallara muy mayor temperancia, y diversidad en las estrellas y en las aguas; no porque yo crea que allí donde es la altura del extremo sea navegable ni agua, ni que se pueda subir allá, porque creo que allí es el paraíso terrenal adonde no puede llegar nadie, salvo por voluntad divina.[6]
>
> [I have no doubt that if I could pass below the equinoctial line, [...] I should find a much milder temperature, and a variation in the stars and in the water; not that I suppose that elevated point to be navigable, nor even that there is water there; indeed, I believe it is impossible to ascend thither, because I am convinced that it is the spot of the earthly paradise, whither no one can go but by God's permission.][7]

It is also worth mentioning that the seventeenth-century Spanish historian and jurist Antonio de León Pinelo wrote a two-volume work entitled *El Paraíso en el*

Nuevo Mundo: comentario apologético, historia natural y peregrina de las Indias Occidentales [*Paradise in the New World: Laudatory Commentary, Natural and Strange History of the Western Indies*] (1656).[8] León Pinelo defended the thesis that the biblical paradise was located in South America, specifically in the Amazon. However, although the Spaniard praised the richness and magnificence of the region, he believed in the superiority of Europeans over indigenous peoples,[9] an ideological position that would be the basis for the eighteenth-century European intellectual debate regarding the inferiority of indigenous populations and the superiority of Western cultures. This controversy was to form part of the Spanish Black Legend,[10] promoted by enlightened European naturalists and historians such as Georges-Louis Leclerc (Count of Buffon), Cornelius de Pauw, William Robertson, and Guillaume Raynal, who questioned the effectiveness and morality of Spain's colonial enterprise in America.

Apart from the influence of the Christian myth of the earthly paradise in the utopian perception of the Spanish American colonies, the narrative concept of travel and discovery underlying the utopian genre can be seen as corresponding to the historical circumstances of Spain's policies of expansion and colonization. This aspect becomes relevant in considering the practice of experimental utopia that defines an important strand in eighteenth-century Spanish utopian fiction. Thus, a central premise is the predominance of a practical or empirical utopia in enlightened Spain as a correlative of the imperial imperative of domination: the Spanish expansionist policy is historically determined by the founding of a real utopia. Such an objective would be principally reflected in the construction of a new historiography of the New World during the eighteenth and nineteenth centuries, 'one constructed in the name of the nation rather than the monarchy'.[11] The most relevant text in this respect was Juan Bautista Muñoz's *Historia del Nuevo Mundo* [*History of the New World*] (1793), a revised history of Spanish colonization as a way of undermining the Spanish Black Legend created by foreign adversaries.

The impact of the colonization process of the New World on the Spanish utopian impulse is visible in the significant practical utopian projects that were envisioned by Spanish missionaries at around the time of the publication of More's pioneering text. The events to be highlighted are the ones related to the Christian mission of evangelization after the conquest of America, which corresponds to what Stelio Cro describes as an empirical utopia or the second stage in the development of the Spanish utopian tradition. The perception of a Spanish empirical utopia from the discovery of the New World until the late colonial period entails the idea that Spaniards were never searching for a utopia because they were always creating one and acting according to its rules. Cro gives important insight into this assumption:

> Mientras la utopía de Platón, como la de Moro y de la mayoría de los utopistas europeos, se basa en una tradición literaria, la utopía española arranca de una experiencia vital. De allí que se distinga netamente de la otra por su carácter empírico. Esto puede haber influido también en la escasez de las elaboraciones teóricas de la utopía española. Al percibir a la utopía como ideal de reforma inspirado en la realidad del Nuevo Mundo, los españoles tuvieron un punto de referencia que otros no conocieron. Al desconocer la utopía empírica, otros pueblos elaboraron la utopía teórica.[12]

[While Plato's utopia, like that of More and most European utopians, is based on a literary tradition, Spanish utopias start from a lived experience. Hence, they clearly differ from the other utopias by their empirical character. This may have also led to the lack of theoretical thinking in Spanish utopias. In perceiving utopia as a reformist ideal inspired by the reality of the New World, Spaniards had a point of reference that other people did not know about. Because of a lack of acquaintance with empirical utopias, other cultures elaborated theoretical ones.]

In the Italian scholar's view, the first stage in the evolution of Hispanic utopianism is the discovery and conquest of the New World or the encounter with a real utopia; the third refers to the replacement of the experimental utopia by literary utopias during the Spanish Golden Age, represented by *Don Quixote*; the fourth and final stage, according to Cro, is marked by the composition of the anonymous and undated *Descripción de la Sinapia, península en la tierra austral*, the only true example, in his opinion, of the utopian genre in Spain.[13]

Given the assumption that the Christianization of the newly discovered peoples was a primitive form of utopian vision, there are at least three socio-religious experiments that are worth focusing on: Father Bartolomé de las Casas's 1516 reform plan to obtain new legislation for protection of the natives (coincidentally in the same year that More's *Utopia* was published); Vasco de Quiroga's *pueblos-hospitales* [hospital-villages] of Santa Fe in Mexico during the period from 1532 to 1539, set up in an attempt to create a new republic of Indians; and the Paraguayan Jesuit *reducciones* [Indian mission settlements] established in 1609. These proposals can be understood as defiant reformist programmes, but the plausibility of conceiving of them as utopian plans lies in their aim to have a meaningful impact on entire communities. Of these three projects, the last two are of special importance, and in fact the Jesuit *reducciones* were apparently inspired by the *pueblos-hospitales*.[14] Both were complex models of a new type of community with a strong Christian ethos.

In contrast with León Pinelo's derogatory view of the otherness of the inhabitants of the New World, Bartolomé de las Casas formulates an anthropological interpretation of the laudable, sophisticated beliefs and practices of the indigenous inhabitants. Las Casas argues that the natives are perfectly rational because their physical constitution is determined by the clemency of the weather and the favourable conditions of the territory. Their rational nature not only makes them self-governing, prone to accept the Catholic faith, and capable of doing without other countries' protection, but also makes them in no way inferior to European nations:[15]

[C]on muchas naciones del mundo señaladas y nombradas por políticas y razonables se igualaron, y a otras muchas más sobrepujaron, y a ningunas fueron inferiores, y entre las con quien[es] se igualaron, fueron los griegos y romanos, y en muchas buenas y mejores costumbres, los vencieron y sobrepujaron. Sobrepujaron también a los ingleses y franceses y a algunas gentes de nuestra España, y a otras innumerables fueron tan superiores en las costumbres, tenerlas buenas y carecer de muchas malas, que no merecieron con las de estas Indias compararse.[16]

[They were equal to many nations of the world that were singled out and described as political and reasonable, and outdid many others; they were not inferior to any of them, and among those with whom they were equal were the Greeks and Romans, and in many good and better customs they overcame and surpassed them. They also outdid the English and the French, and some Spaniards, and they were so superior to countless others in their customs, having good ones and lacking many bad ones, that they did not deserve to be compared to those of the Indies.]

Las Casas's reform programme called for the abolition of all forms of subjugation and the restoration of indigenous states, their rulers, and their population, who was the legitimate owner of the land. Instead of an oppressive conversion process,

> Las Casas hoped for a peaceful colonization of the New World by Spanish farmers who would live side by side with the natives, teach them to farm and live in the European way, and gradually bring into being an ideal Christian community.[17]

The materialization of More's imaginary society was first undertaken by the Spanish humanist and Bishop of Michoacán Vasco de Quiroga with the founding of three experimental towns in New Spain: Santa Fe de los Altos, Santa Fe de la Laguna, and Santa Fe del Río.[18] In fact, he translated *Utopia* into Spanish, but the manuscript is apparently lost.[19] Quiroga's plan was to introduce European civilization into the New World by organizing the natives into villages where they would live according to Catholic doctrine and acquire the habits of virtue. As Silvio Zavala asserts, '*Utopia*, for Quiroga, had a realistic meaning; it was something that could be applied, not an idle dream'.[20] The objectives of utopia turned into an organizational strategy in Quiroga's humanistic programme. Besides the immediate influence of More's work, it is possible to draw a parallel between Bacon's utopia and Quiroga's project on the grounds that the Spanish reformer wanted to establish an ideal community supported by the virtues of science and regulated by a Christian government.[21]

Quiroga's thought was also based on his reading of the play *Saturnalia*, written by the second-century Greek satirist Lucian of Samosata and translated into Latin by Thomas More.[22] In his *Información en derecho* [*Information on the Law*] (1535), Quiroga claimed that the behaviour of the indigenous people of the New World was similar to that of the men of the Golden Age described by Lucian in his work, but he intensified the utopian features of that ideal era of abundance and equality in order to extol the virtues and qualities of the New World's population.[23] His social experiment of the *pueblos-hospitales* exhibited the fundamental ingredients of the utopian model: communities settled in communal lands in which families were the political unit and dedicated to farming and Christian education.[24] The civilizing process of reshaping the natives was intended to protect them from the corrupt customs of the conquistadors and to turn them into the agents of a restored Christianity:

> [S]e pudiese reformar y restaurar y legitimar [...] la doctrina y vida cristiana [...] en esta reneciente Iglesia en esta edad dorada entre estos naturales; pues que en la nuestra de hierro lo repugna tanto nuestra y casi natural soberbia, codicia, ambición y malicia desenfrenadas.[25]

[Christian doctrine and life [...] could be reformed, restored, and legitimized [...] in this renascent Church, in this golden age, among these natives; for in our iron age it is rejected by our own, almost natural and unbridled pride, greed, ambition, and malice.]

In the same vein, the system of Jesuit *reducciones*, an exercise in applied utopianism that spanned the period from 1607 to 1767 in Spanish America, was implemented in Paraguay in 1609 with the purpose of organizing the indigenous population according to a social model subscribing to Christianity, an ideological pattern that permeates the characterization of Spanish utopian thought. The growth of the Paraguayan Jesuit missions has been seen in connection with the decadence of the Spanish Empire, which not only interested the French *philosophes* [philosophers], but was also noted by the Spanish authorities who expelled the Order from Hispanic lands in 1767.[26] The Jesuit model consisted of the division of the Guarani population into thirty villages, in which the regulatory principles were the belonging of the land to the indigenous families and the guarantee of their freedom in the *reducciones*.[27] However, the majority of the opponents of the Jesuits claimed that the Guarani Indians were actually slaves in the missions.[28] In response to such a defamatory statement, the Spanish Jesuit missionary José Manuel Peramás identified a correspondence between the utopian dimension of Plato's *Republic* and the structural aspects of the programme of *reducciones* in his work *La 'República' de Platón y los guaraníes* [Plato's 'Republic' and the Guaraní] (1793), which was originally written in Latin. Anticipating the rejection that his comparison might generate, Peramás argues that his analogy is based on his personal observation of the Paraguayan Jesuit missions and on authorized writings.[29] Nevertheless, the similarity between Plato's utopian model and the system of *reducciones* could be just a mere coincidence.

The utopian nature of the *reducciones* can also be noted not only in their attempt to create a parallel society in which the economic and social lives of the Indians would be strengthened and free of an interfering civil administration,[30] but also in the reactions that such an attempt sparked among certain dissenting sectors of society: 'The effectively utopian character of the Reduction system is clear from the many antagonisms it excited — from Spain's colonial competitors, from the civil authority, from the settlers (deprived of access to Indian labour) and from the diocesan church, among others'.[31]

Moreover, the missionary discourse behind these projects brings up the myth of the good savage or idealized indigenous inhabitant who has not been corrupted by contact with so-called civilization. The image of the good savage is a recurring motif in utopian fiction, and especially in the Spanish utopian tradition, because the possibility of an individual whose mind is a blank slate over which civilization has not exercised its influence is certainly a suitable feature in the building of a happy and perfect society. In fact, the noble or virtuous savage is not an actual person, but a mythical construct, a fable according to which man can live happier in a primitive state and in harmony with nature. Although the concept was outlined by Montaigne in 'Des cannibales' as a means of working out a critique of French culture by opposing it to the virtues of non-European peoples, it was Jean-

Jacques Rousseau who redefined it and brought it into mainstream thinking in the eighteenth century. Rousseau's theory of natural man[32] emphasizes the innate and amoral goodness of humanity in its natural state, which is actually neither good nor bad as morality only develops through education in a civil state. It is against this backdrop, in which Christian conversion merges with the idea of a pristine Other uncorrupted by the vices of an unnatural political society, that the utopian experiments in the Spanish colonies of America sought to protect the rights of their Christianized 'good savages'.

The Tradition of the *Arbitristas*

In the context of the actualization of utopia — a 'concrete utopia' in Ernst Bloch's terms[33] — and the civilizing colonial enterprise as essential elements of Spanish utopianism, it is important to identify the relationship between the characteristics of the Enlightenment and utopia in Spain in order to deconstruct the supposed absence of both utopian and Enlightenment thinking in eighteenth-century Spain.[34] Enlightenment thought in Spain was essentially an ideology of social criticism that implied a rupture with scholastic theology and a desire, in part, to employ secularizing values in the fight against ignorance, superstition, and injustice.[35] This was a way of thinking particularly defended by a group of Spanish political economists called *arbitristas* (1600–50).

The seventeenth-century Spanish current of thought labelled *arbitrismo* was an important ideological precedent for the emergence of Iberian utopianism in the subsequent era of Enlightenment. In spite of being frequently depicted as outlandish charlatans whose supposedly irrational projects[36] did not constitute effective solutions to the problems of the Spanish monarchy, the *arbitristas* can be regarded as the intellectual predecessors of Spanish Enlightenment utopian thinkers by virtue of their vision of social reform. Jean Vilar underlines the original seventeenth-century meaning of *arbitrio* as 'remedy', 'trick', or 'stratagem', that is, the artifice of thinking up alternatives to Spain's problems, especially in the economic sphere.[37] Far from being constrained, the suggestions of the *arbitristas* were tolerated and encouraged by the government due to the lack of an economic theory applicable to the needs of the Spanish nation.[38]

The literary representation of the *arbitrista* as a fictional character in novels and plays portrays him as extravagant, lunatic, and unsuccessful. Such a description did not necessarily conform to reality as the negative image of the *arbitristas* might rather have been the result of their condition as misunderstood thinkers.[39] The nineteenth-century Spanish historian and economist Manuel Colmeiro also recognized the dual characterization of these intellectual figures, whose supposedly unrealistic proposals were simultaneously seen as stimuli for feasible reform plans:

> Los arbitristas eran (como dijo algún escritor del siglo pasado) las sirenas del golfo político, o una secta disidente de los verdaderos economistas; pero en medio de los sueños de felicidad pública, de los delirios de su imaginación exaltada, de sus proyectos no siempre desinteresados, y algunas veces disparatados o imposibles, todavía merecen bien de la ciencia económica, porque excitaban la controversia

y se purificaban las doctrinas favorables al aumento de la riqueza pública y a la reforma de las contribuciones.[40]

[The *arbitristas* were (as some writer of the past century said) the sirens of the political gulf, or a sect dissident from true economists; but in the midst of the dreams of public happiness, of the delusions of their exalted imaginations, of their not always disinterested projects, sometimes foolish and impossible, they still well deserve their place in economic science because they provoked controversy and refined doctrines favourable to the increase in public wealth and to the reform of taxation.]

The definition of *arbitrista* given by the *Diccionario de autoridades* [*Dictionary of Authorities*] in 1726 highlights the concern with economic issues and the widespread negative opinion of the proposed remedies:

El que discurre y propone medios para acrecentar el erario público o las rentas del príncipe. Viene del nombre 'arbitrio'; pero esta voz comúnmente se toma en mala parte, y con universal aversión, respecto de que por lo general los arbitristas han sido muy perjudiciales a los príncipes, y muy gravosas al común sus trazas y arbitrios.[41]

[Someone who imagines and proposes ways of increasing public wealth or the income of the monarch. The term comes from 'arbitrio'; but this word is usually understood in a negative way, and with universal aversion, in that *arbitristas* have generally been very harmful to monarchs, and their plans and remedies have been very burdensome to the common man.]

However, as Henry Kamen explains, 'Los arbitristas provenían de una amplia gama de profesiones: soldados, funcionarios, clérigos, comerciantes, juristas. [...] Su temática era predominantemente económica — comercio, despoblación, inflación, agricultura, pobreza — pero también entraban en problemas morales, religiosos y políticos' [*Arbitristas* came from a wide range of professions: soldiers, bureaucrats, clerics, merchants, lawyers. [...] Their subject matter was predominantly economic — trade, depopulation, inflation, agriculture, poverty — but they also considered moral, religious, and political problems].[42] This wide range of criticism demonstrates the freedom of expression allowed by the government at the time. The main solutions to the Spanish crisis proposed by the *arbitristas* included prohibiting foreign manufactures and increasing domestic production, abolishing harmful taxes, and creating a trading company to stop foreign merchants from controlling Spain's commerce.[43]

In attempting to delineate the parameters of *arbitrismo* as a genre, Juan Ignacio Gutiérrez Nieto, like Kamen, clarifies the fact that the movement's interests comprised different thematic areas: governmental finance, the economic system, politics, society, and manufacturing.[44] As seen from the perspective of utopianism, the involvement of the *arbitristas* in the field of social reform is especially relevant: '[S]us propuestas reformistas inciden de manera directa en la sociedad, bien propugnando un cambio de valores sociales, bien proponiendo medidas que significarían una radical transformación del orden estamental' [Their reformist proposals have a direct impact on society, either by promoting a change in social values or by proposing measures that would mean a radical transformation of the social order].⁴⁵ Moreover, Gutiérrez Nieto distinguishes a utopian spirit in programmes resulting from the practice of social *arbitrismo*, in particular in relation to social inequality: the *arbitristas* condemned the excessive wealth of certain social groups and encouraged the rise of the middle classes.⁴⁶ More than a simple moral issue, the importance of developing a bourgeois sector in society lay in the capacity of such people to secure a more balanced social class system and other societal changes. The utopian quality of these incipient and idealistic reform plans is equally perceived by Evaristo Correa Calderón, who chiefly focused his attention on utopia-like schemes that were created to reform the running of Galicia.⁴⁷

The practical mentality of the *arbitristas* can also be seen as a reason underlying the pragmatic configuration of Spanish utopianism. In this respect, Mariano Baquero Goyanes wonders why *arbitristas*' futuristic vision did not lead to a more substantial production of literary utopias in Spain. His explanation is that the Spanish nation tends to live in a perpetual present that prevents it from projecting itself into an imaginary and ideal future: '[L]os españoles vivimos muy ligados al presente y estamos dotados de escasa capacidad de futurición, ahincados en el momento fugaz y asidos a las cosas, hechos y gestos que componen nuestro vivir más inmediato' [We Spaniards live in a way closely attached to the present and are endowed with little ability to envision the future, being allied to the fleeting moment and attached to things, facts, and actions that comprise our more immediate way of life].⁴⁸ According to the scholar, this immediacy that turns into an extreme materialism corroborates the Spanish tendency towards the promotion of an existential hyperrealism.⁴⁹

To avoid falling into Baquero's radical perspective, it can be said that utopianism in Spain would take a discursive form shaped by the necessity of taking care of immediate socio-political matters in the midst of a reformist and progressive environment. As Amable Fernández Sanz points out regarding Gaspar de Jovellanos's state project, Spanish utopian ideology was more the consolidation of a utopian reality than of an illusionist utopia.⁵⁰ For Spanish Enlightenment ideologues, utopian projects were valuable and justifiable on the basis of their potential degree of concrete realization. This ideological filter seems to be stressed by Maravall when he explains that utopia was a historical product of the renewed man of the Renaissance and that the utopian spirit was anything but an ineffective fantasy.⁵¹

The Spanish Translation of *Utopia*

Although the purpose of this chapter is to discuss the ideological circumstances that prepared the ground for the manifestation of a Spanish utopian awareness in the eighteenth century, it is inevitable that reference be made to the publication of the first translation of More's *Utopia* into Spanish during the seventeenth century as a key moment in the history of utopian thinking in Spain. In 1637, the nobleman Jerónimo Antonio de Medinilla y Porres published his Spanish version of *Utopia* with an introduction by the famous writer Francisco de Quevedo,⁵² who encouraged him to embark on the translation project and who, two years earlier, in 1635, had translated a passage of *Utopia* and included it in his political work *Carta a Luis XIII* [*Letter to Louis XIII*]. However, Medinilla translated only Book II of *Utopia*, which contains the description of the utopian island made by Raphael Hythloday. Medinilla did not include Book I — which consists of the conversation about the problems of injustice and poverty in English society between More (the narrator), the fictional character of the Flemish humanist Peter Giles, and Hythloday — and did not translate certain passages of the second book in anticipation of possible censorship by the Inquisition, which had already banned the original version of More in Latin.[53] The edition includes a statement by the notary of the Inquisition Bartolomé Jiménez Patón, who saved the translation from being censored.[54]

A second edition of Medinilla's Spanish text was not published until 1790. This re-edition included a new statement by Jiménez — presumably preserved and added by the printer — indicating that More's work was enlightening in terms of Christian experience: '[P]uede y debe imprimirse sin escrúpulo, ni sospecha de mala doctrina; antes su lección es de curiosidad cristiana y piadosa' [It can and should be printed without scruple or suspicion of being bad doctrine; rather, its lesson is one of Christian and pious curiosity].[55] The edition also included a biographical summary of More's life based not on the well-known biography written by Fernando de Herrera in 1617, but on the one published by the Jesuit Pedro de Ribadeneyra in his *Historia eclesiástica del cisma del reino de Inglaterra* [*Ecclesiastical History of the Schism of the Kingdom of England*] in 1588. In the prologue to his edition, Medinilla emphasizes the spiritual and ethical dimensions of More's conception of the ideal state: 'Fundó la felicidad de un Estado perfectamente dichoso, estableciendo la virtud, y destruyendo el vicio; y cortó la raíz de competencias entre los hombres, reduciéndolos a vivir en común, sin poseer alguna cosa en particular' [He created the happiness of a perfectly contented state, establishing virtue and destroying vice, and destroyed the roots of competitiveness among humans, obliging them to live in common, without possessing anything of their own].[56] The translator also underscores the usefulness of introducing his compatriots to such a valuable work and its equally praiseworthy author.

It is clear that Medinilla attributed a practical and utilitarian function to More's proposal for a model republic of virtuous, happy citizens. In this sense, Medinilla's viewpoint connects with the pragmatic thought of the *arbitristas*. His selective translation of *Utopia*, due to the repressive action of the Inquisition, ultimately offered the portrayal of a country in which England's problems had been solved by the application of social remedies that could be of use in all nations. The fact that a third edition of Medinilla's text was published in 1805[57] reveals its continuing popularity for Spanish readers.

The appearance of utopian writings in eighteenth-century Spain was preceded by historical circumstances and ideological currents that sought to change or improve the Spanish empire and its society through the application of practical reform projects. Not only would the social experiments of the Spanish evangelizing mission in the New World foster the advent of a utopian mentality in the next few decades, but the reformist initiatives undertaken by the *arbitristas* in the face of Spain's declining power in Europe would also contribute to the evolution of isolated reform efforts into the presentation of integrated utopian writings. In this context of renewal, the late translation of More's *Utopia* during this period seems to have responded to the intellectual thirst for new and effective economic and social solutions to Spain's perceived decadence.

The Scientific and Philosophical Movement of the *Novatores*

In the name of civilization, the *novatores* ('innovators' in Latin), or early Enlightenment thinkers (approximately 1675–1725), sought to separate empirical argumentation in the field of science from religious revelation.[58] Writing in the wake of the reformist texts of the *arbitristas*, the *novatores* were a group of scientists and humanists concerned with the backwardness of Spanish science in relation to the rest of Europe. In fact, they aimed to establish the foundations and principles of a modern conception of knowledge.[59] Thus, the diverse disciplines of human knowledge should be subject to rigorous critical enquiry. Nevertheless, the *novatores* covered areas of knowledge beyond scientific disciplines, such as social history, political economy, and legal theory.[60]

While François Lopez sees the *novatores* as a small intellectual elite, Jesús Pérez Magallón acknowledges their consciousness as a group, which was noticeable in the fact that they were constantly exchanging writings and ideas.[61] This sense of collective identity in being members of the privileged thinking classes was reflected in the subsequent organization of the *novatores* into institutionalized academies under royal patronage.[62] The fact that these intellectual circles were engaged in the global advance or reform of knowledge — aimed at banishing myths and superstitions — made them the initiators not only of Spanish Enlightenment thought, but also, to some degree, of the new spirit of Spanish utopian thought.

The definition of *novator* by the *Diccionario de autoridades* gives the term a negative meaning in the sense that it refers to someone who adds to established ideas: 'Inventor de novedades. Tómase regularmente por el que las inventa peligrosamente en materia de doctrina' [Inventor of novelties. It usually refers to someone who invents things that are dangerous from a doctrinal point of view].[63] However, this view of the *novatores* contrasts with the fact that, in retrospect, they have been vindicated and seen to be the originators of a scientific methodology and rational thought in Spain. The secularization of philosophical and scientific matters carried out by the *novatores* led to their condemnation as heretics by the Spanish theologian Francisco Palanco in his work *Dialogus physico-theologicus contra philosophiae novatores* [*Physico-Theological Dialogue Against the Philosophy of the Novatores*] (1714). As Abellán explains in this respect:

> [L]a nueva mentalidad supone una intrusión del laicismo en las investigaciones filosóficas y religiosas, que puede resultar peligroso para la fe. [...] [Palanco] [s]e escandaliza [...] de la arrogancia de estos filósofos que todo lo quieren medir con su mente, sin darse cuenta de que sólo la mente de Dios es medida de las cosas; motivo por el que acaba considerando su actitud como una temeridad impía y sacrílega.[64]

[The new mentality involves the intrusion of secularism in philosophical and religious research, which can be dangerous to belief. [...] [Palanco] is shocked [...] by the arrogance of philosophers who want to measure everything with their own minds, without realizing that only the mind of God is the measure of things; this is the reason why he ends up considering their attitude as impious and sacrilegious recklessness.]

The *novatores* denied such accusations by claiming that their intention was to restore ancient doctrines distorted by scholasticism in order to arrive at modern methods and truths.[65]

Suspicions concerning the intellectual aims of the *novatores* might have been increased by the fact that their activities started outside the official university establishment.[66] Following the empirical approach introduced by the Valencian physician Juan de Cabriada, a medical *tertulia* [gathering] would meet in Seville to discuss modern and experimental methods of medicine. The innovative perspective of this group of physicians consisted in making knowledge accessible to citizens: '[E]llos sacaron la ciencia del claustro académico a la plazuela pública' [They took science out of the academic cloister and into the public square].[67] This led to the creation of the Royal Academy of Medicine and Surgery of Seville in 1700, an institution conceived for the physical well-being of mankind in general and of Spaniards in particular.[68]

The Reformist Heritage of the *Proyectistas*

As previously mentioned, the seventeenth-century phenomenon of *arbitrismo* was subject to a pejorative interpretation in some of the writings of the period. However, it experienced a change when it was replaced by the concept of *proyectismo* in the eighteenth century. José Muñoz Pérez suggests that the presentation of a project can be seen as a textual genre covering a series of writings dealing with reform plans in accord with the reformist impetus of Carlos III's reign (1759–88).[69] The difference between *arbitrio* [remedy] and *proyecto* [project] lies in the improvised conjectures of the former and the rationalist, more empirical basis of the latter:

> El arbitrio viene a ser [...] una argucia ingeniosa y sencilla, [...] destinada a solucionar con un solo medio todos los males generales del Reino [...]. En los datos que [los arbitristas] manejaban no había ningún contacto con fuentes ni documentos; eran puramente estimativos. [...] El proyectista empezó a utilizar otro procedimiento. [...] Su proyecto ha surgido del manejo de los papeles.[70]
>
> [An *arbitrio* is seen as [...] a simple, ingenious trick, [...] designed to solve at a single stroke all the ills of the Kingdom [...]. In the data that the *arbitristas* handled, there was no contact with sources or documents; it was purely guesswork. [...] The *proyectista* began to use another procedure. [...] His project emerged from the handling of documents.]

Unlike the temporary and immediate solutions devised by the *arbitristas*, the *proyectistas* [planners] focused on concrete problems and proposed solutions applicable in the long term. It is important to bear in mind that eighteenth-century *proyectistas* prompted the work of Spanish economic societies,[71] a group of organizations created and defined by the reformist mentality of the period, as will be explained later in this chapter.

In trying to overcome their connection with discredited *arbitrios*, eighteenth-century projects were based on an optimistic and creative attitude towards the idea of modernizing the Spanish economy and society.[72] Moreover, as José Luis Gómez Urdáñez argues, while the theses of the *arbitristas* remained as impracticable utopian schemes, the programmes of the *proyectistas* were eventually put into practice:

> Si en el siglo XVII las ideas de los arbitristas quedaron en la utopía y en el lamento y la nostalgia, en el reinado de Fernando VI la mayor parte de las ideas de los más prestigiosos proyectistas, desde Gerónimo de Ustáriz y Bernardo Ulloa a Bernardo Ward o Miguel Antonio de la Gándara, pasando por las ideas de los que alcanzaron el gobierno como José del Campillo o [...] [José de] Carvajal, fueron llevadas a la práctica, si no a lo largo del corto reinado, sí no mucho después de la muerte del rey Fernando VI.[73]
>
> [If, in the seventeenth century, the ideas of the *arbitristas* were equated with utopia, lament, and nostalgia, in the reign of Ferdinand VI the majority of the ideas of the most prestigious *proyectistas*, from Gerónimo de Ustáriz and Bernardo Ulloa to Bernardo Ward or Miguel Antonio de la Gándara, including the ideas of those who reached government level like José del Campillo or [...] [José de] Carvajal, were put into practice, if not during his short reign, then not long after the death of King Ferdinand VI.]

In this respect, there were large-scale reform plans such as those of Bernardo Ward, Gaspar de Jovellanos, and León de Arroyal. One highly significant, unpublished reform project was set out by Miguel Antonio de la Gándara in *Apuntes sobre el bien y el mal de España* [*Notes on Good and Evil in Spain*] (1759), a text that influenced the reformist ideas of the government minister Pedro Rodríguez, Count of Campomanes (1723–1803), and other Enlightenment *proyectistas*.[74]

Campomanes was a major reformist figure in the reign of Carlos III. His admiration for the *arbitristas* led him to reprint some of their works in order to bring back into circulation the proposals of key reformers from the past and to emphasize their contemporary relevance.[75] He especially contributed to the re-edition of texts by Miguel Álvarez Osorio y Redín, Francisco Martínez de la Mata, and Sancho de Moncada.[76] Campomanes's initiative corresponds to an interest in preserving a connection with positive aspects of the national tradition, a recurring characteristic of the Spanish Enlightenment. He saw a direct link between the problems of civil order and those of the economy of the country, an idea that is in tune with the development of political economy as the paradigmatic science of the Enlightenment.[77] Although the reformist spirit pervaded Spanish Enlightenment thought, the two most relevant areas were education and the economy. Ignorance was considered to be a cause of poverty and social injustice, hence the need for educational reform, almost as a prerequisite for economic improvement.[78] Furthermore, many progressive thinkers believed that the problems of the national economy could only be remedied if certain radical reforms of a socio-political nature, ones that related to privileged groups such as the Church and the nobility, were put into effect. Reformism related to social structures was, however, already evident in the reign of Carlos II (1665–1700), the moment when *Sinapia*, a major utopian text that will be the subject of the next chapter, was probably written. The fact that, two centuries later when it was rediscovered, the work could be thought to be as much a product of the 1680s as the 1770s reveals the relevance of its ideas to the whole of the period in question. The text was not published, but was preserved by Campomanes in his personal library.

Henry Kamen was one of the first scholars to identify a reformist attitude in the decades prior to 1700. According to him, it is in the reign of Carlos II that the origins of recovery from Spanish decadence[79] and the beginnings of a critical spirit should be located.[80] Kamen also reveals how the reformist spirit was further encouraged by the Bourbon accession to the Spanish throne. The new monarchs had the challenge of dealing with the decline of Spain, a situation profoundly problematic for the generation of *arbitristas*.[81] Since Spaniards were seen as being opposed to the introduction of novelties, Felipe V appointed foreign ministers who began the reform of governmental practices. The effectiveness of monarchical control over institutional reformism tended to focus on making the operations of the state function better.[82] Despite this desire for greater efficiency, the reformist spirit did not attack powerful existing institutions, which were argued to be fundamental to Spain's very identity: the monarchy, the Church, and the nobility.

However, even in the early decades of the eighteenth century, there were writers who questioned central aspects of the organization of Spanish society. Foremost among these was Melchor de Macanaz (1670–1760), the most important Spanish administrator during the War of Succession and secretary of the Council of Castile. Macanaz was entrusted with the reform of the finances and administration of Valencia. A promoter of regalism, he advocated a more significant intervention of the Crown in the actions of the Church and especially in diminishing the power of the Inquisition. His writings mostly remained in manuscript and circulated only to restricted members of the society of the time because their bold character made them susceptible to political censorship.[83] Among his most distinctive works are *Auxilios para bien gobernar una monarquía católica* [*Instructions for the Good Government of a Catholic Monarchy*] (1722) and *El deseado gobierno, buscado por el amor de Dios para el reino de España* (pre-1760).[84] In fact, the latter can be read as a utopian text, as will be highlighted in the next chapter.

The reformist current of thought flourished throughout the eighteenth century, increasing in intensity in succeeding decades, especially after the mid-century. New writings were built on the works of previous authors, often going back several generations. Yet major economic texts like Jerónimo de Uztáriz's *Teórica y práctica de comercio y de marina* [*Theory and Practice of Commerce and Maritime Affairs*] (1724), Miguel de Zavala y Auñón's *Miscelánea económico-política* [*Economic-Political Miscellany*] (1749), Bernardo Ward's *Proyecto económico* [*Economic Project*] (1762), Campomanes's *Discurso sobre el fomento de la industria popular* [*Discourse on the Promotion of Popular Industry*] (1774), and León de Arroyal's *Cartas económico-políticas* [*Economic-Political Letters*] (1786–95) dialogued with one another and kept debate alive. The writings of these authors focused on finding solutions for Spain as a whole, conscious of the need to balance the demands of both the rural and urban population. They were increasingly aware of Spain's backwardness in comparison with neighbouring countries, but their texts attempted to provide detailed remedies for what they saw as a lamentable situation, one that required urgent action on the part of government.[85]

Recent research highlights the fact that the powerful impetus to reform Spain can be seen to start during the rule of Fernando VI (1746–59). While the king himself did not seem as dynamic as his successor, he appointed ministers who attempted reform in areas where it was thought possible.[86] During this period, some rejected ideas of the *arbitristas* were reformulated and improved by the *proyectistas*, like José del Campillo, whose most representative work was *Lo que hay de más y de menos en España, para que sea lo que debe ser y no lo que es* [*What Is Redundant and Absent in Spain, for Spain to Be What It Must Be and Not What It Currently Is*] (1741–42). As Gómez Urdáñez points out,

> Muchas de las despreciadas tesis de los arbitristas del xvii — que ya se empiezan a publicar antes de que lo haga Campomanes — se ven corroboradas con prácticas incipientes que han sido puestas al día por los proyectistas, algunos de los cuales dispondrán del gobierno para llevarlas a cabo.[87]
>
> [Many of the despised proposals of the *arbitristas* of the seventeenth century — which were already beginning to be published before Campomanes did so — were corroborated by the updated early practices of the *proyectistas*, some of whom would have the power of government at their disposal to carry them out.]

The Spanish reformers knew that the central problem of the empire was the uneven distribution and exploitation of land. The peasantry did not have the means of improving farming techniques and the profits derived from the produce of farming, while the Church and the nobility owned and controlled the use of most of peninsular Spain's territory. Fernando VI's reign was not long, and his personal psychological problems seriously affected its final years, but the reformist spirit visible in government circles carries over into the new reign of his half-brother Carlos III. Given that four of the utopian texts examined in this book were published in the final three decades of the eighteenth century, it is notable that the period also marked a high point of reformist thinking.

The reign of Carlos III was especially relevant for reformism: he had led reform as King of Naples before ascending the throne of Spain in 1759.[88] Unlike Britain and France, the Spanish monarchy was infrequently the object of criticism. Religion and absolute monarchy could not be questioned publicly. The Bourbons theoretically legitimized their absolute authority upon the principle of natural law.[89] Thus, the ruler can be a despot who embodies all the power attributed by a social contract according to which that power must increase the happiness of the nation.[90] However, although the monarchy proved untouchable, the nobility and the clergy were to become the target of attacks before 1789.[91] In the context of the rational utilitarianism that characterized Enlightenment thought, the main criticism against the nobility was its lack of social usefulness. To counteract this negative judgement, those who supported the existence of the nobility tried to demonstrate its positive role in society through participation in governmental projects such as the activities, both theoretical and practical, of economic societies, which were fostered by Campomanes as, in part, a way of occupying the idle nobility:

> La nobleza de las provincias, que por lo común vive ociosa, ocuparía en estas sociedades económicas [...] últimamente su tiempo; y sin desembolso alguno del Estado serían los nobles los promovedores de la industria, y el apoyo permanente de sus compatriotas.[92]
>
> [The provincial nobility, who usually live in a state of idleness, would finally occupy their time [...] in these economic societies; and without any investment from the state, nobles would be the promoters of industry and a source of permanent support to their compatriots.]

Although the economic and legal privileges of the nobility and Church constituted an obstacle to the development of productive activities, the acceptance of a highly unequal social stratification was general: privileged classes were the norm, not the exception.[93] The economic power of these two sectors was not seriously challenged before the Courts of Cadiz, in the wake of the Napoleonic invasion that led to the Spanish War of Independence.

Many reformist thinkers in Spain were not anti-monarchical, since they saw the monarchy as a potential guarantor of order in society, an aspect that will be especially relevant for the representation of monarchy in utopian texts. The power of the monarchy, according to some progressive historians of the period, was reinforced by its reluctance to facilitate social reform: '[L]a realidad del despotismo ilustrado es la de un intento de afianzar el poder de una monarquía cuya naturaleza está divorciada del cambio social' [The reality of enlightened despotism supposes an attempt to strengthen the power of a monarchy whose nature excludes social change].[94] Many of the reform projects failed, but those that were successful seem designed to protect the interests of the dominant classes. Social pressure came from middling groups in society who demanded greater powers for themselves. Tax reform, whose foundations were laid during the rule of Fernando VI when he approved the *Catastro* [census of property] carried out by his chief minister the Marquis of Ensenada, would have meant an authentic and progressive advance by making an impact on the system of privileges of the nobility and the clergy, but of course this would have interfered with the monarchy's centralized control of the territory.[95] In a broad sense, the Bourbon regime seemed not to be prepared to undertake social projects or experiments, such as the unsuccessful establishment of the new settlements of the Sierra Morena promoted by Campomanes, as will be discussed later in this book.

Changes in Mentality: Enlightenment Thought

The manifestation of Spanish Enlightenment thinking via ideological renovation, introduced by the *novatores*, contrasts with the idea that Spain did not implement projects or create institutions in order to detach itself from the Old Regime.[96] In fact, the absence of a strong middle class was a principal argument for claiming that there was no Spanish Enlightenment.[97] However, the political discourse of key thinkers under Bourbon rule advocated the modernization and scientific progress of the country, as well as a high level of social improvement, similar to the one achieved by other European nations. In this sense, there was an interest in reinterpreting and rewriting the history of Spain, especially towards the end of the century when Nicolas Masson de Morvilliers wrote the article on Spain for the *Encyclopédie méthodique* [*Methodical Encyclopaedia*], questioning Spain's historical cultural contribution to Europe. This was a debate in which the concept of nation acquired an intense political significance, making evident the logical tension between nationalism and cosmopolitanism, and one in which the apologists of traditional Spanish values perceived foreign influence as a threat to their view of national identity.[98]

Before their expulsion in 1767, the Jesuits tended to be seen as on the side of traditionalists who opposed the progressive thinking of the Enlightenment.[99] One of the triggers for their expulsion was the threat represented by the 1766 riots, the climactic symptom of the ineffectiveness of some of Carlos III's reformist policies.[100] These acts of rebellion responded to the discontent of the masses against the restrictions that the social and economic structures imposed over them. In general terms, the traditionalist or anti-Enlightenment sector of Spain's educated classes consisted of reactionary minorities, such as the Jesuits and the apologists for Spain's historical legacy in the 1780s, who relied for their power on an institution like the Inquisition. For these groups, the Enlightenment was synonymous with anti-Spanish or foreign culture, especially French.[101]

To a certain extent, the utopian thrust in the period is a response to the events resulting from the reformist mentality of the monarchy.[102] The paternalistic nature of the government and its supposedly divine origin reinforced its power at the expense of the rights of the citizens. Therefore, there was a conflict between public happiness and the interests of the absolute monarchy, which resulted in what is called 'enlightened despotism'.[103] However, the form of government was only absolute, not despotic, because it was not always tyrannical, but rather repressive of the desire for freedom of the mass of the population.[104] *El Censor*, the major critical periodical of the 1780s, was condemned because it revealed the contradictions and limitations of governmental reforms.[105] Radical change in the university sector should have been a priority in the programme of the Bourbon reforms, but instructing the country in the new values and knowledge they needed would have potentially implied greater emancipation for Spanish citizens. That is why, instead of teaching how to improve their condition as individuals and as a society, the emphasis was put on the inculcation of utilitarian skills in order to create better workers and thus contribute to the economic growth of the country. As denounced by *El Censor*, governmental action sought to protect the privileges and benefits of the nobility and the Church to the detriment of the rights of the bourgeoisie. This objective of giving prominence to members of the Spanish elite is especially noticeable in the constitution of the economic societies, as stated by Campomanes in his *Discurso sobre el fomento de la industria popular*.[106]

Although a gradual change in mentality among Spain's intellectual classes can be detected from the 1680s, the more dynamic spirit of renewal does not seem to break into broader areas of intellectual debate in the public sphere until the second half of the eighteenth century. The new mentality of the Enlightenment period is described by Peter Gay as 'the recovery of nerve' because 'it was a century of decline in mysticism, of growing hope for life and trust in effort, of commitment to inquiry and criticism, of interest in social reform, of increasing secularism, and a growing willingness to take risks'.[107] This renewed attitude was also determined by an imperial rivalry that led to intellectual exchanges among European states and transnational borrowings of successful practices. Such a phenomenon of emulation responded to the challenges of international competition and cosmopolitanism.[108]

For Spain, however, the appropriation of foreign ideas was not always a fortunate experience, as when the internal colonization scheme of the Sierra Morena used Prussian and Russian precedents as a model. England, in particular, was considered as the greatest power to be emulated, especially in terms of its agricultural system. Pablo de Olavide y Jáuregui's agrarian reform plans encouraged imitation of English agriculture, seen as a guaranteed path to improvement.[109] Bourbon reformist ideology aimed to restore state power through a restructuring of society inspired by the British geopolitical model.[110] Works of British political economy were widely disseminated by Bourbon reformers (Jovellanos and especially Campomanes) who 'sought to attract the public's attention to meritorious institutions and practices of other nations'[111] in order to achieve public happiness and the growth of the state.

The debate widened from the 1750s when more Spaniards became interested in questioning the status quo and in speculating on ways in which society could be changed. In this context, the importance of *tertulias* resided not only in the promotion of writers and intellectuals as functional collaborators in society, but also in the creation of spaces for critical reflection on general issues:

> Eran las tertulias [...] lugares de encuentro y comunicación en los que se podían debatir y difundir ideas, creando un estado de opinión, y donde, saltando la vigilancia de la censura sobre los escritos, se discutía y conocían las novedades políticas, estéticas e ideológicas.[112]
>
> [*Tertulias* were [...] meeting places and venues for dialogue in which ideas could be debated and disseminated, creating public opinion, and, in bypassing the oversight and censorship of writings, political, aesthetic, and ideological novelties were discussed and made known.]

Similarly, academies, although set up with royal approval, became centres of discussion, often encouraged by the government. These institutions were founded during the reign of Carlos II with the official establishment of the Royal Academy of Medicine and Surgery of Seville and came to an end with the setting up of economic societies initiated in the 1760s.

One very effective spur to such wider debate came in advances in the field of publication and printing. Some restrictions on publication were lessened, and new institutions had rights that supposed easier access to public forums of intellectual interchange. Thus, one dynamic new centre of debate able to spread innovation and questioning was the periodical press. According to Richard Herr, alongside universities and economic societies, the periodical press contributed to the dissemination of enlightened and contemporary thought, especially through the journals and newspapers that flourished in the latter years of Carlos III's rule, many of which provided news of innovations from abroad.[113] The conception of periodicals as a tool for the immediate presentation of current debates is also highlighted by Inmaculada Urzainqui, who sees this characteristic as a revolutionary feature of the Spanish press. She equally describes as unprecedented the fact that these periodicals provided a wide network of communication that allowed an increased effective flow of ideas on a national and international scale.[114] In his definition of the genre of *papeles periódicos* [periodicals] published in 1787, Juan Sempere y Guarinos underlined the innovative nature of this new cultural vehicle.[115] The convenience of conveying great amounts of information in a compact format was indeed an important feature of periodical publications. Drawing on Urzainqui's research, it can be said that the periodical press was the emblematic instrument of the Spanish Enlightenment and the facilitator of the connection between Spain and Europe. At the same time as it emphasized links between Spain and the world outside, it powerfully encouraged dialogue between Spaniards:

> [L]a Ilustración española, en lo que tuvo de programa de apertura a Europa, de renovación y de cambio, encontró en el periódico el instrumento más idóneo [...]. Como ningún otro canal anterior, la prensa estaba en las mejores condiciones para allegar información, seleccionarla y filtrarla ofreciendo un medio dúctil y cómodo, además de asequible [...] económicamente. Europa podía estar ahora mucho más vívidamente en España, al tiempo que a España le era permitido también manifestarse con mucha mayor claridad ante los ojos de fuera.[116]
>
> [The Spanish Enlightenment, in as far as it constituted an opening out towards Europe, as a programme of renewal and change, found in periodicals its most suitable mechanism [...]. Like no other previous channel, the press was in the best position to gather, select, and filter information, offering a ductile and comfortable vehicle, besides being economically [...] accessible. Europe could now be much more vividly present in Spain, while Spain could also be much more visible to the eyes of outsiders.]

Almost all areas of social change had their arguments aired and promoted in the periodical press. In the 1760s, this seems limited to individual social action and practices, but in the 1780s this can be seen in what is now referred to by cultural historians as the critical press. In contrast with journals that sought to entertain or criticize social manners and that were promptly discontinued, two publications stood out for the depth of their critical observations of Spanish society: *El Pensador* [*The Thinker*] (1762–67), edited by José Clavijo y Fajardo, and *El Censor* (1781–87), edited by lawyers Luis García del Cañuelo and Luis Marcelino Pereira. Both periodicals attacked the privileges of the nobility and the Church. However, *El Censor* adopted a more radical and comprehensive approach to all aspects of society, including the legal system.[117] It criticized the foundations of Spanish social structures and defended the role of the bourgeoisie as the social stratum with better chances to achieve happiness.[118] Along with the disapproval of the inherited wealth of the aristocracy, the periodical also attacked the unacceptably wealthy Spanish Church. This potentially dangerous turn was commented on by the ever perceptive Sempere:

> Hasta ahora el *Pensador* y los autores de otros papeles periódicos no se habían propuesto otro que el de ridiculizar las modas y ciertas máximas viciosas introducidas en la conducta de la vida. *El Censor* manifiesta otras miras más arduas y más arriesgadas. Habla de los vicios de nuestra legislación, de los abusos introducidos con pretexto de religión, de los errores políticos, y de otros asuntos semejantes.[119]

> [Until this point the *Thinker* and the authors of other periodicals had set out to do nothing more than ridicule fashions and certain prejudicial ideas affecting everyday life. *The Censor* manifests other more complex and riskier views. It deals with the vices of our laws, the abuses that have advanced under the cover of religion, political errors, and other such matters.]

The fact that two of the five works studied in this book originally appeared in periodicals, neither of them indicating the author's name, further underlines the suitability of the press for the expression of unorthodox ideas like the ones proposed in utopian texts.

Nonetheless, the press interacted with pamphlets that advanced the debate further. Although periodicals implied that they might include replies from readers to articles published, when editors ignored the replies, the authors who thought they had something to offer could get their pamphlets published with little difficulty, reacting to articles in the press, sometimes in agreement, but often in opposition.[120] Such texts were frequently published under pseudonyms,[121] but their effect was clear. Paul-Jacques Guinard offers an extensive list of the publications that appeared in reaction to *El Censor*,[122] including the periodical *El Corresponsal del Censor*, written by Manuel Rubín de Celis under the fictional name of Ramón Harnero.

In addition to the periodical press, Herr sees Spanish economic societies as a major contributing element to what he characterizes as the eighteenth-century revolution in Spain. Dating from the 1760s, these institutions received government backing in the 1770s. The mentality that gave rise to the Economic Societies of Friends of the Country was identical to, and chronologically parallel to, that of major utopian writings in Spain. In fact, the system of Solomon's House in Francis Bacon's *New Atlantis* can be identified as the primitive rudiments of these societies, as the Royal Society of London, inspired by the organization of the society of Solomon's House, has been considered a direct influence on them. Thus, foreign societies, such as the ones in Dublin and Bern, motivated the founding of the Basque Society, the first Spanish economic society established in 1765.[123]

Economic change was seen as essential to promoting the happiness of all members of society. However, the activities of the economic societies also entailed social reform that perhaps surprisingly would be carried out almost exclusively by members of the Spanish elite belonging to the economically dominant classes:

> ¿[A]caso el pueblo ignorante de las zonas rurales y el pueblo pervertido de las

ciudades podía comprender que lo que se pretendía era hacerles felices? De ahí la paradoja de un gobierno reformador condenado a apoyarse en una opinión pública hecha de privilegiados para combatir a múltiples privilegios.[124]

[Could the rural population and corrupt city dwellers understand that what was intended was to make them happy? Hence the paradox of a reformist government, condemned to rely on a public opinion made up of privileged people, with the aim of combatting a multitude of privileges.]

The improvement plans should address areas such as agriculture, industry, commerce, and education.[125] The results of the analysis and remedies for the agrarian question in Spain by Madrid's economic society, based in many instances on data requested by government from provincial authorities, were published in Jovellanos's *Informe en el expediente de ley agraria* [*A Report on the Dossier Concerning Agrarian Law*] (1795),[126] a text in which social institutions such as those that produced Church entailment and noble *mayorazgos* [primogeniture] were seen as major impediments in the way of progress. It is significant that among the sources of key information that fed into Jovellanos's *Informe* was the report written over two decades earlier by Olavide, about which more will be argued in Chapter 7.

The Spanish societies primarily comprised members of the nobility and the clergy, but also included middle-class individuals involved in commerce and leading intellectuals (Nicolás Fernández de Moratín, Valentín de Foronda, Juan Meléndez Valdés, Manuel de Aguirre, José de Cadalso, Jovellanos, and many others) who took part in their meetings and activities. The education of noblemen was an important objective of Campomanes's project because he was convinced that a cultured nobility would be the means of achieving social stability.[127] The teaching of political economy was particularly crucial because Spanish universities did not offer this subject. However, although aristocrats were meant to be the patrons of the economic societies, not enough of them responded to the call.[128] In a similar attitude, sections of the clergy were hostile to the purposes of the economic societies and refused to collaborate with them. This was the case with the Aragonese Society in Zaragoza,[129] but not with the Basque Society in Azkoitia, which received the support of the more enlightened members of the Church.[130] Many members of economic societies belonged to the clergy, from bishops to parish priests. Some key archbishops acted energetically to promote economic societies, donating money for prizes and encouraging priests to participate. Only in the late 1780s and 1790s — especially once the French Revolution got underway, and particularly when it began to attack fundamental elements of the social structure such as the monarchy, the nobility, and the Church — did concern for the socio-political status quo provoke some clerics to voice their opposition and the membership of the economic societies to decrease. Some members of the clergy had fears concerning economic reform and their livelihood if questioning of privileges continued. This negative response would eventually lead the Church to place a major reformist text such as Jovellanos's *Informe* on the Inquisition's index of banned books in 1825.

Despite the reticence of certain members of the Church, in the early years of the economic societies, an enlightened clergy was willing to participate in what has subsequently been described by certain scholars as the Catholic Enlightenment. The goal of this movement was especially reflected in the type of education imparted by the clergy, who aimed to integrate the teaching of morality and religion with the training in practical sciences:

> Para que la formación que da el clero sea humanamente integral, es preciso que esté construida en las ciencias útiles al Estado. [...] Se trata, en definitiva, de hacer realidad la síntesis que exigían los tiempos de un cristianismo ilustrado. [...] En la mítica exaltación de lo experimental, jamás se olvida que el principio de la felicidad individual y colectiva no está en el conocimiento puramente científico.[131]

> [In order for the formation provided by the clergy to be humanly comprehensive, it must be built on the sciences useful to the state. [...] In short, it is a question of realizing the synthesis demanded by an age of enlightened Christianity. [...] In the mythical exaltation of the experimental, it is never forgotten that the principle of individual and collective happiness is not in purely scientific knowledge.]

In this context of Catholic Enlightenment, a major reformist line of thinking and action within the Church in Spain received the label 'Jansenist', although the thinking cannot be easily related to the European Jansenist tradition: 'They had been given the name because of their views on the limited authority of the papacy and not for accepting the heretical beliefs of the French Jansenists'.[132] The Spanish sense of the term 'Jansenist' basically implied opposition to the religious teachings of the Jesuit Order and to excessive papal power. Although the Jesuits had partially defended Spanish regalism, they were fundamentally defenders of the power of the pope. There seems to have been some confusion between Jansenism and regalism in this respect. They were both related by virtue of a concern with authority, power, and reforms among laymen and clergy.[133]

Regalists argued that interdependence between the Church and the state was necessary in order for both institutions to prosper in accordance with the requirements of public happiness.[134] However, rather than mutual dependence, the state sought to reform and mould the Church according to its own political interests.[135] The attempt to turn the Church into a political tool reduced religious reform plans to a mechanism that fulfilled the regalist objectives of the Crown.[136] In addition to its spiritual function, it was argued that the Church should co-operate with the modernization of the kingdom: 'The clergy were seen as agents of the State promoting economic development, improving education, building public works, and, in general, advancing the utilitarian policies formulated in Madrid'.[137] The regalist policy of the Spanish Bourbons and the 'Jansenist' orientation of some leading intellectuals undermined the authority of the Church and stimulated the spread of enlightenment in Spain.[138] Thus, the Spanish Enlightenment was marked by more progressive attitudes within Catholicism, sponsored by the monarchy with the intention of benefitting the country as a whole. Andrea Smidt concludes that Catholic Enlightenment in Spain encompassed a useful and civilizing Catholicism that would bring renewal to society: 'As studies have exposed the intersection of regalist policy and Catholic Enlightenment, much room exists to uncover the enlightened efforts of Spaniards who [...] campaigned out of genuinely religious motivations for Catholic renewal and renovation'.[139] The examination of the spiritual role of the Church in the context of Enlightenment thought is a recurring topic in the utopian texts that will be analysed in this book.

A utopian consciousness would emerge in both negative and positive reactions to the restrictive and unfinished governmental plans during the early Bourbon period. It would therefore seem logical to expect that utopian writings concerned with changing important aspects of society should be produced in Spain in the eighteenth century. Not only is the spirit of *proyectismo* and the impulse behind economic societies going to influence the imagining in narrative form of alternative social systems, but the emergence of a critical attitude towards questionable features of institutions such as the nobility and the clergy as well as their interaction with the state's interests were going to find in utopian texts a forum for debate, rather than condemnation or rejection. In this sense, a utopian text only indirectly suggests that something is not right in the existing status quo; it is not a direct attack against the actual order of things. New ideas can be presented to a receptive public for debate and modification without being rejected out of hand or condemned as dangerously revolutionary. At the same time, a strong religious consciousness would pervade most Spanish utopian texts, not only because a significant number of their authors were clerics, but also because Christianity was at that time a fundamental aspect of the identity of Spaniards. As will be shown in the next chapters, this spiritual orientation of Spanish utopianism is in accord with the Catholic utopia proposed by More, but it also tends to equate a utopian Christian ideal with eternal salvation.

Notes to Chapter 2

1. Lucienne Domergue, *La Censure des livres en Espagne à la fin de l'Ancien Régime* (Madrid: Casa de Velázquez, 1996), pp. 226–29.
2. José Antonio Maravall, *Utopía y reformismo en la España de los Austrias* (Madrid: Siglo Veintiuno de España, 1982), p. 4.
3. Abellán, *Historia crítica del pensamiento español*, II: *La Edad de Oro* (1979), p. 384.
4. See Stelio Cro, *Realidad y utopía en el descubrimiento y conquista de la América Hispana (1492–1682)* (Troy, MI: International Book Publishers, 1983).
5. Frank E. Manuel and Fritzie P. Manuel, *Utopian Thought in the Western World* (Cambridge, MA: Harvard University Press, 1979), p. 61.
6. Christopher Columbus, *Select Letters of Christopher Columbus, with Other Original Documents, Relating to his Four Voyages to the New World*, ed. and trans. by Richard Henry Major (London: Hakluyt Society, 1870), p. 141.
7. Ibid. This is a bilingual edition with English translations alongside the Spanish originals.
8. Only the title page and the table of contents were published in 1656. The first edition of both volumes was made by the Peruvian historian Raúl Porras Barrenechea in 1943. See footnote 2 in Carlos Rey Pereira, 'El Paraíso en el Nuevo Mundo. Entre el ejemplo y la excepción', *Cuadernos para Investigación de la Literatura Hispánica*, 29 (2004), 141–59 (p. 141).
9. Abellán, II, pp. 377, 381.
10. The term was coined by the Spanish historian Julián Juderías in *La leyenda negra y la verdad histórica* (1914).
11. Christopher Schmidt-Nowara, *The Conquest of History: Spanish Colonialism and National Histories in the Nineteenth Century* (Pittsburgh, PA: University of Pittsburgh Press, 2008), p. 30.
12. Stelio Cro, 'El mito de la ciudad ideal en España: *Sinapia*', in *Actas del VI Congreso Internacional de Hispanistas*, ed. by Evelyn Rugg and Alan M. Gordon (Toronto: University of Toronto, 1980), pp. 192–94 (p. 192).

13. Stelio Cro, *The American Foundations of the Hispanic Utopia, 1492–1793*, 2 vols (Tallahassee, FL: DeSoto Press, 1994), I: *The Literary Utopia. 'Sinapia', A Classical Utopia of Spain and the 'Discurso de la educación'*, pp. 28–29. According to the author, the peculiar utopian dimension of *Don Quixote* is that the main character, instead of a place, acts as a mechanism of social criticism and symbolizes the disillusionment caused by the Spanish social situation (Cro, *The American Foundations of the Hispanic Utopia*, I, p. 29). A similar perspective is proposed by José Antonio Maravall, who sees in the indeterminacy of the geographical place in which Don Quixote's actions occur a significant feature for the utopian nature of the novel (José Antonio Maravall, *Utopía y contrautopía en 'El Quijote'* (Madrid: Visor Libros, 2006), p. 236).
14. Silvio Zavala, *Recuerdo de Vasco de Quiroga* (Mexico City: Porrúa, 1987), p. 161.
15. Abellán, II, pp. 421–22.
16. Bartolomé de las Casas, *Obras escogidas*, 5 vols (Madrid: Atlas, 1957–58), IV: *Apologética historia*, ed. by Juan Pérez de Tudela Bueso (1958), pp. 430–31.
17. Benjamin Keen and Keith Haynes, *A History of Latin America*, 2 vols (Boston, MA: Wadsworth/Cengage Learning, 2013), I: *Ancient America to 1910*, p. 82.
18. A copy of More's *Utopia* underlined and annotated by Quiroga was found in the personal library of Bishop Juan de Zumárraga, who probably lent that copy to Quiroga. See Abellán, II, p. 392.
19. Julie Greer Johnson, *Satire in Colonial Spanish America: Turning the New World Upside Down* (Austin: University of Texas Press, 1993), p. 4.
20. Silvio Zavala, *Sir Thomas More in New Spain: A Utopian Adventure of the Renaissance* (London: Hispanic and Luso-Brazilian Councils, 1955), p. 12.
21. Juan Pimentel, *Testigos del mundo: ciencia, literatura y viajes en la Ilustración* (Madrid: Marcial Pons, 2003), p. 92.
22. Raúl Villaseñor, 'Luciano, Moro y el utopismo de Vasco de Quiroga', *Cuadernos Americanos*, 68 (1953), 155–75 (p. 157).
23. Vasco de Quiroga, *Información en derecho*, in Rafael Aguayo Spencer, *Don Vasco de Quiroga: pensamiento jurídico. Antología*, ed. by José Luis Soberanes (Mexico City: Porrúa, 1986), pp. 82–212 (p. 189).
24. Abellán, II, pp. 394–96.
25. Vasco de Quiroga, p. 194.
26. Stelio Cro, *The American Foundations of the Hispanic Utopia*, II: *The Empirical Utopia*, p. 138. See also Pedro Rodríguez, Conde de Campomanes, *Dictamen fiscal de expulsión de los jesuitas de España*, ed. by Jorge Cejudo and Teófanes Egido (Madrid: Fundación Universitaria Española, 1977); Teófanes Egido and Isidoro Pinedo, *Las causas 'gravísimas' y secretas de la expulsión de los jesuitas por Carlos III* (Madrid: Fundación Universitaria Española, 1994).
27. Abellán, II, pp. 404–05.
28. Rubén Bareiro Saguier and Jean-Paul Duviols, eds, *Tentación de la utopía: la república de los jesuitas en el Paraguay* (Asuncion: Servilibro, 2012), p. 172.
29. José Manuel Peramás, *La 'República' de Platón y los guaraníes* (Buenos Aires: Emecé, 1946), pp. 19–20.
30. Josep M. Barnadas, 'The Catholic Church in Colonial Spanish America', in *The Cambridge History of Latin America*, ed. by Leslie Bethell, 11 vols (Cambridge: Cambridge University Press, 1984–95), I (1984), pp. 509–40 (p. 533).
31. Ibid., p. 534.
32. Rousseau never used the term 'good savage' (*bon sauvage*) or 'noble savage', but *l'homme naturel* [natural man]. The expression 'noble savage' first appeared in English in 1670 in *The Conquest of Granada*, a heroic play by the English writer John Dryden.
33. Concrete utopia foresees the actualization of a utopian society in the future, as opposed to a merely abstract utopia. While abstract utopia expresses desire, concrete utopia carries hope. See Ernst Bloch, *The Principle of Hope*, trans. by Neville Plaice, Stephen Plaice, and Paul Knight, 3 vols (Oxford: Blackwell, 1986), I, p. 157.
34. See Jesús Astigarraga, ed., *The Spanish Enlightenment Revisited* (Oxford: Voltaire Foundation, 2015).

35. Francisco Sánchez-Blanco, *La Ilustración en España* (Madrid: Akal, 1997), p. 5.
36. The misrepresentation of the *arbitristas* as lunatic liars coincides with Fredric Jameson's negative impression of utopian writers: 'The Utopians, whether political, textual or hermeneutic, have always been maniacs and oddballs: a deformation readily enough explained by the fallen societies in which they had to fulfil their vocation' (Fredric Jameson, *Archaeologies of the Future: The Desire Called Utopia and Other Science Fictions* (New York: Verso, 2005), p. 10). The proposal of irrational projects as solutions to the problems of the Spanish monarchy caused the *arbitristas* to be depicted as charlatans who used the pseudoscience of astrology. In her analysis of the interrelation of utopia and astrology in the popular literature of Enlightenment Spain, Iris Zavala puts forward the existence of a scholarly utopia as opposed to a popular one, the latter being fuelled by the predictive and imaginative power of astrology and its impact on the harmony of the social order. The contents of the almanacs and their creator (the *piscator*) sought to provide the lower middle-class reader with an idealistic or ironic portrayal of society's institutions, through which the disenchanted popular audience could escape from the injustice of an unequal social structure (Iris M. Zavala, 'Utopía y astrología en la literatura popular del setecientos: los almanaques de Torres Villarroel', *Nueva Revista de Filología Hispánica*, 33 (1984), 196–212 (p. 197)). What is of interest here is that astrological utopia is proof that fantasy functioned as a means of relieving social frustration and, therefore, as a way of restraining potential civil conflicts. It can be argued that this form of folk utopia was the vehicle of useless charlatanism aimed at misguiding the public, but instead it was intended to offer practical advice to help citizens achieve happiness and economic welfare. Among various Spanish astrological fictions, Zavala features Diego de Torres Villarroel's works, which are utopian fabulations about the correct use of laws and social institutions. In that sense, Torres Villarroel's utopia has a strong didactic and critical impulse.
37. Jean Vilar, *Literatura y economía: la figura satírica del arbitrista en el Siglo de Oro* (Madrid: Revista de Occidente, 1973), pp. 31–32.
38. Werner Krauss, 'Algunos aspectos de las teorías economistas españolas durante el siglo XVIII', *Cuadernos Hispanoamericanos*, 246 (1970), 572–84 (p. 572).
39. Vilar, p. 221.
40. Manuel Colmeiro, *Biblioteca de los economistas españoles de los siglos XVI, XVII y XVIII* (Madrid: Real Academia de Ciencias Morales y Políticas, [1954]), p. 7.
41. *Diccionario de autoridades*, 6 vols (Madrid: Real Academia Española, 1726–39; facsimile edition, Madrid: Gredos, 1969), I (1726), p. 373.
42. Henry Kamen, *Vocabulario básico de la historia moderna*, trans. by Montserrat Iniesta (Barcelona: Crítica, 1986), p. 14.
43. Henry Kamen, *Spain, 1469–1714: A Society of Conflict* (London and New York: Longman, 1983), p. 233.
44. Juan Ignacio Gutiérrez Nieto, 'El pensamiento económico, político y social de los arbitristas', in *Historia de España*, ed. by Ramón Menéndez Pidal and José María Jover Zamora, 42 vols (Madrid: Espasa-Calpe, 1935–2003), XXVI: *El siglo del Quijote (1580–1680): religión, filosofía, ciencia* (1986), pp. 233–351 (p. 237).
45. Ibid.
46. Ibid., pp. 282, 293.
47. Evaristo Correa Calderón, *Registro de arbitristas, economistas y reformadores españoles (1500–1936): catálogo de impresos y manuscritos* (Madrid: Fundación Universitaria Española, 1981), p. 9.
48. Mariano Baquero Goyanes, 'Realismo y utopía en la literatura española', *Studi Ispanici*, 1 (1962), 7–28 (p. 14).
49. A more extreme view is expressed by the Spanish philosopher José Ortega y Gasset, who thinks that utopia is a false image of reality in the sense that it proposes an ideal but non-existent truth. Ortega y Gasset conceives of a reality composed of multiple perspectives, each equally true and authentic, and where the sole false perspective is that which claims to be the only one there is. Utopia is then regarded as a kind of invalid comprehension of external reality, and, consequently, utopians are doomed to undermine their own authorial image because their discourse is based on misconceptions (José Ortega y Gasset, *El tema de nuestro tiempo* (Madrid: Tecnos, 2002), p. 133).

50. Amable Fernández Sanz, 'La utopía solucionista de Jovellanos', *El Basilisco*, 21 (1996), 25–27 (p. 26).
51. Maravall, *Utopía y reformismo en la España de los Austrias*, p. 3.
52. Thomas More, *La 'Utopía' de Tomás Moro, gran canciller de Inglaterra, vizconde y ciudadano de Londres*, trans. by Jerónimo Antonio de Medinilla y Porres (Cordova: Salvador de Cea, 1637).
53. Francisco López Estrada, 'La primera versión española de la *Utopía* de Moro, por Jerónimo Antonio de Medinilla (Córdoba, 1637)', in *Collected Studies in Honour of Américo Castro's Eightieth Year*, ed. by Marcel P. Hornik (Oxford: Lincombe Lodge Research Library, 1965), pp. 291–309 (p. 304).
54. Regarding the Inquisition's attitude towards More's *Utopía*, see López Estrada, *Tomás Moro y España*, p. 65.
55. Thomas More, *La 'Utopía' de Tomás Moro, gran canciller de Inglaterra, vizconde y ciudadano de Londres*, trans. by Jerónimo Antonio de Medinilla y Porres, 2nd edn (Madrid: Imprenta de Pantaleón Aznar, 1790), n. pag.
56. Ibid., n. pag.
57. Thomas More, *La 'Utopía' de Tomás Moro, gran canciller de Inglaterra, vizconde y ciudadano de Londres*, trans. by Jerónimo Antonio de Medinilla y Porres, 3rd edn (Madrid: Imprenta de Mateo Repullés, 1805).
58. Joaquín Álvarez Barrientos, *Ilustración y neoclasicismo en las letras españolas* (Madrid: Síntesis, 2005), p. 59.
59. François Lopez, 'La vida intelectual en la España de los novatores', *Anejos de Dieciocho*, 1 (1997), 79–90 (p. 86).
60. François Lopez, 'Los novatores en la Europa de los sabios', *Studia Historica. Historia Moderna*, 14 (1996), 95–111 (p. 96).
61. Jesús Pérez Magallón, *Construyendo la modernidad: la cultura española en el 'tiempo de los novatores' (1675–1725)* (Madrid: Consejo Superior de Investigaciones Científicas, Instituto de la Lengua Española, 2002), p. 14.
62. Pedro Álvarez de Miranda, 'Las academias de los novatores', in *De las academias a la enciclopedia: el discurso del saber en la modernidad*, ed. by Evangelina Rodríguez Cuadros (Valencia: Alfons el Magnànim, 1993), pp. 263–300 (p. 273).
63. *Diccionario de autoridades*, IV (1734), p. 683.
64. Abellán, III, pp. 343–44.
65. Ibid., III, p. 344.
66. Francisco Sánchez-Blanco, *La mentalidad ilustrada* (Madrid: Taurus, 1999), p. 24.
67. Ibid., p. 35.
68. Álvarez de Miranda, 'Las academias de los novatores', pp. 273–74. For a comprehensive history of the institution, see Antonio Hermosilla Molina, *Cien años de medicina sevillana: la Regia Sociedad de Medicina y Demás Ciencias, de Sevilla, en el siglo XVIII* (Seville: Diputación Provincial de Sevilla, 1970).
69. José Muñoz Pérez, 'Los proyectos sobre España e Indias en el siglo XVIII: el proyectismo como género', *Revista de Estudios Políticos*, 81 (1955), 169–95 (p. 171).
70. Ibid., pp. 179–80.
71. Luis Miguel Enciso Recio, *Las sociedades económicas en el Siglo de las Luces* (Madrid: Real Academia de la Historia, 2010), p. 10.
72. Pedro Álvarez de Miranda, 'Proyectos y proyectistas en el siglo XVIII español', in *La Ilustración española: actas del Coloquio Internacional celebrado en Alicante, 1–4 octubre 1985*, ed. by A. Alberola and E. La Parra (Alicante: Instituto Juan Gil-Albert, Diputación Provincial de Alicante, 1986), pp. 133–50 (p. 137).
73. José Luis Gómez Urdáñez, *Fernando VI* (Madrid: Arlanza, 2001), p. 194.
74. Jacinta Macías Delgado, 'Estudio preliminar', in Miguel Antonio de la Gándara, *Apuntes sobre el bien y el mal de España*, ed. by Jacinta Macías Delgado (Madrid: Instituto de Estudios Fiscales, 1988), pp. xiii–clv (pp. cxxxi–cxxxvi).
75. Vicent Llombart, *Campomanes, economista y político de Carlos III* (Madrid: Alianza, 1992), pp. 344–45.

76. Abellán, III, p. 559. Several texts by Martínez de la Mata were included with Campomanes's *Discurso sobre la educación popular de los artesanos y su fomento*, 5 vols (Madrid: Imprenta de Antonio de Sancha, 1775–77).
77. See Enrique Fuentes Quintana, ed., *Economía y economistas españoles*, 9 vols (Barcelona: Galaxia Gutenberg, 1999–2004), III: *La Ilustración* (2000).
78. Abellán, III, p. 552.
79. Henry Kamen, *The War of Succession in Spain, 1700–15* (London: Weidenfeld and Nicolson, 1969), p. 33.
80. Henry Kamen, *Spain in the Later Seventeenth Century, 1665–1700* (London and New York: Longman, 1980), p. 317.
81. Kamen, *The War of Succession in Spain*, p. 26.
82. Ibid., pp. 118–19.
83. For a detailed description of Macanaz's writings, see Kamen, *The War of Succession in Spain*, pp. 415–19.
84. The work was first put into print in 1789. This date is clearly significant for understanding the possible influence of the text on utopian writing late in the century.
85. Macías Delgado, pp. lxxi–lxxii.
86. For a well-researched overview of the reign of Fernando VI, see Gómez Urdáñez's *Fernando VI*.
87. Gómez Urdáñez, p. 152.
88. Carlos Gutiérrez de los Ríos, Conde de Fernán Núñez, *Vida de Carlos III*, ed. by Alfred Morel-Fatio and Antonio Paz y Meliá, 2 vols (Madrid: Fernando Fé, 1898; facsimile edition, Madrid: Fundación Universitaria Española, 1988), I, pp. 39–105.
89. Francisco Sánchez-Blanco, *El absolutismo y las Luces en el reinado de Carlos III* (Madrid: Marcial Pons, 2002), p. 16.
90. Sánchez-Blanco, *La Ilustración en España*, p. 40.
91. José Antonio Maravall, 'Las tendencias de reforma política en el siglo XVIII español', in José Antonio Maravall, *Estudios de la historia del pensamiento español (siglo XVIII)*, ed. by María del Carmen Iglesias (Madrid: Mondadori España, 1991), pp. 61–81 (p. 67).
92. [Pedro Rodríguez, Conde de Campomanes], *Discurso sobre el fomento de la industria popular* (Madrid: Imprenta de Antonio de Sancha, 1774), p. lxi.
93. Antonio Domínguez Ortiz, *Las clases privilegiadas en la España del Antiguo Régimen* (Madrid: Istmo, 1973), p. 12.
94. Equipo Madrid de Estudios Históricos, *Carlos III, Madrid y la Ilustración: contradicciones de un proyecto reformista* (Madrid: Siglo Veintiuno de España, 1988), p. 22.
95. Ibid., pp. 10–11. See also Gómez Urdáñez, pp. 163–66.
96. Francisco Aguilar Piñal, *La España del absolutismo ilustrado* (Madrid: Espasa-Calpe, 2005), pp. 12–13.
97. Ortega y Gasset was convinced that the Enlightenment did not flourish in Spain: 'Cuanto más se medita sobre nuestra historia, más clara se advierte esta desastrosa ausencia del siglo XVIII. Nos ha faltado el gran siglo educador. [...] Éste ha sido el triste sino de España, la nación europea que se ha saltado un siglo insustituible' [The more we meditate on our history, the clearer becomes the perception of this disastrous absence of the eighteenth century. We have missed out on the great educational century. [...] This has been the sad destiny of Spain, the European nation that has skipped an irreplaceable century] (José Ortega y Gasset, 'El siglo XVIII, educador', in José Ortega y Gasset, *Obras completas*, 12 vols (Madrid: Revista de Occidente, 1946–83), II: *El espectador (1916–1934)* (1946), pp. 599–601 (pp. 600–01)).
98. Álvarez Barrientos, *Ilustración y neoclasicismo en las letras españolas*, p. 23.
99. François Lopez, 'El pensamiento tradicionalista', in *Historia de España*, ed. by Ramón Menéndez Pidal and José María Jover Zamora, 42 vols (Madrid: Espasa-Calpe, 1935–2003), XXXI: *La época de la Ilustración: el Estado y la cultura (1759–1808)* (1987), pp. 813–51 (pp. 835–36).
100. Lluís Roura i Aulinas, 'Expectativas y frustración bajo el reformismo borbónico', in *Historia de España, siglo XVIII: la España de los Borbones*, ed. by Ricardo García Cárcel (Madrid: Cátedra, 2002), pp. 167–221 (p. 188).

101. Teófanes Egido, 'Los anti-ilustrados españoles', in *La Ilustración en España y Alemania*, ed. by Reyes Mate and Friedrich Niewöhner (Barcelona: Anthropos, 1989), pp. 95–119 (pp. 96–97).
102. Franco Venturi identifies a complementary dynamics between the realms of utopia and reform: '[My concern] is rather the history of political ideas, the relationship between the forces of social enthusiasm, to quote Shaftesbury, the forces of the burgeoning utopias of a human society able to solve "le mot de l'énigme métaphysique et morale" [the message of the metaphysical and moral riddle] and the concrete determination to modify this or that aspect of the societies inherited from the past, to bring about practical change. In short, the relationship between utopia and reform' (Franco Venturi, *Utopia and Reform in the Enlightenment* (London: Cambridge University Press, 1971), p. 99).
103. Sánchez-Blanco, *El absolutismo y las Luces en el reinado de Carlos III*, p. 50.
104. François Lopez, 'La resistencia a la Ilustración: bases sociales y medios de acción', in *Historia de España*, ed. by Ramón Menéndez Pidal and José María Jover Zamora, 42 vols (Madrid: Espasa-Calpe, 1935–2003), XXXI: *La época de la Ilustración: el Estado y la cultura (1759–1808)* (1987), pp. 767–812 (p. 811); Aguilar Piñal, *La España del absolutismo ilustrado*, p. 31.
105. Marcelino Menéndez Pelayo, *Historia de los heterodoxos españoles*, 8 vols (Buenos Aires: Emecé, 1945), VI, pp. 343–44.
106. Antonio Elorza, *La modernización política en España: ensayos de historia del pensamiento político* (Madrid: Endymion, 1990), p. 17.
107. Peter Gay, *The Enlightenment: An Interpretation*, 2 vols (London and New York: W. W. Norton, 1966–69), II: *The Science of Freedom* (1977), p. 6.
108. Gabriel B. Paquette, *Enlightenment, Governance, and Reform in Spain and its Empire, 1759–1808* (Basingstoke: Palgrave Macmillan, 2008), p. 30.
109. Pablo de Olavide y Jáuregui, *Informe sobre la ley agraria*, in Pablo de Olavide y Jáuregui, *Obras selectas*, ed. by Estuardo Núñez (Lima: Banco de Crédito del Perú, 1987), pp. 483–531 (pp. 488–89).
110. This is evident throughout Antonio Elorza's *La ideología liberal en la Ilustración española* (Madrid: Tecnos, 1970).
111. Paquette, p. 40.
112. Joaquín Álvarez Barrientos, 'Los hombres de letras', in Joaquín Álvarez Barrientos, François Lopez, and Inmaculada Urzainqui, *La república de las letras en la España del siglo XVIII* (Madrid: Consejo Superior de Investigaciones Científicas, 1995), pp. 19–61 (p. 53).
113. Richard Herr, *The Eighteenth-Century Revolution in Spain* (Princeton, NJ: Princeton University Press, 1958), p. 183. See also Paul-Jacques Guinard, *La Presse espagnole de 1737 à 1791: formation et signification d'un genre* (Paris: Centre de Recherches Hispaniques, Institut d'Études Hispaniques, 1973).
114. Inmaculada Urzainqui, 'Un nuevo instrumento cultural: la prensa periódica', in Joaquín Álvarez Barrientos, François Lopez, and Inmaculada Urzainqui, *La república de las letras en la España del siglo XVIII* (Madrid: Consejo Superior de Investigaciones Científicas, 1995), pp. 125–216 (pp. 126, 129). See also Inmaculada Urzainqui, 'Diálogo entre periodistas (1737–1770)', in *Francisco Mariano Nipho: el nacimiento de la prensa y de la crítica literaria periodística en la España del siglo XVIII*, ed. by José María Maestre Maestre, Manuel Antonio Díaz Gito, and Alberto Romero Ferrer (Alcañiz: Instituto de Estudios Humanísticos; Madrid: Consejo Superior de Investigaciones Científicas, 2015), pp. 375–418.
115. Juan Sempere y Guarinos, *Ensayo de una biblioteca española de los mejores escritores del reinado de Carlos III*, 6 vols (Madrid: Imprenta Real, 1785–89; facsimile edition, Madrid: Gredos, 1969), IV (1787), p. 176. See also Joaquín Álvarez Barrientos, *Los hombres de letras en la España del siglo XVIII. Apóstoles y arribistas* (Madrid: Castalia, 2006), pp. 98–101.
116. Urzainqui, 'Un nuevo instrumento cultural', p. 130.
117. Sempere y Guarinos, II (1785), pp. 131–32.
118. Elorza, *La ideología liberal en la Ilustración española*, p. 215.
119. Sempere y Guarinos, IV (1787), p. 191.
120. Philip Deacon, 'La prensa dieciochesca española como agente de las Luces', in *Francisco Mariano Nipho: el nacimiento de la prensa y de la crítica literaria periodística en la España del siglo XVIII*, ed. by

José María Maestre Maestre, Manuel Antonio Díaz Gito, and Alberto Romero Ferrer (Alcañiz: Instituto de Estudios Humanísticos; Madrid: Consejo Superior de Investigaciones Científicas, 2015), pp. 225–44 (p. 237).
121. Philip Deacon, 'El autor esquivo en la cultura española del siglo XVIII: apuntes sobre decoro, estrategias y juegos', *Dieciocho*, 22 (1999), 213–36 (pp. 225–26).
122. Guinard, *La Presse espagnole de 1737 à 1791*, pp. 318–22.
123. Robert Jones Shafer, *The Economic Societies in the Spanish World (1763–1821)* (Syracuse, NY: Syracuse University Press, 1958), pp. 24–25.
124. Jean-Pierre Amalric and Lucienne Domergue, *La España de la Ilustración (1700–1833)* (Barcelona: Crítica, 2001), p. 121.
125. Sempere y Guarinos, V (1789), p. 140.
126. Enciso Recio, p. 156.
127. Ibid., p. 170.
128. Herr, p. 162.
129. François Lopez, 'Un sociodrama bajo el Antiguo Régimen: Nuevo enfoque de un suceso zaragozano: el caso Normante', in *Actas del I Symposium del Seminario de Ilustración Aragonesa*, ed. by María-Dolores Albiac Blanco (Zaragoza: Diputación General de Aragón, 1987), pp. 103–16.
130. Herr, pp. 160–61.
131. Vicente Rodríguez Casado, 'El intento español de "Ilustración Cristiana"', *Estudios Americanos*, 9 (1955), 141–69 (p. 158).
132. Herr, p. 35.
133. Charles C. Noel, 'Clerics and Crown in Bourbon Spain, 1700–1808: Jesuits, Jansenists, and Enlightened Reformers', in *Religion and Politics in Enlightenment Europe*, ed. by James E. Bradley and Dale K. Van Kley (Notre Dame, IN: University of Notre Dame Press, 2001), pp. 119–53 (pp. 131–32).
134. Paquette, p. 73.
135. Luis Sánchez Agesta, *El pensamiento político del despotismo ilustrado* (Madrid: Instituto de Estudios Políticos, 1953), p. 174.
136. María Giovanna Tomsich, *El jansenismo en España: estudio sobre ideas religiosas en la segunda mitad del siglo XVIII* (Madrid: Siglo Veintiuno de España, 1972), p. 30.
137. William J. Callahan, *Church, Politics, and Society in Spain, 1750–1874* (Cambridge, MA, and London: Harvard University Press, 1984), p. 5.
138. Herr, p. 36.
139. Andrea J. Smidt, 'Luces por la fe: The Cause of Catholic Enlightenment in 18th-Century Spain', in *A Companion to the Catholic Enlightenment in Europe*, ed. by Ulrich L. Lehner and Michael Printy (Leiden: Brill, 2010), pp. 403–52 (pp. 448–49).

PART II

Characterizing the Spanish Utopian Tradition

CHAPTER 3

Sinapia:
A Foundational Spanish Utopia

In much the same way that some scholars still see More's *Utopia* as an enigmatic work,[1] the anonymous Spanish utopian text *Sinapia*[2] has provoked a similar critical response in its readers since being discovered in the mid-1970s. Moreover, the fact that the name of its author and the precise date of its composition are unknown compounds the mystery surrounding this surprising work. As will be discussed later in this chapter, however, the current consensus among informed critics is that the text belongs to the period of the *novatores* and that a date in the early 1680s seems quite likely.

While the Spanish text overtly demonstrates that it interacts with the extensive utopian tradition established by Thomas More, it is no less evident that some of its key ideological concerns can be related to attitudes and intellectual sensibilities that were prominent in the eighteenth century, which for many critics marks the high point of the flowering of enlightened debate in Spain. It is the purpose of this chapter to explore the convergences and divergences between the political, social, and religious features of *Sinapia* and those of the major utopian models, that is to say, the works by Thomas More, Francis Bacon, and Tommaso Campanella. However, before entering into an analysis of the text, an overview of the discovery of the manuscript of *Sinapia* as well as the scholarly suppositions about the date of composition and authorship of the text need to be set out.

The Text and the Author

The previously unknown manuscript of *Sinapia* was discovered in the mid-1970s among the private papers of Campomanes, after their transfer to the archive of the Fundación Universitaria Española [Spanish University Foundation] in Madrid. The manuscript was first described in the *Catálogo del Archivo del Conde de Campomanes* [*Catalogue of the Archive of the Count of Campomanes*] compiled by the librarian Jorge Cejudo López in 1975,[3] and the revelation of its existence resulted in the almost simultaneous editions of the text prepared by Stelio Cro in Canada in 1975[4] and by Miguel Avilés Fernández in Spain in 1976.[5]

Cro's volume included a facsimile reproduction of the manuscript, as well as a transcription and facsimile of a text entitled *Discurso de la educación* [*Discourse on*

Education], also deposited in the Campomanes Archive, and which suggested to him that the same person transcribed both *Sinapia* and the *Discurso*. The connection led Cro to speculate on the ideological profile of the author, who, he suggested, could have been a priest due to the strong religious component of both texts. He also argued that the author was a contemporary of Diego de Torres Villarroel (1694–1770) and Gregorio Mayans y Siscar (1699–1781) because of the alleged resemblance between their ideas and those of the anonymous author. This comparison in turn led Cro to believe that the two writings (*Sinapia* and the *Discurso*) were composed in the late seventeenth or early eighteenth century. However, a year later in his book *A Forerunner of the Enlightenment in Spain*, Cro suggested a composition date for *Sinapia* of around 1682, based on two additional manuscripts in the same handwriting as that of *Sinapia*, both of which he also discovered in the archives of the Fundación Universitaria Española.[6]

For his part, Avilés focused initially on spatial and geographical aspects of the text that resulted in a hypothetical map of Sinapia, traced in accordance with the geographical information given in the work. Claiming, though without much evidence, that the themes of *Sinapia* echo certain aspects of Enlightenment thinking in Spain — such as the reformism of the Spanish economic societies and physiocratic economic principles — Avilés concluded that the text could have been written in the last third of the eighteenth century.[7] He even thought that *Sinapia* followed the utopian model of Olavide's socio-economic project, begun at government instigation in 1767, and that Campomanes might therefore have been the author, as he supported the project. Although their findings provided a starting point for further research, neither Cro nor Avilés had any previous specialization in eighteenth-century Spanish cultural history, and hence their claims should be treated with caution.[8]

In spite of various other scholars having subsequently shown interest in exploring the utopian nature of *Sinapia*,[9] Stelio Cro is undoubtedly the scholar who has published most on the work. The introduction to his edition of *Sinapia* centres on the analysis of the manuscripts that he used in order to put forward a date of composition of the anonymous work. Cro saw in the evangelization of colonial Spanish America the foundations of Hispanic utopias in general — already discussed in Chapter 2 of this book — and of *Sinapia* in particular.[10] In an article published in 1980, Cro offered a more focused examination of the thematic and ideological aspects of *Sinapia*, underlining the educational dimension as a key element in its utopian system and the fact that, unlike other Spanish Catholic utopias, *Sinapia* sets out a political blueprint grounded in Christian doctrine, but according to a supposedly more authentic Christianity, at variance with the orthodox Catholic European tradition.[11] In a similar line of thought, Avilés highlighted the religious nature of the utopian features of the text, while specifying that religion was not seen as conflicting with the actions of the state. He also claimed that, in a strict sense, *Sinapia* is an 'antitopia' because it is the antipodes of Spain, not actually a non-existent place.[12]

Among leading recent critics of Spanish eighteenth-century culture, François Lopez has devoted detailed attention to attempting to identify the author of *Sinapia*.

Lopez supported Cro's dating of the manuscript after conducting a lexical analysis that would place its composition before the end of the seventeenth century,[13] leading him at one point to suggest that the author was the Valencian Manuel Martí (1663–1735), mentor of Mayans y Siscar. Although Lopez subsequently rejected this hypothesis after realizing that, according to Cro, the author and the scribe of the manuscript were the same person — which disqualified Martí from being the author since his handwriting did not match that of the manuscript[14] — he later resumed his speculations, arguing that Cro might have been wrong in not assuming that the author dictated the text to a scribe.[15]

Like Lopez, Pedro Álvarez de Miranda has been especially interested in fixing the date of composition of the utopian text by means of a linguistic analysis that corroborated its possible origin in the seventeenth century, specifically during the period of the *novatores*.[16] In fact, the current critical consensus of scholars acquainted with eighteenth-century Spain, as stated earlier, is that the anonymous text belongs to the period of the reign of Carlos II (1665–1700). In spite of the scholarly work of Lopez and Álvarez de Miranda, in his 2013 edition of *Sinapia*, the specialist in philosophy of law Miguel Ángel Ramiro Avilés takes for granted that the text was composed during the Enlightenment, but he does not explain why. His approach is primarily concerned with the representation of laws in the utopian model.[17]

Following Lopez's idea that the manuscript is not an autograph copy, José Santos Puerto set out the claim that the author might be Father Martín Sarmiento (1695–1772), an intellectual close to Benito Jerónimo Feijoo. In a long article in which he challenges the hypotheses of Cro, Avilés, and Lopez regarding the authorship of *Sinapia*, Santos Puerto provides reasons for and against Sarmiento being the author.[18] Although he seems to have identified similarities between Sarmiento's mentality and that of the author of *Sinapia*, they may be merely coincidental or a result of ideological influence. In his extensive monographic study on Sarmiento's work, Santos Puerto also indicates that, although it may be proved that the cleric was not the author, what matters most is that Sarmiento's enterprise could be symbolically understood as a 'Great Sinapia', in contrast to the anonymous 'little Sinapia' found in the Campomanes papers.[19] In both cases, Santos identifies a polemical reaction against the status quo of the time. However, such an ideological response might rather be seen as a mere variety of intellectual stances in writers who advocated change.[20]

Finally, it should be pointed out that, based on Avilés's 1976 edition, the Spanish philosopher and writer Fernando Savater wrote in 1983 a free theatrical adaptation of *Sinapia* entitled *Vente a Sinapia: una reflexión española sobre la utopía* [*Come to Sinapia: A Spanish Reflection on Utopia*], a work that was performed in Madrid in the same year. As the subtitle of the text indicates, Savater's purpose was to reflect on the subject of utopia from a Spanish perspective, even though he undervalued the literary qualities of *Sinapia* and regarded it as an imperfect example that confirmed his conviction that utopian literature did not flourish in Spain.[21]

As opposed to criticism focused on dating the manuscript and speculating about the identity of the author, the present chapter will concentrate on examining the narrative and ideological features of *Sinapia*. Critics do not enter into the political or ideological considerations of the text; the religious aspect is equally overlooked or underplayed in their analyses. Assuming that the text was written after 1680, in agreement with Cro's, Lopez's, and Álvarez de Miranda's arguments, the placing of the text in the period of the *novatores* will determine the interpretation of its ideas, which, in fact, can be shown to conform to some defining aspects of the spirit of that period, as will be argued in the analysis below.

The Narrative Features of the Text

In comparing *Sinapia* with the formal features of a typical utopian text, the first element that stands out is the absence of the representation of a visitor arriving in the utopian country and from whose perspective the new territory and its ideal society are described. Instead of portraying the interaction between a traveller and the utopian space visited, the narrative voice purportedly retransmits some travel notes (*apuntamientos*) concerning Sinapia, made as a result of the journey to *Terra Australis Incognita* by the Dutch navigator Abel Tasman (1603–1659) — the first European to reach New Zealand, in 1642 — via a Spanish translation of a French version of the original manuscript, presumably written in Dutch. The narrative voice will be referred to here as the author or translator, even though the text that the 'author' is using to set out the description was supposedly written by Tasman.

Sinapia's technique corresponds to the Cervantine strategy in *Don Quixote* of claiming that the text is not first-hand but found: 'No sé cómo me vinieron a las manos algunos apuntamientos que Abel Tasman había hecho en su viaje, traducidos, por algún curioso, de holandés en francés' [I do not know how some of the notes that Abel Tasman had made during his journey, and translated from Dutch into French by some curious person, came into my hands].[22] As few believed Cervantes's words, few would be expected to believe the words of the Spanish author. However, *Sinapia* avoids this situation because of the fact that Tasman actually existed and explored the geographical area in question. If the story is indeed based on some of Tasman's travel notes, it could be thought that *Sinapia* is the result of writings originally composed before 1659, the year of Tasman's death. If this were the case, the text would turn out to be a largely implicit comparison of an early seventeenth-century Sinapia and late seventeenth-century Spain, which would entail a gap of at least twenty years between both contexts. This difference in time would not affect the fictional plausibility of *Sinapia*, regardless of the actual date of composition of the work, whether in the reign of Carlos II or later.

Not only does the leitmotif of *Terra Australis Incognita* situate *Sinapia* in the tradition of voyages of discovery and utopias, but the very first sentence of the text situates the overall work in a literary context: 'Grande ha sido la curiosidad que hasta ahora han tenido los aficionados a las letras de saber los secretos de la Tierra Austral' [Great has been the curiosity that until now enthusiasts of literature have had to know the secrets of the Southern Land].[23] The objective of conceiving the text as a travel account is reflected in the mention of a group of Spanish and

Dutch navigators who have unsuccessfully explored the land before indicating that Tasman's writings contain information about the existence of a republic in that area. What supposedly most attracts the author to translating Tasman's notes is the fact of Sinapia being a flourishing and happy republic where the people practise Christian virtue, as well as its contrast with Europe and ideas of political organization derived from the writings of Tacitus and Machiavelli.

Given that the description of Sinapia is the product of Tasman's *apuntamientos*, the structure of the text is divided into fragments. In this respect, the author imitates More's organization of the features of Utopia into sections, but the subdivisions in *Sinapia* are more numerous, and many are much shorter. The description is divided into thirty-three numbered and subheaded sections, including the introductory section explaining the lucky find of Tasman's notes and the closing section entitled 'Reflexiones' ['Reflections'], in which it is not clear if it is the translator or Tasman who expresses his opinion about the description of the utopian nation that has been presented in the preceding sections. However, the very last sentence of the text stating that Sinapia is the antipodean version of Spain is undoubtedly a judgement of the Spanish translator. This results in a remarkable counterpoint between the voice of the translator in the initial and final sections and that of Tasman throughout the rest of the descriptive parts of the text. The variation in length of these sections could be argued to respond to Tasman's preference to devote more space to aspects that he finds more interesting, probably because of their contrast with the European context.

Nevertheless, although the text supposedly has input from two figures, Tasman and the anonymous Spanish translator, some lapses made by the latter burst into the translation of the 'French' version, which interferes with the continuity or coherence of the text being translated. In sections 25, 30, and 33, the use of the word *nosotros* [us] seems to refer to Spaniards, which is reinforced by the expression *nuestra Hispaña* [our Spain] in the last sentence of section 33 or 'Reflexiones', as already observed. Such a phrase would probably not be used by a translator of an originally Dutch text. Similarly, explicit references to Tasman's journey in sections 2 and 26 turn the translation into a not entirely coherent narrative.

The depiction of the utopian place is not presented in the form of a dialogue, as in More's *Utopia*, Campanella's *La Città del Sole*, and Bacon's *New Atlantis*. The preference for a descriptive narration over a dynamic conversational structure denotes the predisposition of the Spanish implied author to avoid any confrontation with the reformist ideas proposed. Moreover, he anticipates that his text could be seen as fictional due to the inherently unrealistic nature of the utopian principles that rule Sinapian society: 'Determineme, pues, a traducirla [la descripción de Sinapia], a riesgo de que pase por novela,[24] por la dificultad con que los que nos hemos criado con lo mío y lo tuyo podemos persuadirnos que pueda vivirse en perfecta comunidad' [Hence, I decided to translate it [the description of Sinapia] at the risk of the text being considered a novel because of the difficulty with which those of us who have been brought up with the concepts of mine and yours can be persuaded that it is possible to live in perfect communion].[25] This scepticism about the possibility of the perfect state, to be revealed in the text, could undermine belief in the utopian system that Sinapia represents. The key factor in making a contemporary audience not believe it is the absence of differentiation between 'lo mío y lo tuyo' [mine and yours], that is to say, ownership of property, as the text will proceed to make clear.

However, the translator has opted for a convenient objective viewpoint in order to give the impression that there is no need to persuade the reader of the validity of a social system that has proven to be effective in practice. Since its utilitarian objective has been successful, the question of the feasibility of Sinapia turns out to be of no consequence, and this leads the author to strongly believe that it is a model to follow.[26] The aim of giving the text a non-fictional appearance is rightly observed by Marie Laffranque when she considers the impact of this narrative strategy on the reader: 'La surprise et l'incrédulité du lecteur vont cesser. Il va aborder sans hésitation la terre de Sinapia. Il va croire à l'ensemble harmonieux de son histoire, de ses institutions et de ses coutumes' [The reader will no longer be surprised or incredulous. He will approach the land of Sinapia without hesitation. He will believe in the harmonious whole of its history, institutions, and customs].[27]

Like Utopia, the City of the Sun, and Bensalem, Sinapia functions as an autonomous and exemplary nation-state that implicitly stands in contrast with an existing form of government at a specific historical time. However, while the utopian commonwealths imagined by More, Campanella, and Bacon appear to be socio-political models of possibly universal implementation, the Sinapian republic is conceived exclusively in terms of its antagonistic relationship with Spain in every possible aspect — although some of these differences might be questioned — especially with regard to religion because almost everything in this area is the same as in Spain: '[E]n el sitio como en todo lo demás, es esta península [Sinapia] perfectísimo antípode de nuestra Hispaña' [In its location, as in everything else, this peninsula [Sinapia] is the perfect antipodes of our Spain].[28] The fact that this declaration is only included at the end of the narration would seem to oblige the reader to return to the beginning of the text and reread its description in the light of the claim that Sinapia is a geographically inverted and programmatically subverted Spain in real time; hence, the word 'Sinapia' is a near-anagram of Hispania, the Latin name of Spain. While the author takes Christianity for granted, other aspects of Spanish society might be better if changed to be in accordance with Sinapia.

The tendency to interpret a new geographical, political, military, religious, and social set-up in terms of an already existing society echoes the alienating European consciousness through which the Spanish conquistadors reinvented the New World in their chronicles of discovery and colonization. Perhaps this atavistic gesture operates in accordance with the filtering of Tasman's travel notes through the act of translation, whose narration is controlled by the Spanish translator. *Sinapia*'s apparently objective narrative voice contrasts with the literary figure of the utopian traveller created by More. As Peter Giles says when taking More's fictional alter ego out of his misconception about Raphael Hythloday, Utopia's visitor is essentially a traveller, or rather a philosopher:

'In that case', said I [More], 'my guess wasn't a bad one, for at first glance I supposed he was a ship's captain.'
'Then you're far off the mark', he [Giles] replied, 'for his sailing has not been like that of Palinurus, but more that of Ulysses, or rather of Plato.'[29]

As to the narrative element of the discovery and exploration of a perfect but remote and inaccessible place, *Sinapia* does not comprise the representation of a utopian space in the process of being observed and assessed. What the Spanish text lacks is the recreation of experiencing the newly discovered land, which would provide the opportunity to discuss the suitability of the form of government proposed. However, this characteristic is in accord with the fact that the text is meant to be a description of different aspects of Sinapian society. Therefore, its descriptive tone is for the most part unemotional and neutral as the author's intention is not to assertively recommend the implementation of the Sinapian model in Spain.

The author of *Sinapia* is less enthusiastic in promoting his utopian society than More was. As opposed to the inquisitive and questioning Hythloday or the perplexed members of a European crew after their shipwreck in the *New Atlantis*, *Sinapia*'s narrator is focused on briefly explaining the framework of its utopian system. What ultimately motivates his account is the probable curiosity of his compatriots.[30] The interest of the author seems to be to make details of this society known, and in particular for those who read their books in Spanish. As far as the author is concerned, the state of Sinapia contrasts with Spain, but that is clearly up to the reader to judge.

The significance of the structural components of the republic of Sinapia that are meant to positively turn upside down the existing Spanish system will be explored in the next sections of this chapter. These components are described from the second section of the anonymous text onwards, when readers are presented with a detailed and objective description of Sinapia, without being aware of the transition effected by the author from the mention of the discovery and translation of Tasman's *apuntamientos* to their actual insertion in the text.

The Political and Social Structure of Sinapia

Sinapia reveals its distance from the utopian tradition in the puzzling genesis of Sinapian society. Sinapia is a monarchy, based on a mixture of aristocratic and democratic elements, in which the monarch is the prince, the nobles are the magistrates, and the common people are the families, who make up the majority. The republic was founded by the Persian prince Sinap Ardxird, the Christian patriarch Joseph Codabend, and the Chinese philosopher Siang,[31] and it is the result of a complex amalgam of diverse peoples: Malay, Peruvian, Chinese, and Persian. Christianity arrived with the Persians, whose exodus to Sinapia, in Cro's view, makes the text divert from the traditional utopian models:

> [E]l motivo del éxodo de los persianos a Sinapia y el de la reunificación simbólica en la utopía cristiana representa un paso ulterior en la tradición del género utópico en relación a los modelos clásicos y humanísticos prevalentes en la utopía renacentista de Moro, Campanella y Bacon.[32]

[The motifs of the exodus of Persians to Sinapia and of the symbolic reunification in a Christian utopia represent a further step in the tradition of the utopian genre in relation to the classical and humanistic models prevalent in the Renaissance utopias of More, Campanella, and Bacon.]

The Christian orthodoxy introduced by the Persians and the intervention of sophisticated cultures in the constitution of the Sinapian nation produce an innovative system based on the achievements of former dominant cultures and less dominant ones. In fact, the text suggests that the Malay and Peruvian peoples were subjected to civilizing processes whose final goal was Christian conversion.[33] Civilization and Christianity are presented as interactive forces that enhance the viability and the strength of the system proposed.

The suggestive description of Sinapia's progressive establishment can be interpreted as the birth of a superior civilization consisting of the amalgamation of social groups with colonizing purposes, some of which have escaped from the tyranny of their previous rulers:

> De cuatro naciones toman su origen los habitadores de esta península: malayos, peruanos, chinos y persianos. Los primeros, con el uso de las armas de hierro que trajeron, obligaron a los sencillos negrillos zambales que la habitaban a pasar la cordillera y retirarse con los lagos.[34] Aquéllos trajeron también el uso de vestirse y de cultivar la tierra y navegar. Los peruanos aportaron echados de una tempestad a estas marinas, habiendo salido huyendo del Inca. [...] Uniéronse con los malayos así por ser pocos como por gozar de las comodidades que los primeros con su industria ya tenían.
>
> Después vinieron los chinos y éstos fueron en gran número, por haber salido una armada de ellos huyendo de la tiranía de Kieu [...]. Estos, como gente política e industriosa, con maña fueron haciéndose lugar, de modo que adquirieron la veneración de las otras dos naciones y con el uso de la pólvora se hicieron formidables a los lagos [...].
>
> La última nación fueron los persas, los cuales trajeron la luz del evangelio y con ella la verdadera política.[35]

> [The origin of the inhabitants of this peninsula is from four nations: Malay, Peruvian, Chinese, and Persian. The first of these, using the iron weapons that they brought with them, forced the simple negroes of Zambales, who were already there, to cross the mountain range and go away with the *lagos* [Gauls]. They also brought with them the custom of wearing clothes, cultivating the land, and sailing. The Peruvians were thrown onto these shores by a storm, having fled the Incas [...]. They united with the Malays because they were few and wanted to enjoy the comforts that the Malays already enjoyed thanks to their industry.
>
> Then came the Chinese, and in great numbers, because an army of them had fled from the tyranny of Kieu [...]. These, as civilized and industrious people, with skill began to carve out a place for themselves so that they received the veneration of the other two nations, and with the use of gunpowder they became formidable to the *lagos* [Gauls] [...].
>
> The last nation was the Persians, who brought the light of the Gospel and with it correct ways of behaving.]

It is in this peculiar founding of the utopian community that *Sinapia* shows its originality and desire to underscore the beneficial irruption of civilization into contexts of uncivilized anarchy. Thus, Malays did not exactly conquer and submit the *negros zambales* [negroes of Zambales] (a cross between a Negro and an Indian), who were presumably the original inhabitants of Sinapia's geographical settlement, but rather displaced them by using their civilized and violent weapons. This initial displacement of the first dwellers of the peninsula can be seen to be in keeping with the punishment of exile applied to those who deviate from civil norms and deserve to return to their natural and instinctive environment. The symbolic reference to imposing civilization by means of such features as weapons, clothing, agriculture, and navigation makes it apparent that Sinapia is the product of an advanced process of socio-cultural adaptation and integration. Furthermore, the fact that Peruvians and Chinese ran away from the tyrannical regimes of their respective nations suggests the imperfections of existing systems of government, even though *Sinapia*'s utopian political order is rather an absolutist system prone to commit political abuses with respect to individual freedoms.

However, the text attempts to create the impression of a struggle among these three nations with the aim of correcting the flaws in their original governments and making of the heterogeneous Sinapia an improved version of them. The Chinese colony will end up dominating the other two groups because of the supremacy of its highly developed culture and crucial invention of gunpowder. All in all, there is a competitive relationship among these cultural groups, of which only the strongest will survive. Far from problematizing the question of national identity, this kind of transculturation reinforces the idea of culture as a dynamic historical process instead of as a fixed and unchanging phenomenon with which a community identifies. *Sinapia*'s author subscribes to the thought that a utopian society must be multiracial and multicultural:

> [S]iendo el pueblo de esta república formado de estas naciones, ha de participar de sus cualidades y así la fisionomía es varia, como mezclada de las cuatro más universales: etiópica de los zambales; indiana de los malayos; tartárica de los chinos y peruanos; y asiática y europea de los persas.[36]
>
> [Since the people of this republic are composed of these nations, they necessarily share their qualities, and thus their physiognomy is varied, a mixture of the four most universal types: Ethiopian from the negroes of Zambales; Indian from the Malays; Tartar from the Chinese and Peruvians; and Asian and European from the Persians.]

The contradiction in including the *negros zambales* as one of the racial groups involved, after having said that they were expelled from the peninsula by the Malays, is justified by their required participation in the building of an ideal and universal republic. Although *Sinapia* endorses this kind of terrestrial cultural fantasy without compromising the Sinapians' identity, its nationalism is largely dogmatic and intolerant of foreign influences or contributions, as will be detailed below. Such dogmatism is enhanced by the strong religious component that dominates the socio-political structure of Sinapia, as will also be seen later in this chapter.

Sinapia's repressive consciousness is only exceeded by the solipsistic self-conception of Campanella's City of the Sun in that its prince is called 'Sun' or, in the language of the Solarians, 'Metaphysician' because 'He is both their spiritual and their temporal chief, and all decisions terminate with him'.[37] The totalitarian intervention of the head of state makes him the measure of all things and nothing can be thought outside of his domain. Campanella and the anonymous Spanish author appear to subscribe to Plato's criticism of democracy as a free republic that may descend into degeneration and later into tyranny. However, neither author provides a form of governmental alternative to the democratic or tyrannical excesses, but rather both authors distort the image of the ideal city-state proposed in Plato's *Republic*, in which the philosopher is identified as the only person entitled to rule a utopian city: 'Until philosophers are kings, or the kings and princes of this world have the spirit and power of philosophy, and political greatness and wisdom meet in one, [...] cities will never have rest from their evils'.[38] Sinapia's form of government is not only hybrid and contradictory ('Es la forma de esta república monárquica, mezclada de aristocrática y democrática' [The nature of this republic is monarchical, a mixture of aristocratic and democratic rule]),[39] but also radicalizes the dehumanization of the monarch as he is a metonymic representation of the laws.

The administrative and spatial organization of Sinapia is considerably complex, but the important aspect to note is that families are the institution on the basis of which the layout and running of the peninsula is designed. Each family lives in a house and cannot have more than twelve members, including a slave couple and their children. Ten houses form a neighbourhood, and eight neighbourhoods constitute a village. A city has the same composition as a village, but is divided into parishes (*parroquias*). Of these cities, the one located in the centre of the region is the metropolis, where the church and the bishops are based. In turn, the court is the metropolis of the province of Ni-sa, which is in the centre of the peninsula and is the place of residence of the prince (or *sinapo*), the senate, and the archbishop. Echoing More's precise words when he describes the cities of Utopia,[40] the Spanish author asserts that all the settlements in Sinapia look exactly the same, except for a few constructional details:

> Quien ha visto una villa, las ha visto todas, pues todas son iguales y semejantes; y quien ha visto éstas, ha visto las ciudades, las metrópolis y la corte misma, pues sólo se diferencian en el número de los barrios, en la mejoría de los materiales y en la grandeza de los edificios públicos; y en todo lo demás son uniformes.[41]

> [Whoever has seen one village has seen them all, for they are all equal and alike; and whoever has seen these has seen the cities, the metropolises, and the court itself because they differ only in the number of neighbourhoods, in the improvement of materials, and in the grandeur of public buildings; and they are uniform in every other respect.]

Sinapia's social structure is organized in a pyramidal hierarchy with the prince at the top and the families at the bottom. The middle part of the pyramid is formed by the magistrates, who are all called *padres* [fathers]: 'padres de familia, padres de barrio, padres de villas, padres de ciudad, padres de provincia' [fathers of families, neighbourhood fathers, village fathers, city fathers, provincial fathers].[42] The senate is composed of the 'padres de Sinapia' [fathers of Sinapia] and is headed by the prince. Apart from being described as a sentinel who supervises the actions of the magistrates, the prince is portrayed as having a colonizing function: 'Naturaliza a los forasteros, da la libertad a los esclavos, [...] hace enviar fuera de la isla colonias cuando sobra el número de los moradores, hace venir de las colonias el número de moradores que faltan' [He naturalizes foreigners, grants freedom to slaves, [...] sends colonies of people out of the island when the number of the inhabitants is too many or brings from the colonies the number of inhabitants lacking].[43] Each category of magistrate wears a ribbon of a specific colour attached to their heads, and they are all elected from among themselves, except for the *padres de familia*, who are designated by divine power.

Sinapians dedicate six hours to work, seven hours to sleep, and one hour to the three meals of the day. They have eight spare hours of leisure to entertain themselves: '[L]es quedan libres ocho, las cuales gastan en repasar las lecciones, aprender algún arte o ciencia, leer o jugar algún juego de los permitidos, en cultivar el jardín común y los tiestos de las galerías' [They are free for eight hours, which are spent revising the lessons, learning some art or science, reading or playing some permitted game, cultivating the common garden, and tending to the flowerpots in the galleries].[44] In this respect, the author provides Sinapians with recreational activities similar to those of More's Utopians. In terms of education, the heads of households are responsible for teaching good manners to their children, while schoolteachers are in charge of training them, in the skills thought necessary, from the age of five. Agriculture and other manual occupations are learned at home, whereas Christian doctrine and the basic learning of literacy and numeracy are acquired at school.

Laws and military actions are the means for the preservation of peace and prevention of war. Sinapians avoid war by all possible means, except when they have to act in self-defence. Prisoners of war become slaves, and Sinapians make every effort to release the captured soldiers from their captivity. They try not to destroy houses or trees, or to hurt women, children, or the elderly. Considering that war is seen as opposing the principles of civilization, they judge it more rational and Christian to resolve conflicts by resorting to proven effective stratagems: '[S]i pueden vencer con los beneficios, con la cortesía y con la clemencia, lo estiman, premian y juzgan por más digno de cristianos y de racionales y al mismo tiempo más conveniente y seguro' [If they can find solutions via rewards, courtesy, and mercy, they esteem such a solution, grant it, and judge it worthier of Christians and rational people, and at the same time appropriate and secure].[45]

The Christian Commonwealth of Sinapia

In spite of social equality being the fundamental principle of a utopian republic, *Sinapia* promotes an ideal nation based on the contemplation of divine dictate and subject to the established ideology. The only way of reaching a perfect social balance is by living in conformity with Christian values. In other words, it is imperative to behave within the desired parameters in order to obtain divine salvation. Ultimately, the teleological objective of Sinapia is 'vivir templada, devota y justamente en este mundo aguardando la dicha prometida con la venida gloriosa de nuestro gran Dios' [to live moderately, devoutly, and justly in this world awaiting the promised bliss at the glorious coming of our great God],[46] and the means of attaining it are 'la vida común, la igualdad, la moderación y el trabajo' [common life, equality, moderation, and work].[47] These qualities are, in fact, the essential pillars of every utopian community.

Sinapia's system is determined by a Christianity that might apparently have had its roots in Persian religion. No matter how sophisticated the other three founding nations are, Persians manage to impose their culture because of the compatibility of their religious ideology with the project of Christendom envisioned by Sinapia. According to the anonymous narrator, regardless of history and culture, the Gospel is the real and proper basis of politics for Sinapians, represented by the agglomeration and cultural symbiosis of the four nations that are the constitutive foundations of Sinapian society. Therefore, the justification of the institution of slavery, which will be discussed below, is likely to be rooted in the fact that the Bible does not condemn slavery, but rather supports its regulated practice. Nevertheless, it is more likely that the justification is in the fact that slavery was accepted as normal by European countries until the end of the eighteenth century, when it began to be questioned.

Although the roles of the state and the Church are clearly separate and complementary, the religious sphere prevails in the functioning of Sinapia's utopian system. Spanish Enlightenment thinking developed essentially within the framework of Catholic culture, but the diffusion of science and critical thinking shook the foundations of Christian orthodoxy. However, a sign of new religious vitality was the renewal of missionary activity in America during the seventeenth and eighteenth centuries, especially in the western territories of North America and the missions in Paraguay until the expulsion of the Jesuit Order in 1767. This resurgent impulse of Christian goals was greatly supported by the idea that religion conquers peacefully and has the most effective and convincing means of instilling new principles and practices of government.

What appears to be remarkable in the eminently Christian political doctrine sustained in *Sinapia* is not only the relevance given to Christian virtue, but also its significance in the political sphere. The anonymous author refers to the mutual dependence of the political and the religious: '[E]l ejercicio de la virtud cristiana es más a propósito para hacer una república floreciente y una nación dichosa que cuantas redomadas políticas enseñan Tácito o Machiavelli, o practican los europeos' [The exercise of Christian virtue is more suitable for building a flourishing republic and a happy nation than many policies taught by Tacitus or Machiavelli, or put into practice by Europeans].[48] Civic and religious virtue can be reached through faith and contemplation: 'El empleo más apetecible y digno del hombre creen los sinapienses que es la contemplación de las grandezas de Dios y después las de sus obras' [Sinapians believe that the most desirable and worthy activity is the contemplation of the greatness of God, and afterwards that of his works].[49]

Thus, the utopian scope covered by Sinapia's organization is perceived through the spiritual filter of Christianity. Since the final end of the inhabitants is their salvation and their entry into the most utopian place to live, their compliance with Sinapia's maxims is only a vehicle to succeed in reaching their future destination: '[E]l fin de este gobierno no es dilatar su dominio, enriquecer sus súbditos ni extender su fama, sino hacerlos vivir en este mundo justa, templada y devotamente, para hacerlos felices en el otro' [The purpose of this government is not to extend its dominion, to enrich its subjects, or to spread its fame, but to make people live justly, moderately, and devoutly in this world in order to make them happy in the other].[50] Apart from the constant assessment of virtue, what is persistently pondered is the rational configuration of the Christian religion and the assertion that it is not contaminated by superstition, hypocrisy, and vanity. Sinapia is, then, a Christian commonwealth[51] where the equation of reason with nature prevails, and this, in turn, equates to virtue.

Moderation and simplicity are the principal qualities that constitute the virtuous nature of Sinapians. A human nature of this kind, governed by reason and sobriety, was exactly what the Jesuit *reducciones* in Spanish America, particularly in Paraguay, sought to achieve. Some critics, especially Cro, have stressed the ideological correlation between *Sinapia* and the evangelical reform programme in view of the similarities concerning institutional organization and the educational system. As in the *reducciones*, family is the fundamental social, political, and economic unit in Sinapia: 'Del buen gobierno de las familias, de la buena educación y del acierto de los matrimonios, pende la conservación y felicidad de la república' [The preservation and happiness of the republic depend on the good government of families, good education, and success in marriage].[52] Agricultural and industrial activities are supported by the family structure as the core of society, and only the father can be elected to the magistracy because 'Son los *padres de familia* magistrados naturales, dados por Dios, no elegidos por los hombres' [*Fathers of families* are natural magistrates given by God, not chosen by men].[53]

The Sinapian family is strictly patriarchal and acts as a balancing force in the communal system. Ultimately, the nuclear family replicates the mechanism of the whole society, and the *pater familias* [head of household] is expected to apply the overall model of social control in his household:

> Ejercitan su jurisdicción en todas las personas de la familia, a quien mandan absolutamente y castigan con prisión, ayuno y azotes. A ellos incumbe guardar y hacer guardar la ley de Dios, las leyes sinapienses [...] y aumentar la iglesia con buenos cristianos y la república de buenos ciudadanos.[54]

> [They exercise their jurisdiction over all members of a family, whom they command absolutely and punish with imprisonment, fasting, and lashes. It is their duty to keep and enforce respect for the law of God, Sinapian laws [...], and to expand church membership with good Christians and the republic with good citizens.]

Despite Sinapia's rejection of the use of violence, the use of Christian mortification or penance is contemplated as a valid part of its political-religious system. The analogy between good Christians and good citizens not only echoes the likely problematic interaction between civic and spiritual virtue, but is also in line with the location of the church at the centre of the urban plan and with the fact of using the word *padres* to name both ecclesiastical and governmental authorities. Nonetheless, it must be pointed out that there is a gender issue implied in the sense of patriarchy that ends up precluding any genuine sexual equality.

Another important point of comparison between Sinapian society and the Jesuit theocracy in Paraguay is the non-existence of private property, interpreted as a primitive and purer stage of Christianity in which all possessions are held as collective state property. Echoing the constitutive tenets of the Jesuit *reducciones*, *Sinapia* is a response to a technocratic utopia: 'a controlled economy organized for universal well-being'.[55] What this kind of utopia pursued was a nostalgic vision of nature and natural man and a disapproval of religious superstition; its intention was not to justify a systematic set of reforms. Cro's observation sums up the logic of the *reducciones* that might be seen as a template for Sinapia's design:

> Las Reducciones representaban todo lo que la ilustración voltairiana combatía con más vehemencia: la unidad del poder temporal y espiritual bajo una casta sacerdotal, la economía comunitaria y planificada que excluía el beneficio individual, la exclusión del capital privado, la limitación del poder del monarca, la supeditación de la razón a la fe.[56]
>
> [The *Reducciones* represented all that the Voltairean Enlightenment fought against most vehemently: the unity of temporal and spiritual power under a priestly caste, a planned and communal economy that excluded individual benefit, the exclusion of private capital, the limitation of the power of the monarch, the subordination of reason to faith.]

Sinapia is described as 'una nación sencilla, que carece de las maliciosas máximas de la política interesada' [a simple nation, which lacks the malicious maxims of selfish politics],[57] and that is why its governmental superstructure does not produce socio-economic crises. However, Sinapia's very conservative Christian blueprint restricts its inhabitants' free will. Since vice and corruption are deeply rooted in civilized man, those who try to sabotage the established order are necessarily punished, as will be explained below. The spiritual impetus is the essential factor in maintaining moral virtue, but it is not the entity that administers society because the Church is subject to the state in all that is not related to moral conscience. Under Sinapia's utopian scheme, politics and ethics work together to provide citizens with the happiness that justice and equality bring. The acceptance of a pre-existing political administration is chiefly associated with the sublime institution of family in which parents are natural magistrates elected by divine power, as previously mentioned. A Christian utopia, then, seems to undermine the utopian aspect of free election of rulers and lawmakers by citizens.

The duality of reason and spiritual progress must be examined in relation to the belief held by some, especially the advocates of capitalism, that collective happiness depends on material progress. In order for civilization to develop, happiness must be achieved through the improvement of man's spiritual, not material, world. This phenomenological premise underlies the allegedly rational Christianity that *Sinapia* defends as the starting point of its utopian model. The characterization of a rational Christian plan is also reflected in the brevity and concision of Sinapia's laws, as in More's *Utopia*, even though their origins and implications are not supposed to be questioned or explained at all. This restrictive aspect is an indicator of the blinkered attitude towards other ways of creating a perfect society. In this respect, Ramiro Avilés posits that the utopian style allows the narrator to persuade the reader of the effectiveness of the socio-political measures that have already been applied, rather than using a direct descriptive style through which the audience is offered a series of experimental and uncertain reforms, contingent upon their successful application in the future:

> The utopian literary form allowed the author of *Sinapia* to avoid presenting his readers with reform policies to be legitimated and adopted. Instead, the readers were offered a political project already implemented and legitimized by the rationality, fairness and justice of its arrangements as they were vividly experienced in the lives and characters of the populace.[58]

Despite the fact that utopia is largely a political creation, its aesthetic features should not be overlooked. In doing so, its discursive complexity is reduced to a mere impulse or wish, as Fredric Jameson points out: 'It has often been observed that we need to distinguish between the Utopian form and the Utopian wish: between the written text or genre and something like a Utopian impulse detectable in daily life and its practices'.[59]

Although the configuration of a utopian civic Christendom is more coherent and technical in *Sinapia*, the same target is observed in other Spanish utopian texts, such as *El deseado gobierno, buscado por el amor de Dios para el reino de España* (pre-1760) by Melchor de Macanaz. The protagonist is a pilgrim who embarks on a fantastic journey to a utopian country called *Deseado Gobierno* [Desired Government], a kingdom of truth where nobody tells lies and where the practice of virtue is enshrined in law. The pilgrim believes that the remedy for the decline in politics and social behaviour 'would not come out of the outdated ideas on which the current regime operates, but that it is necessary to undertake reforms based on new ideas. This is the origin of his pilgrimage towards enlightened ideas'.[60] The desired government is naturally one that fully complies with the requirements of Christian doctrine because '[s]in ella bien sabida, creída y ejecutada, no puede haber gobierno que agrade ni a Dios ni a los hombres' [without it being well known, believed in, and carried out, there can be no government that pleases God or men].[61] However, the narrator sadly recognizes the vacuous character of any plan of government, real or imaginary. His reflection on the fact that both a good government and a good governor are speculative creations reinforces the sense of negativity that tends to appear in *Sinapia* and other Spanish utopias.[62]

Civilization and Social Norms

Since the institution of private property has been abolished in Sinapia, there are virtually no conflicts between the members of the community. However, in order for a system of shared goods to succeed, it is necessary to have enough supplies in stock to fulfil the needs of all the citizens. Any surplus is exchanged among the cities, the metropolis, and the court. To enhance the sense of community and equality in all areas of life, there are a number of civic and religious activities through which the citizens are expected to strengthen their friendship and co-operation. In addition to gathering in the church to celebrate religious festivities, these communal events include weddings and baptisms.

Sinapians also meet every Sunday to share a meal in the house of the father of the neighbourhood (*barrio*). Although these meals are meant to be special occasions in which the best food and drinks are served, moderation is always the norm. In this respect, the voice of the Spanish translator is made present in the narration in comparing Sinapian banquets with those in Spain. The important element to highlight regarding such social activities is that individualism is unthinkable in Sinapia's system. A constant interaction between its citizens is required to maintain an efficient and happy society.

As a result of pursuing social equality, hereditary nobility does not exist in Sinapia. The absence of an aristocracy not only prevents Sinapians from experiencing feelings of arrogance and ambition, but also eradicates the existence of poor people and plebeians from their social composition, as well as the potential threat of uprisings. Such a disdain for the traditional institution of aristocracy is in direct opposition to the conventional social organization in Spain, in which the hereditary nobility played a central role. As in Utopia, the absence of nobility, money, and private property is a fundamental component in Sinapia. Furthermore, as in the case of Utopians, it is possible to think that virtue is the only conceivable notion of nobility in Sinapia.

It is clear that *Sinapia* advocates a civilized coexistence of the members of the community. However, the notion of a civilized citizen can be problematic because he or she is susceptible to be corrupted by society itself. Oddly enough, the text of *Sinapia* blames corruption on rational and cultural conceptions resulting from supposedly civilizing processes, such as money and private property. In order to protect the integrity of the system, the authorities are called on to restrain the irrational excesses that are hard to banish from human nature. This is mostly the case when dealing with public celebrations, both sacred and secular. In describing the severity with which unacceptable behaviour is punished, the absolutist regime contemplated by *Sinapia* becomes more than evident:[63]

> En todas se prohíben, por las leyes, todos los desórdenes de bandos o parcialidades, de palabras o acciones poco honestas, de murmuraciones picantes o doctrinas contrarias a la república y buenas costumbres, para lo cual hay nombrados celadores que asisten para notar los excesos, castigándolos al punto y sin remisión.[64]
>
> [In each of them, by law, all disorder caused by groups or factions, dishonest

words or actions, racy rumours or doctrines contrary to the republic and good customs is forbidden, for which there are appointed overseers who are present in order to note the excesses, punishing them immediately and without remission.]

The distortion of pseudo-civilizing instruments of civil discipline makes the use of the utopian label more problematic. Laws and rules are intended to repress the natural freedom of the human will, and the effectiveness of force and punishment is fully legitimized by the government, despite the fact that crime rarely occurs in Sinapia. Jorge Pérez-Rey argues that the totalitarian nature of the spatial configuration of *Sinapia* is the result of the repressive colonization of the urban space.[65]

Sinapia's system conceptualizes the hostile side of nature as a space of punishment and degradation. In that regard, the sentence of exile, which is the highest sentence given in Sinapia, consists in being abandoned in the middle of the vast space and inhospitable area of the desert:

> La pena de destierro [...] se da a los rebeldes a Dios y a la república [...]. Ésta se ejecuta llevando al reo a una de muchas islas desiertas que hay hacia el oriente, donde lo dejan con víveres para un mes, instrumentos para cavar y cortar madera y para hacer fuego, vasos y semillas.[66]

> [The punishment of exile [...] is imposed on rebels against God and the republic [...]. It is executed by taking the prisoner to one of the many deserted islands that lie towards the east, where they leave him or her with provisions for a month, tools to dig and cut wood and to make fire, as well as vessels and seeds.]

It is interesting that the outcast is provided with the minimum civilized tools necessary to enable him or her to survive. In other words, the exiled person is sentenced to a reencounter with their pre-civilized self, but this regression necessarily implies a negative and degrading connotation of nature to the extent that the condemned will be sentenced to death if he or she attempts to return to Sinapia. The emptiness of a desert island as opposed to the fertility of the Sinapian peninsula, or of any primitive place with abundant natural resources, apparently alludes to the desire to suppress any external and contending pre-societal reality.

Alongside exile, slavery acts as a significant disciplinary control in Sinapia. Perpetual slavery replaces the death penalty in cases of serious offences, which are not specified in the text. This aspect connects to the fact that the relationship between utopia and reform brings about the complicated question of the right to punish. The topic permeates the entire utopian tradition, and the functionality and legitimacy of punishment appear to be based on the mechanism of social control that is inherent to utopian projects. In More's *Utopia*, slavery is the most common type of punishment and is understood as more effective than the death penalty because slave labour is of greater benefit to the community than the death of slaves could be:

> Generally, the gravest crimes are punished with slavery, for they think this deters offenders just as much as getting rid of them by immediate capital punishment, and convict labour is more beneficial to the commonwealth. Slaves, moreover, contribute more by their labour than by their death [...]. If

the slaves rebel against their condition, then, since neither bars nor chains can tame them, they are finally put to death like wild beasts.[67]

In a similar way to *Sinapia*, *Utopia* implies that those who are unable to bear their sentences must be treated as savages incapable of being kept in order and, therefore, deserving of death. Nonetheless, Utopians can get their liberty back or, at least, have their slavery mitigated by gift of the prince or the people's intercession, which can be equated to the temporary slavery to which Sinapians are subjected when they commit certain serious transgressions. A point not tackled by the text of *Sinapia* and notably highlighted by More is the imposition of slavery when adultery is committed. Both the adulterer and the adulteress must comply with the labour to which slaves are condemned, but, once again, the repentance of the offender, together with the benevolence of both the prince and the injured person, allows him or her to be pardoned. However, those who relapse are punished with death.

The necessity of eradicating all actions contrary to moral principles by means of slavery points to the idea that civilization prevents men from developing their human nature in a context untouched by the artificiality and tyranny of civil society, but *Sinapia* does not seek to change human nature or the interactions between humans and the natural world. The Spanish text favours a contemplative experience of nature instead of discussing the critical confrontation between mankind and nature. Paradoxically, going back to the Sinapian use of exile as a humiliating return to a pristine but barbaric primitivism, the kingdom of nature can be equally tyrannical and an unsuitable basis for government planning. Ultimately, natural man and moral man become indistinguishable since they belong to axiological spheres susceptible to the same degree of suspicion in terms of their value and viability.

The Relations of Sinapia with the Outside World

In Sinapia, the prevention of harmful innovations that could be spread by contact with foreigners results in an aversion to letting the citizens leave the country or to allowing visitors to enter the Sinapian territory:

> Logra esta república con lo demás del mundo de un comercio ventajosísimo, pues, pudiendo tener todo lo bueno que hay fuera de ella, está libre de que se le introduzca lo malo y, sacando todo lo inútil y sobrado, se queda con todo lo útil y provechoso. Esto consiguen teniendo prohibido a los naturales el salir de la península sin licencia del senado y toda comunicación con extranjeros y a éstos, el poner pie en la península sin permiso.[68]
>
> [This republic achieves a very advantageous trading relationship with the rest of the world because, being able to access all the good outside of it, it is free from receiving anything bad, and, by removing all useless and unnecessary things, it retains all the useful and beneficial ones. They achieve this by forbidding the natives to leave the peninsula without the permission of the senate and by forbidding all communication with foreigners, who are banned from entering the peninsula without permission.]

The reluctance to overtly interact with other nations distinguishes the Spanish text from the *New Atlantis*, where a critique about the absence of the practice of travelling in Bensalem is formulated:

> [T]his happy island where we now stood was known to few, and yet knew most of the nations of the world [...]. This we found wonderfully strange; for that all nations have inter-knowledge one of another either by voyage into foreign parts, or by strangers that come to them [...]; for that it seemed to us a condition and propriety of divine powers and beings, to be hidden and unseen to others, and yet to have others open and as in a light to them.[69]

Nevertheless, both Bensalem and Sinapia have the capacity to obtain goods and knowledge from other cultures without endangering their own supplies and wisdom. Under the guise of reciprocity, Sinapia's trading is contradictorily unilateral:

> Lo que sale de la península es lo que en ella sobra de frutos y manufacturas [...]. Lo que se trae son drogas medicinales, materiales para algunas manufacturas, las nuevas invenciones de artes y ciencias, buenos libros, modelos de artificios que no hay en Sinapia y mapas puntuales y cartas de marear de todas partes.[70]

> [What is exported from the peninsula is what is surplus in produce and manufactures [...]. What are imported are medicines, materials for some manufactured products, new inventions of the arts and sciences, good books, models of artefacts that Sinapia does not have, and detailed maps and navigational charts from everywhere.]

A similar attitude is held by the people of the City of the Sun, who send spies to other nations to learn their customs and, by doing so, improve their own. Although it may seem paradoxical, the insularity that gives a utopia its autonomy and self-sufficiency does not mean a growing apart or an estrangement from other nations. On the contrary, as Bacon's shipwrecked travellers say, knowledge acquired through direct observation and physical contact with the territories to be explored constitutes the most appropriate type of interaction between countries.

The objective of voyages is not only an educational process that provides the traveller with a symbolic cultural capital, but also a dialectical encounter between the traveller and the socio-historical situations faced in the course of travel. As a consequence, the practice of voyaging entails a transformative experience that refers to an open-minded pedagogy, which evidently conflicts with the ideological narrowness of Sinapia's programme. Any human activity that involves changes in the way people think would only mean danger to the established order of government. Thus, the omission of the practice of productive travelling activity is perplexing by virtue of the highly civilizing nature of the act of travel in itself. Voyages have usually become an act of decentring through which individuals can better get to know themselves. Anthropological otherness allows civilizations to discover their uniqueness by entering into dialogue with each other's differences. The observation of other societies turns travel into a conciliatory force between physical and social environment. However, the fact that *Sinapia* does not recreate the act of travelling through which the novelty of the utopian society can be unveiled reaffirms its disdain for the epistemological function of travel experience, a belief at variance with the assertion of such an idea at the high point of Enlightenment debate in late eighteenth-century Spain.

The Arts, Sciences, and Culture

Unlike Utopia and Bensalem, the development of the arts in Sinapia is not as valuable as that of the sciences because they are seen as probably deceitful and useless. The only way Sinapians can access true knowledge is by using rational methods:

> Válense para descubrir la verdad [...] de las vías matemáticas de división y de unión, procurando evitar todos los errores de los sentidos, de las pasiones y de la educación [...]. Del artificio retórico hacen poco caso, como de cosa que disminuye el crédito y sólo tiene eficacia mientras engaña. La poesía usan por la armonía y agrado de la música, pero muy natural, quitando todo relumbrón, juego de palabras y agudeza pueril.[71]

> [They use the mathematical techniques of division and addition [...] in order to discover the truth, trying to avoid all errors of the senses, passions, and education [...]. They do not care about rhetorical artifice as it diminishes credibility and is only effective when it deceives. They use poetry because of the harmony and enjoyment of its music, but in a very natural way, removing all ostentation, play on words, and childish wit.]

Any kind of intellectual or practical invention is condemned because of mistrust and only permitted after official approval from the authorities. Moreover, banned inventions are recorded in writing, an action that resembles the Inquisition's procedures in compiling lists of prohibited literary creations, though here applied to practical invention. Thus, *Sinapia* is characterized by a strong disapproval of the cultivation of creative skills because they constitute the germ of innovative and alternative projects that may threaten the ideological uniformity of the state. As an apparent believer in utilitarianism, *Sinapia*'s author stresses the importance of always keeping a rational objective, especially in the area of aesthetics. Poetry, painting, architecture, and sculpture must be primarily appreciated by virtue of their contributions to pragmatic ways of improving the lives of Sinapians:

> La arquitectura en los edificios particulares atiende sólo a la comodidad y duración; en los públicos, también a la magnificencia y en todos a la hermosura, que no consiste en los adornos, sino en la observancia de la simetría que agrada. En la pintura y escultura no sólo atienden a la imitación, sino a la propiedad en fisionomía, trajes, usos, animales y plantas.[72]

> [The architecture of private buildings focuses only on comfort and durability; in public ones, it also focuses on magnificence, and in all of them on beauty, which consists not in adornments, but in the observance of a symmetry that pleases the eye. In painting and sculpture, they pay attention not only to imitation, but to the appropriateness of physiognomy, clothing, traditions, animals, and plants.]

The value of the arts acquires an ambiguous characterization in *Sinapia*. Although all of these artistic disciplines are natural manifestations of human needs and thinking, they are treated as superfluous and corrupting areas of knowledge, which leads to questioning as to what extent the Enlightenment debate about the confrontation between nature and culture is involved in the author's utopian vision. The sciences are divided into the natural, the moral, and the divine. These three, in their turn, are subdivided into more categories, but the relevant point is that they are all simplified into history and doctrine because the interplay between these two legitimizes the utilitarian character of Sinapia's scheme. History provides the facts used to formulate doctrinal theorems.

The two major institutions dedicated to promoting the cultivation of science are an academy and a college, both epitomizing 'el espíritu que vivifica la república, pues de ellos salen las buenas máximas con que se gobierna y las buenas invenciones con que socorre sus necesidades y alivia sus trabajos' [the spirit that gives life to the republic, because from them emerge the good maxims that are used to govern and the good inventions that attend to its needs and lighten its toil].[73] While the academy consists of scholars versed in various disciplines of the arts and humanities and supervised by the interests of the senate, the college is comprised of a group of sages who are committed to making advances in the scientific field to a point where it would be difficult to maintain the belief in pre-existing knowledge. Their mission is to come up with useful inventions for the conservation of human life, preventing the implantation of harmful innovations that could be spread by contact with foreigners. The only foreign knowledge accepted is that derived from the valuable products of other nations and adequately filtered by the mediation of the translation process into Sinapia's language.

To carry out a beneficial trade in knowledge, a network of intellectuals conducts the meticulous task of organizing and refining the information gathered: the merchants of light[74] (*mercaderes de luz*) go on a pilgrimage to collect all the pertinent material from written sources; the harvesters (*recogedores*) decide what data will be of use; the distributors (*repartidores*) classify the information; the miners (*mineros*) infer or correct scientific definitions; the distillers (*destiladores*) formulate theorems based on the definitions; the benefactors (*bienhechores*) solve problems by using both definitions and theorems; and the magnifiers (*aumentadores*) draw out new and illuminating conclusions from all the findings. This description resembles the concept of 'invisible college' that became influential in seventeenth-century Europe. The invisible college in England consisted of a group of natural philosophers led by Robert Boyle and is generally regarded as a precursor to London's Royal Society. It was essentially a network of scientists and philosophers exchanging ideas in order to acquire knowledge through experimental research. Bringing up the comparison serves to show that the exclusive transfer of thought functions in Sinapia not so much as a kind of secret society, but as an intellectual defence against any questionable institutional authority. This attitude would point to an ideal or utopian dimension where a new system for the circulation of knowledge could be founded. In any event, neither the college nor the academy is envisioned as a selective scholarly association. The attention paid to the sciences and arts is notably prioritized in *Sinapia* compared to the customary treatment of the topic in the utopian genre.

The influence on Sinapia's college of Francis Bacon's Solomon's House or The College of the Six Days' Works as described in the *New Atlantis* should also be pointed out. Bacon's ideal college prided itself on having achieved mastery over nature through a rational and collaborative undertaking. However, as is the case with the potential dissenting citizens of Sinapia, Bacon's scientists are also fallible and corruptible human beings. By hampering improvement, *Sinapia* limits all possibility of historical progress and, in that sense, differs from Solomon's House, where artificial measures are implemented to achieve the creation of a superior society. However, the fact that these measures result from the observation of nature is persistently stated. The Father of Solomon's House explains to the shipwrecked crew that the logic of his utopian community is based on the imitation and representation of nature, but with the intention of establishing a better social system:

> We have also engine-houses, where are prepared engines and instruments for all sorts of motions. There we imitate and practise to make swifter motions than any you have [...] and to make them stronger, and more violent than yours are; exceeding your greatest cannons and basilisks. We represent also ordnance and instruments of war [...]. We imitate also motions of living creatures, by images of men, beasts, birds, fishes, and serpents.[75]

Thus, in opposition to *Sinapia*'s repressive perspective on human progress, Bacon's utopian perception of an ideal state entails the capacity to expand and enrich knowledge, which requires a rethinking of ingrained human practices. As the Father of Solomon's House indicates, 'The end of our Foundation is the knowledge of causes, and secret motions of things; and the enlarging of the bounds of Human Empire, to the effecting of all things possible'.[76]

The prevalence of a scientific culture in *Sinapia* is highlighted by the explicit reference to the French 'new philosopher' René Descartes (1596–1650), whose philosophical methodology is the basis for the practice of logic, even though Sinapians are not aware of his existence. Their innate connection with Descartes lies in the sole use of reason as a universal faculty. Just as in Descartes's thinking, the sciences in Sinapia are reduced to logic, medicine, and mechanics. Although the science of ethics conceived of by Descartes as the last degree of wisdom is not expressly included in Sinapia's institutional system, it is represented in the constant presence of moral virtue in Sinapia's political system. However, interestingly enough, Avilés remarks that the scribe of the manuscript crossed out the following segment on the list of sciences: 'Moral, que cura las pasiones y vicios y enseña las virtudes. Y ésta nace de la metafísica, dialéctica' [Morality, which cures passions and vices and teaches virtues. And this is born of metaphysics, dialectics].[77] This detail confirms the ideological adherence of Sinapia to the Cartesian axioms.

The Functions of the Sinapian Language

To consolidate the unity and equality of Sinapians, it was seen as imperative to achieve linguistic unity. The Sinapian language is a mixture, although not in equal parts, of the languages of the four founding nations: 'La lengua, aunque mezclada de todas las de estas gentes, mucho más participa de la dulzura y simplicidad china y de la elegancia persiana' [The language, although mixed with all the languages of these peoples, takes much more from the sweetness and simplicity of Chinese and the elegance of Persian].[78] The proposal of a universal language is utopian in itself, but it certainly was a key feature of the new order imposed by Felipe V (r. 1700–46) after coming to power in the wake of the War of the Spanish Succession when a policy of Castilianization was established. If not universal, the use of Spanish in administration, trading, and legal actions meant, at least, that Spanish became the most prestigious and widely used language. The aim of the linguistic reform was the extinction of subordinate languages in Spanish colonies and in parts of Spain with their own language, which implied that only Spanish would be spoken. The Crown never completely abandoned its utopian plan to hispanicize the peoples of America, and, in fact, the colonial linguistic policy responded to Antonio de Nebrija's classic formulation that 'la lengua fue compañera del imperio' [language was the companion of the empire],[79] included in his *Gramática de la lengua castellana* [*Grammar of the Castilian Language*] (1492).

The main function of monolingualism is naturally reflected in its convenience for the legal system. In Sinapia, linguistic and political authoritarianism are tied to each other:

> El libro de las leyes sinapienses, hecho por los tres fundadores de la república y añadido o alterado por las cortes generales de la nación [...], está escrito en purísimo estilo y lengua sinapiense, en verso suelto. Las leyes son breves, claras, sin dar causas ni alegar razones, sino mandando o vedando absolutamente.[80]
>
> [The book of Sinapian laws, made by the three founders of the republic, and enlarged or modified by the general courts of the nation [...], is written in a very pure style and in the Sinapian language, in free verse. The laws are brief and clear, without giving causes or alleging reasons, but commanding or prohibiting absolutely.]

The use of free verse to write Sinapia's laws must be regarded not as a desire to achieve an aesthetic effect, but as a plain, memorable, brief, and direct style through which orders and prohibitions are issued. However, Avilés explains that Tartessos, an early civilization in southern Spain, wrote their laws in verse.[81]

The importance conceded to language is significantly more elaborate in *Sinapia* than in any other utopia. Not only do Sinapians have a culturally hybrid language that they use in their daily lives, but they have created a language to formulate their philosophical ideas:

> [H]an formado artificiosamente una lengua filosófica, acomodada a las ideas simples o compuestas de las cosas, según la observación estudiosa de ellas, no según el uso o antojo de la gente y de ésta usan en la explicación de la naturaleza.[82]
>
> [They have artificially formed a philosophical language, adapted to simple or compound ideas of things, according to the careful observation of them, not according to the habits and whims of people; this language is used for the explanation of nature.]

Because everyday language is suspect and easily manipulated, a more reliable and exclusive communication code is needed to transmit ideological or scientific knowledge. This double communication system is applied to Sinapians' writing style. They use Persian characters while paying attention to the linguistic form of words, whereas Chinese writing is preferred when dealing with the content of thoughts:

> Tienen dos maneras de escribir: una, con caracteres arábigos, a la persiana; otra, con símbolos chinos. De ambas usan, pero de la última sólo en inscripciones públicas y en aquellos escritos en que no se atiende tanto a cómo se dice la cosa como a lo que se dice.[83]
>
> [They have two ways of writing: one, with Arabic characters, in the Persian style; the other, with Chinese symbols. They use both, but the latter only in public inscriptions and in those writings in which one pays less attention to how something is said than to what is said.]

It is evident that *Sinapia*'s author is aware of the interrelation between language and political power, as well as of the advantages of linguistic unity in achieving hegemony and dominance. Sinapia's utopian mindset is basically the result of a process of conquest and colonization, and the introduction of rules and regulations is fundamentally peaceful and gradual. This non-violent method of submission is mainly due to the religious basis of Sinapia's government and its primary policy of ideological and spiritual conversion.

The linguistic aspect also underlies the evangelical interests that define the utopian system of Sinapia. The study and interpretation of the Holy Scriptures as well as the teaching of divine wisdom are carefully regulated by the clergy and protected from misinterpretation through their translation into the Sinapian language:

> No puede nadie valerse de otra traducción de la Escritura que de la que hicieron en lengua sinapiense los tres héroes sinapienses, Sinap, Codabend y Siang, aprobada por el primer sínodo y sacada del texto hebreo en el Testamento Viejo y del griego en el Nuevo, de un manuscrito traído de la Persia.[84]
>
> [Nobody can use a translation of the Scriptures except the one based on a manuscript brought from Persia and written in the Sinapian language by the three Sinapian founders, Sinap, Codabend, and Siang, which was approved by the first synod and taken from the Hebrew text in the Old Testament, and from the Greek one in the New.]

Language and religious legislation find themselves intertwined in an enterprise that seeks to ensure the ideological acceptance of Christianity.

The strictness of language use in Sinapia relates to the radical but apparently effective closed-minded administrative policies of the society. In this regard, *Sinapia* refuses to follow a Christian model like the one used in *Christianopolis*, a utopian community devised by the German theologian Johann Valentin Andreae in 1619. Christianopolis is an ideal state where science and Christian tenets are the key elements of social order and where all citizens are free:

> Three principles stand out in the political and public life of Christianopolis: preserving the peace, equality of citizens, and contempt for large possessions. The practice of these principles guards the state and its citizens against the three greatest evils: war, slavery, and corruption in public affairs.[85]

Nevertheless, the use of slavery may not be as strong a sign of intolerance as is the ban on foreign contact in Sinapia, as was pointed out above regarding the dynamics of trading strategies.

In trying to elucidate the features of Spanish utopianism and its interpretive framework, the discourse of *Sinapia* can be seen as a response to the need to reorganize and improve Spain's existing situation, except in terms of the religious sphere. Its affiliation with a patriarchal social system based on Christianity points to the possibility that the author was a priest who defended an active participation of the Church in the running of society. However, despite the support of traditional values, *Sinapia* offers a progressive approach to how the Spanish system can be enhanced by means of an effective development of knowledge and science. The importance given to culture and education turns the republic of Sinapia into a sophisticated civilization with exemplary Christian citizens. Regardless of the lack of certainty about its compositional context, *Sinapia* represents a pivotal moment in the progression of Hispanic utopian writing, while, at the same time, eluding any fixed categorization within the genre.

Notes to Chapter 3

1. George M. Logan and Robert M. Adams, 'Introduction', in Thomas More, *Utopia*, ed. by George M. Logan and trans. by Robert M. Adams (Cambridge: Cambridge University Press, 2006), pp. xi–xxix (p. xiii).
2. Although the full title is *Descripción de la Sinapia, península en la tierra austral*, the abbreviation *Sinapia* is generally used in this book.
3. Jorge Cejudo López, *Catálogo del Archivo del Conde de Campomanes (fondos Carmen Dorado y Rafael Gasset)* (Madrid: Fundación Universitaria Española, 1975), p. 34.
4. Stelio Cro, ed., *'Descripción de la Sinapia, península en la tierra austral': A Classical Utopia of Spain* (Hamilton, Ontario: McMaster University, 1975). There is a plain, unannotated reproduction of Cro's transcription of *Sinapia* in Stelio Cro, 'La utopía de las dos orillas (1453–1793)', *Cuadernos para Investigación de la Literatura Hispánica*, 30 (2005), 15–268 (pp. 212–39).
5. Miguel Avilés Fernández, ed., *'Sinapia': una utopía española del Siglo de las Luces* (Madrid: Editora Nacional, 1976). Avilés's edition was republished with a new prologue by Pedro Galera Andreu in 2011 (Madrid: Círculo de Bellas Artes). The 1976 edition is used in this book.
6. Stelio Cro, *A Forerunner of the Enlightenment in Spain* (Hamilton, Ontario: McMaster University, 1976), p. 16.
7. Carlos Sambricio agrees with Avilés that the text was written towards the end of the eighteenth century, based on *Sinapia*'s replication of the principles of city planning in late eighteenth-century Spain. See Carlos Sambricio, '*Sinapia*: utopía, territorio y ciudad a finales del siglo XVIII', *Scripta Nova: Revista Electrónica de Geografía y Ciencias Sociales*, 18 (2014), <http://www.ub.es/geocrit/sn/sn-475.htm> [accessed 12 August 2015]. See also the English version of this article in Carlos Sambricio, '*Sinapia*: Utopia, Territory, and City at the End of the Eighteenth Century', in *Views on Eighteenth-Century Culture: Design, Books and Ideas*, ed. by Leonor Ferrão and Luís Manuel A. V. Bernardo (Newcastle-upon-Tyne: Cambridge Scholars Publishing, 2015), pp. 44–77.
8. A detailed account of Cro's and Avilés's research work on *Sinapia* can be found in Francisco López Estrada, 'Más noticias sobre la Sinapia o Utopía española', *Moreana*, 4 (1977), 23–33.
9. For a review of the perspectives of Cro, Avilés, Lopez, López Estrada, and Abellán, see Ángel González Hernández and Juan Saez Carreras, '*Sinapia* o la Ispania utópica de la Ilustración: claro-oscuro de una polémica', in *Educación e Ilustración en España: III Coloquio de Historia de la Educación* (Barcelona: Universidad de Barcelona, 1984), pp. 90–100.

10. In an unpublished undergraduate dissertation, Carolina Varela Sepúlveda evaluates *Sinapia* in the light of Dutch expansionism and argues that the referential reality of the utopian text was not America, but New Holland, which is how the Dutch referred to Australia. See Carolina Varela Sepúlveda, 'La Ilustración europea: el racionalismo de las letras en el siglo XVIII. Utopías en la España del siglo XVIII: *Sinapia* y el expansionismo holandés' (unpublished *licenciatura* thesis, Universidad de Chile, 2007), <http://www.repositorio.uchile.cl/tesis/uchile/2007/varela_c/html/index-frames.html> [accessed 3 November 2015]. It is worth mentioning that there is another unpublished thesis on *Sinapia*, written by Rebecca Foust. See Rebecca A. Foust, '*Sinapia*: An Enlightened Ideal' (unpublished master's thesis, University of North Carolina at Chapel Hill, 1988).
11. Cro, 'El mito de la ciudad ideal en España: *Sinapia*'.
12. Miguel Avilés Fernández, 'Introducción', in *'Sinapia': una utopía española del Siglo de las Luces*, pp. 13–65 (p. 24).
13. François Lopez, 'Considérations sur *La Sinapia*', in *La Contestation de la société dans la littérature espagnole du Siècle d'Or: actes de colloque de la R. C. P.*, ed. by Centre National de la Recherche Scientifique (Toulouse: Université de Toulouse–Le Mirail, 1981), pp. 205–11.
14. François Lopez, 'Una utopía española en busca de autor: *Sinapia*. Historia de una equivocación. Indicios para un acierto', *Anales de la Universidad de Alicante. Historia Moderna*, 2 (1982), 211–21.
15. François Lopez, 'Une autre approche de *Sinapia*', in *Las utopías en el mundo hispánico*, ed. by Étienvre, pp. 9–18.
16. Pedro Álvarez de Miranda, 'Vuelta a *Sinapia*', in *Littérature et politique en Espagne aux siècles d'or: colloque international*, ed. by Jean-Pierre Étienvre (Paris: Klincksieck, 1998), pp. 349–60.
17. Miguel Ángel Ramiro Avilés, ed., *Descripción de la Sinapia, península en la tierra austral* (Madrid: Dykinson, 2013).
18. José Santos Puerto, 'La *Sinapia*: luces para buscar la utopía de la Ilustración', *Bulletin Hispanique*, 103 (2001), 481–510 (p. 508).
19. José Santos Puerto, *Martín Sarmiento: Ilustración, educación y utopía en la España del siglo XVIII*, 2 vols (La Coruña: Fundación Pedro Barrié de la Maza, 2002), II, pp. 357–58.
20. José Gómez-Tabanera does not dismiss the possibility of a collective authorship of *Sinapia* as a form of 'divertimento intelectual' [intellectual entertainment], a supposition that lacks scholarly evidence in its favour (José Gómez-Tabanera, 'La *Sinapia*, una España imposible en el mundo austral o la forja de una utopía hispana en el siglo XVII', in *España y el Pacífico*, ed. by Antonio F. García-Abásolo (Cordova: Asociación Española de Estudios del Pacífico, 1997), pp. 121–34 (p. 128)). The author was apparently intending to publish his own edition of *Sinapia*.
21. Fernando Savater, *Vente a Sinapia: una reflexión española sobre la utopía*, in Fernando Savater, *Último desembarco; Vente a Sinapia* (Madrid: Espasa-Calpe, 1988), pp. 77–138 (p. 80). For an analysis of the play, see María Lastenia Valdez, 'Fernando Savater y el género utópico en España: de *Sinapia* (siglo XVII) a *Vente a Sinapia* (siglo XX)', in *Actas del XV Congreso de la Asociación Internacional de Hispanistas 'Las dos orillas'*, ed. by Beatriz Mariscal and María Teresa Miaja de la Peña, 4 vols (Mexico City: Fondo de Cultura Económica, 2007), III, pp. 417–25.
22. *Descripción de la Sinapia*, p. 69.
23. Ibid.
24. It should be assumed that the author interprets the term *novela* as a long short story or narrative, according to Cervantes's seventeenth-century understanding of the concept. Eloy Navarro Domínguez approaches the study of *Sinapia* by relating it to real travel accounts and argues that the author of *Sinapia* was prejudiced against the novelistic genre and other fictional forms, which resulted in a failed utopian account. However, his assertions on *Sinapia* lack textual underpinning. See Eloy Navarro Domínguez, 'Relaciones de viajes y ficción novelesca en la *Descripción de la Sinapia*', in *Utopía: los espacios imposibles*, ed. by Rosa García Gutiérrez, Valentín Núñez Rivera, and Eloy Navarro Domínguez (Frankfurt am Main: Peter Lang, 2003), pp. 131–46.
25. *Descripción de la Sinapia*, p. 70.
26. Ibid.
27. Marie Laffranque, 'La *Descripción de la Sinapia, Península en la Tierra Austral*', in *La Contestation de la société dans la littérature espagnole du Siècle d'Or*, pp. 193–204 (p. 197).

28. *Descripción de la Sinapia*, p. 134. The original word in the manuscript is *Hespaña*, which is transcribed thus by Cro in his edition. However, Avilés changes the spelling to *Hispaña* without justifying his amendment.
29. More, *Utopia*, ed. by Logan and trans. by Adams, pp. 9–10.
30. *Descripción de la Sinapia*, p. 69.
31. Navarro Domínguez thinks that Siang might be the equivalent of Confucius (Navarro Domínguez, p. 137).
32. Stelio Cro, '*Sinapia*, el Viejo Testamento y la teocracia cristiana', in *Actas del XII Congreso de la Asociación Internacional de Hispanistas*, ed. by Jules Whicker, 2 vols (Birmingham: University of Birmingham, 1998), II, pp. 130–36 (pp. 130–31).
33. *Descripción de la Sinapia*, p. 75.
34. Avilés specifies that the *lagos* have already been related to the *galos* [the Gauls], the barbarian Celtic invaders of the Iron Age. See footnote 21 in Avilés, 'Introducción', p. 27.
35. *Descripción de la Sinapia*, pp. 72–73.
36. Ibid., p. 75.
37. Campanella, *La Città del Sole*, pp. 31, 33.
38. Plato, *The Republic* (University Park: Pennsylvania State University Press, 1998), pp. 156–57.
39. *Descripción de la Sinapia*, p. 86.
40. 'If you know one of their cities you know them all, for they're exactly alike.' (More, *Utopia*, ed. by Logan and trans. by Adams, p. 44)
41. *Descripción de la Sinapia*, p. 85.
42. Ibid., p. 86.
43. Ibid., p. 91.
44. Ibid., p. 103.
45. Ibid., p. 102.
46. Ibid., p. 70.
47. Ibid.
48. Ibid., pp. 69–70.
49. Ibid., p. 124.
50. Ibid., p. 134.
51. According to Stelio Cro, 'Por lo que se refiere a la tradición de la ciudad ideal cristiana en España se conocen los ejemplos de la *Ciudad de Dios* de San Agustín o el *Blanquerna* de Raimundo Lulio, primer ejemplo literario en España de una concepción utópica, según la definición de Marcelino Menéndez y Pelayo de "utopía cristiano-social"' [As far as the tradition of the ideal Christian city in Spain is concerned, there are known examples such as *The City of God* by Saint Augustine or *Blanquerna* by Ramon Llull, the first literary example of utopianism in Spain, according to the definition of 'Christian-social utopia' put forward by Marcelino Menéndez y Pelayo] (Stelio Cro, 'La utopía en España: *Sinapia*', *Cuadernos para Investigación de la Literatura Hispánica*, 2–3 (1980), 27–40 (p. 37)).
52. *Descripción de la Sinapia*, p. 102.
53. Ibid., p. 86.
54. Ibid.
55. Manuel and Manuel, p. 328.
56. Stelio Cro, 'Las reducciones jesuíticas en la encrucijada de dos utopías', in *Las utopías en el mundo hispánico*, pp. 41–56 (p. 42).
57. *Descripción de la Sinapia*, p. 134.
58. Miguel Ángel Ramiro Avilés, '*Sinapia*, A Political Journey to the Antipodes of Spain', in *Utopian Moments: Reading Utopian Texts*, ed. by Miguel Ángel Ramiro Avilés and J. C. Davis (London: Bloomsbury Academic, 2012), pp. 80–85 (p. 82).
59. Jameson, *Archaeologies of the Future*, p. 1.
60. Alex-Alban Gómez Coutouly, 'Spanish Literary Utopias: *Omnibona* and *The Desired Government*', in *Nowhere Somewhere: Writing Space and the Construction of Utopia*, ed. by José Eduardo Reis (Porto: Universidade do Porto, 2006), pp. 71–85 (p. 73).
61. Melchor de Macanaz, *El deseado gobierno, buscado por el amor de Dios para el reino de España*,

Huesca, Biblioteca Pública de Huesca, MS 141, Miscelánea, 1855, fols 57^v–94^r (fol. 68^v), <http://bibliotecavirtual.aragon.es/bva/i18n/catalogo_imagenes/grupo.cmd?posicion=122&aceptar=Aceptar&path=1000180&presentacion=pagina> [accessed 21 February 2016].

62. In this respect, it should be noted that the ideas of impossibility and negativity have long been part of the definition of utopia in the Royal Spanish Academy's dictionary. While the first appearance of the term in 1869 highlights its encouraging theoretical contribution, although overshadowed by its non-existent practical dimension ('Plan, proyecto, sistema o doctrina que halaga en teoría, pero cuya práctica es imposible' [Plan, project, system, or doctrine that pleases in theory, but whose practical application is impossible]), the latest definition from 2014 reiterates the difficulty of its implementation ('Plan, proyecto, doctrina o sistema deseables que parecen de muy difícil realización' [Plan, project, doctrine, or system that is desirable and seems very difficult to accomplish]). See *Diccionario de la lengua española*, 23rd edn (Madrid: Real Academia Española), <http://dle.rae.es> [accessed 7 July 2017].

63. In *Memoria sobre espectáculos y diversiones públicas* [*Memoir about Spectacles and Public Amusements*] (1790), Jovellanos acknowledges that there is a blurred line between liberty and licence, but condemns the fact that Spanish magistrates confuse surveillance with oppression: Spanish power and justice, far from ensuring order and stability, are intended to subjugate and enslave the citizens by imposing social control through fear (Gaspar Melchor de Jovellanos, *Memoria sobre las diversiones públicas*, in Gaspar Melchor de Jovellanos, *Obras completas*, ed. by Elena de Lorenzo Álvarez, 14 vols (Oviedo: Ayuntamiento de Gijón, Instituto Feijoo de Estudios del Siglo XVIII, KRK Ediciones, 1984–2010), XII: *Escritos sobre literatura* (2009), pp. 191–318 (pp. 252–53)).

64. *Descripción de la Sinapia*, pp. 111–12.

65. Jorge Pérez-Rey, 'Sinapia, una utopía en el mundo hispánico del siglo XVIII: la imagen especular invertida de la nación real', in *Communautés nationales et marginalité dans le monde ibérique et ibéro-américain* (Tours: Université de Tours, 1981), pp. 49–57.

66. *Descripción de la Sinapia*, p. 114.

67. More, *Utopia*, ed. by Logan and trans. by Adams, p. 81.

68. *Descripción de la Sinapia*, p. 123.

69. Bacon, pp. 161–62.

70. *Descripción de la Sinapia*, p. 124.

71. Ibid., p. 128.

72. Ibid.

73. Ibid., p. 125.

74. 'Merchants of light' is the exact term used by Bacon in the *New Atlantis* to describe the explorers who collect knowledge from around the world (Bacon, p. 183).

75. Bacon, pp. 182–83.

76. Ibid., p. 177.

77. *Descripción de la Sinapia*, footnote 145, p. 127.

78. Ibid., p. 75.

79. Antonio de Nebrija, *Gramática sobre la lengua castellana*, ed. by Carmen Lozano (Madrid: Real Academia Española, 2011), p. 3.

80. *Descripción de la Sinapia*, p. 116.

81. See footnote 141 in *Descripción de la Sinapia*, p. 116.

82. *Descripción de la Sinapia*, pp. 75–76.

83. Ibid., p. 76.

84. Ibid., p. 98.

85. Andreae, *Christianopolis*, p. 35.

CHAPTER 4

❖

Social Satire and Utopia in the *Suplemento de los viajes de Enrique Wanton al país de las monas*

Terra Australis Incognita is the name given to a hypothetical great southern continent that was used in European cartography between the fifteenth and eighteenth centuries. The notion of what is now known as the continent of Oceania was introduced by Aristotle and based on the hypothesis that the landmasses of Europe, Asia, and North Africa must have been balanced by a large continent in the southern hemisphere. However, despite the geographical knowledge provided by several expeditions of discovery, such as those of the Dutch explorer Abel Tasman and the English navigator James Cook,[1] the mythical representation of the Unknown Southern Land continued to be a favoured utopian and literary setting for European writers until well into the eighteenth century.

As has been seen in *Sinapia*, Spanish authors were no exception and took advantage of the old legends of *Terra Australis Incognita* as a framework to create utopian societies. A Spanish work that was representative of the narrative of imaginary travel to the Unknown Southern Land in the second half of the eighteenth century was the *Suplemento de los viajes de Enrique Wanton al país de las monas* by Gutierre Joaquín Vaca de Guzmán y Manrique. Unlike *Sinapia*'s structure, which clearly follows More's utopian narrative model, Vaca de Guzmán's text mostly conforms to the conventions of the imaginary voyage as characterized by Jonathan Swift in his eighteenth-century satirical text *Travels into Several Remote Nations of the World. In Four Parts by Lemuel Gulliver*, commonly known as *Gulliver's Travels* (1726), as will be explained in the analysis below. Nevertheless, it should not be forgotten that Swift's literary method was noticeably inspired by More's textual model.

The work consists of four volumes: the initial two, first published in 1769 and 1771 respectively, are a Spanish translation made by Vaca de Guzmán of the original text published in Italian by Zaccaria Seriman in Venice in 1749 and called *Viaggi di Enrico Wanton alle terre incognite australi, ed al paese delle scimmie* [*The Travels of Henry Wanton to Unknown Southern Lands and to the Country of the Monkeys*],[2] while the last two appeared in 1778 and are entitled *Suplemento de los viajes de Enrique Wanton al país de las monas*; they are by Vaca de Guzmán himself and not a translation of the additional two volumes published by Seriman in 1764, supposedly in Bern.³ Although the purpose of this chapter is to discuss the nature of Vaca de Guzmán's *Suplemento* as a sequel to Seriman's story, an examination of the two translated volumes needs to be made in order to assess the thematic continuity and discontinuity between the narrative by the Italian author and the complementary text by the Spanish imitator.

The Spanish Translation of Seriman's *Viaggi di Enrico Wanton*

The conceptualization of the southern continent in Seriman's original work not only resembles the imagined narrative of the discovery of America or that of the Northwest Passage, but also reinforces the depiction of an antipodean world as a suitable fictional space in which to rethink and critically analyse the existing order of things in a specific society.⁴ This image of a world turned upside down constitutes the basis for the development of the satirical and utopian components that structure Vaca de Guzmán's work. As a preliminary observation, it should be noted that the fact that the first two volumes are a translation does not imply a lack of creativity on the part of the Spanish author. In fact, as various critics have pointed out, the two translated volumes and the two written by Vaca de Guzmán are strategically adapted to the eighteenth-century Spanish context, and they can be regarded as a rudimentary expression of nineteenth-century *costumbrismo* [literature of manners and customs].⁵ According to José Escobar and Anthony Percival, the criticism of social customs is comparable to the criticism of a nation and, in that sense, the *Viajes de Enrique Wanton* are ideologically connected with the essayistic literature of Feijoo or Cadalso, as well as with essay periodical writing to be found in *El Pensador* and *El Censor*.⁶

Most imaginary voyages written from the seventeenth century onwards share a homogeneous style and manner of composition, something which is noticeable in the conventions of the genre exploited by Seriman in his *Viaggi* and visible in the Spanish version. In this respect, the *Viaggi* and the *Viajes* are fundamentally influenced by Jonathan Swift's *Gulliver's Travels*⁷ in terms both of the literary elements of the story and the satirical perspective that allows a critical reflection on the validity of cultural, social, and political institutions. In fact, a review of the opening volume of the first Spanish translation of the *Viajes del Capitán Lemuel Gulliver* [*The Travels of Captain Lemuel Gulliver*] that appeared in the *Memorial Literario* [*Literary Record*] in 1794 compared the English text to the *Viajes de Enrique Wanton*:

> La historia de los viajes del Capitán Lemuel Gulliver es una invectiva de la misma especie que los viajes de Enrique Wanton al país de las Monas, el viaje a la luna de Cirano de Barbeirac [*sic*], del Saturnino Micromegas y otros.⁸

> [The story of the travels of Captain Lemuel Gulliver is an invective of the same kind as the travels of Henry Wanton to the country of the Monkeys, the voyage to the moon of Cyrano de Bergerac, the journey of Micromegas to Saturn, and others.]

Swift's emblematic novel is primarily a satire on human nature and social behaviour, precisely targeted through the parodic portrayal of the shortcomings of eighteenth-century English society. It can be said, then, that the ironic and subverted social system presented by Vaca de Guzmán echoes not only the enlightened critical attitude of Spanish thinkers towards their nation, but also that of Swift towards England and Western culture.

In a similar way to *Gulliver's Travels*, the story of the *Viajes* begins with a biographical description of Enrique Wanton's family circumstances and personal situation. Enrique is an Englishman who, like Lemuel Gulliver, was destined to enter a profession he is not truly interested in, which makes him feel extremely unhappy in his home circumstances. In the attempt to escape from a reality that does not satisfy him, Enrique decides to abandon his homeland and put out to sea on an adventure voyage to the East Indies, during which he meets another young Englishman, a merchant called Roberto who was on a business trip on his father's behalf. A close friendship develops between the two young men, and the relationship of this kind of Cervantine duo consists of that of a master and his pupil. Indeed, after their shipwreck, the imaginary travel account turns into a *Bildungsroman* in which Enrique's instinctive apprehension of the new reality encountered is dispelled by the enlightened guidance of the practical and knowledgeable Roberto. The only belongings salvaged by the two friends are their firearms and some books, elements that symbolize the irruption of Western civilization into the society with which they will make contact. After reaching the shore of a land that they identify as the mysterious region of the southern hemisphere known as *Terra Australis Incognita*, the castaways live on the seashore for several months. However, their fortune changes the day that they accidentally arrive in the country of the monkeys, which is a satirical representation of the peculiarities of the lifestyle of European aristocrats and intellectuals — Spanish noblemen for the purpose of Vaca de Guzmán's translation. From this moment on, the narration makes it clear that the rational or logical conventions of a consensual worldview are ironically inverted. The two young travellers are treated as exotic and ridiculous creatures in a world dominated by inferior beings:

> ¡Qué bueno era entonces ver a dos hombres nacidos en el país más culto de la Europa, que es por cierto la parte del mundo más cultivada incomparablemente que las demás; qué buena vista, repito, dos hombres sirviendo de materia de juguete a unos animales que, por el contrario, en la común estimación, son los más viles y despreciables del universo![9]

> [How good it was, then, to see two men born in the most cultured country of Europe, which is certainly the region of the world incomparably more cultivated than other parts; what a good image, I repeat, of two men serving as playthings for animals, which, according to popular belief, are by contrast the most vile and despicable beings in the universe!]

This last sentence not only reaffirms the parodic or, in Bakhtinian terms, carnivalesque nature of the subsequent story, but also makes the axiomatic statement that the pretension to alter the traditional order of social roles and hierarchies should not be pursued. Although this initial principle is not an obstacle to the inclusion of utopian features in the conception of Simiópolis (the capital of the country of the monkeys), it can be argued that, in line with Swift's anthropological perspective, the *Viajes* presuppose the existence of a superior reason as unrealistic. In his letter to Alexander Pope of 29 September 1725, Swift confesses:

> I have ever hated all nations, professions, and communities; and all my love is toward individuals [...]. But principally I hate and detest that animal called man [...]. I have got materials toward a treatise, proving the falsity of that definition *animal rationale*, and to show it should be only *rationis capax*. Upon this great foundation of misanthropy, [...] the whole building of my travels is erected.[10]

By offering a new definition of man not as a rational animal (*animal rationale*), but rather as an animal capable of reason (*rationis capax*), Swift attributes a utopian element to the concept of rationality itself and problematizes the value of an abstract understanding of man, as opposed to the concrete crystallization of the concept in individuals.[11] This critical approach to the teleological justification of mankind can be seen as related to the paradoxical supremacy of a utopian community over its inhabitants for its own sake. In turn, the relegation of individualism in favour of a collective consciousness entails a degree of fuzziness in the way identity is determined.

The confrontation between civilization and barbarism is constantly referred to by Enrique and Roberto when stating that they have the privilege of being endowed with reason, which is precisely why the monkeys do not trust them. Nevertheless, Roberto ironically recognizes that the apes[12] also possess the ability to reason and that both species[13] can benefit from the exchange of knowledge and experiences:

> [P]odremos agradarnos unos a otros; porque vosotros, participándonos todo lo bueno y brillante que en estas provincias se goza, conquistaréis en nosotros dos sinceros panegiristas, y os quedaremos muy agradecidos. Y nosotros, comunicándoos nuestros conocimientos y todo lo mejor que se practica en la Europa, no seremos de poco provecho a estas provincias, añadiendo a las perfecciones de estos países las maravillas del nuestro.[14]

> [We will be able to please each other, because you, in providing us with all the good and brilliant things that are enjoyed in these provinces, will gain through us two sincere panegyrists, and we will be very grateful to you. And we, giving you our knowledge and all the best that is practised in Europe, will not be of little benefit to these provinces, adding to the perfections of these countries the wonders of ours.]

According to the two Englishmen, the monkeys are aware of their rational condition and fear their potentially dangerous actions. In order to minimize the threat that the visitors pose, the monkey-people decide to imprison them. Although the two friends are welcomed at the beginning, the morning after their arrival they awake to find themselves bound in chains in a stable. The monkeys had apparently put a sleep-inducing substance in the drinks offered to Enrique and Roberto. It is obvious that this scene is based on the similar reception experienced by Gulliver in Lilliput.[15] In fact, the monkeys can be compared with the Houyhnhnms or rational talking horses, encountered by Gulliver in his fourth voyage, while the humanoid

Yahoos, who are the slaves of the Houyhnhnms, are comparable to Enrique and Roberto. In the same way that the two Englishmen try to be accepted into the world of the monkeys in order to be safe, Gulliver makes every effort to be like the Houyhnhnms, but they see no difference between him and the Yahoos and sentence him to exile.[16]

If the power of Gulliver lies in his physical superiority over the Lilliputians, the dominant position of the two European travellers resides in their rational faculties and their possession of firearms with which to defend themselves in case their lives are in danger. However, like Gulliver, they do not want to take advantage of their favourable situation, not only because the end of their imprisonment would mean the collapse of the pivotal fictional event in the story, but also because their escape would be interpreted as antagonistic to their rational nature. As Roberto explains, as long as they keep together, protected by the wisdom of their friendship, they can remain in captivity without compromising their dignity or their humanity:

> ¿Porque estemos en una caballeriza; porque nos sujeten ridículas monas; porque al pie nos rodeen estas cadenas, hemos perdido por esto el ser hombres? No, amigo; pues aún podemos obrar con entendimiento, y nos es conforme a razón vivir unidos, y gozar del placer de la amistad.[17]

> [Have we lost, because we are in a stable, our condition as men? Because we are restrained by ridiculous monkeys, because our feet are surrounded by these chains? No, my friend; we can still act with understanding, and for us it accords with reason to live together and enjoy the pleasure of friendship.]

Therefore, it is not only the act of reasoning in itself but also the knowledge resulting from human interaction that prevents Enrique and Roberto from being deprived of their civilized qualities. The importance given to friendship in the *Viajes* reveals the fact that the literary eighteenth century was more intensely concerned with the matter than any previous or subsequent historical period.[18] Friendship and the pursuit of happiness were basic ideals promoted by Enlightenment thinking because they are two motors for human development.[19]

What is relevant to the question of rationality in Vaca de Guzmán's text is the attribution of a superior reason to the two English visitors over that of the monkeys. Since the hierarchical roles between humans and animals have been exchanged, the monkeys are provided with a level of reasoning presumably equivalent to human rationality, but far from giving up their rational condition, Enrique and Roberto are supposed to be vested with a superior rationality. Even in his *Suplemento*, Vaca de Guzmán makes Enrique affirm his superiority and the amusing distraction that the monkeys represent to him. This fictional characteristic may be a direct influence of Gabriel de Foigny, who in *La Terre Australe connue* [*The Known Southern Land*] (1676) attributes an extraordinary reasoning ability to his hermaphrodites, the inhabitants of Foigny's austral utopia. In fact, the ideological influence of Foigny's novel has also been noted in the themes and motifs of *Gulliver's Travels*.[20]

A negative aspect of the presumed benefits of superior reason is the potential risk of dehumanization implied in any social system that is ruled by a perfect rationality. Unlike Foigny's Australians who constitute a kind of anti-society governed by a debilitating rationalism and relentless deism, the two English friends do not lack desires or passions; nevertheless, they mould their actions according to the dictates of reason and God. The universalizing principles of their philosophical doctrine seem to be contained in a book entitled *Ensayos del Señor de Montaña* [*The Essays of Mr Mountain*], an apparent reference to the *Essais* [*Essays*] (1580) of Michel de Montaigne,[21] which furnishes Enrique and Roberto with the necessary knowledge to tackle their difficult situation in a place governed by animals:

> La continuación en la lectura que habíamos hecho Roberto y yo [Enrique] en el [libro del] Señor de Montaña, único libro que tuvimos en la prisión, y alivio de aquellas desgracias, me había despertado la atención a las cosas naturales, y particularmente a las que pertenecen a las acciones de las bestias.[22]

> [The continuation of the reading that Roberto and I [Enrique] had made of [the book by] Mr Mountain, the only book that we had in prison and a relief from those misfortunes, had awakened my attention to natural things and particularly to those that belong to the actions of beasts.]

Enrique's cognitive journey comprises, then, not only Roberto's teachings, but also the practical implementation of the wisdom enshrined in a book with an arguably sceptical orientation. The parable-type stories of the *Ensayos del Señor de Montaña* are meant to instruct and inspire both young men to act in the right way in order to eventually dominate the monkeys and force them to accept their inferiority. The reference to Montaigne can be associated with the fact that his essays focused on criticism of human behaviour from a sceptical perspective. His essay 'Des cannibales' is especially applicable to the situation of Enrique and Roberto in that both characters represent the values of the Western world in confrontation with a new civilization, which in Montaigne's text turns out to be a utopian characterization of the New World as an unspoiled space where Europeans could turn their dreams into reality.

The spiritual or religious component is inevitably present in the *Viajes*, as in other Spanish imaginary voyage or utopian accounts published in the eighteenth century. However, in this text in particular, religion acts as a vehicle to ensure the consolidation of the civilizing process. Enrique, who has received religious inspiration from Roberto, explains how religion and rationality work together against the uselessness of passions and delusions:

> [L]os proyectos contrarios a los preceptos de la religión de cuando en cuando se ponían delante de mis desesperados pensamientos; mas en llegando la pasión a ciertos grados, presto desvanece todos los sentimientos juiciosos, y reincide en los primeros delirios; así se mezclaban mis desesperadas resoluciones y las reflexiones piadosas que iluminaban mi alma en las llamaradas de la razón.[23]

> [Projects contrary to the precepts of religion took pride of place in my desperate thoughts from time to time; but when passion reaches certain levels, it promptly dispels all judicious feelings and returns to the first state of madness; in this way, my desperate resolutions mingled with the pious reflections that illuminated my soul in the flames of reason.]

It is interesting to observe the interrelation between spiritual and rational reflections as if they were two sides of the same coin. The application of reason to religion refers to a deistic perspective, but it is the civilizing effect of religion that must be associated with its rational attributes. In this sense, it is important to remember that the term 'civilization' first appeared in 1756 in *L'Ami des hommes, ou traité de la population* [*The Friend of Men; or, Treatise on Population*] by Victor de Riqueti, Marquis of Mirabeau. According to Mirabeau's vision, religion is the impulse for civilization because it restrains humanity from vain pleasures.[24] Considering the formative and pedagogical function of religion, the spiritual realm can certainly be understood as a fundamental supporting tool for the success of civilization's progress. The practice of religious virtue surpasses any other good qualities.

In spite of the fact that there is no explicit mention of the Christian religion, the use of expressions such as *Providencia* [Providence], *Altísimo* [the Almighty], and *Dios* [God] would appear to link the text to the precepts of Christianity, even though such terms also seem perfectly compatible with a deistic outlook. The attitude of the castaways/travellers in commending their lives to God resembles an important element of the traditional narrative of the Spanish conquest of America.[25] Nevertheless, along with a providentialist interpretation of their experiences, Enrique and Roberto acknowledge the intervention of nature in the course of their vicissitudes. The reconciliation between the laws of nature and divine law leads Enrique to accept that tolerance is an indispensable civic value when it comes to understanding other customs and ways of living. In other words, different or inferior forms of civilization must be respected as they are all a creation of God:

> Yo enteramente me había puesto en manos de la Providencia [...], admirando sus operaciones para con las infinitas criaturas de innumerables especies que se hallan esparcidas sobre la tierra. Cuando llegábamos a cualquier país de aquellos en donde son las costumbres tan diversas de las nuestras, y en cuyos pueblos parecen los hombres como de especie diferente de nosotros, ya por el color y configuración del cuerpo, ya por el modo de pensar y pasar la vida, no caía yo en la culpa de aquella vergonzosa e injusta maravilla [...], y que es efecto de una ciega y ambiciosa ignorancia. De aquí es que sabía compadecerme de los yerros que hallaba cerca de las leyes de la humanidad; y sin violencia alababa aquellas costumbres y obras que veía conformes a la razón. Huía la necia temeridad de apellidar bárbaro y extravagante a un pueblo, o porque seguía máximas discordes de las nuestras, o porque desterrados el lujo y superfluidades, vivía en una natural simplicidad, o porque los usos, vestidos, mantenimientos, habitaciones y otras cosas semejantes me parecían nuevas.[26]

> [I had entirely placed myself in the hands of Providence [...], admiring its operations in relation to the infinite creatures of innumerable species that are scattered across the earth. When we arrived in any of those countries where the customs are so different from ours, and in whose towns men seem to be of a different species from ours, either because of the colour and configuration of their bodies or because of their way of thinking and spending their lives, I did not fall into the guilt of that shameful and unjust wonder [...], and which is the consequence of a blind and ambitious ignorance. That is why I knew how to sympathize with the errors that I found in the laws of humanity, and without violence I praised those customs and works that I considered consistent with reason. I rejected the foolish temerity of calling a people barbaric and

extravagant because it followed rules different from ours or because, having abolished luxury and excess, it lived in a natural simplicity, or because the habits, clothing, food, rooms, and other such things seemed new to me.]

This extensive quotation is key to the thematic and ideological framework of Vaca de Guzmán's translation: the statement that unfamiliar cultures or peoples should not be misjudged on the basis that they are perceived as new and different. Unknown customs and mental attitudes cannot be labelled barbaric as they are a product of divine Providence or natural laws. To corroborate his assertion, Enrique resorts to a philosophical or anthropological explanation according to which the importance of otherness in defining self-identity and the abolition of self-love are the essential principles to be followed in the eradication of sociological misconceptions:

> [N]o se llega a tal término sin un atento estudio de sí mismo y de los demás. Para adquirir esta indiferencia filosófica, no se necesita más que suspender los juicios que produce el amor propio. Consistiendo este adelantamiento en deshacerse de aquellas preocupaciones [...] que no tienen otro principio que una temeraria ambición, mediante la cual solo aprobamos las cosas que dicen alguna relación con las nuestras y desaprobamos las que no la tienen.[27]

> [One does not come to such a conclusion without a careful study of oneself and others. In order to acquire this philosophical indifference, one only needs to suspend the judgements produced by self-love. This achievement consists in getting rid of those prejudices [...] that have no other basis than reckless ambition, by which we only approve things that have some relation to ours and disapprove of those that do not.]

However, as the French philosopher Paul Ricœur states in his essay about universal civilization and national cultures, when we discover that there are several cultures instead of just one and, therefore, when we foresee the end of a kind of cultural monopoly, we feel overwhelmed by a subtle danger that threatens us. We ourselves are an Other among others, and this discovery is never a harmless experience; it rather entails an undesirable process of disillusionment.[28] While this approach provides a sociological critique of cultural encounter, the satirical viewpoint of Vaca de Guzmán's text prevents the English characters from upsetting themselves with the thought that their cultural predominance may be affected by a plurality of civilizations. The superiority of their cultural status is reasserted throughout the entire narration. Ricœur's concept of a universal civilization originating from the illusion that European culture was a superior and global one is worth bringing up here:

> [L]a rencontre des autres traditions culturelles est une épreuve grave et en un sens absolument neuve pour la culture européenne. Le fait que la civilisation universelle ait procédé pendant longtemps du foyer européen a entretenu l'illusion que la culture européenne était, de fait et de droit, une culture universelle. L'avance prise sur les autres civilisations semblait fournir la vérification expérimentale de ce postulat.[29]

> [The encounter with other cultural traditions is a serious and, in a way, an absolutely new test for European culture. The fact that, for a long time, universal civilization was thought to originate in Europe sustained the illusion

that European culture was, both in reality and by right, a universal culture. The lead taken over other civilizations seemed to provide the experimental verification of this premise.]

Ultimately, the philosophical strategy proposed by the *Viajes* relies on the hypothesis that human differences are neutralized when civilization or humanity is thought of as a universal phenomenon. As Escobar and Percival indicate in this regard,

> [T]ravellers of the eighteenth century saw things in universal terms. Beneath the surface differences in habits and customs from country to country, they found in human nature a common denominator. Everything in humanity is different but deep down everything is the same.[30]

In the introductory preface to the first volume of the text, Enrique — presented as the author of the book — implies that he has been a traveller of the world and that his reliable observations enable him to testify that customs are basically similar in their essence, although they vary in the ways of putting them into practice. His travel experience gives him the authority to open his European readership's eyes and present the land of the monkeys as convincing proof that unknown or remote communities do not have to be savage or irrational by definition:

> [S]e podría creer que los países que la naturaleza separó enteramente de nuestro continente, y en los que yo he sido el primer hombre que puso el pie, debieran variar en lo que mira a las costumbres por encontrarse poblados de habitadores que siempre hemos tenido por faltos de razón y entendimiento. [...] Pero mis aventuras me han desengañado, y [...] he visto que en todo lugar [...] la naturaleza viciada inclina a obrar lo peor, y que estamos generalmente engañados en el modo de juzgar. El país de las monas, que se tuvo hasta ahora por un ente imaginario, es la prueba que confirma esta verdad.[31]

> [It might be thought that the countries that nature separated entirely from our continent, and in which I was the first man to set foot, should vary with regard to customs because they are populated by people whom we have always considered as lacking in reason and understanding. [...] But my adventures have opened my eyes, and [...] I have seen that [...] corrupt nature tends to do the worst everywhere, and that we are generally deceived in the way we judge. The country of the monkeys, which until now has been considered an imaginary place, is the proof that confirms this to be true.]

Misjudgement and disillusionment are the leitmotifs that pervade the *Viajes*, and, thanks to Enrique's discovery enterprise, the land of the monkeys transcends its fictional reality to become irrefutable proof that civilization expresses itself in various forms throughout the world. Enrique's appraisal of a universal civilization must derive from Roberto's cosmopolitan worldview, which is expressly pointed out in the text when Roberto defends his theory of the citizen of the world:[32]

> El hombre [...] debe considerarse ciudadano del mundo, y no es razón encarcele sus propios afectos en los estrechos términos de una ciudad y de su familia. Nosotros [...], que habitamos sobre la tierra, somos todos hijos de un solo padre, que es Dios; por esto, todos los hombres son hermanos; y cualquier lugar es su patria para aquel que se considera como es en sí, esto es, hombre. [...] La divina bondad no ha limitado sus beneficencias a sola nuestra patria; en todas partes las

ha difundido, y a todos los vivientes ha suministrado con abundancia los dones necesarios para la vida, y mil placeres que la hagan deleitable.³³

[Man [...] should consider himself a citizen of the world, and there is no reason for him to imprison his personal affection within the narrow limits of a city or his family. We [...], who inhabit the earth, are all children of one father, who is God; therefore, all men are brothers; and any place is a homeland for the person who thinks of himself as he is in himself, that is to say, a man. [...] Divine goodness has not limited its beneficence to our country alone; it has spread it everywhere, and has supplied, in abundance, all living beings with the gifts necessary for life, and a thousand pleasures that make it delightful.]

It follows from this passage that a cosmopolitan citizen is not only one who believes in a global civil society, but also someone who advocates a common and egalitarian humanity based on the idea of a homogeneous religious community in which all men are members of a single family. A universal citizen, then, is one who sees mankind as a spiritual and physical homeland because humans share their condition as men in the first place. Joaquín Álvarez Barrientos correctly interprets the aforementioned passage in terms of a utopian project of social equality among all human beings and also stresses the presence of a deistic influence due to the emphasis placed on natural order rather than on the social one.³⁴

Even though the notion of a universal community is utopian in itself, the problematic aspect of such an ideal concept resides in conceiving global civilization not as universal, but rather as uniform. The promotion of a perfectly homogenized civilization belittles any kind of progress that can be achieved by so-called uncivilized peoples. Brett Bowden highlights this argument when thinking of cosmopolitanism as a form of dystopia:

[A]n element of danger is inherent in the very idea of a cosmopolitan, globalized, peaceful international society. While this end might sound desirable and the general intent admirable, the pursuit of a 'realistic utopia' has very real implications for those peoples and societies that do not measure up or conform to the norm.³⁵

Despite the fact that the *Viajes* appeal to the premise that all nations are analogous in terms of the divine nature of their habits, the thorny question of a superior civilization is concealed by the satirical intention of the author. In the prologue, Vaca de Guzmán defines his translated text as a sharp satire aimed at ridiculing the vices that affect all nations. The depiction of nations as a universal civilization functions as a narrative strategy to make the point that the translation of the Italian original is applicable to the Spanish context. The fact that the point of convergence that unifies all nations is a very negative one — the idea that most humans suffer from the same follies — restates the ironic configuration of the text. However, Vaca de Guzmán makes sure that the reader is aware that certain linguistic adjustments have been made to the Italian text in order for the translation to be intelligible to the Spanish audience, in the same way that the supposed Italian translator omitted some expressions of the fictitious English original.

Although the Spanish version has frequently been regarded as a satire, its ascription to a specific genre turns out to be problematic. The most accurate description of the text could be an imaginary travel account tinged with utopian, novelistic, and satirical elements. Nonetheless, Álvarez Barrientos conceives of the *Viajes* as a novel because of the complexity of its narrative structure as well as of the narrative evolution of both Enrique and Roberto and their intervention in the utopian world.[36] In other earlier utopian texts, the visitor barely interacts with the inhabitants of the territory to be explored, and he does not take an active part in their socio-political system. He is a mere observer or witness, and, as a result, his way of thinking does not change or evolve in the context of the story. The passive role of the visitor in the utopian country is thus not applicable to Enrique or Roberto. Álvarez Barrientos's interpretation is in accord with the fact that Vaca de Guzmán's work can be seen as a *Bildungsroman* or novel of education in which Enrique goes through a process of learning and personal evolution. A similar opinion was expressed by Elena de Lorenzo Álvarez, who saw the text as a novel, but organized according to the conventions of travel literature. She also related the satire of social customs included in Enrique's fantastic voyage to the literary genre of *costumbrismo*.[37] However, bearing in mind its affiliation with *Gulliver's Travels*, it would be more correct to think of the *Viajes* as a satirical imaginary voyage with a secondary utopian undercurrent.

As a matter of fact, Seriman's *Viaggi* and the several editions of Vaca de Guzmán's translation are included in Philip Gove's list of imaginary voyages, as well as in other catalogues of travel literature. Gove draws attention to the remarks made in 1878 by the Danish scholar Julius Paludan, who found Seriman's text intolerably prolix and commonplace, especially the moral reflections of the first volume, but he also believes that the romantic element predominates strongly over the satirical. Another comment featured is the one made in 1825 by the French bookseller and publisher Louis-Gabriel Michaud, for whom the *Viaggi* was the best and only philosophical novel written in Italian.[38]

What must be emphasized is that the intellectual discussion about the concept of civilization in the *Viajes* is meant to be focused on criticism of social customs, not of political structures. As José Escobar explains, the verbs *civiliser* [to civilize] and *polir* [to polish] have been treated as synonyms since their appearance in the French dictionaries of the seventeenth century.[39] The refinement of manners is of course susceptible to being reinforced by the intervention of religion in social life, as Mirabeau posits: '[La religion] nous prêche et nous rappelle sans cesse la confraternité, adoucit notre cœur, élève notre esprit' [Religion constantly calls to mind and advocates brotherliness, softens our hearts, elevates our souls].[40] After all, *civiliser*, *polir*, and *adoucir* are conceived of as interrelated actions. In the Enlightenment period, then, the new meaning of civilization was closely related to a refinement of social behaviour:

> La acción de refinar y mejorar las costumbres de un pueblo se entiende [...] como progreso de la moral social, expresión ideológica de una nueva moralidad ilustrada y revolucionaria. Es una acción moral dirigida al perfeccionamiento de la sociedad civil a lo largo del desarrollo histórico de la humanidad. [...] Es decir que el concepto dieciochesco de *civilisation* se construye sobre la base semántica establecida por las virtudes civiles propias de la nueva sociedad burguesa.[41]

[The action of refining and improving the customs of a people is understood [...] as the progress of social morality, the ideological expression of a new, enlightened and revolutionary morality. It is a moral action aimed at perfecting civil society in the course of the historical development of humanity. [...] That is to say, the eighteenth-century concept of civilization is built on the semantic basis established by the civil virtues belonging to the new bourgeois society.]

Before giving examples of the customs satirized in the *Viajes*, it is worth mentioning that the topic of *Terra Australis Incognita* does not act as a backdrop to the development of the story. It is a mere excuse to introduce the idea of a world turned upside down, which is the necessary backdrop for social criticism. After their shipwreck, the initial geographical observations that Roberto and Enrique make are carried out in conformity with modern practical methods and lead them to suppose that they have reached the antipodes in the Unknown Southern Land, but the purpose of their explorations does not affect the fictional domain of their experiences. As Suzanne Kiernan points out, 'Seriman's book [...] has nothing at all to do with actual antipodean travel and exploration in the South Pacific'.[42] This kind of incoherence may be due to the fact that, at the time in which Seriman was writing his story, the southern hemisphere had emerged from classical myth and mythical geography and could scarcely be thought of any longer as unknown. In any case, Seriman's work combines two themes that appear together in other imaginary voyages of the Enlightenment period: the fictional location of *Terra Australis Incognita* and the arrival of travellers in a republic of apes or other animals. A couple of relevant examples of this thematic tradition are *Songes philosophiques* [*Philosophical Dreams*] (1746) by Jean-Baptiste de Boyer — a clear forerunner of the *Viaggi* — and *La Découverte australe par un homme-volant, ou le Dédale français* [*The Discovery of the Southern Land by a Flying Man; or, The French Daedalus*] (1781) by Nicolas-Edme Rétif de la Bretonne. As is the case with the writing of Aesopic fables during the Enlightenment period, the objective behind the use of animals in order to criticize social behaviour involves a didactic intention with regard to the culture and society of the time.

Another noteworthy factor is the peculiar satirical technique employed in the *Viajes*. Vaca de Guzmán reappropriates Seriman's narrative technique, which consists of a game of identity and difference, that is, a world where the alienation of the Other is the condition required to make a subtle satirical device work. A strange and ironic reciprocity connects visitors and natives. As Kiernan asserts regarding the Italian version, 'In their manners, fashions, and social organization, the apes who are the dominant race in these Antipodes are recognizable as Seriman's compatriots'.[43] That is to say, the circumstances of humans and apes are exactly the same in their respective ontological contexts, but this is precisely the reason why they reject each other. While Enrique and Roberto take an estranged view of their simian counterparts, the apes similarly regard them as monstrous. Their human appearance excites derision, fear, and contempt. In a sense, the encounter between the two species replicates the typical response of Europeans to the primitive in the long age of exploration. In line with this view, Escobar and Percival formulate the concept of satirical perspectivism to explain Enrique's ingenuousness in the face of scenes and actions that are repeatedly presented as if they were extravagant. Confronted with what seems to be strange to him, Enrique is warned by Roberto not to be surprised by follies that are as likely to be found in the country of the monkeys as anywhere else in the world:

> La perspectiva satírica de los *Viajes de Enrique Wanton* surge de la asombrada ingenuidad de Enrique que contempla las escenas de costumbres y lo que ocurre normalmente como si fueran raras y extravagantes al verlas representadas por actores extraños que invierten la normalidad. Las acciones habituales de los humanos, al ser ejecutadas por los monos, se ridiculizan. [...] En una sociedad alegóricamente simiesca, los raros son los dos seres humanos que aparecen en ella de no se sabe dónde.[44]

> [The satirical point of view of the *Travels of Henry Wanton* derives from the astonished innocence of Enrique, who contemplates the scenes of customs and what normally happens as if they were rare and extravagant, on seeing them carried out by strange actors who invert normality. The usual actions of humans, when carried out by monkeys, are ridiculed. [...] In an allegorically simian society, the strange human beings are the two who appear in it from no one knows where.]

Indeed, Enrique and Roberto acknowledge their hostile role of invaders in a world that parodies their own cultural conventions. However, they remain passive intruders who do not interfere with a reality that could easily be subverted by relying on their presumed superiority because doing so would mean perpetrating an act of uncivilized violence. They need to recover their liberty so urgently that they degrade themselves in trying to imitate their antagonistic compatriots; in fact, their impersonation is so astonishing that they begin to be called 'dos monos del otro mundo' [two monkeys from the other world].[45] Roberto and Enrique's plan is to become famous across the simian nation, so that a rich monkey-citizen can be interested in buying them and, as an involuntary consequence, release them not only from their prison, but also from the inhuman treatment received from their provincial and savage captors. They will unfortunately find out that there is no actual difference between the monkeys from the city and those from the provinces.

Following the traditional tactic used by European colonizers, the two visitors — in spite of being primarily prisoners — ingratiate themselves with the monkeys by learning the simian language, in contrast with which the English language is called 'idioma natural' [natural language].[46] This also echoes Gulliver's learning of several imaginary languages during his travels. Alleging the ridiculous nature of the language of the monkeys, Enrique excuses himself from providing a grammatical description of this new language, as all travellers do in every place they visit. However, this can actually refer to the ostentatious erudition of studying foreign grammars and customs.

Only when the two Europeans are able to prove to their hosts/captors that they are rational animals — most of all after their acquisition of the simian language — are they released from their detention in the stable and allowed to circulate freely in society, subsequently making their way to the capital, Simiópolis, and ultimately into the social circle of the prime minister. He tells them a long tale about his youthful travels to the kingdom of the parrots and the empire of the frogs, undertaken in the spirit of the Grand Tour and in the company of his tutor and his dancing teacher. In a metanarrative attempt to recreate the immediate circumstances in which Enrique and Roberto find themselves, the moral of the tale is that, when abroad, it is wisest to conform to the customs of the locals if one wants to be socially accepted and even obtain some benefits: the tutor in rhetoric learned to parrot so fluently that he was offered a chair in philosophy, and the dancing instructor was a success among the frogs. According to the minister, it is no use trying to impose one's own beliefs and values on a foreign society; it is better to naturally and temporarily adapt oneself to local conditions rather than trying to alter them because 'la distinción no conduce más que a los peligros y al último exterminio' [the distinction leads only to dangers and ultimate extermination].[47] In the hope that they will return safely to their homeland, the two Englishmen are certainly aware of the effectiveness of the minister's advice and conform to simian practices, although they seem unnatural and irrational to both of them, who pride themselves on coming from the most civilized nation.

Throughout the four Spanish volumes, a concern with contemporary manners and customs is evident, as well as the programmatic purpose of demonstrating the dangers that extreme refinement can pose to civil society. This aspect can be noticed in the description that Roberto gives of a rich monkey-lady who has the intention of buying him and Enrique as servants and to whom they have been recommended by Oliva, the female monkey who acts as their master and ally, and who teaches them the simian language and tells them what they want to know about simian society: '¡Oh, cuánto más afortunada sería aquella loca si, en vez de los ricos vestidos y joyas que adornaban su cuerpo, estuviera su espíritu dotado de aquella preciosa luz de razón que excede a todos los dones de la fortuna!' [Oh, how much more fortunate this madwoman would be if, instead of the rich dresses and jewels that adorned her body, her spirit were endowed with that precious light of reason that surpasses all the gifts of fortune!].[48] Roberto's first impression of the lady was to insult her frivolous and arrogant personality: Oliva's refined friend should be more concerned with the cultivation of her intellectual faculties than with the sophistication of her external appearance, which is reflected in her pretentious clothing and jewellery. Instead of showing off her wealthy apparel, she should brag about the richness of her enlightened knowledge, if only she possessed such a virtue. This passage of the text seems to allude to the Spanish popular saying 'Aunque la mona se vista de seda, mona se queda' [Although a monkey be dressed in silk, she is still a monkey], which is included in the *Diccionario de autoridades*.[49] Regardless of whether or not Seriman was aware of this proverb, it is very likely that Vaca de Guzmán knew it well.

The crucial element to be highlighted here is the distinction between urban dwellers — who live in Simiópolis, the capital — and those who live in the country. On the basis of Roberto's argument, the apes of the peripheral regions are negatively influenced and corrupted by the monkey-people of the metropolis.

Thus, the internal exchange of customs and values is not beneficial at all, which proves the degenerating effect of allegedly more civilized manners on a space predominantly ruled by a natural consciousness. In turn, the deplorable cultural state of the urban centre is the result of the preference for the application of foreign knowledge in the field of the arts and sciences. The disdain for the local potential and the uncertainty about the possibility of generating better and more valuable material and intellectual capital lead simian society to its self-destruction:

> Se ha introducido entre los Simiopolitanos el fanatismo de no dar estimación sino a las cosas que vienen de lejos. Los profesores de las ciencias que se aprenden en esta ciudad no tienen mérito; para que sean estimados, es necesario que vengan de países extranjeros, y a proporción de la distancia de nuestra patria crece la reputación que de ellos se forma. No se cree poder hallar artífices excelentes sino fuera de estos dominios; lo propio se entiende de músicos, pintores y de todos aquellos que se emplean en cualquier ciencia, o arte liberal o mecánico. Esta necedad se extiende a todas las cosas; [...] el dinero sale del Estado, que por consiguiente se va empobreciendo, y entre tanto los forasteros se ríen y triunfan de nuestra ignorancia.[50]

> [What has been introduced among the Simiopolitans is the fanaticism of appreciating only things that come from distant parts. The teachers of the sciences that are learned in this city have no merit; to be esteemed they need to come from foreign countries, and in proportion to the distance from our country, their reputation grows. It is thought impossible to find excellent teachers except those from outside these domains; the same applies to musicians, painters, and all of those who are employed in any science or liberal or mechanical art. This folly extends to all things; [...] money is exported from the country, which consequently becomes impoverished, and meanwhile strangers laugh at us and enjoy success as a result of our ignorance.]

Taking into account the fact that the land of the apes is the satirized version of Spanish (or Venetian, in the original) society, the indiscriminate assimilation of foreign habits referred to in the passage above alludes to the unnecessary influence from other apparently superior European countries, and from England in particular.

There are a few episodes in Vaca de Guzmán's text that directly establish the parallel between Spanish/English (European in a broad sense) customs and their parodic reflection, such as the episode of Madama Betónica, who praises not only the similarities between European and ape-like women, but also the fact that the plebeians follow the customs and fashion of the nobles, who must always be a social model for them:

> Mucho me agrada, añadió Madama, que las mujeres tengan el exquisito gusto de las monas, y no desapruebo la conducta de la plebe que sigue las ideas de la nobleza pues esta debe ser siempre el modelo de las operaciones de aquella.[51]

> [I am much pleased, added Madam, that women share the exquisite taste of the monkeys, and I do not disapprove of the behaviour of the masses who follow the ideas of the nobility because the latter must always be the model for the behaviour of the former.]

In view of Enrique's bewilderment at the nonsensical reproduction of the same vain customs in England and the nation of the monkeys, Madama Betónica explains that it is perfectly logical that the same rational and praiseworthy customs are put into practice in different countries, even without having news of their existence, because rational thinking is a universal and innate faculty:

> [A]quel uso debe creerse sabio y racional, que es generalmente abrazado por todas las naciones, y no pudiera ciertamente haberse puesto en la cabeza a las señoras de vuestro país el imitarnos en tan útil invento sin conocernos si la naturaleza, la verdad y la razón no las hubiera suministrado la idea.[52]

> [That custom, which is generally embraced by all nations, should be considered wise and rational, and the idea of imitating us in such a useful invention could not have been put into the heads of the ladies of your country without them knowing us if nature, truth, and reason had not suggested to them such an idea.]

Enrique, of course, disapproves of what Madama Betónica means by 'rational'. Actually, the definition becomes complicated when Enrique notes that European women pierce their ears to wear earrings, which the female monkeys do not do; they do wear earrings, but they do not alter their bodies for the sake of beauty because 'aún no las había podido persuadir la vanidad a que se agujereasen su propia carne para parecer más bellas' [they had not yet been persuaded by vanity to have their own flesh pierced in order to appear more beautiful].[53] This European custom, then, could be seen as a retrogressive attack against civilization, which swaps the roles between monkeys and humans and makes the latter look like barbarians.

At the same time, since Enrique adds that the European custom of ear piercing resembles the practice of nose piercing by Indian women in order to wear precious metals, this anecdote confirms Madama Betónica's theory that rational customs are universal. However, Europeans judge those Oriental women to be savages without realizing that they carry out the same practice, which is incisively condemned by Enrique, who complains about their inability to recognize themselves in other cultures: '¡Oh, qué fácil es desaprobar y escarnecer en otros nuestros mismos defectos, y dar título de bárbaras a aquellas propias costumbres que entre nosotros llamamos civilización y política!' [Oh, how easy it is to disapprove of and mock our own defects when found in other people and to describe as barbaric those very customs that among us are called civilized and politic!].[54] It needs to be pointed out that Vaca de Guzmán translates the Italian word *coltura* [cultivation][55] as *civilización* [civilization],[56] not as *cultura* [culture].

The satire of coffee houses can be regarded as another important criticized custom of eighteenth-century Europe. From Enrique's perspective, the coffee house is presented as an enigmatic place frequented by a great variety of monkeys. Coffee ('aquel amargo y negro licor' [that bitter, black liquor])[57] makes Enrique feel nauseated, and he later learns that it is a popular drink among the monkeys, who gather at the coffee house to basically waste their time in fruitless conversations. The institution of the coffee house as a regular place of meeting was a literary theme that appeared in the eighteenth-century Spanish press, although it featured even more prominently in the English essay-periodicals of the early eighteenth century.[58]

Thus, the criticism of customs is one of the ideological techniques by which the enlightened intellectual minority in Spain fulfilled its ambition of reforming the practices of a society that claimed to be sunk in a state of national decadence. The new concept of civilization based on customs and manners is essential to the structure of the *Viajes*, whose multiple reprints and wide circulation imply its popularity and favourable reception among Spanish readers of the period.[59] While Donald White and Philip Gove describe five editions of Vaca de Guzmán's work between 1769 and 1831,[60] Francisco Aguilar Piñal records an edition published in 1846,[61] and José Montesinos adds a later one in 1871.[62] Not only did the two translated volumes benefit from a positive reception, but the two-volume sequel created by Vaca de Guzmán also received a notable response from readers, which turned the work into an important Spanish bestseller.[63]

The Contribution of the *Suplemento*

The translation and continuation of Seriman's *Viaggi* by Vaca de Guzmán struck Pedro Álvarez de Miranda as a complex textual and bibliographical tangle: Vaca de Guzmán published the Spanish versions of the first two volumes of Seriman's work in 1769 and 1771 respectively (the two volumes were originally published by the Italian author in 1749), but instead of translating the other two Italian volumes that appeared in 1764 in an edition that included the first two volumes, the Spanish author published his own two-volume continuation in 1778.[64] According to Álvarez de Miranda, the two-volume sequel created by Vaca de Guzmán not only ultimately shows the superiority of the Spanish writer's literary skills over those of Seriman, but also attracts the attention of the Spanish audience in directly portraying the reality of Spanish society.[65]

The author seemed to be in control of his text, deciding who should print it and making it clear right until 1785 that the bookshop of Bernardo Alberá sold it, possibly exclusively. A relevant point that would support this view is that Vaca de Guzmán presumably owned the plates that were used to provide engravings in the later editions and made them available to each printer. These illustrations, produced by the Spanish engraver José Patiño, represent scenes from the narrative and present humanized simians dressed in eighteenth-century clothes, but they are not as numerous as the plates that appeared in the Italian version (more than thirty in some editions); in fact, the two volumes of the Spanish supplement have only two engravings each, but they illustrate significant moments in the story.[66]

Álvarez de Miranda thinks that the original Italian work is not utopian at all, but rather a satirical criticism of social customs.[67] However, he does not indicate whether he believes the same is true for the Spanish supplement to the Italian volumes. Unlike Álvarez de Miranda, Escobar and Percival, the scholars who have studied in greatest detail the *Viajes*, consider that Seriman's two final volumes, which describe Enrique's visit to the land of the *cinocefali* [dog-headed men], constitute a utopia that complements the apparent anti-utopia depicted in the land of the monkeys. As to Vaca de Guzmán's two original volumes, the authors regard them as a transformation of the land of the monkeys into a 'near-utopia', in which the unproductive life of the Spanish aristocracy is especially criticized.[68] Another scholar who has questioned the utopian features of the *Viajes* and their *Suplemento* is Claude Morange, who sees the text as a traditional satire of social life,[69] similar in its moralizing tone to Cadalso's *Cartas marruecas*, a work completed in manuscript in the 1770s, but not published until seven years after the author's death, in 1789.[70] Despite his detailed analysis of the idealized rural life in Vaca de Guzmán's *Suplemento*, Morange does not recognize the Spanish work as a utopia and proposes to interpret it in the socio-political and cultural context of 1778.[71]

Vaca de Guzmán boasts about the success of his translation at the beginning of his *Suplemento, o sea tomo tercero de los viajes de Enrique Wanton al país de las monas* [*A Supplement, or Rather the Third Volume, to the Travels of Henry Wanton to the Country of the Monkeys*], a work of his own authorship. It was the reception of his two-volume translation of Seriman's text that encouraged him to compose the sequel to the Italian author's *Viaggi* in two more volumes.[72] The Spanish author disregards the continuation to the story published by Seriman and instead substitutes his own satire of the customs and manners of Spain for Seriman's alternative story. The author's friends — Monsieur Riregüet (an anagram of Gutierre) and Doctor Boicocéfalo ('cabeza de vaca' [cow's head] in Greek), that is, the fictional splitting of Gutierre Vaca de Guzmán into two characters — defend the publication of his story claiming that the Italian author was not able to get a copy of Enrique's manuscript describing the continuation of his travels to the land of the apes, but instead he found a manuscript with Enrique's adventures in the country of the dogs.

Combining historical facts and literary fiction, Vaca de Guzmán, in the introduction to his third volume, makes reference not only to the anonymous publication of the Italian original, but also to the peculiarity that his sequel to the *Viaggi* is equally based on a (fictional) manuscript of Enrique himself, called *Apuntaciones y borradores pertenecientes a mis Viajes al País de las Monas* [*Notes and Drafts Pertaining to my Travels to the Country of the Monkeys*] and to the fact that his two supplements were finished before he was informed of the (real) existence of the other two Italian volumes, published along with the two previous volumes in 1764 and entitled *Viaggi di Enrico Wanton alle terre incognite australi, ed ai regni delle scimmie, e dei cinocefali, nuovamente tradotti da un manoscritto inglese* [*The Travels of Henry Wanton to Unknown Southern Lands and to the Kingdoms of the Monkeys and the Cynocephali, Newly Translated from an English Manuscript*]. However, as Vaca de Guzmán argues, this unexpected discovery is no reason for him not to publish his own text.

To support his argument as to the convenience of dismissing Seriman's satire about the realm of the cynocephali, the Spanish author goes into the detailed and complex explanation that the Italian continuation suffers from some incongruities, which is not the case with his Spanish version since it is based on 'el verdadero original, escrito de mano del mismo viajero, aun en los propios borradores y apuntaciones que tenía prevenidos para poner en limpio y que, impedido por algún accidente, no pudo ejecutar' [the true original, handwritten by the traveller himself, even the very drafts and notes that he had planned to put into a final version, which were prevented from appearing there by some accident and which he was unable to complete].⁷³ The fictional method of writing following the primary source of Enrique's travels destroys Seriman's strategy of the found original English manuscript. However, irrespective of his advantageous position to offer a more reliable narration, Vaca de Guzmán adopts a cautious attitude towards the possible negative reception of his two new volumes, which explains the use of the word *Suplemento* in the title pages to both of them:

> [N]o he dudado en trabajar en dicha obra con cuanto cuidado he podido, arreglándome lo posible al estilo que en los tomos antecedentes sigue su docto autor, y no alterando en un ápice las noticias de los dichos borradores; pero, por si la delicadeza de los paladares de algunos lectores melindrosos no halla estos tomos con tanta sazón como los anteriores, he usado en el frontispicio de la obra del defensivo de la voz *Suplemento*.⁷⁴

> [I have not hesitated to work on this text with as much care as I have been able, adapting myself as much as possible to the style that its learned author follows in the previous volumes and not altering at all the news conveyed in these drafts; but, in case the delicacy of the palates of some fussy readers does not find these volumes as good as the previous ones, I have used in my defence the word *Supplement* in the frontispiece of the work.]

Vaca de Guzmán's third and fourth volumes certainly attempt to imitate Seriman's writing style, but it is less easy to claim that they function as a supplement to the other two books. The *Suplemento*'s chapters are normally double the length of the *Viaggi*'s. Vaca de Guzmán's linguistic style is mostly fluent and confident. He uses popular sayings: 'Es el amor ciego' [Love is blind],⁷⁵ 'Los guapos y el buen vino duran poco, dice un adagio vulgar' [Handsome men and good wine last briefly, says a common adage],⁷⁶ '[M]eter la hoz en mies ajena' [To put the sickle in someone else's field],⁷⁷ '[P]ara que pasen lo blanco por tinto, y compren gato por liebre' [To pass white wine for red wine, and to buy a cat instead of a hare].⁷⁸ He even appears to use neologisms, such as *hoidiarista*⁷⁹ to describe old people who praise the past and condemn the present time (*hoy día* [today]). Volume IV seems more fluent in technique than volume III: whereas volume IV shows the constant novelty that a good text requires if it is to maintain the continued attention of the reader, volume III can often seem less engaging. The use of dialogue in the text is minimal; rather, the reader is subject to extensive expositions of ideas or principles. Vaca de Guzmán's is an intellectual work, one that draws the reader in. The author expects the reader to share many of the points of view argued for in the text, but ultimately readers are allowed to form their own judgements. In this sense, Vaca de Guzmán uses a technique that is common to the novel, an aspect that makes the text more modern to a reader today.

In line with the connection of the *Viaggi* to the Swiftian tradition, the *Suplemento* includes paratextual references to Spanish satirists in the epigraphs of each volume — the poets Jorge Pitillas, pseudonym of José Gerardo de Hervás (?–1742), and Lupercio Leonardo de Argensola (1559–1613) — which implies the relationship of the text to the Spanish satirical tradition. The two previous translated volumes contained epigraphs by Francisco de Quevedo (1580–1645) and Juan Gregorio

Morillas Osorio (?–1599). However, Vaca de Guzmán also explicitly refers to Thomas More in volume III, in a letter in which Roberto explains to Enrique that the soul is always free and productive when the body has been confined to prison: 'No adquirió tanto crédito para con patricios y extranjeros el incomparable Tomás Moro entre las felicidades de su libertad como entre los horrores de su prisión' [The incomparable Thomas More did not receive as much credit from patricians and foreigners in the happiness of his freedom as in the horrors of his imprisonment].[80] This would seem to claim that Vaca de Guzmán saw his text as in the utopian generic tradition and was convinced of the importance of reminding the reader of that link. He experiments most effectively with the utopian model as he retains the inherited framework, but his authorial originality is evident in his handling of details. In fact, the Spanish author has the ingenious idea of making Enrique travel around the country of the monkeys allowing him to undergo a variety of experiences, which might be regarded as a modernized idea of utopia. As will be seen below, Enrique's tour reveals that the country is not uniform because different provinces each seem to have their own character, as is evident in their practices. Although Vaca de Guzmán keeps up the pretence of depicting another world at all times, the acute reader can easily apply the social criticism to Spain and perceive possible equivalences. Despite the fact that Enrique's story is originally intended for a reader back home in England, the vision presented in the *Suplemento* can be allowed to reflect back on Spain.

Vaca de Guzmán and Seriman are distinguishable in the way in which the approach to society is treated. Although it is true that criticism of European customs is a constant feature throughout the four Spanish volumes, the last two strengthen the critical approach to civilized moral and social codes by portraying the developing friendship between Enrique and Tulipán [Tulip], the youngest son of Enrique's protector in the land of the apes. Building on Seriman's critical representation of social aspects of the country of the monkeys, Vaca de Guzmán strongly underlines the ethical dimension of simian society through substantial discussion by Enrique of the inhabitants' social behaviour (*costumbres*), while Roberto is presented as being concerned with the political aspects of this society.

Enrique is usually a trustworthy witness, although he can occasionally be led astray by Tulipán. He is an acute and ostensibly reliable observer of many social foibles and is always concerned to get to the bottom of matters and discover the truth without prejudice, but he maintains his moral focus and makes judgements on the behaviour that he witnesses. Although he reveals himself as a constant thinker, his human fallibility is evident in that he can sometimes fall into traps that he regrets having succumbed to in retrospect. As Vaca de Guzmán allows Enrique to be flawed or fallible, he becomes more credible to the reader. The author even allows him to appear to reflect on his own behaviour, in addition to letting Roberto criticize his actions. Moreover, the sophisticated personality that Enrique projects can be seen as close to the potential reader, who the author hopes will be influenced by the same set of experiences of life as Enrique has in another country with a somewhat, though not very, different culture.

Although social structures are configured in the text, the Spanish author is more interested in actual behaviour, placing the emphasis on individuals' free choice as to how to behave. In this sense, the author contrasts good behaviour with bad according to the topic he is dealing with. While sometimes the satire is so strong as to stretch credibility, at other times it is clear that Vaca de Guzmán portrays genuine first-hand experience and describes what he sees accurately and without exaggeration. Thus, the *Suplemento* is wide-ranging in the aspects of society that it covers, such as life at court, extravagance (especially luxury spending, which is also present in the provincial capitals that Enrique visits), how the legal system operates, social types (such as *pretendientes* [petitioners] and *petimetres* [dandies]), how education functions, what activities universities engage in, false beliefs (in the influence of eclipses or in ghosts), social gatherings (*tertulias*), the behaviour of a nobility obsessed with rank and privilege, noble ancestry, idleness and hard work, among various other characteristics. This survey of an evolving social system results in a detailed picture of the new society explored by Enrique. The reader is not informed that specific socio-political structures are in existence as a scenario for human action as is the case in *Sinapia*. Vaca de Guzmán describes a society that seems to have changed over time and has now reached the stage of development that his text carefully describes.

The satirical construction of the land of the apes comprises a metropolitan, a cosmopolitan, and a parochial outlook. The systematic rupture between the centre and the periphery in the simian country is especially depicted in the character of Tulipán, a young monkey-apprentice and son of one of the principal citizens, who sheltered Roberto and Enrique in his palace after they were released from their imprisonment. While Seriman's third and fourth volumes concentrate on life in Simiópolis, Vaca de Guzmán's continuation deals with the journey undertaken by Enrique and Tulipán along the roads of various regions of the country. The relationship between Enrique and Tulipán reproduces not only the 'didactic friendship' between the former and Roberto, but also the leitmotif of travel as a cognitive and educational instrument. However, it is Enrique who benefits most from this new instructional journey. Tulipán is the tool used to improve Enrique's observations of the Simiopolitans because he can witness their natural interaction with his young friend; that is why, in order to fully succeed in his role of anthropological observer, Enrique takes advantage of his friendship and of the fact that the young monkey confides in and completely depends on him:

> [S]in su amistad y compañía no podría yo tener un conocimiento tan exacto; él ha sido el único medio de mi instrucción en este punto; [...] para lograr mis intentos no podía menos de irme estrechando en su amistad, y para esta intimidad era fuerza seguirle y acompañarle adonde violentamente he sido muchas veces conducido. Él me ha fiado enteramente su corazón; nada sabe ya emprender, ni aun dar un paso sin mí.[81]
>
> [Without his friendship and company, I could not have acquired such accurate knowledge; he has been my sole source of instruction in this matter; [...] in order to achieve my aims, I could only strengthen our friendship, and to achieve this intimacy, it was necessary to follow and accompany him where I

have been violently led many times. He has given me his heart completely; he does not know how to undertake anything or even take a step without me.]

According to Escobar and Percival, Tulipán is a representative figure of a Simiopolitan young man, corresponding to what the Spanish satirical writers of the eighteenth century called a *petimetre* (a word derived from the French *petit-maître*). The concept suggests 'the aping of foreign ways typical of these characters, their vain superficial enslavement to the dictates of fashion and their complete lack of moral depth'.[82] In Enrique's words, these members of the aristocracy can be characterized as follows:

> [N]o son buenos para otra cosa que para ir de estrado en estrado trayendo y llevando chismes con otros como ellos; para andar de baile en baile, donde sueltan los diques a su desenfreno; para marchar por esas calles con el mayor atolondramiento; y en fin para aprender y ejecutar con gran estudio cuantas gesticulaciones ven a los extranjeros, [...] haciendo en todo un increíble esfuerzo para diferenciarse del resto de sus compatriotas.[83]

> [They are not good for anything except for going from podium to podium supplying and conveying gossip with others like them, for going from ball to ball, where they unrestrainedly allow all freedoms, for marching along those streets with the greatest bewilderment, and, in short, for diligently learning and carrying out all the gesticulations that they see in foreigners, [...] putting an incredible effort into everything in order to distinguish themselves from the rest of their compatriots.]

Therefore, *petimetres* strive to copy foreign behaviour because they seek to differentiate themselves from the masses and their own compatriots. For *petimetres*, becoming civilized entails abandoning ancient and uncouth customs in order to acquire the refinement of modern manners. In a social and historical context, rusticity is identified with old Spain in contrast to the social sophistication of modern Europe. As Escobar and Percival conclude,

> [I]f we set the comparison in the broad panorama of eighteenth-century Spain, we can see in the affected attitude of the *petimetres* a frivolous caricature of a deeper problem posed in Enlightenment Spain: the pressing need on the part of the enlightened few of finding remedies for Spain's backwardness in regard to more developed countries.[84]

The satire of *petimetres* is complemented by the satire of the *cortejo* [extramarital close friendships] phenomenon, a well-known eighteenth-century custom among men of high society that consisted in paying court to a married woman.[85] In the simian language, this practice is called *mutuo obsequio* [mutual deference],[86] and it is a significant activity in which the young Simiopolitans engage. Enrique identifies this social custom as the chief activity of Tulipán's idle moments. The young ape usually visits the Marquesa de la Mielga [Marchioness of Alfalfa] in the absence of her husband:

> Una de sus más preferidas visitas, o por decir lo más cierto, la principal, era a la Marquesa de la Mielga, joven hermosa, pero boba; rica, pero presumida; bien nacida, pero mal criada; estaba casada con un caballero mono, juicioso, prudente y arreglado.[87]

[One of his most favourite visits, or, to be more exact, the main one, was to the Marchioness of Alfalfa, a beautiful young woman, but a fool; rich, though arrogant; well born, but badly raised; she was married to a gentleman monkey who was judicious, prudent, and orderly.]

Enrique is surprised at the mismatched qualities between the Marquesa and her noble husband, but this kind of marriage seems to respond to the philosophical discussion about effective marriages contained in the second volume of the *Viajes*. In Roberto's view, since love, the greatest irrational passion, is not the most suitable basis for marriage, the monkey-fathers are in charge of a rational selection of the best husbands for their daughters:

> Nuestros monos, reflexionando los inconvenientes que suele producir una mala elección sugerida por la pasión únicamente, [...] quisieron hacerse árbitros de los verdaderos intereses de sus hijas, eligiendo aquellos partidos que [...] juzgan ser los más útiles. Así pues, el que estos vínculos no se formen por el amor, sino por la razón, que es una guía más iluminada y segura, no veo deba ser motivo de tanta extrañeza.[88]

> [Our monkeys, reflecting on the inconveniences that a bad choice, suggested by passion alone, usually causes, [...] wanted to act as arbiters of the true interests of their daughters, choosing those catches that [...] they think most useful. Hence, I do not think that the fact that these bonds are formed not by love, but by reason, which is a more enlightened and safe guide, should be the cause of so much concern.]

It can be deduced, then, that the satire of the *cortejo* custom and *petimetres* is a representation of a more profound eighteenth-century problem resulting from the change in values from a traditionalist to a modern Spain.

Vaca de Guzmán's interest in social behaviour links to the use of reason and, in some measure, to Enlightenment thought. Reason is the touchstone for behaviour, and behaviour can be enlightened. It is argued that animal behaviour is rational in that it is mediated by a choice between good and bad consequences. Enlightenment is mentioned several times in the *Suplemento* in the forms of *ilustrar* [enlighten], *ilustrado* [enlightened], and *ilustración* [enlightenment]. There is even a direct reference to the Enlightenment period: '[N]o hay ciencia ni arte en que [los monos] no hayan puesto la pluma con notable felicidad en el día; por lo que con razón llaman muchos al presente el siglo ilustrado' [There is no science or art that they [the monkeys] have not currently written about without remarkable success; that is why, with good reason, many think that the present century is enlightened].[89] In his interpretation of Seriman's text, Vaca de Guzmán translates *illuminati* [knowledgeable group][90] by *iluminados* [visionaries],[91] as was common before the 1770s.

The cultivation of the sciences is another important aspect of the kingdom of the apes. There is a province called Polymathía that is exclusively dedicated to the teaching of areas of knowledge such as philosophy, law, medicine, and the grammar and rhetoric of the simian language. This city is also referred to as *Estudio General* [General Study] and *Ciudad de las letras* [City of Letters], but it is thought that the learning of impractical theories and principles does not turn out to be useful for the progress of society. The absence of an effective practical implementation of the sciences studied does not fit the parameters of the utopian model, but it also emphasizes the Manichean perspective that permeates the *Suplemento*.

Since reason is made the criterion for judging behaviour, religious principles are not evoked as a measure in such respect. In fact, no mention of religious worship is made in the *Suplemento* at all. God is very occasionally referred to, but usually in deistic terms. Thus, a notable absence in Vaca de Guzmán's Simiópolis is organized religion; no mention is made of clerics or of formal Church activity. There are various references to divine Providence made by Enrique, but almost in terms of the deistic conception of a supreme being. There is also a mention of the spirituality that Roberto was endowed with by Seriman. However, leaving aside the beliefs of the two visitors, a generalized religious orientation does not exist in the nation of the monkeys. In this respect, Vaca de Guzmán would seem to be following in the footsteps of Thomas More.

Appropriating Seriman's narrative style and subject matter, the Spanish author introduces in his two original volumes a new perspective in which the refined life of the capital is contrasted with the crude life of the provinces. Not for nothing does Enrique's patron in this new set of adventures describe Simiópolis, in a remarkable image, as an insatiable entity — in fact, a whale — that simultaneously appropriates and annihilates the marginal sectors of the simian nation to enhance its power:

> Simiópolis, aquella insaciable ballena que en el gran mar que forman los pueblos de este continente todo lo devora, todo se lo traga, después que nos apura el dinero ya en contribuciones, ya en préstamos, ya en moños para nuestras antojadizas monas.[92]
>
> [Simiopolis, that insatiable whale that in the great sea formed by the peoples of this continent devours everything, swallows everything, after taking our money in taxes and loans or for hair buns for our capricious female monkeys.]

The governmental system of the monkeys is, then, an unequal society in which the poorest are the most oppressed.

In Chapter VIII of the third volume, Vaca de Guzmán, by means of the philosophical reflections of Señor Moral [Mr Morality], gives a long description of the socio-political system of the nation of the monkeys, in which the author includes a clear allusion to the oppressive political order. The initial structure of the simian republic complies with the traditional elements of a utopian society to a great extent, but Señor Moral's description progressively shows the cultural decadence of a rootless nation, which constitutes a kind of anti-utopia: 'De la abundancia pasó la nación al tedio del trabajo; del tedio al ocio; patrocinó a este el jefe principal, y quedó el país aletargado' [The nation passed from abundance to the drudgery of work; from drudgery to leisure, sponsored by the chief ruler, and this left the country lethargic].[93] An important factor in the decline of Simiópolis was the uneven division of land and labour, which opposes one of the basic principles of a utopian system. The resulting inequality provoked poverty and social oppression.

In the same way, the allocation of *señoríos* [seigneurial rights] to certain individuals as a reward from the king for helping in the restoration of the provinces had detrimental effects on the equal prosperity of every citizen in the nation.

Although public recognition for good actions promotes the production of further good actions, some possessors of seigneurial rights use such powers in their own interests instead of contributing to the happiness of those under their authority. The *señoríos* were a major issue concerning privilege and a constant topic of complaint by eighteenth-century social reformers in Spain such as Jovellanos.[94] However, there are good and bad *señores* according to Vaca de Guzmán, which implies that the structure seems not to matter as much as the attitude of the individual. This perspective is quite modern as it reflects the individuality of humans. Despite the ethical dimension involved in the choice of personal behaviour and its social implications, the country of the monkeys is characterized by a social immobility that prevents the lower classes from climbing higher up the social ladder, in which it is the masses that keep the other social classes functioning:

> [A]quella clase de gente que se tiene por incivil y grosera, pero que en la sustancia es el nervio del Estado, el fundamento de las artes y el comercio, y a quien debe el Príncipe su subsistencia, los poderosos su descanso, su lujo y sus relumbrones, las capitales su brillantez. Por último, en el cuerpo místico de la República, así como el Soberano tiene las veces de la cabeza, y las milicias togada y armada la de los brazos, esta clase ejerce la del estómago, oficina desde donde se fomentan todos los miembros, y se les da vigor para que puedan cumplir con las funciones de su cargo.[95]
>
> [The kind of people that is thought to be uncivil and coarse, but in essence is the nerve of the State, the basis of the arts and commerce, and to which the Prince owes his survival, the powerful their rest, luxury, and ostentation, and the capitals their brilliance. Finally, in the mystical body of the Republic, in the same way that the Sovereign serves as the head and the qualified militia and armed militia function as arms, this class works as the stomach, an office from which all the members are encouraged and given the strength to carry out the duties of their posts.]

In relation to the metaphorical representation of society as a human body in the last part of this passage, Claude Morange points out that Enlightenment thinkers often resorted to such a metaphor, which in turn supported the idea of resignation to a social status assigned by divine Providence.[96] It is precisely the dissatisfaction with one's social position that leads to the utopian desire for a better society with equal opportunities for happier citizens.

A controversial perspective about the notion of civilization is implied in the custom of tiger-fighting (equivalent to a Spanish bullfight) in the city of Fastuaria, a place invented by Vaca de Guzmán and identifiable as a parodic version of Seville, according to Escobar and Percival.[97] Although it represents an expression of barbarous behaviour, Enrique attends a tiger-fight, but in accord with his policy of avoiding misjudgements, prefers not to judge the appropriateness of such a foreign tradition. However, he admires the bravery of the contestants. Another public spectacle that is criticized as barbaric is a show of acrobatics observed by Enrique in the city of Eschenobacia. In *Gulliver's Travels*, the danger involved in performing acts to entertain the emperor and gain favour at the English court, such as rope dancing, is highly reprehensible.[98] From a similar point of view, Enrique condemns the fact that the audience at this kind of spectacle enjoys the performance only because of the risk involved in the dangerous behaviour of the acrobats. The supposedly irrational nature of these uncivilized acts unveils the inhumane and unsympathetic instincts of the monkeys, a characteristic that conflicts with Enrique's values.

In his journey across the provinces of the land of the apes, Enrique meets many members of the simian aristocracy, who are often referred to in negative terms. In fact, hereditary nobility is strongly questioned in a dialogue between Tulipán and the mayor for the nobility (*alcalde del Estado noble*), a role labelled in the same way as in Spain. Although both characters recognize the established tradition of the *nobleza de sangre* [nobility of blood], the mayor argues that an inherited status of nobility (*nobleza natural o heredada* [natural or inherited nobility]) can be maintained only through the practice of virtuous actions (*nobleza personal* [personal nobility]) in favour of the community. During the eighteenth century, the criticism of hereditary nobility was a recurring topic in Spain. The theme was treated in searing terms in *El Censor*, especially in the utopian account of the Ayparchontes, which appeared in this periodical and will be analysed in the next chapter.

The anti-utopia that the country of the monkeys has principally signified for Enrique starts to turn into a potential utopia when he arrives in Polypiticon, a city in the southern part of the country, and identifiable as Cadiz, according to Escobar and Percival, because this monkey-city is portrayed as a prosperous bourgeois centre.[99] Unexpectedly enough, the character who welcomes Tulipán and Enrique on behalf of Polypiticon's most distinguished class, called Señor Plátano [Mr Banana], is not a nobleman as in the previous cities that they have visited, but an influential and captivating merchant. When Señor Plátano offers a splendid banquet in his house, Enrique has the opportunity to reassess the aristocratic conceptions about business and businessmen that he has picked up in Simiópolis:

> Mucho me alegré de haber presenciado este banquete, en que pude desimpresionarme de algunas de las necias ideas que tienen y oí varias veces en Simiópolis acerca del comercio y de los individuos a él dedicados en este y otros puertos de aquellos dominios. Estos son unos sujetos [...] criados en el seno de la abundancia, que jamás vieron el rostro a la necesidad y, por tanto, con mucha dificultad pueden dar entrada a pensamientos ruines y villanos, por lo común hijos de la pobreza.[100]

> [I was very glad to have witnessed this banquet, in which I was able to disabuse myself of some of the foolish ideas that they have and that I heard several times in Simiopolis concerning trade and the individuals dedicated to it in this and other ports of those domains. These are subjects [...] raised in the bosom of abundance, who never saw the face of necessity, and, therefore, they can hardly countenance bad and evil thoughts, which are usually the result of poverty.]

It is the existence of such a wealthy and unpretentious lifestyle in a bourgeois setting that makes Enrique think of the possibility that the country of the monkeys may be considered a utopian society. Enrique had criticized aristocrats' unproductive luxurious lives, but the monkey-businessman convinces him that a life of luxury enjoyed by rich merchants like him, who have accumulated wealth thanks to their own industry, is actually beneficial to the country as it contributes to the creation of jobs and the circulation of money.[101]

In addition to this revelation, it is significant that, before returning to England, Enrique is exposed to a discussion between Señor Brusco [Mr Rudeness] and Señor Camueso [Mr Fool] about the confrontation between Simiópolis and a city that is supposed to be its antagonistic version, called Micópolis. While Camueso describes the place as an ideal world, Brusco thinks that it is a copy of the simian republic:

> Encendiéronse en la altercación el famoso Moni-Mico [Camueso], que sostenía que en Micópolis todo era bueno, todo agradable, y todo embeleso de los sentidos; y el cerrado Anti-micancio Brusco, que aseguraba que allí nada había siquiera mediano, nada que no fuese desagradable, y nada que pudiera servir de halago o atractivo, a no ser lo que habían llevado o imitado de Simiópolis.[102]

> [The argument became very heated between the famous Monkey-Mico [Camueso], who held that everything in Micopolis was good, agreeable, and a delight to the senses, and the closed-minded Anti-mico Brusco, who asserted that there was nothing even mediocre there, nothing that was pleasant, and nothing that could be considered flattery or attractive, except for what they had taken or imitated from Simiopolis.]

Thus, a constant interaction of opposing reflections in a context of utopian and dystopian tension can be identified in Vaca de Guzmán's *Suplemento*. The variety of urban spaces and their respective inhabitants and social customs turn this text into a significant satirical portrayal of Spanish society in the reign of Carlos III.

The continuation written by Vaca de Guzmán differs significantly from the translation of Seriman's story in both the literary and ideological aspects. Not only is the prose of the Spanish author more sophisticated, yet dense, but his narration adopts a more socio-critical perspective, as opposed to Seriman's strongly philosophical and anthropological approach — not in vain did the Italian writer translate Alexander Pope's poem *An Essay on Man*. In the light of the substantial tradition of satirical imaginary travel accounts, the *Viajes* serve as a corrective contribution aimed at making Spanish people aware of the increasing decline in their social behaviour and practices, something that is reflected in the superficiality of their questionable civilized customs. In this regard, Vaca de Guzmán's satire seeks to condemn the practice of cosmopolitan habits that may hamper the construction of a Spanish identity. However, far from being mocking or insulting, his satire claims to be 'alma de la rectitud y freno de los vicios' [the soul of righteousness and a restraint on vice].[103] Roberto and Enrique travel through villages and cities letting their own stereotypical beliefs be challenged while trying to interpret manners and opinions in the spirit of a critical reformism guided by reason, one typical of Enlightenment social thought.

Vaca de Guzmán's satirical and didactic objectives do not prevent his story from developing a utopian vision as a counterpart to Enrique's observations of the simian republic. The land of the apes is not a dystopia because there are positive and negative aspects that the visitors observe and comment on. Overall, the work shows the flexibility of the utopian model, which builds on the interplay between utopia and dystopia in the satire of English society presented by Swift in *Gulliver's Travels*. The typical characteristics of the genre are present to make sure that the reader understands the idea that the main model is More's *Utopia*, but the variations are so great both in literary and social terms that Vaca de Guzmán is able to reveal himself as a literary experimenter with a strong satirical bent.

Notes to Chapter 4

1. On Spanish expeditions to *Terra Australis Incognita*, see David Fausett, *Writing the New World: Imaginary Voyages and Utopias of the Great Southern Land* (Syracuse, NY: Syracuse University Press, 1993) and Mercedes Maroto Camino, *Exploring the Explorers: Spaniards in Oceania, 1519–1794* (Manchester: Manchester University Press, 2008).
2. The full title is *Viaggi di Enrico Wanton alle terre incognite australi, ed al paese delle scimmie, ne' quali si spiegano il carattere, li costumi, le scienze, e la polizia di quegli straordinari abitanti. Tradotti da un manoscritto inglese, con figure in rame* [*The Travels of Henry Wanton to Unknown Southern Lands and to the Country of the Monkeys, Which Explains the Character, Customs, Sciences, and Norms of Those Extraordinary Inhabitants. Translated from an English Manuscript, with Illustrations on Copper*]. The Spanish title is *Viajes de Enrique Wanton a las tierras incógnitas australes y al país de las monas, en donde se expresan las costumbres, carácter, ciencias y policía de estos extraordinarios habitantes. Traducidos del idioma inglés al italiano, y de este al español, por D. Joaquín de Guzmán y Manrique. Con láminas que representan algunos pasajes de la historia* [*The Travels of Henry Wanton to Unknown Southern Lands and to the Country of the Monkeys, in Which the Character, Customs, Sciences, and Norms of These Extraordinary Inhabitants Are Expressed. Translated from English into Italian, and Thence into Spanish, by D. Joaquín de Guzmán y Manrique. With Illustrations that Represent Some Passages of the Story*].
3. An important listing of Seriman's editions and their Spanish translations is included in the Appendix C to Donald Maxwell White, *Zaccaria Seriman (1709–1784) and the 'Viaggi di Enrico Wanton': A Contribution to the Study of the Enlightenment in Italy* (Manchester: Manchester University Press, 1961), pp. 141–49.
4. For the representation of the antipodes in *Terra Australis Incognita*, see Alfred Hiatt, 'Terra Australis and the Idea of the Antipodes', in *European Perceptions of Terra Australis*, ed. by Anne M. Scott and others (Farnham, UK, and Burlington, VT: Ashgate, 2011), pp. 9–44.
5. Vaca de Guzmán's translation was acknowledged by nineteenth-century *costumbristas* [writers of literature of manners and customs] such as Mariano José de Larra and Ramón de Mesonero Romanos. Both writers highlight the importance of the *Viajes* as a portrayal of Spanish customs. See Mariano José de Larra, '"Panorama matritense". Cuadros de costumbres de la capital observados y descritos por un Curioso Parlante. Artículo segundo y último', in Mariano José de Larra, *Fígaro: colección de artículos dramáticos, literarios, políticos y de costumbres*, ed. by Alejandro Pérez Vidal (Barcelona: Crítica, 1997), pp. 544–48 (p. 545). See also Ramón de Mesonero Romanos, *Panorama matritense. Cuadros de costumbres de la capital, observados y descritos por un Curioso Parlante*, 3 vols (Madrid: Imprenta de Repullés, 1835–38), I (1835), p. xi; Ramón de Mesonero Romanos, 'Memorias de un setentón', in Ramón de Mesonero Romanos, *Obras de Ramón de Mesonero Romanos*, ed. by Carlos Seco Serrano, 5 vols (Madrid: Atlas, 1967), V, pp. 1–247 (p. 187).
6. José Escobar and Anthony Percival, 'An Italo-Spanish Imaginary Voyage: Zaccaria Seriman (1709–1784) and Joaquín Vaca de Guzmán (1733–1808)', in *The Enlightenment in a Western Mediterranean Context*, ed. by Frederick Gerson, Anthony Percival, and Domenico Pietropaolo (Toronto: Benben Publications, 1984), pp. 87–96 (p. 88).
7. The first Spanish translation of *Gulliver's Travels* by Ramón Máximo Spartal was made from a French edition and published over the period from 1793 to 1800. The announcement of the publication of volume I of the text can be found in the *Gaceta de Madrid*, No. 103, 24 December 1793, pp. 1353–68 (p. 1367). The coincidence of Swift's four voyages in *Gulliver's Travels* being supplemented by an additional voyage in the French translation is a curious parallel with Vaca de Guzmán's supplement to Seriman's work. See Philip Deacon, 'La novela inglesa en la España

del siglo XVIII: fortuna y adversidades', in *Actas del I Congreso Internacional sobre novela del siglo XVIII*, ed. by Fernando García Lara (Almería: Universidad de Almería, 1998), pp. 123–39 (p. 133). Although Swift's text was a bestseller in Europe, the extent of its impact on Spanish readers is unknown because of the lack of information about the number of copies that were printed of each of the two Spanish volumes (Eterio Pajares Infante, *La traducción de la novela inglesa del siglo XVIII* (Vitoria: Portal Education, 2010), p. 382).
8. *Continuación del Memorial Literario, Instructivo y Curioso de la Corte de Madrid*, February 1794, pp. 161–239 (p. 216).
9. Zaccaria Seriman, *Viajes de Enrique Wanton al país de las monas*, trans. by [Gutierre] Joaquín [Vaca] de Guzmán y Manrique, 2 vols, I (Alcalá: Imprenta de María García Briones, 1769), p. 36.
10. Jonathan Swift, 'To Mr Pope', in Jonathan Swift, *Epistolary Correspondence. Letters from September 1725 to May 1732* (Edinburgh: Archibald Constable, 1824), pp. 3–6 (p. 4).
11. This standpoint is close to Kant's view of enlightenment in his famous essay 'Beantwortung der Frage: Was ist Aufklärung?' ['An Answer to the Question: What is Enlightenment?'] (1784). See Immanuel Kant, 'An Answer to the Question: What is Enlightenment?', in Immanuel Kant, *Political Writings*, ed. by Hans Reiss and trans. by H. B. Nisbet (Cambridge: Cambridge University Press, 1991), pp. 54–60.
12. The terms 'monkey' (*mono*) and 'ape' (*simio*) are used interchangeably throughout the translated text, including Vaca de Guzmán's continuation.
13. It should be pointed out that Georges-Louis Leclerc, Count of Buffon, in his monumental work *Histoire naturelle, générale et particulière* [*Natural, General, and Particular History*] (1749–88), formulated a nomenclature for monkeys and apes as part of his definition of species. Buffon rejected any possible lineage between apes and humans.
14. Seriman, *Viajes de Enrique Wanton*, I, pp. 77–78.
15. Jonathan Swift, *Gulliver's Travels*, ed. by Claude Rawson (New York: Oxford University Press, 2005), p. 17.
16. Ibid., pp. 205–57.
17. Seriman, *Viajes de Enrique Wanton*, I, p. 42.
18. See Frederick Gerson, *L'Amitié au XVIIIe siècle* (Paris: La Pensée Universelle, 1974).
19. See Anthony Pagden, *The Enlightenment: And Why It Still Matters* (Oxford: Oxford University Press, 2015), pp. 199–203.
20. David Fausett, *Images of the Antipodes in the Eighteenth Century: A Study in Stereotyping* (Amsterdam: Rodopi, 1994), p. 49.
21. Montaigne was usually referred to as 'Señor de la Montaña' [Mr Mountain] in Spain, especially by Francisco de Quevedo, who was one of the first readers and admirers of the French philosopher in seventeenth-century Spain.
22. Seriman, *Viajes de Enrique Wanton*, I, p. 98.
23. Ibid., p. 29.
24. Victor de Riqueti, Marquis de Mirabeau, *L'Ami des hommes, ou traité de la population* (Avignon: n. pub., 1756), p. 136.
25. See Beatriz Pastor, *Discurso narrativo de la conquista de América: ensayo* (Havana: Casa de las Américas, 1983).
26. Seriman, *Viajes de Enrique Wanton*, I, pp. 16–17.
27. Ibid., p. 17.
28. Paul Ricœur, 'Civilisation universelle et cultures nationales', in Paul Ricœur, *Histoire et vérité* (Paris: Seuil, 1964), pp. 274–88 (pp. 277–78).
29. Ibid., p. 277.
30. Escobar and Percival, 'An Italo-Spanish Imaginary Voyage', p. 89.
31. Seriman, *Viajes de Enrique Wanton*, I, p. xi.
32. In 1760, the Anglo-Irish writer Oliver Goldsmith published a series of essays in the journal *The Public Ledger* under the title of *Chinese Letters*. These essays were later collected as *The Citizen of the World* in 1762. It could be thought that this work had some influence on Vaca de Guzmán's text.
33. Seriman, *Viajes de Enrique Wanton*, I, pp. 8–9.

34. Joaquín Álvarez Barrientos, 'Sobre utopías y viajes imaginarios: Gutierre Joaquín Vaca de Guzmán', in *Historia de la literatura española*, ed. by Ricardo de la Fuente, 50 vols [incomplete] (Madrid: Júcar, 1991–97), XXVIII: *La novela del siglo XVIII* (1991), pp. 131–41 (p. 136).
35. Brett Bowden, *The Empire of Civilization: The Evolution of an Imperial Idea* (Chicago, IL, and London: University of Chicago Press, 2009), p. 99.
36. Álvarez Barrientos, 'Sobre utopías y viajes imaginarios', pp. 140–41.
37. Lorenzo Álvarez, 'Literatura de viajes y utopías', pp. 12–13.
38. Philip Babcock Gove, *The Imaginary Voyage in Prose Fiction* (London: Holland Press, 1961), p. 316.
39. José Escobar, 'Más sobre los orígenes de *civilizar* y *civilización* en la España del siglo XVIII', *Nueva Revista de Filología Hispánica*, 33 (1984), 88–114 (p. 89). See also 'The Defense of Civilization', in Pagden, pp. 204–46.
40. Mirabeau, p. 136.
41. Escobar, pp. 90–91.
42. Suzanne Kiernan, 'The Exotic and the Normative in *Viaggi di Enrico Wanton alle Terre Australi Incognite* by Zaccaria Seriman', *Eighteenth-Century Life*, 26 (2002), 58–77 (p. 61).
43. Ibid.
44. José Escobar and Anthony Percival, 'Viaje imaginario y sátira de costumbres en la España del siglo XVIII: los *Viajes de Enrique Wanton al país de las monas*', in *Aufstieg und Krise der Vernunft: Komparatistische Studien zur Literatur der Aufklärung und des Fin-de-Siècle*, ed. by Hans Hinterhäuser, Michael Rössner, and Birgit Wagner (Vienna: Hermann Böhlaus Nachfolger, 1984), pp. 79–94 (p. 86).
45. Seriman, *Viajes de Enrique Wanton*, I, p. 53.
46. Ibid., p. 108.
47. Ibid., p. 175.
48. Ibid., p. 65.
49. *Diccionario de autoridades*, IV, p. 594.
50. Seriman, *Viajes de Enrique Wanton*, II, pp. 152–53.
51. Ibid., p. 158.
52. Ibid., pp. 158–59.
53. Seriman, *Viajes de Enrique Wanton*, I, p. 59.
54. Ibid., pp. 59–60.
55. Zaccaria Seriman, *Delli viaggi di Enrico Wanton alle terre australi*, 4 vols (London: Tommaso Brewman, 1772), I, p. 66.
56. Seriman, *Viajes de Enrique Wanton*, I, p. 60.
57. Ibid., p. 134.
58. For the subject of English coffee houses and their link to periodicals, see John Brewer, *The Pleasures of the Imagination: English Culture in the Eighteenth Century* (London: HarperCollins, 1997), pp. 34–40.
59. The *Gaceta de Madrid* advertised the publication of volume I in No. 32, 8 August 1769, pp. 257–64 (p. 264); volume II in No. 44, 29 October 1771, pp. 371–82 (p. 382); volume III in No. 9, 3 March 1778, pp. 77–88 (p. 88); and volume IV in No. 35, 30 April 1779, pp. 293–300 (p. 300).
60. White, pp. 141–49; Gove, pp. 314–15.
61. Francisco Aguilar Piñal, *Bibliografía de autores españoles del siglo XVIII*, 10 vols (Madrid: Consejo Superior de Investigaciones Científicas, 1981–2001), VIII (1995), p. 238.
62. José F. Montesinos, *Introducción a una historia de la novela en España en el siglo XIX* (Valencia: Castalia, 1972), p. 246.
63. Apart from the multiple Spanish editions, Seriman's first volume was translated into Portuguese and published in Lisbon in 1799. It seems that the *Viaggi* were not translated into other major languages.
64. Álvarez de Miranda, 'Sobre utopías y viajes imaginarios en el siglo XVIII español', p. 371.
65. Ibid., p. 372.
66. In a 1799 issue of the *Diario de Madrid* [*Madrid Daily*], an avid reader of Vaca de Guzmán's work suggested to the editor of the newspaper that a new edition of the *Viajes* improving the

engravings of the edition by Antonio de Sancha should be published (*Diario de Madrid*, No. 79, 20 March 1799, pp. 321–24 (p. 322)). In fact, an edition containing new illustrations by the Spanish engraver Miguel Gamborino was published by the Imprenta Real [Royal Press] in 1800.
67. Álvarez de Miranda, 'Sobre utopías y viajes imaginarios en el siglo XVIII español', p. 372.
68. Escobar and Percival, 'An Italo-Spanish Imaginary Voyage'; Escobar and Percival, 'Viaje imaginario y sátira de costumbres en la España del siglo XVIII'. This second article is a translation of the English one cited first, although it includes a list of the Spanish editions of the *Viajes* that does not appear in the English version.
69. Claude Morange, 'Variations sur un thème: le monde rural dans le *Suplemento* [...] *de los viages de Enrique Wanton* (1778)', in *Les Voies des Lumières: le monde ibérique au XVIIIe siècle*, ed. by Carlos Serrano, Jean-Paul Duviols, and Annie Molinié (Paris: Presses de l'Université de Paris-Sorbonne, 1998), pp. 79–111 (p. 110).
70. See Nigel Glendinning, 'New Light on the Circulation of Cadalso's *Cartas marruecas* before its First Printing', *Hispanic Review*, 28 (1960), 136–49.
71. Morange, p. 111.
72. It is interesting to note that, in a comparable case, the French philosopher Denis Diderot wrote his *Supplément au voyage de Bougainville* [*A Supplement to Bougainville's Voyage*] inspired by Louis Antoine de Bougainville's *Voyage autour du monde* [*A Voyage Around the World*] (1771). Diderot's text was written in 1772, but officially and posthumously published in 1796. The full title is *Supplément au voyage de Bougainville, ou dialogue entre A et B sur l'inconvénient d'attacher des idées morales à certaines actions physiques qui n'en comportent pas* [*A Supplement to Bougainville's Voyage; or, A Dialogue between A and B on the Drawback of Attaching Moral Ideas to Certain Physical Actions that Bear None*]. In this philosophical dialogue, often read as a primitive utopian text because of its description of Tahiti as a natural society, Diderot emphasizes the necessity of eradicating all actions contrary to moral principles by means of exile and slavery (Denis Diderot, *Supplément au voyage de Bougainville* (Rosny-sous-Bois: Bréal, 2002), p. 72). Diderot questions not only the goodness of nature, but also the very concept of nature, which he defines as a referent in a state subject to constant change. This Heraclitean view of the natural world releases human nature from being judged as intrinsically good or bad, and, consequently, it is deemed as incongruous with any policy of moralizing.
73. [Gutierre] Joaquín [Vaca] de Guzmán y Manrique, *Suplemento, o sea tomo tercero de los viajes de Enrique Wanton al país de las monas* (Madrid: Antonio de Sancha, 1778), p. viii.
74. Ibid., p. vi.
75. Ibid., p. 25.
76. Ibid., p. 167.
77. Ibid., p. 224.
78. [Gutierre] Joaquín [Vaca] de Guzmán y Manrique, *Suplemento, o sea tomo cuarto y último de los viajes de Enrique Wanton al país de las monas* (Madrid: Antonio de Sancha, 1778), p. 23.
79. [Vaca] de Guzmán, *Suplemento, o sea tomo tercero*, p. 135.
80. Ibid., p. 191.
81. Ibid., pp. 29–30.
82. Escobar and Percival, 'An Italo-Spanish Imaginary Voyage', p. 90.
83. [Vaca] de Guzmán, *Suplemento, o sea tomo tercero*, p. 29.
84. Escobar and Percival, 'An Italo-Spanish Imaginary Voyage', p. 91.
85. See Carmen Martín Gaite, *Usos amorosos del XVIII en España* (Madrid: Siglo Veintiuno de España, 1972).
86. [Vaca] de Guzmán, *Suplemento, o sea tomo tercero*, p. 12.
87. Ibid., p. 13.
88. Seriman, *Viajes de Enrique Wanton*, II, pp. 184–85.
89. [Vaca] de Guzmán, *Suplemento, o sea tomo tercero*, p. 50.
90. Seriman, *Delli viaggi di Enrico Wanton*, I, p. 112.
91. Seriman, *Viajes de Enrique Wanton*, I, p. 104.
92. [Vaca] de Guzmán, *Suplemento, o sea tomo tercero*, p. 202.

93. Ibid., p. 96.
94. See Gaspar Melchor de Jovellanos, 'Discurso sobre la necesidad de unir al estudio de la legislación el de nuestra historia y antigüedades', in Gaspar Melchor de Jovellanos, *Obras publicadas e inéditas de Don Gaspar Melchor de Jovellanos*, ed. by Cándido Nocedal, 5 vols (Madrid: Atlas, 1952–63), I (1963), pp. 288–98 (p. 294). On the *régimen señorial* [seigneurial regime], see also Antonio Domínguez Ortiz, 'El ocaso del régimen señorial en la España del siglo XVIII', in Antonio Domínguez Ortiz, *Hechos y figuras del siglo XVIII español* (Madrid: Siglo Veintiuno de España, 1973), pp. 1–62.
95. [Vaca] de Guzmán, *Suplemento, o sea tomo tercero*, pp. 194–95.
96. Morange, p. 107.
97. Escobar and Percival, 'An Italo-Spanish Imaginary Voyage', p. 92.
98. Swift, *Gulliver's Travels*, pp. 33–34.
99. Escobar and Percival, 'An Italo-Spanish Imaginary Voyage', p. 92.
100. [Vaca] de Guzmán, *Suplemento, o sea tomo cuarto y último*, p. 117.
101. This viewpoint can be related to Bernard Mandeville's *The Fable of the Bees; or, Private Vices, Public Benefits* (1714), which conceives of luxury and other vices as being necessary for public prosperity and welfare. For the debate on luxury in Spain, see Hans-Joachim Lope, '¿Mal moral o necesidad económica? La polémica acerca del lujo en la Ilustración española', in *La secularización de la cultura española en el Siglo de las Luces: actas del Congreso de Wolfenbüttel*, ed. by Manfred Tietz and Dietrich Briesemeister (Wiesbaden: Harrassowitz, 1992), pp. 129–50. See also Christopher J. Berry, *The Idea of Luxury: A Conceptual and Historical Investigation* (Cambridge: Cambridge University Press, 1994).
102. [Vaca] de Guzmán, *Suplemento, o sea tomo cuarto y último*, p. 162.
103. [Vaca] de Guzmán, *Suplemento, o sea tomo tercero*, p. 55.

CHAPTER 5

Utopianism in the *Monarquía de los Ayparchontes* and Related Periodical Texts of the 1780s

A Spanish utopian text first published in 1784–85, which will be referred to here as the *Monarquía de los Ayparchontes*,[1] joins *Sinapia* and the *Viajes de Enrique Wanton* in the use of the imaginary southern continent, or *Terra Australis Incognita*, as the setting for its utopian story. Unlike Seriman's more novelistic work, the utopia of the Ayparchontes is fundamentally the depiction of an alternative political and religious system, which relates it to the measured reformist programme of *Sinapia*. More importantly, what distinguishes this anonymous utopian account from the texts analysed in Chapters 3 and 4 is its inclusion in the pages of *El Censor*, the most combative periodical of late eighteenth-century Spain.[2]

Without having a specific title, the story of the Ayparchontes is split between three non-consecutive *discursos* [essays] in the journal, of which the first two (Discurso 61 and Discurso 63) were published in 1784, and the final one (Discurso 75) in 1785, after a break resulting from a clash with the state censorship system of the Council of Castile. As is the case with many of the *discursos* that comprise *El Censor*, the author of this utopian narrative is unfortunately unknown. Leaving aside the intractable issue of the authorship, the purpose of this chapter is to examine the significance of the *Monarquía de los Ayparchontes* within the Spanish utopian tradition and to explore its relationship with other literary texts and publications of the period. However, before dealing with the text in question, some background details concerning the importance and impact of *El Censor* as well as the use of literary devices in some of its essays are required.

Radicalism and the Literary Imagination in *El Censor*

El Censor was first published in Madrid in 1781 and continued to appear weekly, though with two substantial suspensions, until its final closure by the Council of Castile in 1787. Modelled to some degree on *The Spectator* — the English daily paper founded and edited by Joseph Addison and Richard Steele, which lasted from 1711 to 1714 — the Spanish publication comprised 167 serious and often satirical *discursos* that criticized a wide variety of aspects of Spanish life and institutions, which makes it an outstanding example of Spanish Enlightenment writing. The editors, Luis García del Cañuelo and Luis Marcelino Pereira, were lawyers approved by the Royal Councils (*abogados de los Reales Consejos*) who, from the launch of the journal, showed themselves cautious in revealing their identities and those of their collaborators, perhaps due to potential hostility generated by the frankness with which their publication tackled features of Spanish society.[3]

In relation to the focus and openness that firmly characterized *El Censor*, even after its first two suspensions (in 1781 and 1784),[4] Juan Sempere y Guarinos highlights the unprecedented critical nature of the periodical in comparison with previous ones,[5] such as *El Pensador*: 'Su autor no ha mudado de tono en los posteriores [discursos] a la prohibición. La misma entereza, la misma libertad se observa ahora en ellos que en sus principios' [Its author has not changed tone in the ones [essays] published after the prohibition. The same integrity, the same freedom is present in them as in the first ones].[6] What turns out to be somewhat unexpected is the fact that, despite publications such as *El Censor* being subject to censorship, a 1785 *Real Orden* [Royal Order] supported their objectives: '[C]ontribuyen en gran manera a difundir en el público muchas verdades o ideas útiles, y a combatir por medio de la crítica honesta los errores y preocupaciones que estorban el adelantamiento en varios ramos' [They contribute greatly to disseminating many truths or useful ideas among the public and to combatting, by means of honest criticism, the errors and prejudices that hinder progress in various fields].[7]

Although the editors used pseudonyms (Luis Castrigo and Mariano Heredia) to keep their anonymity when signing official documentation, the Spanish authorities were aware of who the persons responsible for the daring publication were.[8] However, the varied writing styles of the *discursos* suggest a collaborative work between the editors and other authors, a suggestion first put forward by Alberto Gil Novales.[9] According to José Miguel Caso González, the conjecture about the multiple authorship follows from the fact that the reports of the censors make reference to the stylistic changes from one essay to the next. Hypothesizing further, Caso González believes that the intellectual circle surrounding the Countess of Montijo was involved in the writing of *El Censor*. What cannot be denied is that essays known to come from the pens of Gaspar de Jovellanos, Félix María Samaniego, and Juan Meléndez Valdés appeared anonymously in its pages. The most significant objective of this group of enlightened thinkers was to change the mentality and practices of Spaniards.[10]

Irrespective of the names behind individual *discursos*, what is certain is that Cañuelo and Pereira were well respected among the Spanish intellectual elite. Their bold spirit and example inspired the appearance of other periodicals such as *El Apologista Universal* [*The Universal Apologist*] (1786–88) by the Augustinian monk Pedro Centeno, *El Corresponsal del Censor* [*The Censor's Correspondent*] (1786–88) by Manuel Rubín de Celis, and *El Observador* [*The Observer*] (1787–90) by José Marchena. It is significant that a pamphlet was published defending the aims of *El Censor*, namely the *Diálogo crítico-político sobre si conviene desengañar al público de sus errores y preocupaciones, y si los que son capaces de ello arriesgarán algo en hacerlo* [*A Critical-Political Dialogue about Whether It Is Appropriate to Disabuse the Public of its Errors and*

Prejudices, and about Whether Those Who Are Capable of It Will Be at Risk in Doing So] (1786) by Joaquín Medrano de Sandoval, a text that endorsed the periodical's critical attitude towards religion in Spain.[11]

Various fictional resources, including utopian frameworks, may have been used by *El Censor* in order to avoid problems with the censorship system, of which the periodical was repeatedly a victim, but it is also legitimate to probe such a narrative impulse in relation to the publication of utopian fictions and imaginary travel literature throughout the Enlightenment period as techniques for stimulating thought about social and political change. Interestingly enough, this view is supported by the fact that, after the final governmental suspension of *El Censor* in 1787, Cañuelo started work on a text called *Viaje al mundo inteligible* [*A Voyage to the Intelligible World*], but the introduction to that text was censored because of its attempt to discredit the foundations of the sciences in trying to establish a new metaphysics.[12] As a result, the author was unable to finish the work.

Contrary to the assumption that utopias or dreams deal with illusions, the anonymous voice of *El Censor* claims that the content of the periodical conforms to the precepts of reason as the only means of carrying out an effective critical examination of Spanish society. In Discurso 1, the narrator introduces himself as a martyr to reason: '[T]odo lo que se aparta un poco de la razón me lastima; el más pequeño extravío de la regla y del orden me causa un tedio mortal' [Everything that diverges even slightly from reason offends me; the smallest deviation from the rule and from order causes me acute tedium].[13] Nevertheless, far from being limited to the criticism of social customs, *El Censor* sought to question many aspects of the existing socio-political system. This is precisely the purpose of the *Monarquía de los Ayparchontes*, as the analysis below will attempt to demonstrate.

In accordance with the literary trends of the time, *El Censor* also includes, in parallel to the utopia of the Ayparchontes, five *discursos* (89, 90, 101, 106, and 107) about the dystopian life in a place called Cosmosia (1786) and two dreams that comprise Discurso 50 (1783) and Discurso 161 (1787). Other literary forms such as apocryphal letters or dialogues are the vehicle for conveying a strong reformist attitude towards the political status quo. By appealing to the didactic function of fiction in Discurso 161, the author praises the ability to dream methodically, a talent shared by the enlightened members of his family. Being called a dreamer is no longer an insult, but a goal to achieve.[14] Dreams and the power of the imagination can be used as a constructive force to effectively question the socio-political system and offer a more rational and just state of affairs. The Enlightenment utopia appropriates the intellectual function of the dream, but uses it to portray a better everyday world instead of distorting or escaping from the conventional restraints of society.[15] In this respect, the utopian approach aims at exploring and understanding better the mechanisms underlying socio-political processes.

The Narrative Techniques of the *Monarquía de los Ayparchontes*

The narrative framework that links the three parts of the utopia of the Ayparchontes[16] is complex in terms of the interaction between the voice of the traveller (or the anonymous author of the manuscript containing the utopian story), the voice of the fictional editor of the traveller's story (who assumes the role of *el censor*), and the potential readership of this particular episode of *El Censor*. In Discurso 61, the editor claims that he bought the manuscript from a bookseller in the Spanish court in 1781. However, the fact that the description of such an interesting unexplored country, as the land of the Ayparchontes appears to be, has been unpublished until then makes him believe that the story is only fiction, which is reinforced by the fact that the author/traveller does not specify the exact geographical location of the country described. By expressing two incompatible points of view, the editor provokes the reader to think and decide for him or herself.

The manuscript, in fact, contains the description of several nations visited by the traveller, but the editor decides to reproduce only the most relevant parts of the account concerning the country of the Ayparchontes. At the end of Discurso 61, the editor justifies the interruption of his transcription by stating that the story is long and that it will be continued in a future *discurso*. This break allows the narration to introduce an amusing anecdote at the beginning of Discurso 63: an anxious reader goes to a bookshop that sells the works of the supposed editor to buy the continuation of the story, but the customer becomes angry when he realizes that Discurso 62 does not continue the story; the editor happens to be in the bookshop when this scene occurs and decides to publish the rest of the text that same week, motivated not so much by the reader's complaint as by the interest of the ideas expressed in the manuscript.

Finally, in Discurso 75, published a year after the appearance of Discurso 61, the editor announces that he is going to copy another passage of the manuscript, without giving any details of the nature or the relevance of the section to be transcribed. The omission of a narrative context in which to present the new passage can be understood as a neutral way of addressing the tricky topic of religion that is going to be treated in this final instalment. When considered in retrospect, it is clear that those responsible for the publication of *El Censor* could not have foreseen such a large gap in time between the publication of the first two instalments of the story of the Ayparchontes and the concluding one. For that, one has to place the blame with the Council of Castile for suspending the appearance of the journal after Discurso 67, giving rise to a wait of seventeen months before allowing the publication of Discurso 68 and the final sequence of issues. However, it is noteworthy that the periodical was allowed to continue and that the editors felt emboldened to publish the final part of the Ayparchontes utopia, which happens to be the most ambitious component of the whole story because of its questioning of the powers and privileges of the Church.

The System of Meritocracy

In Discurso 61, having recourse to the standard utopian image of the shipwrecked traveller in the mysterious southern region, the author introduces the description of the nation of the Ayparchontes, whose monarchical system has many similarities with Spain, according to the editor of the story who acts as *el censor*. Since the narrative technique is that of the found manuscript, the account is therefore filtered for the reader through the perspective and judgements of the editor. The simplicity with which the author presents the description of the country implies its authenticity, but the fact that such an important discovery has remained unknown for so long makes the editor doubt whether the story is true.

Despite the supposed shortcomings of the manuscript, the journal editor gives a brief summary of the nature of the piece of text that he is going to transcribe, material that he considers worthy of interest to his readers: 'Es una descripción moral y política de las tierras australes incógnitas' [It is a moral and political description of the unknown southern lands].[17] In both social and political terms, the objectives of the description of the country of the Ayparchontes are similar to those of *Sinapia*. In fact, both imaginary nations can be seen as different versions of Spain, even though their utopian territories correspond to random and arbitrary places. In addition to the uncertainty about the plausibility of the narration contained in the found manuscripts, the fictional and anonymous editors of both utopian accounts stress the fact that the societies depicted are capable of awakening the curiosity of their readership because of a close resemblance to the reality of Spain.

Using a Socratic dialogue technique, the fictional author (*el Autor*) of the manuscript, who is the unnamed Western traveller or visitor, and Zeblitz, an enlightened native of the land of the Ayparchontes, initiate a question-and-answer conversation about the differences between the social structure of the unnamed nation of the shipwrecked traveller and that of the remote southern country, which is defined as a vast empire. Zeblitz's community is divided into three social classes: 'Todos los habitantes de aquel vasto imperio están [...] comprendidos en tres clases: o son nobles, o plebeyos, o infames' [All the inhabitants of that vast empire are [...] included in three classes: they are either nobles, plebeians, or despicable].[18] Each class corresponds to specific criteria, with the nobility being the most cultivated group, thanks to which the society of the Ayparchontes is characterized as 'sumamente culta' [highly educated].[19]

In opposition to the recovery of the idyllic concept of the good savage in the project of a utopian society, the Ayparchontes' world is a highly civilized reality in which the pristine and virtuous nature of primitive man has no functionality at all. The category of despicable citizens comprises the lawbreakers who commit the most serious crimes, but are nevertheless supposed to have a certain level of education. Since such a marginalized status is always acquired by one's actions in the society of the Ayparchontes, the condition of infamy is not inherited by the descendants of the criminals. Furthermore, convicts can redeem their infamy by doing useful jobs such as working as hangmen or soldiers. They are so eager to amend their contemptible behaviour that their service to the patriotic cause results in a rise of the nation's splendour. In other words, the despicable inhabitants, once rehabilitated, are partly responsible for the magnificence of this utopian empire. The attribution of a key role to the lowest stratum of their society reveals the advanced state of civilization that dominates the ideal monarchy of the Ayparchontes.

The explanation of the most inferior class's constitution is the preamble to the argument that meritocracy is the only valid and fair system to determine the belonging of individuals to a particular social group. Social position must be based on merit rather than on inheritance.[20] Thus, the possibility of social mobility is always present in the formation of any class, especially that of nobles and plebeians. Zeblitz explains that meritorious acts are the only measure used to assign a profession to a plebeian over a noble:

> Los empleos [...] y las dignidades no deben darse al mérito presunto, sino al acreditado. Y hallándose este en igual grado en un noble y un plebeyo, no debe ser preferido aquel sino este que por necesidad tuvo menos facilidad y mayores estorbos que vencer para adquirirlo.[21]
>
> [Posts [...] and honours should not be given on presumed merit, but to worth that is deserved. And since this merit exists in the same degree in a nobleman as in a plebeian, the former should not be preferred to the latter, who, by necessity, had less ease and greater obstacles to overcome in order to acquire it.]

The fact that a plebeian faces more difficulties in getting an appropriate job gives their efforts more weight and credit. Because a concrete difference between nobles and plebeians is not seen in terms of work skills, the common people have access to the same positions to which members of the nobility aspire.

Plebeians are basically artisans, farmers, or merchants, and all these occupations are compatible with the rank of aristocracy. For its part, the nobility is divided into six levels, each of which corresponds to a specific degree of merit that is not inherited but awarded according to the type of occupation performed, a system that has certain logical limitations: a first-class nobleman will necessarily have second-class children and third-class grandchildren, and so on. In consequence, some descendants of nobles are born with the status of plebeians. Noblewomen change their condition depending on the social rank of their husbands, a feature that denotes the patriarchal character of the Ayparchontes' society. In any case, the possibility of getting a job in a competitive environment is the only way of ascending socially. However, it is possible to reach a higher social status through special privileges granted by the prince in return for exceptional services rendered. This, nevertheless, bears a great resemblance to the situation in Spain and other European monarchies. Those rewarded with access to the highest level of society benefit from exclusive civil prerogatives.

Compared with the functioning of the social hierarchy in his country — Spain, presumably — the Western traveller finds the Ayparchontes' system very strange, and, in his turn, Zeblitz is surprised at the illogical and unjust hereditary principles of the nobility in the traveller's homeland. By basing his viewpoint on a detailed argumentation, Zeblitz rejects the premise that the descendants of an honourable and hardworking nobleman, who may themselves be only distant relatives of the original benefactor, are automatically entitled to enjoy the same prestigious reputation. It should not be assumed that all the members of a noble family must be virtuous and, therefore, worthy of recognition. In contrast with this ideology surrounding the policies of the nobility in the traveller's country, the Ayparchontes' social doctrine first prioritizes the advantages of the original nobleman and, secondly, those of his close relatives. In spite of his sharp criticism of such an incoherent system,[22] Zeblitz acknowledges that it can act as an incentive for citizens to try to reach the highest positions in order to pass on privileges to their offspring.

What equates the conception of aristocracy in both Zeblitz's and the visitor's society is the existence of the nobility as a political support to the Crown, and hence as a kind of necessary component. However, the nobility is not an essential piece in the machinery of the Ayparchontes' monarchy because the aristocrats see themselves as not being required to contribute to the progress of society since they will always keep the same social status and fortune without making any effort. On the contrary, plebeians are the ones who are most encouraged to progress. In the traveller's opinion, idleness may be associated with the majority of noblemen, but they are still an important part of socio-political life. They act as a link or intermediary between the prince and the plebeians,[23] and they also serve as an instrument of resistance against despotism:

> [L]os más de nuestros nobles parten toda su vida, como hacía un europeo bastante célebre llamado *la Fontaine*,[24] la mitad en dormir bien y la otra en no hacer nada. Mas no por eso dejan de ser muy útiles a la sociedad. La perpetuidad en la nobleza es una cosa, en el sentir de nuestros políticos, tan esencial en una monarquía que yo no sé cómo sin ella subsiste la vuestra [la monarquía de los Ayparchontes]. La nobleza es una cadena que une la plebe con el soberano, y al mismo tiempo que es el más firme apoyo del trono, es una barrera la más fuerte contra el despotismo.[25]

> [Most of our nobility divide their lives, as did a very famous European man called *La Fontaine*, by sleeping well half the time and doing nothing in the other half. But that does not prevent them from being very useful to society. The survival of the nobility is something, in our politicians' view, so essential to the monarchy that I do not know how yours [the Ayparchontes' monarchy] survives without it. Nobility is a chain that links the masses to the sovereign, and while it provides the strongest support for the throne, it is also the strongest barrier against despotism.]

Merit and virtue are the sole determinants of social success and influence. As Carlos III laid down in 1775 in law 21, book 6, title 1 of the *Novísima recopilación de las leyes de España* [*The Newest Compilation of the Laws of Spain*],

> En las consultas que hiciere la Cámara sobre mercedes de títulos de Castilla, tendrá presente haber reparado en algunas que los pretendientes fundan su mérito en su nobleza y alianzas, o en las de sus antepasados, sin probar ni alegar méritos propios ni servicios personales; y que no tengo por conveniente se hagan dignos de tan alta distinción de títulos de Castilla los que no me hayan servido por sus personas y al público.[26]

> [In the consultations that the House might make about the concession of titles

of Castile, it will notice some in which the applicants base their merits on nobility and connections, or on those of their ancestors, without proving or claiming merits of their own or personal services; and that I do not consider it appropriate that those who have not served me and the public should become worthy of such a high distinction as the titled nobility of Castile.]

Carlos III's reformist agenda certainly sought to dignify some occupations of the masses, allowing plebeians to occupy municipal posts. As stated in a *Real Cédula* [Royal Decree] of 1783 (law 8, book 8, title 23 of the *Novísima recopilación de las leyes de España*),

> Declaro que no solo el oficio de curtidor, sino también las demás artes y oficios de herrero, sastre, zapatero, carpintero y otros a este modo son honestos y honrados, que el uso de ellos no envilece la familia ni la persona del que los ejerce, ni la inhabilita para obtener los empleos municipales de la República [...], y que tampoco han de perjudicar las artes y oficios para el goce y prerrogativas de la hidalguía.[27]

> [I declare that not only the occupation of tanner, but also other arts and crafts such as blacksmith, tailor, shoemaker, carpenter, and the like are honest and honourable, that the exercise of them demeans neither the family nor the person who carries them out, nor does it even disqualify them from obtaining municipal posts in the Republic [...], nor should exercising arts and crafts be an obstacle to the enjoyment and prerogatives of nobility either.]

The same statute confirms the assignation of social distinctions to the lowest classes based on personal achievement. It can be said, then, that the socio-juridical norms of the land of the Ayparchontes are a utopian improvement of the legal measures contained in some of the reforms of Carlos III. This ideological interconnection turns the fictitious monarchy of the Ayparchontes into a more advanced version of the existing Spanish socio-political system.

The Social Legislation

The subsequent Discurso 63 deals with the implementation of a legal framework to control the power of the nobility. Reaffirming the implicit postulate of Discurso 61, the epigraph for the new Discurso is a verse from one of Juvenal's satires that reads: 'Nobilitas sola est, atque unica, virtus. [...] La virtud es la única nobleza' [Virtue is the only nobility],[28] a maxim that equates social rank to virtuous behaviour, fostering the empowerment of disadvantaged groups through the practice of outstanding actions because virtue is the only true nobility.[29] In this sense, the *Monarquía de los Ayparchontes* echoes *Utopia*'s understanding of virtue, a concept that was commented on earlier in this book.

Zeblitz warns the traveller that appropriate legislation applicable to both plebeians and aristocrats is necessary in order to avoid undesirable outcomes resulting from civic idleness and to allocate capable citizens to state positions. Nobility is hereditary in both Zeblitz and the visitor's reality, but the presence of vices and the incompetence of people who form the nation's workforce are the two main factors that differentiate the essence of that social class in their respective societies. Zeblitz's perspective demonstrates the constant confrontation between an 'us' (*nosotros*) and a 'you' (*vosotros*), emphasizing the better administration of the same parallel social model by the Ayparchontes. The apparent didactic dialogue that constitutes the utopian story is rather an instructive account of the efficiency of the Ayparchontes' system and of how that system has been distorted by governmental practices in the visitor's country. In this regard, Ismael Piñera Tarque highlights the narrative counterpoint of the two characters' thoughts and the inability of the fictional author/traveller to refute Zeblitz's arguments:

> [E]n la confrontación entre el Autor y el sabio nativo Zeblitz, éste parece imponerse sobre el primero, quien no encuentra oposición a sus argumentos sobre la idoneidad del mundo Ayparchonte y sus críticas al sistema europeo, pese a que le parezcan discutibles.[30]

> [In the confrontation between the Author and the native sage Zeblitz, the latter seems to impose himself on the former, who cannot summon counter-arguments concerning the suitability of the Ayparchonte world and Zeblitz's criticism of the European system, even though they appear to be questionable to the Author.]

In view of the failure to formulate counter-arguments or impose his judgements over those of his instructor-friend, the foreign traveller ironically hopes that European politicians will prove the pointlessness of Zeblitz's utopian vision of society. Such a frustrated dialogue acts as a textual strategy, but it is also an indicator of the author's discomfort with his social reality. According to Zeblitz, two serious consequences derive from the careless administrative programme that the author vainly tries to defend: the oppression of the masses and the disrepute of the nobility. The discrediting of the elite class derives from the fact that virtually every citizen is capable of acquiring a noble rank. That is, nobility becomes common, and this popularization may lead to its progressive decline as a symbol of social and personal importance and value. In contrast with this scenario, the Ayparchontes' utopian society strives to reduce the permanence of noble families as a way of avoiding potential corruption, although noblemen are always highly regarded. By using again the linguistic play of *nosotros* versus *vosotros*, Zeblitz states:

> Entre nosotros podrá extinguirse o disminuirse la nobleza de una casa, pero los nobles en general se conservan siempre en un mismo grado de estimación. Pero entre vosotros no pudiendo salir la nobleza de la familia en que una vez entró, e introduciéndose cada día en otras nuevas, no puede menos de hacerse despreciable por su vulgaridad.[31]

> [The nobility of a house may be extinguished or diminished among us, but nobles in general are always entitled to the same degree of esteem. But among you nobility cannot be separated from the family that it once belonged to, and, in its possession by other new families every day, it can only be despised because of it being common.]

Antonio Elorza's critical synthesis of the three utopian *discursos* underscores the transformative intention of the story of the Ayparchontes regarding the socio-political redefinition of the aristocracy: '[L]a descripción de la sociedad en los

Ayparchontes muestra una cierta estratificación en que el *status* adquirido prevalece sobre el adscrito. Sin desaparecer, la nobleza se ve relativizada, transformada, terminando por ser accesible para todo ciudadano' [The description of the society of the Ayparchontes shows a certain stratification in which acquired status prevails over the ascribed one. Without disappearing, nobility is relativized and transformed, ending up being accessible to all citizens].[32] Seen in this light, the utopia of the Ayparchontes is a clear condemnation of the drawbacks of a useless nobility based on an absurd longing for power, especially economic power. In the European world, society itself is the dangerous agent that leads to the incongruous accumulation of wealth and the empowerment of the aristocratic class, while, at the same time, stimulates the loss of social exclusivity of the elite by democratizing access to the benefits of the upper classes. The utopia of the Ayparchontes, then, adopts a critical attitude that differs from the satirical angle that often defines the standpoint of *El Censor*. Instead of concealing social criticism by means of irony, the editor transcribes a story that gradually develops into a doctrinal attack on the mismanagement of Spain's rulers.

The Religious Organization

As a complement to the description of the Ayparchontes' utopian social order, Discurso 75 sets out the complex structure of their religious system. With a gap for the original readers of seventeen months after the beginning of the story, and unlike the other two *discursos* in which dialogue is the narrative vehicle, this last essay is a direct narration from the fictional author's point of view. The introductory outline is intended to be a favourable overview of the Ayparchontes' religion:

> Los Ayparchontes son en extremo amantes de su religión que, si se ha de dar fe a sus historias, conservan desde la más remota antigüedad. Aunque se ven en ella muchas prácticas y creencias supersticiosas, no se hallan aquellas monstruosidades que en la de casi todos los pueblos entre los cuales no ha rayado la luz de la revelación.[33]

> [The Ayparchontes are extreme lovers of their religion, which, if their historical accounts are taken as true, they have preserved since the remotest antiquity. Although it reveals evidence of many superstitious practices and beliefs, one does not find the monstrosities that are present in almost all peoples for whom the light of revelation has yet to dawn.]

Since the author does not say *revelación divina* [divine revelation], this supposes a certain ambiguity that could allow the reader to imagine that the narrator is referring to another form of enlightenment. Moreover, the judgement that many of their religious practices were superstitious but not excessively irrational neutralizes the impression of a barbarous nation expressed, at the beginning of Discurso 63, by the impatient reader who was expecting the continuation of the story:

> ¡Pues no es bueno que después de haberme tenido ocho días enteros con la mayor impaciencia del mundo [...] solo por ver si el Bachiller de Zeblitz tenía aún que responder a la solidísima objeción hecha contra el ridículo sistema de

nobleza de aquellos bárbaros, se nos venga ahora el Señor Censor tratando una materia totalmente inconexa!³⁴

[It is not good that, after having waited eight whole days with the greatest impatience in the world [...] only to see if the graduate Zeblitz was to respond to the very strong objection made against the ridiculous system of nobility of those barbarians, Mr Censor now comes out with a totally unrelated matter!]

Not only does the author not perceive the Ayparchontes as an uncivilized people, but he also attributes to them a firm adherence to rational morality, even though their belief system is not a true religion because for him it is clear that Catholicism is the only acceptable faith: '[P]or lo que toca a la moral, [su religión] es bastantemente conforme a los dictámenes de la razón. En una palabra, entre todas las falsas religiones, no creo haya otra menos extravagante' [As far as morality is concerned, it [their religion] is quite consistent with the dictates of reason. In a word, among all false religions, I do not believe there is another less extravagant one].³⁵ This remark seems to have been designed to appease the Inquisition's censors.

The Ayparchontes' Church has a pyramidal hierarchy in which the base consists of ministers called *Zymbloyes*. Each *Zymbloy*, helped by two assistants, runs a temple that corresponds to one hundred families. For every two or three hundred *Zymbloyes*, there is a *Tuleytz*, who is responsible for observing their behaviour and the carrying out of their duties. The *Tuleytzes* are in charge of the education of young seminarians and are helped by twenty or thirty *Zymleytzes*, advisors elected from among the oldest and wisest *Zymbloyes*. The highest authority is represented by a *Kastuleytz*, whose task is to supervise the conduct of the *Tuleytzes*. He is a supreme *Tuleytz* and the greatest priest of the nation. Within this hierarchy, the different levels have obvious equivalences in the Catholic Church in Spain.

In the Ayparchontes' Church, all priests are called *Tosbloyes*. They have very specific functions within society: they direct religious ceremonies, offer sacrifices, and act as persuasive arbitrators between litigious citizens, especially in religious matters. They may punish a citizen with exclusion from religious gatherings, but this penalty does not mean the loss of civil rights. In general, then, they instruct, persuade, and admonish. *Tosbloyes* do not have administrative jurisdiction or special privileges in the political sphere, in clear contrast to Spain. Rather, they are subject to all social obligations provided that these are compatible with their ministry. They are not allowed to obtain civil employment or accept donations — which could be interpreted as an attack on the clergy occupying positions in universities in Europe, as well as on Church mendicant orders — because the government gives them sufficient income to maintain a basic, though frugal, existence. Moreover, to become a *Tosbloy*, one must give up one's personal fortune. As to the situation in eighteenth-century Spain, the state allowed the Church to collect tithes as well as to own and inherit property such as land and buildings, which both brought in income in the form of rent.

With regard to economic matters in the ethical code of the Ayparchontes' Church, it has to be emphasized that the Spanish Church was a most powerful economic institution in the eighteenth century until the process of disentailment began in 1798. The wealth of the eighteenth-century Spanish Church rested on a complex variety of resources such as legacies, donations, income from agricultural property, and land tenure in urban areas.[36] However, this material prosperity was fragmented in its distribution: 'Revenues produced by real estate, the tithe, *censos* [rents], and other sources can be classified as Church income, but this simply means the accumulated income of a multitude of ecclesiastical institutions — bishoprics, monasteries, convents, and charitable and pious associations'.[37] The frugality prevailing in the religious system of the Ayparchontes can be thus interpreted as an indirect critical judgement on the wealth of the Spanish Church.[38]

Naturally, the author/visitor finds the Ayparchontes' ecclesiastical legislation very strange and inadmissible:

> Mis lectores concebirán fácilmente cuán extraño se me haría este sistema, y sobre todo, cuán admirable me parecía esta contraposición entre la opinión pública y la ley, y un sacerdocio sobre falso, tan poco protegido por la autoridad pública, y por otra parte tan venerado de todos los ciudadanos en particular.[39]
>
> [My readers will easily understand how strange this system would be to me, and, above all, how admirable this opposition between public opinion and the law seemed, and a priesthood not only false, but also so little protected by public authority, and, on the other hand, so revered by all citizens in particular.]

Contrary to the belief of the traveller that this religious system restricts or neglects the status of the Church, Zeblitz asserts that, through the elaborate organization of the clergy, the government shows absolute respect for the Church and its members. The state protects the integrity of the Church's moral authority by keeping it away from privileges and richness. Otherwise, luxury and material comfort would attract worldly and avaricious people who, in turn, would corrupt those who want to dedicate their lives to the priesthood:

> El lujo, la avaricia y toda suerte de desórdenes se introducirían entre los que le profesasen [el sacerdocio]; y aquellos mismos que no con otro fin entrasen en él que la felicidad de su espíritu serían bien presto corrompidos ya por el ejemplo de los demás, ya por la virtud casi irresistible de las riquezas y la opulencia.[40]
>
> [Luxury, greed, and all kinds of disorder would be introduced among those who exercise it [the priesthood]; and those who entered into it for no other purpose than the happiness of their spirit would be promptly corrupted by the example of others or by the almost irresistible virtue of wealth and opulence.]

This passage reflects the author's opinion of the effects of the fiscal situation of the Church in Spain. What is implicitly criticized are those intending to make a career in the Church who are attracted to ecclesiastical service by Church wealth and social status rather than for spiritual reasons. Zeblitz corroborates the disastrous consequences that a religious system corrupted by opulence can cause when he describes the situation that prevailed during a 'dark' period of the Ayparchontes' history: 'En unos tiempos en que la luz que había iluminado a los primeros siglos de nuestra monarquía se había del todo oscurecido' [At a time when the light that had illuminated the first centuries of our monarchy had been completely obscured].[41] This terrible period could be understood as the history of the Spanish Church after the coming of the Habsburg dynasty. However, Zeblitz adds that a good king finally came to the throne and restored religion to its primitive state and purity. The portrayal of the king in question may be interpreted as a reference to Carlos III, who realizes the importance of the situation of the priesthood: 'Es muy justo, solía él decir, que quien sirve al santuario viva de él. Que viva, pero no en el deleite, no en el fausto y la opulencia' [It is very right, he used to say, that whoever serves the sanctuary lives off it. May he live, but not in pleasure, not in splendour and opulence].[42] The allusion to a dark moment in Spanish history can be regarded in terms of a contrast with the metaphor of light in the Enlightenment period.

El Censor disapproves of the fact that the Church, via subsidiary institutions such as the Inquisition, exerts control over Enlightenment thought in Spain because that would imply the development of an ideology contrary to the promotion of the arts and sciences, in spite of the intellectual formation of priests. As Francisco Sánchez-Blanco argues, 'La reforma del clero con que simpatiza *El Censor* consiste en que los sacerdotes se dediquen a predicar bien, abandonen los asuntos mundanos y no anatematicen a los que buscan la verdad, tachándoles de ateos e impíos' [The reform of the clergy *The Censor* sympathizes with consists in priests dedicating themselves to preaching well, abandoning worldly matters, and not anathematizing those who seek the truth, labelling them as atheists and heathens].[43] In fact, the reformist nature of Discurso 75 caused the text to be prohibited by the Inquisition, which was not the case with Discurso 61 or Discurso 63.[44] The desire to reform the clergy and the censorship role that this position entails would validate the hypothesis of Caso González that *El Censor* was, in some measure, supported by Carlos III, especially since it is known that Cañuelo received a pension from the King beginning at approximately the time when the publication of the periodical started.[45] Because Carlos III could have planned to implement reforms in the Church, encouraging the project of *El Censor* would have been in accord with his beliefs. Caso González speculates that the periodical was produced in hitherto unclear circumstances in which a pool of anonymous writers was committed to supporting the plans of the monarch:

> Todo lleva a suponer que nuestro periódico estaba programado, dirigido y redactado por un grupo de ilustrados [...] que ocupaban puestos de relieve en las instituciones de gobierno, y que, si no fue impulsado ni protegido por órganos oficiales, fue una iniciativa de Carlos III, o una iniciativa ajena patrocinada por el Rey.[46]
>
> [Everything leads one to suppose that our periodical was planned, directed, and written by a group of enlightened thinkers [...] who occupied prominent positions in government institutions, and that, if it was not promoted or protected by official bodies, it was an initiative of Charles III or an initiative of others sponsored by the King.]

Aspects such as the absence of Church wealth and the return to the original impoverished state of the priesthood led Richard Herr to indicate that 'Cañuelo was echoing the arguments of the Jansenist clergy, who were friends of the Enlightenment and partisans of reform of the Church by royal order'.[47] Nevertheless, as Caso

González claims, the definition of Jansenism and its imputation of heresy were unclear, and, consequently, it cannot be established whether the utopian principles of the Ayparchontes' religion refer to the acceptance of the Jansenist perspective.[48] In his article on *El Censor*, the French scholar Paul-Jacques Guinard summed up the critical attitude towards the Spanish Church, as set out in various essays of the periodical, in the following way:

> Ce que Pereyra et Cañuelo — ou leurs collaborateurs occultes — fustigent, c'est, dans une perspective économique, la richesse de l'Église, propriétaire [...] de nombreuses et vastes mainmortes [...]. Dans une perspective politique, ils rêvent d'un état où, conformément aux conceptions régalistes en honneur parmi les 'ilustrados', l'Église exercerait son pouvoir, qui est purement spirituel, sans porter atteinte aux prérogatives des autorités civiles. Sur le plan spirituel, ils se montrent [...] fort prudents en ce qui concerne la doctrine, mais ils reprochent au clergé son manque de vocation, son pharisaïsme, son incompétence née de son ignorance. Ils lui reprochent également de faire régner l'obscurantisme et l'esprit d'intolérance chez les fidèles, d'encourager ceux-ci à les pratiques superstitieuses, et de transmettre des traditions sans fondement, des récits de faux miracles qu'aucun chrétien raisonnable et respectueux de sa religion ne saurait accepter.[49]

> [From an economic perspective, what Pereira and Cañuelo — or their secret collaborators — criticize is the wealth of the Church, as the owner [...] of numerous and vast entailed properties [...]. From a political perspective, and in accordance with the regalism favoured by Enlightenment thinkers, they dream of a state where the Church would exercise its power, which is purely spiritual, without infringing on the prerogatives of the civil authorities. In the spiritual domain, they are [...] very cautious about Church doctrine, but they reproach the clergy for their lack of vocation for the priesthood, their Pharisaism, their incompetence born of ignorance. They also reproach them for spreading obscurantism and a spirit of intolerance among the faithful, for encouraging them to adopt superstitious practices, and for passing on unfounded traditions, stories of false miracles that no reasonable Christian who is respectful of his or her religion could accept.]

A crucial element that permeates the utopian vision of the *Monarquía de los Ayparchontes* is the application of rational criteria to the reform of social institutions. The importance of rational practices is a constant in eighteenth-century Spanish utopian texts, but in the case of the utopian monarchy of the Ayparchontes, the interest in social and spiritual transformation is principally focused on a theoretical reformulation of society and not reflected in a correlative spatial organization, which is a key aspect in the ideal constitution of Sinapia, for example. What matters most here is not a sophisticated urban plan, but a social organization based on rewarding individual work and a genuinely spiritual Church. Thus, another contrast with the tradition of Spanish utopias is that the series of utopian *discursos* of *El Censor* are openly emphatic about the unavoidable necessity of both the nobility and the Church as supporting elements of the socio-political regime, as long as they are both subject to rational regulation. In this sense, *El Censor* did not intend to put forward a revolutionary model but to reform the existing one by delineating a positive feasible utopian alternative. As Guinard notes, 'Il ne propose aucunement le rêve d'une société parfaite et radicalement autre. Ce n'est en fait, malgré le respect des certaines conventions, qu'un projet de réformes, bien plus qu'une utopie au sens primitif' [It does not in any way propose the dream of a perfect and radically different society. Despite the respect for certain conventions, it is in fact only a project of reforms, much more than a utopia in the original sense of the term].[50] María Dolores Gimeno Puyol suggests that the radical perspective of the utopia of the Ayparchontes was restrained by the censorial activity of the Spanish Inquisition and the reactionary reception of the reform programme by the Spanish nobility and clergy:

> This reformist programme must have seemed too advanced to the majority of Spanish noblemen and clergy, who were highly conservative and tied to their enormous privileges, therefore *El Censor* could only give an exotic example of a faraway country under a utopian disguise and written by an unknown traveller.[51]

The idea of giving a reformed new shape to an existing system may be in accordance with the fact that the name *Ayparchontes* may derive from the Greek word *huparchontón*, the plural imperative of the verb *huparchó*, which means 'to begin'.[52] The etymology of the name of this utopian community could refer, then, to an exhortation to renew society. However, according to Sánchez-Blanco, the word *Ayparchontes* does not exist in Greek, but would mean 'those who do not exert power'.[53] In this context of linguistic interpretations, the name of the sage Zeblitz is claimed by Francisco Uzcanga Meinecke to have been inspired by Karl Abraham von Zedlitz, an enlightened minister of Frederick II of Prussia and Kant's protector.[54] This possible origin of the native's name would reinforce his rational character, which is also evident in the logical structure of his dialogue with the traveller.

Utopia and Dystopia in *El Censor*

The utopia of the Ayparchontes can be read in parallel with the subsequent dystopia of the Cosmosians in *El Censor*, which is the story of another imaginary community, published in 1786 in five *discursos*. On this occasion, the *discursos* consist of several letters provided by a French gazetteer, and, as in the previous utopian narration, the metatextual narrative voice acts as the editor of those letters describing the nation of Cosmosia, letters written by a traveller called Mr Ennous. The letters are annotated with comments by both the French gazetteer and the editor.

In spite of being a dystopian, chaotic place, Cosmosia is ideologically connected to the land of the Ayparchontes in terms of the exaltation of the moral code that must be obeyed. The social disorder and unhappiness of the Cosmosians are a consequence of their reluctance to put into practice the faculties of reason and freedom given to them by their creator:[55] '¡Cuán grande no será este desorden! ¡Cuán grande no será esta infelicidad! Y he aquí a qué abismo conduce a los Cosmosianos el no uso de los medios con que su Criador les ha dotado para vivir ordenados y felices' [How great this disorder is! How great this unhappiness is!

And here is the abyss to which the Cosmosians are led for not using the means with which their Creator has endowed them in order to live happily in an orderly way].[56] Their distorted judgement prevents them from distinguishing between good and evil, and, as a result, Cosmosians reveal an excessive ambition for frivolous goods. Ultimately, their barbarous existence is caused by their ignorance of God's universal rules. However, their unawareness of a supreme being is acquired, not innate. In other words, they recognize the depravity of their actions, but do not want to abandon their state of deception and falseness, which equates to a life of unlimited material possessions. The Cosmosians' moral world is corrupted due to their self-deception and their will to deceive others: 'No quieren entender porque no quieren obrar bien. Ni les basta el engañarse todos a sí mismos, han menester también engañar a los demás' [They do not want to understand because they do not want to act well. It is not enough that they should all deceive themselves, they also need to deceive others].[57]

Everything in Cosmosia is chaos and anarchy. Although the theological and philosophical attack supposed by this dystopia can be regarded as a direct response to the moral state of the Spanish Church at the time, Cosmosia's spiritual decadence is basically the result of the perversion of the natural law. As Sánchez-Blanco sees it: 'Lo de las "leyes del Hacedor" es un eufemismo para aludir al Derecho natural. Estamos ante una nación que no respeta ni el orden natural ni el cristiano' [The reference to the 'laws of the Maker' is a euphemism to evoke natural law. We are facing a nation that respects neither the natural order nor the Christian one].[58] As a matter of fact, *El Censor* as a whole advocates the constitution of a social organization based on the imitation of the basic rules of nature. The scourge of social inequality in Cosmosia is grounded in the effects of an artificial social superiority, generated by the hellish lifestyle of Cosmosians: '[E]sta superioridad o elevación [...] no es natural, sino facticia. Es un efecto de las monstruosidades que se han formado a causa de la turbación del orden establecido por el Autor del mundo moral' [This superiority or elevation [...] is not natural, but factitious. It is an effect of the monstrosities that have resulted from the disturbance of the order established by the Author of the moral world].[59]

Only a state of superiority coming from the will of God or the law of nature can be beneficial. A paradigmatic example of natural superiority is the vertical relationship between the prince and his vassals, but his power becomes futile when it comes to doing good to the masses because he is unable to overcome their universal error. To simplify the philosophical content behind the calamity that condemns this dystopian society, it can be inferred that the inhabitants of Cosmosia do not follow any laws because they are unaware of the existence of God, the true author and legislator of the moral law. In this sense, José Portillo Valdés opposes the cursed land of Cosmosia to the blessed land of the Ayparchontes, but connects both settings through the common purpose of reinterpreting the bases of the Spanish monarchy from a natural and moral delineation of Catholicism.[60]

Another paradoxical aspect of thematic convergence between the moral disorder of Cosmosia and the social order of the land of the Ayparchontes is the veneration of a hereditary system of wealth and privileges. Although the nobility does not exist as a class in their world, the Cosmosians encourage injustice and inequality by creating insurmountable differences among citizens. What turns out to be striking about the way social hierarchy works in Cosmosia is that power is not measured by how many material things a citizen owns, but by the arbitrary value that the rich decide to give to those acquired properties. Therefore, social inequality is infinite and illegitimate because those who unlawfully hold power set the criteria for social standards according to their own interests. Since fate is the only force that rules this dystopian reality, Cosmosia is certainly an atheist nation. As partisans of atheism and opponents of the plan of salvation, the Cosmosians live indifferent to the system of virtue and merit that governs the country of the Ayparchontes.

Utopian Echoes and Critical Debates in the Eighteenth-Century Spanish Press

Besides the fact that both imaginary societies — Cosmosia and the land of the Ayparchontes — may have been thought up by the same anonymous author, the story of another utopian society was conceived in reaction to the description of Cosmosia and appeared in letters 20 and 21 of *El Corresponsal del Censor* in 1787. The letters are signed by Ramón Harnero (the pen name of Manuel Rubín de Celis), a fictional correspondent who maintains an epistolary communication with the also fictional author(s) of *El Censor*. The circumstances of the arrival in the utopian place are again favoured by a storm that causes a vessel to be thrown against an island, an unnamed and glorious island diametrically opposed to Cosmosia: '[N]o puede lograrse en este mundo gloria mayor que la de vivir y morir en una isla tan diametralmente opuesta a la Cosmosia' [No greater glory can be achieved in this world but that of living and dying on an island so diametrically opposed to Cosmosia].[61]

What is interesting to note about this ideal community is its respect for religion and the law. The religious doctrine of its inhabitants is free of superstition, the major symptom of false religions disapproved of by *El Censor*. Irrational beliefs only produce fearful and unconfident citizens. As to the application of the law, their legal system echoes the rules contemplated by the Ayparchontes in terms of maximizing the growth of society through the arduous and difficult work that can be performed by convicts: '[L]a ley no inventó los suplicios sino por el bien de la sociedad' [The law did not invent torture except for the good of society].[62] In this respect, both Cosmosia and the monarchy of the Ayparchontes share points of convergence with *Utopia*'s conception of lawbreakers as useful manpower for society.

The ethical parameters of the utopian island are strictly based on the code of nature, and the rank of nobility is merely a personal achievement. Noble status can be obtained by fulfilling one of the following activities: fighting against the enemies of the nation, inventing something useful, or pursuing a career in the liberal arts. Talented citizens are protected by the government and are expected to instruct their fellow citizens in how to preserve traditional virtues. Hard work and personal merit are the only way of succeeding and becoming better citizens: 'Entre ellos no se conocen otros padrinos que la justicia o el mérito' [Among them, no other godparents are known than justice or merit].[63] It is important to specify the Enlightenment idea that individual virtue is only valuable insofar as it produces positive effects in other community members. In this regard, Caso González points out that '[n]o es [...] el conjunto de buenas cualidades lo que hace virtuoso al hombre, sino, como sostiene Voltaire [...], el que esas buenas cualidades actúen con relación al prójimo' [it is not [...] the set of good qualities that makes man virtuous, but, as Voltaire maintains [...], the fact that those qualities operate in relation to other people].[64] In order to intensify the collective commitment to achieving an ideal society, the islanders publish a monthly gazette reporting reprehensible actions that have happened on the island and that must be avoided. In this way, Harnero contrasts the pleasurable purpose that underlies Spanish gazettes with the moral objective of utopian newspapers: '[L]a gaceta, que por lo común no sirve en nuestro país más que para diversión de gente desocupada, es en este un fuerte estímulo para adquirir y mantener las buenas costumbres, y un freno que impide abandonarse al vicio' [The gazette, which usually does not serve in our country more than for the amusement of idle people, is here a strong stimulus to acquire and follow good behaviour, and a brake that prevents one from succumbing to vice].[65]

According to the analysis of this utopian account made by José Mariluz Urquijo, the legal and judicial system of the islanders copies the reformist proposals included in the official regulations of the Spanish government. For example, the prohibition to question or interpret the rules replicates the prescriptions regarding the non-examination of the laws of the Indies, in case a hermeneutical perspective provokes an incorrect interpretation or perceptions not in accord with reason. The utopian narration of *El Corresponsal del Censor*, to an extent similar to the dystopia of Cosmosia and the utopia of the Ayparchontes, transcends the fictional subtext and is interwoven with real referents: 'La lectura de estas páginas produce la impresión de estar frente a textos de algún penalista de la época y no de literatura de ficción' [The reading of these pages produces the impression of being faced with texts by some expert in criminal law of that era and not of fictional literature].[66] In the same vein, the debate about the impossible elimination of hereditary nobility was an urgent topic for Spanish Enlightenment writers, apart from the treatment of the discussion in utopian fictions. Especially in the land of the Ayparchontes, the possessions and privileges of the Spanish nobility are seen as a real threat to the social and economic development of the country.

It is also important to mention Discurso 65 of *El Censor*, a letter written by a Moroccan citizen, who describes his Spanish visit to his compatriot and addressee Abu-Taleb. The text was published in 1784 and was undoubtedly inspired by the visit of the ambassador of Morocco, Sidi Hamet Al Ghazzali, to Spain in 1766. Both this historical event and the literary model of Montesquieu's *Lettres persanes* [*Persian Letters*] (1721) were the source of inspiration for Cadalso's *Cartas marruecas*[67] and the fictional letter of *El Censor*.[68] In an attempt to criticize the traditional Spanish insistence on applying erroneous political strategies, Discurso 65 reproaches the

Spanish administration for not having a coherent legal system, which results in the lack of a consistent form of government. The Moroccan visitor explains to Abu-Taleb that all social classes are blended together with the head of the state, but that this sublime situation is probably the cause of the existence of an undefined legislative and political system.[69]

Besides the paternalistic relationship between the prince and his subjects, what stands out as atypical about the political set-up in Spain, according to the Moroccan observer, is the amorphous government plan that ignores the tripartite classification of government models delineated by Aristotle in his *Politics*: monarchy, aristocracy, and democracy. Rejecting Aristotle's classification, Montesquieu's *De l'esprit des lois* [*The Spirit of the Laws*] of 1748 distinguished three types of government: monarchy, republic, and despotism. Aristotle leaned towards a mixed government, specifically the combination of democracy and aristocracy. His reflections curiously made reference to the role that virtue played in the character of the members who composed the oligarchy:

> Aristocracy is thought to consist primarily in the distribution of office according to merit: merit is the criterion of aristocracy, as wealth is the criterion of oligarchy, and free birth of democracy. [...] In most cities the form of government is called 'constitutional government', since the mixture attempted in it seeks only to blend the rich and the poor, or wealth and free birth, and the rich are regarded by common opinion as holding the position of gentlemen. But in reality there are three elements which may claim an equal share in the mixed form of constitution: free birth, wealth, and merit. (So-called 'nobility' of birth, which is sometimes reckoned a fourth, is only a corollary of the two latter, and simply consists in inherited wealth and merit.)[70]

The Aristotelian conception of moral virtue seems to be the basis for the construction of a utopian Spain where the acquisition of values is needed for social transformation. Aristotelian virtue is always a voluntary and deliberate act. As the utopia of the Ayparchontes proclaims and the dystopia of Cosmosia ignores, virtue, not wealth or arbitrary power, is the cornerstone of an enlightened society in which the happiness and well-being of the people are the ultimate objectives of government. This kind of sociological insight of *El Censor* triggered its participation in the heated attack against Spain's apologists that dominated the periodical press from 1786 until 1788. In the rivalry between apologists and anti-apologists, *El Censor* supported the criticism of the factors that were preventing Spain from joining the mainstream of European intellectual life and thought, such as its moral values, deficient legal system, and attachment to scholastic theology. The anti-apologists were categorically opposed to the outdated values defended by the apologists, who also resisted the intellectual work of the nation's enlightened thinkers.[71] The open conflict between the two groups had its origins in France in 1782 when Nicolas Masson de Morvilliers published an article about Spain in the *Encyclopédie méthodique*, a revised and expanded version of the *Encyclopédie, ou dictionnaire raisonné des sciences, des arts et des métiers* [*Encyclopaedia; or, A Systematic Dictionary of the Sciences, Arts, and Crafts*], edited by Denis Diderot and Jean le Rond d'Alembert and published in Paris between 1751 and 1772. In his entry, Masson describes Spain as a backward and ignorant nation whose government is weak and whose clergy is tyrannical.[72] The decline and decadence of the arts and sciences in Spain are also sharply criticized. Masson's rhetorical question was famously repudiated by Spaniards: 'Mais que doit-on à l'Espagne? Et depuis deux siècles, depuis quatre, depuis dix, qu'a-t-elle fait pour l'Europe?' [But what do we owe to Spain? And over the last two, four, or ten centuries, what has Spain done for Europe?].[73] This was a question about the cultural resources of the Spanish nation and the extent of their contribution to European culture, which caused discomfort to many Spaniards.[74]

Among the diverse reactions to the French geographer's polemical article, one that is particularly significant is the *Oración apologética por la España y su mérito literario* [*Discourse in Favour of Spain and its Literary Merit*] (1786) by Juan Pablo Forner, a text whose publication was subsidized by the government. Although *El Censor* includes in its *discursos* explicit replies to Masson's negative evaluation of Spain's potential, it is Discurso 165 that constitutes the emblematic response to the French writer and the Spanish apologists. Printed in 1787 and presented as a parody of Forner's text, the *Oración apologética por el África y su mérito literario* [*Discourse in Favour of Africa and its Literary Merit*] tries to eradicate the excessive and unfounded optimism that only hampers the ability of Spain to judge its achievements in a rational way.[75] What is worth noting in this Discurso is the appeal to the moral dimension, again stating that Spain's adversities reside in the absence of an institutionalized system of social values and moral or religious convictions. Under an ironic gaze, the flattering supporter of the African nation complains about the misinterpretation concerning the spiritual but civilized and rational ruling principles of his people:

> La moral, la divina ciencia del hombre, la doctrina de su orden, de su fin, de su felicidad, la que une a la más noble de las criaturas con su próvido y liberal Criador, no ha sido entre nosotros todavía contaminada con aquellas legislaciones absurdas que hacen al hombre o brutal, o impío, o ridículo.[76]
>
> [Morality, the divine science of man, the doctrine of his order, his purpose, his happiness, that which unites the noblest of creatures with his prolific and liberal Creator, has not yet been contaminated for us with those absurd laws that make man brutal, impious, or ridiculous.]

The tension between the artificial laws of the state and the natural ones of God brings about a barbaric image of religion: '[L]a ciencia de la religión no es de este siglo, y precisamente han de pasar por bárbaras aquellas naciones en que se ha consumido más tiempo, más atención y más papel en hablar de Dios y de sus inefables fines' [The science of religion is not of this century, and precisely those nations in which more time, more attention, and more paper have been dedicated to speaking of God and his ineffable purposes have been considered barbarians].[77] A theological exploration of religious practices tends to be overlooked in this ideological confrontation.

By putting the utopia of the Ayparchontes in dialogue with other texts of the period, it is possible to observe a widespread concern about both the incongruity of the hereditary privileges of the nobility and the existence of a wealthy Church. In spite of not claiming to be a revolutionary model, the account of the monarchy of the Ayparchontes is an invitation to rethink the internal system and dynamics of these two key features of Spanish society. However, the boundaries between utopian and reformist schemes should be seen as separable in terms of the context in which these projects are created and the extent to which their practical application is intended. The account of the Ayparchontes would have provoked its readership to radically question the existing political, social, and religious system of Spain, providing the Spanish utopian tradition with a more significant and dynamic image of the readership of utopian fiction.

Notes to Chapter 5

1. See the justification in note 6 of the Introduction.
2. See the chapter entitled 'La Seconde Génération de "spectateurs": 1. *El Censor*', in Guinard, *La Presse espagnole de 1737 à 1791*, pp. 291–323.
3. Elsa García-Pandavenes, '*El Censor* (1781–1787): A Study of an Essay Periodical of the Spanish Enlightenment' (unpublished doctoral thesis, University of California, Berkeley, 1970), p. 2.
4. Caso González, '*El Censor*, ¿periódico de Carlos III?', pp. 779–80.
5. See Francisco Sánchez-Blanco, '*El Censor*': *un periódico contra el Antiguo Régimen* (Seville: Alfar, 2016).
6. Sempere y Guarinos, IV (1787), p. 191.
7. Quoted in Philip Deacon, '*El Censor* y la crisis de las Luces en España: el *Diálogo crítico-político* de Joaquín Medrano de Sandoval', *Estudios de Historia Social*, 52–53 (1990), 131–40 (p. 135).
8. Caso González, '*El Censor*, ¿periódico de Carlos III?', p. 788.
9. Alberto Gil Novales, 'Para los amigos de Cañuelo', *Cuadernos Hispanoamericanos*, 229 (1969), 291–323 (p. 197).
10. José Miguel Caso González, 'La crítica religiosa de *El Censor* y el grupo ilustrado de la Condesa de Montijo', in *La Ilustración en España y Alemania*, ed. by Reyes Mate and Friedrich Niewöhner (Barcelona: Anthropos, 1989), pp. 175–88 (p. 185).
11. See Deacon, '*El Censor* y la crisis de las Luces en España'. The pamphlet was reprinted in Barcelona by the Imprenta de Sastres in 1793.
12. Caso González, '*El Censor*, ¿periódico de Carlos III?', pp. 790–91.
13. *El Censor*, I [1781]: 'Discurso I', pp. 17–28 (p. 22).
14. *El Censor*, VIII [1787]: 'Discurso CLXI', pp. 565–79 (p. 566).
15. This conceptualization brings up the meaning behind Francisco de Goya's Capricho [Caprice] 43, entitled 'El sueño de la razón produce monstruos' ['The Sleep of Reason Produces Monsters'] (1797–98). 'El sueño de la razón produce monstruos' can be read as a proclamation of Goya's adherence to the values of the Enlightenment. According to the manuscript explaining the subtext of the aquatint, Goya believed that the imagination should never be completely abandoned in favour of reason because the imagination alone produces impossible monsters, but, united with reason, it is the mother of the arts. For Goya, art is the result of the combination of reason and the imagination (Edith Helman, *Trasmundo de Goya* (Madrid: Alianza, 1983), p. 221).
16. The text of the three *discursos* constituting the *Monarquía de los Ayparchontes* that is used in this chapter is included in the facsimile version of the original edition of *El Censor* made by José Miguel Caso González and published in 1989 (*El Censor*, III [1784]: 'Discurso LXI', pp. 225–39, 'Discurso LXIII', pp. 257–70; IV [1785]: 'Discurso LXXV', pp. 131–50). Gimeno Puyol republished the text in 2014 along with two other Spanish utopian works, but it is little more than a transcription of the text, with almost no critical analysis of the society of the Ayparchontes (María Dolores Gimeno Puyol, ed., *Tres utopías ilustradas: 'Viaje al país de los Ayparchontes', 'La isla', 'La utopía de Zenit'* (Nuremberg: Clásicos Hispánicos, 2014), ebook).
17. *El Censor*, III, 'Discurso LXI', p. 225.
18. Ibid., p. 226.

19. Ibid.
20. For a detailed discussion of the critical treatment of the nobility in eighteenth-century Spanish poetry, see Elena de Lorenzo Álvarez, 'La polémica sobre el lujo y *el noble inútil*', in Elena de Lorenzo Álvarez, *Nuevos mundos poéticos: la poesía filosófica de la Ilustración* (Oviedo: Instituto Feijoo de Estudios del Siglo XVIII, 2002), pp. 289–368.
21. *El Censor*, III, 'Discurso LXI', pp. 228–29.
22. The theme of an irrational hereditary nobility is a recurring issue in Cadalso's *Cartas marruecas*, published originally in 1789, after the author's death, in the periodical *Correo de Madrid*. By displaying a refined satirical technique, the Spanish author subscribes to the idea of a renovation of the nobility's education by which noblemen are obliged to undertake specialized studies with the aim of being suitably prepared to fill the highest positions in the army, civil administration, and government. Social classes are structured in agreement with the natural order, and nobody should try to break that pre-established harmony. Cadalso presents an educational method to instruct Spain's idle elite, so that these well-educated people will succeed within the superficial system of manners imposed by society. He also debates issues such as virtue, moderation, and human misery, as well as the confrontation of the virtuous man (*el hombre de bien*) with social evils (José de Cadalso, *Cartas marruecas. Noches lúgubres*, ed. by Emilio Martínez Mata (Barcelona: Crítica, 2008)).
23. The characterization of the nobility as an intermediary force in the monarchical system was pointed out by Montesquieu in *De l'esprit des lois* [*The Spirit of the Laws*] (1748): 'Le pouvoir intermédiaire subordonné le plus naturel est celui de la noblesse. Elle entre en quelque façon dans l'essence de la monarchie, dont la maxime fondamentale est point de monarque, point de noblesse; point de noblesse, point de monarque' [The most natural, subordinate intermediary power is that of the nobility. It is, in a sense, part of the essence of monarchy, whose fundamental maxim is: without the monarch, there is no nobility; without the nobility, there is no monarch] (Charles-Louis de Secondat, Baron de Montesquieu, *De l'esprit des lois*, 6 vols (Paris: Lebigre Frères, 1834), I, p. 46). The translation is adapted from Charles-Louis de Secondat, Baron de Montesquieu, *The Spirit of the Laws*, ed. and trans. by Anne M. Cohler, Basia Carolyn Miller, and Harold Samuel Stone (Cambridge: Cambridge University Press, 1989), p. 18.
24. Apparently, the French fabulist Jean de La Fontaine (1621–1695) was reputed to enjoy a restful life. He spent much of his childhood observing the animal world, which later gave him the inspiration for his fables. For twenty years, he lived in perfect tranquillity under the patronage of Marguerite Hessein, Madame de La Sablière. La Fontaine's primitiveness and laziness were actually harshly criticized by his protector: 'Madame de la Sablière at one time discharged her whole establishment whilst La Fontaine was residing in her house. "What!," said somebody, "have you kept none?" "None," replied the lady, "except *mes trois bêtes* [my three animals] — my cat, my dog, and La Fontaine." Such was her idea of his thoughtless and more than childish simplicity' (Mary Shelley, *Lives of the Most Eminent French Writers*, 2 vols (Philadelphia, PA: Lea and Blanchard, 1840), I, pp. 183–84).
25. *El Censor*, III, 'Discurso LXI', pp. 238–39.
26. *Novísima recopilación de las leyes de España*, 6 vols (Madrid: n. pub., 1805–07), III (1805), p. 6. See also Antonio Domínguez Ortiz, *Carlos III y la España de la Ilustración* (Madrid: Alianza, 1989), p. 122.
27. *Novísima recopilación de las leyes de España*, IV (1805), p. 182.
28. *El Censor*, III, 'Discurso LXIII', p. 257.
29. For an overview of attitudes towards an ineffective nobility in Spain, see the chapter 'Les décevantes classes dirigeantes', in Jean Sarrailh, *L'Espagne éclairée de la seconde moitié du XVIIIe siècle* (Paris: Imprimerie Nationale, 1954), pp. 75–99. See also Part I entitled 'El estamento nobiliario', in Domínguez Ortiz, *Las clases privilegiadas en la España del Antiguo Régimen*, pp. 17–197.
30. Piñera Tarque, p. 157.
31. *El Censor*, III, 'Discurso LXIII', pp. 264–65.
32. Elorza, *La ideología liberal en la Ilustración española*, p. 223.
33. *El Censor*, IV, 'Discurso LXXV', pp. 131–32.
34. *El Censor*, III, 'Discurso LXIII', p. 258.

35. *El Censor*, IV, 'Discurso LXXV', p. 132.
36. Callahan, pp. 38–42.
37. Ibid., p. 43.
38. For criticism of the eighteenth-century Spanish Church, see the chapter 'La Pensée religieuse: I. Le Procès de l'Église', in Sarrailh, pp. 613–61.
39. *El Censor*, IV, 'Discurso LXXV', pp. 137–38.
40. Ibid., p. 140.
41. Ibid., p. 141.
42. Ibid., p. 147.
43. Sánchez-Blanco, *El absolutismo y las Luces en el reinado de Carlos III*, p. 342.
44. *Índice último de los libros prohibidos y mandados expurgar: para todos los reinos y señoríos del católico rey de las Españas, el señor Don Carlos IV* (Madrid: Imprenta de Antonio de Sancha, 1790; facsimile edition, Valencia: Librerías París-Valencia, 1997), p. 50.
45. Gil Novales, p. 205.
46. Caso González, '*El Censor*, ¿periódico de Carlos III?', p. 797.
47. Herr, p. 186.
48. Caso González, '*El Censor*, ¿periódico de Carlos III?', p. 796.
49. Paul-Jacques Guinard, 'Remarques sur une grande revue espagnole du XVIII siècle: *El Censor* (1781–1787)', *Les Langues Néo-Latines*, 212 (1975), 90–105 (pp. 101–02).
50. Guinard, 'Les Utopies en Espagne au XVIII siècle', p. 178.
51. María Dolores Gimeno Puyol, '*Viaje al país de los Ayparchontes*: The Limits of a Spanish Utopia in the Eighteenth Century', in *Trans/Forming Utopia: The 'Small Thin Story'*, ed. by Elizabeth Russell (Bern and Oxford: Peter Lang, 2009), pp. 175–86 (p. 183).
52. Uzcanga Meinecke, p. 158.
53. Sánchez-Blanco, *El absolutismo y las Luces en el reinado de Carlos III*, p. 325.
54. Uzcanga Meinecke, p. 159.
55. The dystopian Cosmosia of *El Censor* had a precedent in Benito Jerónimo Feijoo's 'El gran magisterio de la experiencia' ['The Great Lessons of Experience'] (1733), Discurso II in volume V of his *Teatro crítico universal, o discursos varios en todo género de materias para desengaño de errores comunes* [*Universal Critical Theatre; or, Various Essays on Every Kind of Matter for Disproving Common Errors*]. Feijoo's essay starts with a metaphorical story aimed at proving that experience and experimentation are the only way of getting to the knowledge of the truth. Taking the form of a fable, the episode narrates how the kingdom of Cosmosia — an allegory of the world — is affected by the rivalry between two powerful women: Solidina, who personifies the method of experience, and Idearia, the embodiment of thinking based on reason. The story is a clear criticism of the weakness of Aristotelianism as opposed to the favourable reception of the Baconian method, which is symbolized by Solidina's reintegration into society after her exile from Cosmosia. Although the Cosmosia of Feijoo is not the moral representation of a specific community as is the case in *El Censor*, both Cosmosias insinuate the need to restore a sensible state of things that positively results in a desirable social set-up.
56. *El Censor*, IV [1786]: 'Discurso LXXXIX', pp. 155–84 (p. 182).
57. *El Censor*, IV [1786]: 'Discurso XC', pp. 385–408 (pp. 406–07).
58. Sánchez-Blanco, *El absolutismo y las Luces en el reinado de Carlos III*, p. 340.
59. *El Censor*, V [1786]: 'Discurso CVII', pp. 715–37 (pp. 717–18).
60. José M. Portillo Valdés, 'Los límites de la monarquía: catecismo de Estado y constitución política en España a finales del siglo XVIII', *Quaderni Fiorentini*, 25 (1996), 183–263 (p. 209).
61. Rubín de Celis, p. 175.
62. Ibid., p. 170.
63. Ibid., p. 173.
64. José Miguel Caso González, 'Introducción', in José de Cadalso, *Cartas marruecas*, ed. by José Miguel Caso González (Madrid: Espasa-Calpe, 2007), pp. 11–28 (p. 25).
65. Rubín de Celis, p. 172.
66. Ibid., p. 321.
67. Cadalso submitted the manuscript of the *Cartas marruecas* to the Council of Castile in 1774 in

order to obtain a printing licence, which suggests that the text was finished by the mid-1770s (Nigel Glendinning, *Vida y obra de Cadalso* (Madrid: Gredos, 1962), p. 137).
68. Uzcanga Meinecke, p. 167.
69. *El Censor*, III [1784]: 'Discurso LXV', pp. 289–306 (p. 298).
70. Aristotle, *Politics*, trans. by Ernest Barker, and rev. and ed. by R. F. Stalley (Oxford: Oxford University Press, 2009), p. 152.
71. García-Pandavenes, '*El Censor* (1781–1787)', pp. 269–71.
72. See Clorinda Donato and Ricardo López, eds, *Enlightenment Spain and the 'Encyclopédie méthodique'* (Oxford: Voltaire Foundation, 2015).
73. Nicolas Masson de Morvilliers, 'Espagne', in *Encyclopédie méthodique, ou par ordre de matières*, ed. by Denis Diderot and Jean le Rond d'Alembert, 203 vols (Paris: Panckoucke, 1782–1832), I: *Géographie moderne* (1782), pp. 554–68 (p. 565).
74. For a re-examination of the aesthetic and political content of eighteenth-century Spanish cultural production, see Thomas Cassidy Neal, *Writing the Americas in Enlightenment Spain: Literature, Modernity, and the New World, 1773–1812* (Lewisburg, PA: Bucknell University Press, 2017).
75. For a critical analysis of the clash between Forner and *El Censor*, see Philip Deacon, 'Señas de identidad de Juan Pablo Forner: una aproximación a las *Demostraciones palmarias*', in *Juan Pablo Forner y su época (1756–1797)*, ed. by Jesús Cañas Murillo and Miguel Ángel Lama (Mérida: Editora Regional de Extremadura, 1998), pp. 379–99.
76. *El Censor*, VIII [1787]: 'Discurso CLXV', pp. 629–60 (p. 640).
77. Ibid., p. 641.

CHAPTER 6

Anti-Enlightenment Perspectives in the *Monarquía columbina*

The publication of the short utopian text *Tratado sobre la monarquía columbina* [*Treatise on the Monarchy of Doves*] in 1790, in volume XXX of the Madrid periodical *Semanario Erudito*,[1] coincided with the almost contemporaneous appearance of other utopian texts in the Spanish press, such as the *Monarquía de los Ayparchontes* in *El Censor* and the brief untitled utopias of *El Corresponsal del Censor* and the *Correo de Madrid*,[2] both published in 1787. What the *Monarquía columbina* shares with these other utopian narratives is the explicit division of the story into thematic sections, but, unlike them, the development of the plot is not fragmented into episodes presented in subsequent issues of the periodical.

Although the text originally appeared as an anonymous work — which was also the case with the utopian writings included in other periodicals — in the *Semanario Erudito* edited by Antonio Valladares de Sotomayor, the authorship was made known by the Spanish scholar Pedro Álvarez de Miranda, to whose attention the news of the publication of the same text in the *Revista Calasancia* [*Calasanz Journal*] in 1895 was brought by Francisco Aguilar Piñal. The journal, belonging to the religious order of the Escolapians, gives the text the title of *Monarquía columbina. Su gobierno y causa de su ruina* [*The Monarchy of Doves. Its Government and the Cause of its Ruin*], the work of Father Andrés Merino de Jesucristo, himself an Escolapian, whose non-religious name was Manuel Antonio Merino Irigoyen (1730–1787).[3] This title, which may be that of the manuscript transcribed, certainly announces the theme and unhappy ending of the story. The comparison between the version published in the *Revista Calasancia* and a manuscript of the text found by Álvarez de Miranda in the National Library of Spain (MS 17874, fols 143–66)[4] confirms that the word *tratado* [treatise] was added to the original title by Valladares. The present chapter will demonstrate that a utopian perspective threatened by the imminent imposition of a destabilizing force characterizes the fiction of the *Monarquía columbina*, a text described by Álvarez de Miranda as an anti-Enlightenment utopia, possibly composed by Merino near the date of his death in 1787.

The Organizational Structure of the Text

Despite the fact that the word *tratado* seems to be an editorial addition to the author's title, the *Monarquía columbina* certainly aims to offer an accurate description and reflection of the establishment of the republic of doves in four parts or *discursos* that form a kind of treatise. However, the portrayal of the utopian space and its social system is presented only in the third part of the narrative. The thematic sequence of the four parts of the story is as follows: 1) the voluntary social disintegration of the community of doves; 2) their exodus to the utopian region of the City of the Sun; 3) the establishment of the utopian monarchy of the doves; and 4) the social disintegration of their kingdom due to their subjugation by the birds of prey. As Pedro Álvarez de Miranda[5] and Emilio Palacios Fernández[6] both point out, Merino's text has a cyclical structure because the situation of the doves is the same at the beginning as at the end of the story: their society is destroyed by the power of their enemies. Such a pessimistic perspective implies that the doves are doomed to recurring failure, trapped in a cycle of hope and decline, even though there is a lapse of five hundred years before the eventual demise of their utopian nation.

As in *Sinapia*, the *Monarquía de los Ayparchontes*, or the *Suplemento de los viajes de Enrique Wanton*, the utopian community is defined as a monarchical system, often referred to as a republic in the classical sense of the term. In the *Monarquía columbina*, however, the need to establish a monarchy emerges in response to the existing state of anarchy that damages the natural innocence and goodness of the doves, who are subject to the evil influence of their immediate enemies, the birds of prey:

> Las causas de formarse esta monarquía dimanaron de que vivieron antiguamente las palomas sin forma alguna de república, sin formar cuerpo distinto de las demás aves, hasta que el tiempo las hizo conocer los grandes perjuicios que padecía su natural sencillo e inocente con la comunicación y encuentro de tantas aves de rapiña, que nunca se saciaban de su sangre.[7]
>
> [The causes of the formation of this monarchy derived from the fact that the doves lived previously without any kind of republic, without forming a grouping distinct from other birds, until time made them aware of the great damage that their simple, innocent nature suffered due to their contacts and encounters with so many birds of prey, which were never satisfied with their blood.]

As seen in Chapter 4, the use of animals as inhabitants of the utopian space is a technique equally adopted in the republic of monkeys as depicted by Seriman and Vaca de Guzmán. Such a technique obviously echoes the method of eighteenth-century fables, but the image of the birds also has literary and biblical connotations in the *Monarquía columbina*.

The confrontation between good and evil is the leitmotif that permeates the four parts of the text, which are recounted by a third-person narrator, a strategy that serves to underline the quasi-historical aspect of the story. This impersonal narrator remains unidentified and monopolizes the authority to speak. However, in order to stress the moral dimension that the subject entails, Merino uses several intercalated speeches directed at the doves by one of their number, Calistomos, whose concerns are addressed in the second *discurso* by the phoenix bird Crisorroa. The longest speech, located near the beginning of the story in the first *discurso*, transmits what Calistomos has to say to the community of doves about the barbaric excesses of the birds of prey. Being the wisest of the doves, Calistomos is a key character who foresees the future of the birds and provides them with spiritual guidance and support throughout the whole process of establishing their long-awaited monarchy.

The moralistic nature of Calistomos's vision, and of the text as a whole, results in a prevalence of the development of the historical evolution of the dove society as opposed to the depiction of the political, social, and even religious structures of the utopian society in question. The external narrator judges the world of the doves and makes moralizing comments on the birds of prey and their way of life and wishes for a reformed type of society. In this way, Merino can be seen to underplay the traditional potential of a utopian text and instead emphasize its character as a moral tale. The result for the reader is a focus on a developing story in contrast with an examination of social and political structures that is customary in utopian writings. In fact, as will be analysed later, giving the account a pessimistic ending also distances the *Monarquía columbina* from the traditional utopian model, which usually does not have a conclusive ending, especially not a negative one. The fact that Merino presents Calistomos as, in some measure, a protagonist in the story also replaces the interest of a more traditional utopian account.

A Distorted Concept of Civilization

The first *discurso* sets out the idea of founding a utopian colony in an isolated place far from enemies, instead of undertaking a massive exodus that would only bring about a rupture in the community of birds. As in *Sinapia*, the nuclear family is seen as both the germ of the nation and the institution that keeps society unified. Nevertheless, the humanization of the birds is an inconsistency that is present throughout the story, though it is also a way of making it clear that the nation of doves serves as an allegorical representation of mankind, and more specifically of an autonomous society striving to preserve its identity in the face of the dangers that intruders pose.

In order to determine how to improve their present situation in a space free from the menace of the birds of prey, the doves find shelter in a cave in the middle of a stormy night. The discussion is led by Calistomos, the oldest of the birds, whose gender is actually undetermined 'porque los historiadores están divididos en si era varón o hembra' [because historians are divided over whether it was male or female],[8] although the personal pronoun *él* [he] is used to refer to him in the text. Making use of his eloquence, Calistomos criticizes and condemns the fact that the once infamous birds of prey are now regarded as noble, enlightened, and civilized ('hidalgas, nobles, ilustres, ilustradas, cultas y civilizadas' [honourable, noble, illustrious, enlightened, educated, and civilized]).[9] The wise dove regrets that such a high status has been distorted and corrupted by the introduction of vices, such as greed and lust, which have been transmitted to the birds by foreign communities:

> [T]odas estas aves que llaman nobles [...] antiguamente eran muy templadas y modestas; vivían contentas con una simple comida, y eran humanas y aplicadas al trabajo para buscar alimento; pero después que se introdujo en ellas la gula y la lujuria, que tomaron del comercio con las avestruces del Asia y comunicación con los papagayos Nordestes y guacamayos de Indias, no bastan a saciar su crueldad y codicia cuantos inocentes pájaros crió el Supremo Hacedor de las cosas.[10]

> [All of these birds that are called nobles [...] were formerly moderate and modest; they lived happily with a simple source of food, and were humane, working hard to find sustenance; but after gluttony and lust, which derived from trade with the ostriches of Asia and communication with the parrots of the Northeast and the macaws of the Indies, affected their behaviour, all the innocent birds that the Supreme Maker created were not enough to satisfy their cruelty and greed.]

Similar to the ideological features of Vaca de Guzmán's utopian work, the indiscriminate assimilation of foreign customs or practices is conceived of as a negative factor in the social formation of a virtuous country. The reference to the commercial interaction with Asia, the New World, and possibly France can be interpreted as an allusion to Spain, especially when taking into account the religious character of this allegorical nation. For many opponents of Enlightenment thinking in Spain, the standard source of the moral corruption of Spanish society derived from France. As shown in the quotation above, the disapproval of a life of excess and debauchery, in contrast with a frugal and moderate lifestyle, reveals the evident Christian affiliation of the author. As far as the religious or metaphysical framework of the narrative is concerned, Merino, besides expressly mentioning God (*Dios*), also uses expressions such as *Divina providencia* [Divine Providence], *Criador del Universo* [the Creator of the Universe], or *Supremo Hacedor* [the Supreme Maker].

After presenting a portrayal of the pernicious power that the birds of prey are trying to impose on the doves, Calistomos proposes the abandonment of their homeland as the only effective way of escaping harassment by their enemies. This process of involuntary uprooting is seen as preferable to the extermination of their species. In consequence, the doves will escape to a utopian region, the hyperborean woods, located next to the City of the Sun, an explicit reference to Campanella's *La Città del Sole* (1623).[11] Calistomos describes the woods as an idyllic and unspoiled country whose government is run by the mythical phoenix bird, from whom the doves will request protection:

> Hay, pues, junto a la Ciudad del Sol, unos frondosos bosques, abundantes de cuantas delicias y bienes puede desear nuestra naturaleza. Allí es donde tiene su corte y morada la Reina de las aves, allí donde goza de una tranquila felicidad [...], allí es, en fin, donde todo lo bueno abunda, sin que reine lo malo en parte alguna. A este riquísimo y abundante país es adonde he pensado que debemos pasar, porque allí hasta ahora no entró ni pirata, ni ladrón, ni ladroncillo, ni asesino, ni salteador; porque nuestra Reina, la ave Fénix, nunca dejó llegar allí ave ninguna de rapiña [...]. Allí podremos criar a nuestros hijos en la inocencia y simplicidad. El mal ejemplo no los arrastrará al vicio.[12]

[There are, then, adjoining the City of the Sun, lush forests abundant in all the delights and goods that our nature may desire. That is where the Queen of birds has her court and dwelling, where she enjoys tranquil happiness [...], that is, in short, where all that is good abounds, without evil prevailing anywhere. I have thought that we should move to this very rich and abundant country because there has not been a single pirate, robber, petty thief, murderer, or brigand present, since our Queen, the Phoenix, never let any bird of prey enter [...]. We will be able to raise our children in innocence and simplicity there. Bad examples will not lead them to vice.]

The characterization of the phoenix as the ruler of the utopian territory emphasizes the religious framework of the metaphorical story. As is known, the phoenix has been used as a Christian symbol since the first century, when the myth was related by Saint Clement of Rome in his first Epistle to the Corinthians. The phoenix became a symbol not only of the resurrection of Christ, but also of Christ himself.[13] Apart from signifying virtue, faith, purity, and constancy, the role of the phoenix in the *Monarquía columbina* can be understood as the saviour who is destined to rescue the doves from their suffering and ensure their safety in an imperishable land that symbolizes the triumph of eternal life over death. The hyperborean woods are a pure and indestructible place where the new generations of doves will be raised, unaware of the existence of evil, and where the creation of a prosperous republic is possible.

Continuing with the pseudo-biblical features of the story, the female bird called Polirroa, who attacks and contradicts Calistomos's assertions, can be identified as a version of Judas, as Claire Mercier points out.[14] Described as an arrogant and pretentious bird, Polirroa defends the prestige of the birds of prey and believes that the so-called innocence of the doves is actually ignorance and rusticity, as opposed to the intelligence and industriousness of their enemies:

> Yo nunca llamaré a nuestra rusticidad y torpeza inocencia, candidez y simplicidad, ni a las aves ágiles, civilizadas, diestras, industriosas y vividoras aves de rapiña, ni piratas, ni ladronas, ni homicidas; antes así como alabo su aplicación a la destreza y agilidad, condeno nuestra flojedad y estupidez.[15]

> [I will never call our rusticity and clumsiness innocence, naivety, or simplicity, nor will I call those birds that are agile, civilized, skilled, industrious, and opportunistic birds of prey, pirates, thieves, or murderers; rather, in the same way as I praise their dedication to dexterity and agility, I condemn our laziness and stupidity.]

Polirroa is considered a traitor not only because she strongly rejects the way of thinking of Calistomos — and, as a consequence, of her own species — but also mainly because she is married to one of the opposing birds, a sparrowhawk. Nonetheless, the most important aspect of the dispute resides in the introduction of the recurring topic of civilization versus barbarism, which is frequently treated in utopian fiction.

The concept of civilization is always portrayed negatively in the text and is identified with such features as power and oppression. In this respect, Merino's position seems to reject the conceptual association of the good savage, represented by the doves, with negative notions such as apathy and stupidity. His reaffirmation that the civilizing principles associated with the Enlightenment have been perverted by a vain and snobbish attitude is visible when the narrator sarcastically implies a lack of skilfulness in the birds of prey during their return to the cave where the doves had been holding their meeting. Instead of trying to block the entrance of the cave to prevent the doves from leaving, a group of owls focuses its efforts on finishing off Polirroa. The desire to satisfy their instinctive needs is stronger than their ability to reflect and act wisely. Their irrational behaviour deprives them of any attribute of goodness and compassion.

In addition to the irony and Christian symbolism employed in this *discurso*, the escape of the doves from the dark cave inevitably brings to mind Plato's allegory of the cave,[16] in the sense that their escape forms a prelude to the overcoming of their tribulations and ordeals and leads to their subsequent journey to the utopian country. In his parable, Plato describes the soul's ascent from illusion to enlightenment, from a false understanding to wisdom. The idea that there are several levels of knowledge between the shadowy world of the imagination and the highest truth relates to the gap between the reasoned knowledge of the doves and the supposedly enlightened birds of prey.

The Christian emphasis of the *Monarquía columbina* can also be considered in terms of the ideas appropriated from Campanella's text. Campanella conceived of Christianity as the supreme source of the law and the ultimate reason why Spaniards became the actual discoverers of the New World:

> I conclude [...] that Christianity is the true law and that [...] it will become mistress of the world. I also conclude that for this reason the Spaniards discovered the rest of the world so as to unite it all under one law, even though Columbus [...] was its first discoverer. [...] I see, moreover, that we know not what we do but are instruments of God. Thanks to their hunger for gold, the Spaniards go about discovering new countries, but God has a higher end in mind.[17]

It is also significant that Campanella composed a political work called *Monarchia di Spagna* [*The Monarchy of Spain*] in 1600.[18] This text was written as a form of advice to Felipe III on how to establish a universal monarchy in order to extirpate Protestantism in Europe. Having been written before Campanella's imprisonment by the Spanish Inquisition, such a book constituted proof of his innocence and of the unsoundness of the accusation of rebellion made against him.[19]

A Mythical Utopian Land

The second *discurso*, which might well have been labelled a chapter, recounts the adversities faced by the doves during their journey to a region adjacent to the City of the Sun. The importance given to the narration of the journey leads Ana Baquero to consider that, while in most utopias the travel process is a simple vehicle to arrive in the ideal place, in the *Monarquía columbina* it injects a note of novelistic tension that is not typical of the utopian genre.[20] Half the initial number of doves that started the journey managed to reach the hyperborean woods, while the other half died as a consequence of the assaults of the birds of prey. This episode, however, certainly resembles the biblical account in which Moses leads the Israelites to the Promised Land of Canaan (Numbers 34. 1–12). Not only the long and arduous exodus across the desert, but also the slaughter of a great number of Israelites as a punishment for their sinful adoration of the Golden Calf (Exodus 32. 1–6) are echoed by the odyssey of the doves. Although the doves are not killed because of morally reprehensible behaviour, their sin consists in doubting the promise of Calistomos that they would get to the dreamlike land. Like Moses, Calistomos struggles to make them recover trust in him. To stress the redemptive nature of the act of displacement from the homeland, the journey to the hyperborean woods is said to have been made in six days, which of course recalls the creation of the world in the same period of time. Once the doves have arrived at their new destination, they can feel safe and protected from evil. As Calistomos warns them, the birds of prey are a curse throughout the world; the only territory that they are incapable of invading is the empire of the phoenix.

Having lived oppressed for centuries by the tyranny of the birds of prey, Calistomos offers himself and his people as vassals to Crisorroa, the phoenix bird who acts as the Queen of the hyperborean realm. It is at this point that standard features of utopian narrative assume importance again. Crisorroa shows herself as a compassionate leader and does not accept any form of slavery in her kingdom because that would infringe upon her natural benevolence. In the *Monarquía columbina*, the Queen metonymically represents government and is portrayed as a protective and liberal ruler who is particularly prone to loneliness, 'no porque sea enemiga del género humano, sino por no ver las maldades que ejecutan los piratas con los inocentes' [not because she is an enemy of the human race, but because she does not want to see the evils that pirates commit against the innocent].[21] As is the case with the privileged position of the philosopher-king in his role as ruler of the utopian country, Crisorroa is aware of the superior power that she has been given by Providence, but acknowledges that she identifies with the rest of the world in the universal desire to live in peace, without fear or vices. Although Calistomos represents the patriarchal authority that rules the utopian society, the character of Crisorroa introduces a strong matriarchal component that subverts the gendered view of a male-dominated utopian world. Thus, Merino's text strays from the standard utopian model and contributes a notable feature to the Spanish utopian tradition.

Crisorroa gives the doves full access to the land and the right to delimit their own territory within the country, where they are required to live according to an established set of laws:

> Lo que pedís se os concede sin restricción alguna, porque beneficios con condiciones es verdadera esclavitud. [...] El territorio le elegiréis a vuestro gusto, con toda la extensión que os parezca conveniente; bien entendido que libremente podéis pasearos por todo el reino que pertenece a mi patrimonio. En lo demás se os darán por escrito las leyes que debéis observar para vuestra mayor unión y concordia, que serán pocas, claras y breves, porque la multitud

de leyes es perjudicial, perturba los pueblos, se observa ninguna y ellas entre sí se complican.²²

[What you ask for is granted to you without restriction, because benefits with conditions are true slavery. [...] You will choose the territory to your liking, with all the extension that seems appropriate; it is understood that you can freely walk around the kingdom that belongs to my inheritance. In other respects, you will be given in writing the laws that you must observe for your greatest union and harmony; these will be few, clear, and brief because a multitude of laws is harmful and disturbs people; none is observed, and they complicate each other.]

The strict observance of a few specific laws is a fundamental utopian feature that will be developed in the third *discurso* of the *Monarquía columbina*. However, although Crisorroa is presented as a sympathetic ruler, the imposition of her laws on the newly constituted monarchy of doves without input from the majority may result in the perception of the utopian system as authoritarian and undemocratic because the laws seem incapable of being questioned. This element would seem to turn Merino's work into a counter-utopia.

It is significant to note the construction of Calistomos's monarchy within the boundaries of the phoenix's country, that is to say, the creation of a utopia within another utopia, a system of subordination in which Calistomos's administration depends on Crisorroa's own rules. This parallel configuration of both kingdoms not only implies an indirect form of the process of colonization prior to the materialization of the utopian reality, but also entails the disadvantages of building a utopian space in a human (or animal) context in opposition to the perfectly utopian place created by divine intervention. Worldly happiness is always at risk of failing and bringing about the end of the ideal society. The supernatural character of the utopian enterprise is an aspect that the *Monarquía columbina* clearly shares with *Sinapia*.

The Utopian System of the Kingdom of Doves

In order to ensure an organized application of the laws, Calistomos, having been named governor of the doves, divides them into twelve tribes after choosing a flourishing and fertile valley as the place to establish their own kingdom. However, the division of the land does not promote the practice of private property — a feature contrary to utopian discourse — as such an implementation would constitute a grave mistake in the effective founding of the monarchy. The division of the doves into twelve tribes clearly echoes the twelve Hebrew tribes of Israel that, after Moses' death, settled in the Promised Land of Canaan under the leadership of Joshua (Genesis 49. 1–28), but it could also allude to the twelve apostles, each of whom was meant to rule one of the tribes.

Following the utopian ideal of a rural and egalitarian society, the monarchy of the doves is based on agriculture, and their social structure does not contemplate class hierarchies or honorific treatment. The lack of social privileges and distinctions is in accord with their rejection of practices exercised by the community of birds of prey.

In other words, the *Monarquía columbina* advocates the elimination of the concept of nobility, as opposed to the inclination of other Spanish utopias to merely suppress its hereditary character.

In spite of the laws being considered unnatural due to their restrictive nature, they must be enforced to avoid misconduct and indiscipline, especially in those whose personality is intrinsically corruptible. An abundance of laws is seen as useless and ineffective, hence the convenience of having a small number of them detailing precise instructions to be put into practice. Although they go against natural laws, the artificial rules imposed by any society are necessary to make its members free. Being a Christian monarchy, service to God underlies the sense of freedom in the actions of the doves. A pelican called Argirodoto,[23] one of the ministers of the Queen, is put in charge of ensuring compliance with the seven laws ordered by Crisorroa, which are presented as divine commandments to be carefully obeyed: 1) each day will begin with a service to thank God for their existence; 2) all goods will be communal, and there will be no titles of distinction in order to prevent discord; 3) if a dove is offended by another's actions, the offender must beg forgiveness on bended knee; otherwise, the offender will be exiled; 4) any act of contempt against parents will be severely punished; 5) when a misdemeanour is committed, the parents of the offender are to be punished as well because they have failed to provide their children with a good upbringing and education; 6) parents must educate their children in obedience to God's precepts; 7) there will be no tribunals, judges, or lawyers because there will be no lawsuits due to the absence of private land ownership.

The legislation described is grounded in religion, and the education carried out by parents must instil in children a devotion to God. Each tribe of doves will have only two mediators ('hombres ancianos de piedad y religión' [elderly men of piety and religion])[24] to deal with potential complaints or disputes. While the carrying out of a death sentence can only be authorized by Crisorroa, Calistomos has the power to sentence those found guilty to prison, exile, lashes, or public shaming. Crisorroa's laws only vaguely outline the structural mechanism of the monarchy of the doves and do not cover many aspects of its socio-political system. Similarly, the religious institutions of the doves' utopian society are not specified in the *Monarquía columbina*, a characteristic that distances Merino's text from the narrative tradition of Spanish utopian works in which the concept and organization of the Church are considerably developed. This thematic absence contrasts with the spiritual and moral dimensions that determine the essence of Merino's utopian account. Such an omission could be interpreted as a way of avoiding censorship, but as Álvarez de Miranda explains,

> [D]e la mayor parte de los textos que publicó Valladares en el *Semanario* no quedan noticias [...]. Ante la falta de ellas cabe suponer, pues, que el *Tratado* pasó la censura previa sin problemas, ayudado por la confusión del momento — en que se empezaba a perseguir especialmente la propaganda revolucionaria — y también, probablemente, por su propia ambigüedad ideológica.[25]
>
> [There are no details concerning the majority of texts that Valladares published

> in the *Weekly* [...]. Given this absence, it can be assumed, then, that the *Treatise* passed the prior censorship system without any problems, aided by the confusion of the time — when revolutionary propaganda was beginning to be pursued — and also, probably, because of its own ideological ambiguity.]

With regard to the subjects to be taught, the educational method highlights the cultivation of moral values and respect for the principle of personal dignity. Since the training of children is basically religious and spiritual, the study of the secular sciences is relegated in favour of a learning process focused on the duties to God and man. The main goal is to maintain a just and harmonious communal existence, in which mutual respect is the predominant element. The exclusion of scientific knowledge from the educational system of the doves — which is the opposite in *Sinapia* or *El Evangelio en triunfo*, as will be seen in the next chapter — is an evident denial of the Enlightenment's emphasis on education and for there to be formal education in other areas besides those closely linked to religion. In trying to explain how the *Monarquía columbina* is distinct from the Enlightenment spirit of the reign of Carlos III and from other modern utopias, Álvarez de Miranda argues that the principal dissident gesture of the text against Enlightenment thinking is its radical dismissal of science and the progress that comes with it:

> [S]upone un vivo contraste con la importancia que se concede a la ciencia como motor del progreso — y por ende a la formación científica — en casi todas las utopías, y de manera muy especial en la *Nueva Atlántida* de Bacon. La clara divergencia de nuestro autor se explica aquí por su misma postura de cerrada oposición a los 'civilizados' del momento, defensores inequívocos del progreso científico.[26]
>
> [It supposes a sharp contrast with the importance given to science as the engine of progress — and therefore to scientific training — in almost all utopias, and especially in the *New Atlantis* of Bacon. The clear difference of our author is explained here by his very attitude of strong opposition to the 'civilized' people of the time, unequivocal defenders of scientific progress.]

Merino's anti-Enlightenment position concerning education and knowledge is also apparent in his epic poem in prose *La mujer feliz, dependiente del mundo y de la fortuna* [*The Happy Woman, Dependent on the World and Fortune*], published in three volumes in 1786 under the pseudonym of El Filósofo Incógnito [The Unknown Philosopher]. This work is a kind of continuation of *El hombre feliz, independiente del mundo y de la fortuna* [*The Happy Man, Independent of the World and Fortune*] (1779) by the Portuguese priest Teodoro de Almeida. Although inspired by Almeida's novel, the originality of Merino's essentially didactic text lies in its ideological and stylistic divergence from the story on which it is based: women become the main characters, and the narrative is addressed to a female audience, which reaffirms Merino's inclination towards the representation of a matriarchal society. As the fictional editor states in his prologue about the author,

> [E]l motivo que tuvo para escribir este poema fue el amor a la humanidad, en especial para con las mujeres, que son las únicas que con su ejemplo, virtud y discreción pueden criar sus hijos con la noble y generosa educación que tuvo la

> heroína de esta obra, y mujer incomparable en la prudencia y caridad para con los infelices.[27]
>
> [The reason he had to write this poem was love for humanity, especially for women, who are the only ones who, with their example, virtue, and discretion, can bring up their children with the noble and generous education that the heroine of this work had, an incomparable woman in terms of prudence and charity towards the wretched.]

Merino's epic poem tells the story of Sofronia, Countess of Moravia, a widow commonly known by the nickname of *mujer feliz* [happy woman], and of the events that happened in her house in Olmütz while Princess Sophia of Constantinople stayed there as a guest. Sofronia became a model for other women, and her education was an example to follow by Christian girls and young women.

In *La mujer feliz*, Merino launches an attack against the intellectual activities of the philosophers who dare to enquire into religious matters that he considers inherently inaccessible to human reason. Not only does Merino seem to believe that God is the only source of reason ('Siempre que la razón mande, nos dirigirá al Criador' [Whenever reason dictates, it will lead us to the Creator]),[28] but he also distrusts the philosophers who question the existing ordering of the universe and propose reforms. Merino expresses the same rejection of the questioning of political and social structures in the *Monarquía columbina*. Moreover, in line with his support for a non-scientific educational method, he appears to defend the concept of innate ideas as the best source of knowledge and rejects a modern empiricism based on the evidence of the senses:

> Si en vez de lenguas nos enseñaran matemáticas, organizándonos antes la cabeza, esto es, quitándonos los errores de los sentidos, nos acostumbraríamos a pensar sin ayo en las materias científicas, y romperíamos las cadenas con que estamos aprisionados y que nos hacen infelices.[29]
>
> [If instead of languages, we were taught mathematics, organizing our heads sooner, that is to say, taking away from us the errors of the senses, we would become accustomed to thinking of scientific matters without a tutor and would break the chains that imprison us and make us unhappy.]

A more intense criticism of the supposedly frivolous attitudes and affectations adopted in the name of civilization is displayed in the final *discurso* of the text.

From a Utopian to a Dystopian Social Model

The content of the fourth *discurso* is the narration of what happened to the *Monarquía columbina* five hundred years later when Crisorroa was about to die. During the intervening period, the community of doves was a genuine utopian society, in which happiness and justice were the foundations of its monarchy: 'Quinientos años vivieron en este estado de felicidad, seguras y libres de todo cuidado, gozando libremente y sin recelo de todos los bienes que ofrecía la abundancia del terreno' [They lived in this state of happiness for five hundred years, safe and free of all cares, enjoying freely and without fear all the goods offered by the abundance of the land].³⁰ Nevertheless, as the phoenix predicted, the nation of the doves came to an end when the vicious ideology of the birds of prey infiltrated the system of government of their innocent victims, taking advantage of the weakness of their condition and the unavoidable tendency of human nature to be attracted to bad influences, a clear echo of the Christian concept of original sin. From the perspective of the conventions and expectations of utopian discourse, it is puzzling that nothing is recounted of the five hundred years during which the life of the birds in their new environment was peaceful and prosperous. It is not known how the ideal society of doves was achieved in the new land after its establishment. In a more conventional utopian narrative, an account of how society functioned during this extensive period of peace and normality would be expected to be described in detail and its merits made evident; however, such a component was clearly not thought to be essential by Merino.

After Calistomos's death, the doves got swept up in the curiosity of knowing other countries and their inhabitants as a result of their own prosperity and desire to broaden their vision of the world. Thus appears the questionable idea that abundance and success produce arrogance and corruption, a way of thinking that justifies the importance of a solid moral education. Moreover, this aspect leads to the assumption that the obedience to Calistomos was key to the achievement of the utopian monarchy of the doves because, once their leader died, they unfortunately decided to establish relations with outside birds, which eventually resulted in their moral decline. The hostility towards the encounters with foreign realities is a manifestation of the degree of xenophobia that defines the perspective of other utopias such as *New Atlantis* or *Sinapia*. In this manner, the isolated state that constitutes the essence of utopia turns into an intolerant and closed-minded mentality, a posture that makes it possible to think of Merino, in Álvarez de Miranda's words, as 'un casticista de la España del XVIII' [a purist of eighteenth-century Spain].³¹

Before dying in accordance with the myth, Crisorroa held a meeting with all the species of birds, in which she rejected the request of the birds of prey to live together in harmony with the doves. Their claim was that the imputation of immorality against them was a false accusation and that their only ambition was to protect the doves because their nature was inherently paternalistic. However, the birds of prey managed to convince the group of doves who took over the leadership during the interregnum of the monarchy, that is to say, until Morantia, the new bird born from the ashes of Crisorroa, was able to assume control of the government. The underpinnings of the ruling system subscribed to by the predatory birds totally undermined the tenets of the monarchy of the doves:

> [L]os palomos áulicos patrocinaron su petición diciendo que las señoras aves de rapiña eran gente ilustrada y civilizada, que sabían distinguir los derechos de las gentes maravillosamente, que estaban instruidas en el bello gusto de la moda, que las ciencias cultas les eran familiares. Que en una república bien ordenada debía haber jerarquías para premiar los adelantamientos del entendimiento y del valor. Que eran necesarios tribunales de justicia para que el miserable quedase protegido de la violencia de los grandes. Y finalmente, que era justísimo que

las palomas no fuesen tan absolutas dueñas de sus vidas y haciendas, y para esto se les debía poner algún freno que reprimiese la natural altivez que produce la libertad.[32]

[The courtly doves endorsed their petition by saying that the birds of prey were enlightened and civilized, that they knew how to distinguish the rights of peoples marvellously, that they were trained in the good taste of fashion, that erudite sciences were familiar to them. That in a well-ordered republic there should be hierarchies in order to reward advances in knowledge and valour. That courts of justice were necessary for the wretched to be protected from the violence of the great. And finally, that it was most just that the doves were not the absolute owners of their lives and properties, and for this they should be restrained by a brake that would repress the natural arrogance that freedom produces.]

The ironic, virtually sarcastic tone of this passage reveals that Merino disparages the concepts of enlightenment and civilization, which in his view entail bad taste in the choice of clothing, a superficial understanding of science, and the judgement of advances in knowledge and improvements of value made exclusively by socially superior individuals. He also seems to condemn the interpretation of natural law (the increasingly important concept of *derecho de gentes* or *ius gentium*) by the enlightened classes, who used such legislation to protect the poor (*el miserable*) from the powerful (*los grandes*).[33] The need for the legal protection of all citizens is one of the main reasons to establish a sophisticated system of courts, an anti-utopian element that, according to Merino's thinking, ends up destroying the ideal community of doves. Merino, then, criticizes key ideas of those who wished to enlighten Spain, though without, of course, mentioning Spain by name. By reproducing the model of society supported by their enemies, the doves transform their utopian dream into a dystopian nightmare. This model would appear to be a description of the existing social order in Spain, where the nobility, its privileges, and titles were the political basis of society.

Álvarez de Miranda also rightly asserts that the *Monarquía columbina* outlines a concept of happiness contrary to the proposals for achieving public happiness argued for by Enlightenment thinkers. For them, happiness derived in the first instance from economic prosperity, and it is this aspect that Merino's text criticizes:

Para aliviar, pues, a esta mísera gente se dejó ver otra especie de aves llamadas arpías que publicaron mil proyectos para hacer felices así las tribus de las palomas como el erario, pero al cabo se supo que sólo hacían feliz su buche.[34]

[In order to provide relief for these miserable people, another species of bird called harpies made their appearance and published a thousand projects to make the flocks of doves and the treasury happy, but, in the end, it was discovered that they only filled their own crops.]

The use of the word *proyecto* in this passage may explicitly refer to the works of the Spanish *proyectistas*. The narrator immediately points out that 'un palomo bachiller, y que pagó con el pellejo, dijo que la felicidad consistía en destruir tantos tribunales' [a talkative male dove, who paid with his life, said that happiness consisted in destroying so many tribunals].[35] This decisive statement implies that happiness simply consists in going back to the original state of government of the doves, in which the supposedly confusing system of laws of the birds of prey did not exist. However, modern political theorists would identify increasing civilization and the humanitarian treatment of the whole of society with legal systems designed to produce just laws enforced by effective mechanisms of justice. Merino's utopian vision of laws and justice might be considered dangerously ambiguous in that he seems to reject the effectiveness of a just legal system.

Apart from the establishment of an allegedly complex judicial system, the creation of schools, academies, and universities was implemented through the appointment of foreign instructors. All the arts and sciences were included in the educational programme of the civilized birds, as well as the adoption of the customs and practices of other countries. Each of these three targets would have been familiar to Merino's original readers as allusions to the French influence on prevailing tastes in the Spain of the 1780s. Merino's overtly ironic tone is more emphatic when the decline of the monarchy of the doves is blamed on the taxes that they had to pay to the birds of prey: as the *plebe columbina* [the populace of doves] rapidly evolved into a *plebe rapiñante* [the populace of birds of prey], the payment of taxes became unmanageable. Critics like Jovellanos disapproved of the unjust taxation system in Spain,[36] which was seen as stifling the ability of the labouring poor to improve their situation. This system maintained the upper classes largely exempt from taxation and ensconced in a world of privilege. The additional burden on the agricultural poor of providing for the upkeep of the Church was also seen as unjust, a situation that Merino as a cleric was hardly likely to condemn.

The uncontrollable situation resulted in the disbanding of the community of doves, which was exactly the reason why they escaped from the domain of their enemies in the first place. In addition to being unable to extricate themselves from their bad reputation in an effort to start a new life elsewhere, the new exodus of the victimized doves takes them back to the slavery of the previous era. As a moral of the story, the text concludes with the escape of the doves to the human world and their subsequent oppression by and submission to humans: 'Las palomas, por último, escaparon a las ciudades de los hombres y, huyendo de unos enemigos, dieron en poder de otros peores' [The doves finally escaped to the cities of men, and, fleeing from one set of enemies, they ended up in the power of others who were even worse].[37] In an attempt to restore the coherence of the narrative, this final sentence refers to the fact that the humanization of the doves was part of the allegorical sense of the text and that the birds, and human beings by extension, are always slaves to the inglorious power of superior social groups. Such power derives from the distortion of the common attributes of all the birds:

> Ya veis, queridas palomas, que la naturaleza no nos dio armas algunas para nuestra defensa, porque nunca hicimos otro uso de nuestras uñas y pico sino el que es necesario para la vida, que las aves de rapiña uno y otro lo han convertido en aguzadas cuchillas para rasgar y despedazar a todo viviente.[38]
>
> [As you can see, dear doves, nature did not give us any weapons for our defence because we never made use of our claws and beaks, which the birds of prey have

turned into sharp blades to rip and tear apart any living creature, for anything other than what is necessary to stay alive.]

The main criticism of Merino's text ultimately centres on the misuse that the birds of prey make of the advantages of their own natural constitution — especially their beaks and claws — to cause harm to other birds, which is the metaphorical representation of any damaging agent that can disrupt the smooth functioning of a social order.

The Underlying Connotations of the Text

The utopian perspective of the *Monarquía columbina* takes as its starting point the Manichean dichotomy of good and evil, relying on the Christian symbolism of the dove as the image of the Holy Spirit and on the message of peace, innocence, and purity that this idea implies. Moreover, the 'diaspora' of the doves seems to represent the estrangement of Jesus Christ from his family: '[E]l hijo separado del padre, y la madre de las queridas prendas de sus entrañas' [The son separated from the father, and the mother from the beloved offspring of her body].[39] However, it equally echoes the search for the Promised Land of the children of Israel as narrated in the Old Testament account. The way the metaphorical use of the doves and the phoenix fits the Christian context appears to have been strategically worked out by Merino. In addition, the function of the family as a core social institution is key to the successful development of the monarchy of the doves.[40]

Beyond the religious interpretation, the storyline of the *Monarquía columbina* relates to the idea of a remote Golden Age before the Manichean division of the birds into two contending factions:

> Por lo que toca a la templanza y honestidad con que vivieron en tiempos antiguos, sería temeridad y mala crianza no dar crédito a lo que nos contaron nuestros abuelos y bisabuelos, y más cuando un tatarabuelo mío aseguró haber él alcanzado aquellos felices tiempos y haber vivido juntamente con un sacre muy inocente, y que toda su familia era muy honrada y bienhechora.[41]

> [Regarding the temperance and honesty with which they lived in ancient times, it would be reckless and ill-educated not to give credit to what our grandparents and great-grandparents told us, especially when a great-great-grandfather of mine claimed that he had reached those happy times and lived together with a very innocent saker falcon, and that all members of its family were very honourable and benevolent.]

This depiction of an idyllic past when there was no rivalry among the birds reveals the inspiration behind the desire to recover the utopian coexistence of the species. However, in opposition to the myth of the Golden Age, the doves must work to provide their own maintenance, despite the abundance and fertility of the hyperborean woods. In this sense, the Arcadian life of the doves tends to be rather a form of primitive communism, as Álvarez de Miranda notes: '[A]unque se nos describa el lugar en que las palomas se asientan como un paraíso abundante [...], la intención del autor se inclina hacia lo que [...] podemos llamar colectivismo'

[Although the place where the doves settle is described to us as a fertile paradise [...], the intention of the author leans towards what [...] we might call collectivism].[42]

The symbolic content of Merino's work leads one to think of it as a hybrid story that combines elements from different textual traditions. Aside from making use of material from Christianity and mythology, it is possible that the author had recourse to the compendium of birds in medieval bestiaries in order to outline the personalities of his fictional characters, of which a few distinctive characteristics are explained in Mercier's study.[43] At the beginning of the story, there is a gallery of birds specifying the members that the avian nation comprises: '[T]odas estas aves que llaman nobles, como son águilas, buitres, gavilanes, milanos, azores, neblíes, gerifaltes, sacres, quebrantahuesos, arpías, vencejos, búhos, cornejas, lechuzas, mochuelos, etc.' [All these birds that are called nobles, such as eagles, vultures, sparrowhawks, kites, goshawks, peregrine falcons, gyrfalcons, saker falcons, lammergeiers, harpies, swifts, owls, crows, barn owls, owlets, etc.].[44]

In relation to this cultural — no longer only religious or moral — significance of the birds, it is impossible not to mention Aristophanes' comedy *The Birds* (414 BC) as a potential source of inspiration for the *Monarquía columbina*. In fact, *The Birds* is considered Aristophanes' first utopian play. It narrates the story of two Athenians, Pisthetaerus and Euelpides, who, tired of living in the polis, where people only argue over the law all day, decide to convince the birds that they must create the perfect city in the sky, called Cloudcuckooland, because they were the original gods and should regain their powers and privileges from the Olympian gods. By doing so, the birds would be able to escape the tyranny of humans and dominate them. However, Pisthetaerus and Euelpides realize that their cohabitation with the birds is making them lose touch with their humanity because the citizens of Cloudcuckooland treat the humans who begin coming into the land as enemies and deprive them of their freedom as the birds implement the laws of the new city with excessive zeal. Therefore, Cloudcuckooland entirely depends on law enforcement in order to be a functioning city, which ironically turns it into a tyrannical land.[45] The enmity between birds and mankind in Aristophanes' play is similar to the one between doves and birds of prey, and subsequently to the one between doves and humans in the *Monarquía columbina*. Moreover, the claim of divinity of Aristophanes' birds and the creation of their own empire relate to the establishment of the monarchy of the doves, but the desire for power and domination of these birds and their cumbersome legal machinery connect them with the dystopian world of the birds of prey. *The Birds* is a satire on the running of the law courts and on politics in ancient Athens and uses anthropomorphic birds to parody the members of the political and justice system. In the same vein, the utopian approach of Merino's text is targeted at satirizing the unnecessarily intricate regulations in the mechanisms of government of the birds of prey.

Another significant literary source that could well have influenced the plot of the *Monarquía columbina* is the second imaginary journey of Savinien Cyrano de Bergerac in *Histoire comique des états et empires de la lune et du soleil* (1662).[46] Dyrcona, the protagonist of the story and Cyrano's alter ego (and near-anagram), travels to the sun and arrives at the kingdom of the birds, which make him their prisoner because they hate mankind. He is accused of chasing and killing birds, but, more importantly, of corrupting their ingenuous nature. The phoenix appears in the story as well, but it doesn't have a royal position. The king of the birds is always the most peaceful of them, like the male dove that was governing during the visit of Dyrcona. Coincidentally, Tommaso Campanella also shows up in the tale as Dyrcona's guide and takes him to the Land of the Philosophers.[47]

As can be seen from the possible impact that the above textual references might have had on the *Monarquía columbina*, Andrés Merino made use of his wide-ranging cultural knowledge in order to create his own utopian text. Together with his interest in palaeography, pedagogy, rhetoric, lexicography, engraving, among other disciplines, Merino stood out for his narrative production.[48] One noteworthy literary and pedagogical work by the author is his already mentioned text *La mujer feliz*. A significant link between this didactic work and the *Monarquía columbina* is the fact that *La mujer feliz* interpolates short stories featuring animals as protagonists, stories from which a moral is always drawn. However, even more relevant is Merino's fragmentary manuscript text entitled *Monarquía de los leones* [*The Monarchy of Lions*], which was left incomplete by the author. Unlike the monarchy of doves, the monarchy of lions is not a utopian system because lions, which act as the universal protectors of all the animals, allow the oppression of the inferior species by the superior ones. In spite of this ideological divergence, the lions, like the doves, found their own monarchy in the mythical kingdom of Golconda in order to escape from their enemies, the humans. The parallel between both texts restates Merino's intention of metaphorically recreating the conflicting relationships of power among human beings.[49] However, it is not possible to develop this comparison very far since the *Monarquía de los leones* is a text in embryo only.

Thus, Merino's social ideology is grounded in a pessimistic view of humanity that recalls Thomas Hobbes's gloomy vision of human nature in *Leviathan* (1651), in which human beings are seen as predators and in conflict with one another in a society based on individuals' mutual fear. The absence of a fellow feeling for humanity leads to a natural state of war in which there are no ethical distinctions:

> *In such a war nothing is unjust.* To this war of every man against every man, this also is consequent; that nothing can be unjust. The notions of right and wrong, justice and injustice have there no place. Where there is no common power, there is no law: where no law, no injustice. [...] Justice and injustice are none of the faculties neither of the body nor mind. [...] They are qualities that relate to men in society, not in solitude. It is consequent also to the same condition that there be no propriety, no dominion, no *mine* and *thine* distinct; but only that to be every man's that he can get; and for so long as he can keep it.[50]

The violence used by men to subdue other men automatically annihilates any distinguishing boundaries between justice and injustice, which is the situation depicted by Merino through the rivalry between the doves and the birds of prey. Oddly enough, this state of conflict and hostility equally precludes any sense of private property or attitude of 'mine versus yours', a coinciding point of contact with the utopian model.

The *Monarquía columbina* presents the emergence and demise of an allegorical utopian society in a fabulistic way that is quite unusual for the utopian genre, but appropriately matches its historical moment, appearing at a time when the didactic function of fables was seen as most effective in criticizing the existing order of things. Merino uses the struggle of doves against the despotism of birds of prey to bring awareness of the injustice he alleges is caused by institutionalized socially oppressive practices for the supposed benefit of civilization. Merino's pessimism about the goodness of human nature causes him to be labelled a reactionary writer opposed to what he sees as the erroneous, reforming principles of the Enlightenment. In addition to the anti-Enlightenment stance of the text, the dogmatic ruling system of the doves, governed by the matriarchy of the phoenix bird, causes their utopian scheme to be perceived as authoritarian to some degree. Both a female-dominated society and an overly prescriptive administration reshape the traditional characterization of the utopian model.

Merino's critical approach combines the satirical and utopian spheres to reject social classes and hierarchies in eighteenth-century Spanish society. Thinking of the reaction of his potential readers, perhaps Merino intentionally planned to formulate a convincing critique by creatively rewriting and intertwining elements from religious, cultural, and literary discourses. The ethical and aesthetic position of the author engages the reader, although it may well provoke ideological opposition. In the absence of an outsider who personally visits the utopian monarchy of the doves, the reader is implicitly called on to adopt the role of privileged visitor who witnesses and evaluates the causes of the failure of the society presented in the *Monarquía columbina*. Those who held power in the reign of Carlos III or that of his successor did not carry out the more profound transformational plans put forward by thinkers allied to Enlightenment reformism, and one might imagine that many of the original readers of Merino's text might have sympathized with the author's overt and covert criticism of the mentality that he rejected in his work.

Due to its oscillation between the antithetical realms of utopia and dystopia, Merino's narrative can be seen as confusing. As the author merely states his rejection of features associated with an enlightened society, he prevents the reader from understanding what his specific objections are. Merino's vision is ultimately dogmatic, and full engagement with his ideas is impossible. This unexplained set of values drastically weakens the internal logic of his account and makes it unconvincing to anyone persuaded by the train of thought normally associated with Enlightenment rationalism.

Notes to Chapter 6

1. See the full reference in note 9 of the Introduction to this book. The thirty-four volumes of the periodical appeared in Madrid between 1787 and 1791. Its principal focus was the dissemination of previously unpublished historical writings, few of which were literary in character. See Francisco Aguilar Piñal, *La prensa española en el siglo XVIII: diarios, revistas y pronósticos* (Madrid: Consejo Superior de Investigaciones Científicas, 1978), p. 35. For an overview of the periodical, see Guinard, *La Presse espagnole de 1737 à 1791*, pp. 281–86.
2. See note 13 in the Introduction.

3. Álvarez de Miranda, 'El Padre Andrés Merino', pp. 20–21. Based on the satirical critique of the Enlightenment as the main focus of the text, Nigel Glendinning attributed the authorship of the *Monarquía columbina* to the Spanish reformer, translator, and poet León de Arroyal (1755–1813) (Nigel Glendinning, 'Tendencias liberales en la literatura española a fines del siglo XVIII', *Dieciocho*, 9 (1986), 138–52 (p. 142)).
4. Álvarez de Miranda, 'El Padre Andrés Merino', p. 20. Almost all the known research on the *Monarquía columbina* has been carried out by Álvarez de Miranda, who found the text in the *Semanario Erudito* and decided to draw attention to the work by re-editing it with an extensive introduction and notes in 1980. His intention was to offer a definitive edition of the text based on the three sources that he was acquainted with, but so far no new edition has been published by him (Ibid., p. 39). See footnote 5 on page 21 of 'El Padre Andrés Merino' for a full bibliographical reference of the issue of the *Revista Calasancia* in which Merino's work was published.
5. Pedro Álvarez de Miranda, 'Introducción', in *'Tratado sobre la monarquía columbina': una utopía antiilustrada del siglo XVIII*, pp. v–lviii (p. xxxvii).
6. Emilio Palacios Fernández, 'El Padre Andrés Merino de Jesucristo y la cultura española del siglo XVIII', *Boletín de la Real Sociedad Bascongada de los Amigos del País*, 47 (1991), 3–42 (p. 39).
7. [Merino de Jesucristo], *Monarquía columbina*, p. 3.
8. Ibid., p. 8.
9. Ibid., p. 4.
10. Ibid., p. 5.
11. Campanella's work was written in 1602, and a few copies circulated in manuscript for some time. It was first published in 1623 in a Latin translation made by Campanella himself and entitled *Civitas solis*. The first critical edition of the text in Italian was published by Norberto Bobbio in 1941 and was based on ten of the eleven manuscripts known at the time (Daniel J. Donno, 'Introduction', in Campanella, *La Città del Sole*, pp. 1–21 (pp. 19–20)).
12. [Merino de Jesucristo], *Monarquía columbina*, pp. 7–8.
13. George Ferguson, *Signs and Symbols in Christian Art* (New York: Oxford University Press, 1961), p. 23.
14. Claire Mercier, 'De la alegoría de las aves en *Tratado sobre la monarquía columbina*, del padre Andrés Merino de Jesucristo', *Visitas al Patio*, 5 (2011), 103–19 (pp. 113–14).
15. [Merino de Jesucristo], *Monarquía columbina*, p. 9.
16. The myth of the cave appears in the dialogue between Socrates and Glaucon in Book VII of the *Republic* (Plato, pp. 193–213).
17. Campanella, *La Città del Sole*, p. 121.
18. See Tommaso Campanella, *A Discourse Touching the Spanish Monarchy*, trans. by Edmund Chilmead (London: Philemon Stephens, 1654).
19. Germana Ernst, *Tommaso Campanella: The Book and the Body of Nature*, trans. by David L. Marshall (Dordrecht: Springer, 2010), p. 57.
20. Ana L. Baquero, 'El viaje y la ficción narrativa española en el s. XVIII', in *Libros de viaje: actas de las Jornadas sobre 'Los libros de viaje en el mundo románico', celebradas en Murcia del 27 al 30 de noviembre de 1995*, ed. by Fernando Carmona Fernández and Antonia Martínez Pérez (Murcia: Universidad de Murcia, 1996), pp. 21–29 (p. 28).
21. [Merino de Jesucristo], *Monarquía columbina*, pp. 7–8.
22. Ibid.
23. In Merino's text, the concept of the pelican seems to be devoid of its meaning as a Christian symbol representing Christ's self-sacrifice for human salvation, namely the image of the pelican feeding its young with its own blood.
24. [Merino de Jesucristo], *Monarquía columbina*, p. 19.
25. Álvarez de Miranda, 'Introducción', pp. ix–x.
26. Ibid., p. xxxiii.
27. El Filósofo Incógnito [Andrés Merino de Jesucristo], *La mujer feliz, dependiente del mundo y de la fortuna*, 3 vols (Madrid: Imprenta Real, 1789), I, pp. i–ii.
28. Ibid., I, p. 94.

29. Ibid., II, p. 77.
30. [Merino de Jesucristo], *Monarquía columbina*, p. 22.
31. Álvarez de Miranda, 'Introducción', p. xxxiv.
32. [Merino de Jesucristo], *Monarquía columbina*, pp. 25–26.
33. See the brief overview by Salvador Rus Rufino, 'Evolución de la noción de derecho natural en la Ilustración española', *Cuadernos Dieciochistas*, 2 (2001), 229–59. The theory of natural law was essential to the Enlightenment and stated that certain rights were innate and universally knowable through human reason: 'During the Enlightenment period natural law existed primarily as an alternative system of morality, politics and law — a system that was intended to have the authority of two qualities that were highly prized: universality and rationality' (*The Blackwell Companion to the Enlightenment*, ed. by John W. Yolton and others (Oxford and Cambridge, MA: Blackwell, 1995), p. 351).
34. [Merino de Jesucristo], *Monarquía columbina*, p. 28.
35. Ibid., pp. 28–29.
36. In his *Informe en el expediente de ley agraria*, Jovellanos proposed a taxation system in which the tax burden should be proportional to the ability to pay (Gaspar Melchor de Jovellanos, *Informe de la sociedad económica de esta corte al real y supremo Consejo de Castilla en el expediente de ley agraria* (Madrid: Imprenta de Sancha, 1795), p. 102).
37. [Merino de Jesucristo], *Monarquía columbina*, p. 29.
38. Ibid., p. 6.
39. Ibid., p. 3.
40. Although the importance of the family for society is a constant feature in utopian narrative, this is not the case, oddly enough, with Campanella's *La Città del Sole*, in which the preservation of the family unit is not a crucial component of an ideal social system: after the breastfeeding period is over, the child 'is given into the charge of the mistresses, if it is a female, and to the masters, if it is a male' (Campanella, *La Città del Sole*, p. 44).
41. [Merino de Jesucristo], *Monarquía columbina*, p. 5.
42. Álvarez de Miranda, 'Introducción', p. xxx.
43. Mercier, pp. 111–12.
44. [Merino de Jesucristo], *Monarquía columbina*, p. 5. It is possible that Merino had access to Buffon's *Histoire naturelle, générale et particulière*, in which nine out of thirty-six volumes are on birds. The Spanish translation in twenty-one volumes by José Clavijo y Fajardo only began to appear in 1786.
45. Aristophanes, *'The Birds' and Other Plays*, trans. by David Barrett and Alan H. Sommerstein (London: Penguin, 2003).
46. 'Cyrano no debía de ser desconocido en la España del XVIII, a juzgar por lo que se lee en la propaganda de la traducción española de los *Viajes del Capitán Lemuel Gulliver*: "Invectiva de la misma especie que los *Viajes de Enrique Wanton al país de las monas*, el *Viaje a la luna* de Cyrano de Bergerac, *Micromegas* y otros"' [Cyrano may not have been unknown in eighteenth-century Spain, judging from what one reads in the advertisement of the Spanish translation of *The Travels of Captain Lemuel Gulliver*: 'an invective of the same kind as *The Travels of Henry Wanton to the Country of the Monkeys*, the *Voyage to the Moon* of Cyrano de Bergerac, *Micromegas*, and others'] (Álvarez de Miranda, 'Introducción', p. xliii).
47. Savinien Cyrano de Bergerac, *Œuvres complètes*, 2 vols (Paris: Galic, 1962), I: *Histoire comique des états et empires de la lune et du soleil*.
48. For detailed information about the life and other works of Merino, see Palacios Fernández, 'El Padre Andrés Merino de Jesucristo y la cultura española del siglo XVIII'.
49. Pedro Álvarez de Miranda sees the stories as 'dos relatos gemelos' [two twin stories] (Álvarez de Miranda, 'El Padre Andrés Merino', p. 38). See also Pedro Álvarez de Miranda, 'Un relato inédito e inacabado del P. Andrés Merino: la *Monarquía de los leones*', *Dieciocho*, 16 (1993), 13–23.
50. Thomas Hobbes, *Leviathan; or, The Matter, Form and Power of a Commonwealth Ecclesiastical and Civil*, ed. by Michael Oakeshott (New York: Simon & Schuster, 1997), p. 101.

CHAPTER 7

Between Utopia and Reform: The Educational and Socio-Economic Vision of the 'Cartas de Mariano a Antonio' in *El Evangelio en triunfo*

During the progressive early years of the reign of Carlos III, when legislation and state-led initiatives sought to reform society and regenerate the economy, the Peruvian-born Pablo de Olavide y Jáuregui (1725–1803) was not only a prolific theorist, but also a practical collaborator in governmental activity.[1] In 1767, Olavide was entrusted with the Sierra Morena settlement project, a socio-economic blueprint potentially applicable to the whole of Spain.[2] The plan was implemented not only in response to the problems of depopulation and inefficient agricultural practices, but also as a way of creating useful citizens whose role was essential for the successful realization of the project. Three decades later, Olavide would draw on the plan in the final six letters of his epistolary philosophical text *El Evangelio en triunfo, o historia de un filósofo desengañado*. In 1988, Gérard Dufour argued for this group of letters to be considered a utopian tale separable from the preceding plot of *El Evangelio*,[3] entitling them 'Cartas de Mariano a Antonio' ['Letters from Mariano to Antonio'] in his edition of that year.[4]

By comparing the two stages in Olavide's thinking, the present chapter will analyse the overlap of reformism and utopianism as well as the ideological implications of the educational and socio-economic features of the society described in the 'Cartas'. In response to scholars who dismiss the utopian intention of these letters, the analysis will discuss the degree to which the final sections of *El Evangelio* conform to the parameters of the utopian model. It will also focus on the links between the agenda of Enlightenment reformism and Catholic thought, revealing the Creole administrator as a subtle and original proponent of theological argument in a reactionary clerical environment. In so doing, this chapter draws on José Antonio Maravall's differentiation between reformist and utopian thinking: the first characterized by isolated, piecemeal changes, the second by comprehensive reform.[5]

The *Nuevas Poblaciones* and Olavide's Economic Thought

After graduating with a doctorate in theology and a degree in law by the age of seventeen, Olavide occupied various governmental positions in the Viceroyalty of Peru. However, it was the tragic earthquake that destroyed Lima in 1746, killing his parents and one of his sisters, that first gave him the opportunity to demonstrate his skills as an administrator. He was commissioned to carry out the rebuilding of the city, but was later accused of using funds designated for the restoration of a church to build a theatre, something not considered a priority in the reconstruction of urgent infrastructure. Although Olavide's action may have derived from his literary interests and his desire to provide the citizenry with a place where they could escape the traumatic experience of the earthquake,[6] he was accused of misuse of funds, which led him to present himself in Spain to face trial and possible imprisonment.[7] Nevertheless, his actions during the reconstruction of Lima revealed an ability to apply his intellectual skills to the transformation of physical reality. While some interpreted the earthquake as divine punishment and organized religious processions to placate God's wrath,[8] Olavide tackled the tragic event from a practical and humanitarian perspective.[9]

Olavide continued to demonstrate his administrative expertise by carrying out new duties assigned to him in Spain, such as director of the Hospice of San Fernando in Madrid, representative of the city council, and *Intendente* [royal governor] of Seville,[10] but his most important role was to be as *Intendente* in the socio-political experiment of the *Plan de Nuevas Poblaciones* [Plan for New Settlements] of the Sierra Morena in Andalusia, a task delegated to Olavide by Campomanes. Similar to his work to rebuild Lima after the earthquake, the project gave Olavide the opportunity to reorganize an entire community, but on a larger scale, taking into account sociological factors. Though his task was to repopulate the area and revive the agrarian economy, the project was regulated by the legislative code entitled *Instrucción y fuero de población* [*Population Norms and Rights*], which framed the political, social, and economic life of the settlements from 1767 until 1835. In his study of the scheme, Julio Caro Baroja described Olavide as 'el filósofo creador, el utopista generoso y un poco precipitado' [the creative philosopher, the generous and somewhat hasty utopian].[11] Indeed, the Count of Peñaflorida — founder of the recently established Royal Basque Society of the Friends of the Country — saw the *Nuevas Poblaciones* as 'una nueva Arcadia' [a new Arcadia] or 'verdadero paraíso terrenal' [a true earthly paradise] and called Olavide 'un nuevo Adán' [a new Adam].[12]

The importance of the *Plan de Nuevas Poblaciones* lies in the fact that it allowed Olavide to rethink the spatial organization of a rural community, a plan that acquires a literary utopian form in the 'Cartas de Mariano a Antonio'.[13] The socio-economic reconstruction of the Sierra Morena was the kind of real utopia that Olavide could not have foreseen when thinking of how to improve Lima. In fact, the Sierra Morena project is another example of a political experiment with utopian features,[14] as was the case of the Jesuit missions of Paraguay and their corresponding utopian correlation with the socio-political structure of Sinapia. Bearing in mind that Olavide had a close relationship with Campomanes, it is possible to imagine that the occasional similarities between both experimental projects were due to the former having access to the latter's personal library, where the manuscript of *Sinapia* was housed.

The complex socio-economic experiment was based on a plan suggested by Johann Kaspar von Thürriegel, a Bavarian colonel in the service of Carlos III, whose scheme was originally designed to be put into practice in deserted areas of South America and Puerto Rico. However, Olavide thought that Thürriegel's scheme would be better applied to the underpopulated and unproductive region of the Sierra Morena, and especially to the vast plains of Andalusia that were rife with bandits, a situation that hampered communication with Madrid. Olavide's detailed thinking on the subject initially fed into his *Informe sobre la ley agraria* [*Report on the Agrarian Law*], drawn up in 1768.[15]

The plan consisted in recruiting mainly German, Swiss, and Flemish Catholic farmers and stockbreeders and transporting them to Spain as colonists. The new settlements comprised up to thirty adjacent houses, and each active settler would receive fifty acres of land. Monks and nuns were excluded because they were likely to accumulate wealth and assume land ownership in perpetuity, but priests, along with mayors, deputies, and delegates, would oversee parishes composed of up to five settlements. The participation of foreigners was intended to rouse the lethargic spirit of Spain's farmers, resulting from agrarian failure considered to derive from inadequate agricultural legislation.[16] Nevertheless, the project aimed to include Spanish farmers in order to preserve the Spanish language and Catholic religion.[17] What is more, marriages between Spaniards and foreigners were encouraged in order to stimulate population growth, though equally to incorporate the latter into the labour infrastructure of the region.[18] The plan thus contemplated a calculated process of transculturation with economic objectives as the pillar for the sociological restructuring of rural community life in that part of Spain.

One peculiarity of the repopulation experiment was its eclectic and rootless nature;[19] that is to say, the greater the social and cultural dissimilarity from the Spanish nation, the better the social composition of the ideal society.[20] This tendency to venerate foreign experiences by virtue of their alleged superiority is also visible in the culturally hybrid constitution of the utopian society in *Sinapia*, mainly when it comes to the assimilation of foreign knowledge. Nonetheless, both *Sinapia* and Olavide's programme advocate the indispensable preservation of a Christian identity. Apart from this goal, the Sierra Morena project had as its objective the complete transformation of an unproductive and unsafe territory into a useful and profitable one. The immigrant inhabitants were supposed to eradicate the presence of gypsies and bandits who lived outside the law. In this sense, Marcelin Defourneaux points out that the sociological experiment not only entailed a physical and ideological renovation of the Sierra Morena, but might also have served as a model for the rest of Spain:

> Installer dans ces terres vierges des colons venus d'autres parties de l'Espagne, c'eût été y apporter en même temps les pratiques et les préjugés ancestraux; c'eût

été risquer une rapide 'contamination' des nouveaux venus par les populations des régions immédiatement voisines. Au contraire, le recours à des éléments 'déracinés' offrait, *a priori*, les conditions les meilleures pour la réalisation de l'expérience et la constitution d'une 'société rurale modèle' qui pourrait ensuite être donnée en exemple à toutes les campagnes espagnoles.[21]

[Settling colonizers from other parts of Spain in these virgin lands would have meant bringing at the same time ancestral practices and prejudices; it would have meant risking that the newcomers be promptly 'contaminated' by the populations of the directly neighbouring regions. On the contrary, turning to certain 'rootless' elements afforded in principle the best conditions for carrying out the experiment of creating a 'model rural society' that might then set an example for all of rural Spain.]

In spite of Spanish practices and customs being considered a potentially negative influence on the new immigrants, the exemplary character that Defourneaux attributes to this pilot scheme was eclipsed in its early stages by the impoverished background of the recently arrived migrants, as Cayetano Alcázar Molina demonstrates in his analysis of the *Nuevas Poblaciones*. Because they saw emigration to the Sierra Morena as a way of improving their living conditions, most of the foreigners who enlisted in the scheme were old, in bad health, and ill-clothed. Their pitiful state was not compatible with the high expectations of the government's plan.[22] Campomanes, however, insisted on their acceptance into the colonies claiming that their physical condition did not imply an inability to be good workers. Yet time would prove him wrong, as many colonists turned out to be unskilled and unfit for the task expected of them. The situation would eventually improve as the unsuitable migrant workers were expelled from the colonies and progressively replaced by Spanish farmers,[23] who saw this opportunity as a process of reconquest of their own territory and culture:

[L]os españoles [...] iban ya predominando y reconquistando los territorios que abandonaban los intrigantes, los borrachos, los vagos y las gentes de malas costumbres, y cultivando su propio suelo sin los clamores de lenguas extrañas ni resonancias más allá de las fronteras.[24]

[The Spaniards [...] were already in a majority and repossessing the territories left by schemers, drunks, idlers, and people of bad habits, cultivating their own soil without the clamour of strange languages or echoes from outside.]

Olavide's detailed plan for agricultural reform is set out in his *Informe sobre la ley agraria*, of which the Sierra Morena project forms a part. His solutions to the farming problems of Andalusia complement the plan for new populations contained in the *Instrucción y fuero de población*. In accordance with the *Instrucción*, Olavide outlines a programme to regulate the actions of the foreign inhabitants taking into account the existing conditions of agriculture in Andalusia. Although he did not have practical knowledge of agricultural methods, and the information he relied on came largely from books,[25] the originality of his thought undermined the traditional standards of the ruling administration.[26] In addition to his theoretical understanding, Olavide saw in the pragmatic imitation of effective past experience a reliable and convenient approach to be applied. He urged following the example of England, a country whose economic history he viewed as similar to that of Spain, but which was seen in eighteenth-century Europe as being at the leading edge of successful innovation. It was imperative for Spain to imitate the most important changes introduced in the English rural economy, in particular the equal status of agriculture and stockbreeding.[27]

Once arable farming is identified as a key productive activity, the main point criticized by Olavide is the unsuitable distribution of land and its consequent poor cultivation, as well as the application of bad farming techniques. The lamentable state of agriculture has a negative effect on the social structure of Andalusia, which is divided into four classes: landowners, big and small landlords, and farm workers. Aside from the social inequality that this hierarchy creates, the detachment of owners from their properties constitutes the major issue to be discussed in Olavide's *Informe*. In order to achieve a better exploitation of land and its resources, its redistribution should be based on the possession of plots by tenant farmers (*colonos*) who would settle in their properties and cultivate them using appropriate techniques. Such a system of land tenure could also be applied to land owned by the Church; since the clergy should be expected to devote its time purely to spiritual and missionary work, the cultivation of the land could be taken over by competent farmers.

Although Olavide's plan sought to reduce the socio-economic differences among the social groups in Andalusia, he was aware of the political necessity of a monarchy to preserve wealth inequality, but he also specified that there should be many people with moderate fortunes instead of vast wealth enjoyed only by a tiny minority.[28] The encouragement of individual or private property ownership is a factor that some scholars claim may disqualify Olavide's project from being viewed as utopian. However, the promotion of individualism in this case is justified by the sense of involvement that owning a possession engenders.[29] Furthermore, as Jovellanos would conclude some thirty years later in the *Informe en el expediente de ley agraria* (1795), private property should be seen as a legitimate feature of society.[30] Jovellanos recognizes that, as an individualistic conception of property always implies social injustice, the accumulation of wealth by a privileged few should be avoided. Thus, the notion of land ownership emerges as a norm in which the concept of property as a product of nature legitimizes the natural distinction between social classes. This principle was shared by the French physiocrat and economist Mirabeau in *L'Ami des hommes, ou traité de la population* (1756),[31] a text believed by some to have influenced Olavide's economic thought. Therefore, Olavide's socio-economic experiment can be approached from the idyllic and redemptive status of agriculture, according to which rural society obeys nature's laws and acts as an antagonistic force against a corrupt urban metropolis. The idealistic character of such thinking will now be examined.

El Evangelio en triunfo in Context

Olavide's *El Evangelio en triunfo* was first published in Valencia in 1797–98, being repeatedly reprinted in subsequent decades and becoming a bestseller in Europe and America.[32] The first two volumes appeared in 1797 and the final two in 1798. The subtitle was added from the second edition onwards. Although published anonymously, Olavide was known to be the author by many of his contemporaries. The work was completed at the end of a seventeen-year exile in France, after his escape from confinement by the Spanish Inquisition on being convicted of heresy in 1778, a charge he vehemently denied.[33] Because of his status as a foreigner in France and being suspected of collaboration with the French political elite, Olavide was incarcerated for a few months in 1794. The new imprisonment caused him to witness at first-hand the extreme violence during the period of the French Revolution known as the Reign of Terror. As the prologue to *El Evangelio* states, 'Yo me hallaba en París el año de 1789 y vi nacer la espantosa revolución que, en poco tiempo, ha devorado uno de los más hermosos y opulentos reinos de la Europa' [I was in Paris in 1789 and saw the birth of the dreadful revolution that, in a short time, has devoured one of the most beautiful and opulent kingdoms in Europe].[34] His disapproval of the distorted ideals of the Revolution was expressed in the final four letters of volume IV of *El Evangelio*, which were banned and taken out of the text by the Spanish censors.[35]

The sense of disillusion that Olavide experienced when the Revolution took a violent, anti-Catholic, and irrational turn led him to write *El Evangelio* as a confirmation of his Catholicism in preparation for a possible return to Spain. Scholars such as Jean Sarrailh[36] and Alfred Morel-Fatio[37] see the text as the recantation of a disillusioned Olavide, reflected in the disenchanted protagonist of his fiction. The story indeed reveals autobiographical elements that turn Olavide into the hero of his own narrative. However, as Miguel Benítez argues, rather than a mere defence of Christianity, *El Evangelio* can be read as an invocation of the true spirit of Catholicism, offering a narrative that blends Catholic discourse and Enlightenment humanist thought.[38] Amable Fernández Sanz also believes that a fundamental characteristic of *El Evangelio* is 'la necesidad de añadir un *convencimiento ilustrado* a la natural práctica de la religión en España' [the need to add an *enlightened feeling of conviction* to the natural practice of religion in Spain].[39]

Olavide portrays religion as an essential pillar of society, hence the fact that the settlements were called 'parishes' (*feligresías*) instead of 'towns' or 'villages'. The prologue to *El Evangelio* explains that the memoirs of the *filósofo desengañado* [disillusioned philosopher] are meant to show how religion, not rebellion as in the French Revolution, is the best weapon against ignorance and irrationality:

> Estas memorias deben advertir a los pueblos del peligro a que se exponen si dan oídos a esas sirenas seductoras; deben despertar a los soberanos, haciéndoles ver que no puede ser estable ni tranquila la duración de sus imperios si no preservan a sus pueblos de este fatal contagio, y que el mejor preservativo es extender en ellos la instrucción y el estudio sólido y convincente de la verdad de la religión.[40]

[These memoirs should warn people of the danger to which they expose themselves if they listen to those seductive sirens; they should awaken the sovereign rulers, making them see that the duration of their empires cannot be stable or calm if they do not preserve their peoples from this fatal contagion, and that the best protection is to spread throughout their territories education and the solid and convincing study of the truth of religion.]

In fact, a rational and humanistic Christianity is a basic feature of Olavide's utopianism and derives, in large measure, from *Les Délices de la religion, ou le pouvoir de l'Évangile pour nous rendre heureux* [*The Delights of Religion; or, The Power of the Gospel to Make Us Happy*] (1788) by the French politician Antoine-Adrien Lamourette, an author opposed to traditional theology and committed to reconciling Enlightenment thought with a tolerant Catholicism. *El Evangelio* is, in part, a translation of Lamourette's work, and Olavide acknowledges the use of the French text while looking for creative and entertaining ideas during his prison time. What is more, *El Evangelio* is believed to have inspired the writing of François-René de Chateaubriand's *Génie du christianisme* [*The Genius of Christianity*] (1802), in which the French politician defends the wisdom of the Catholic faith against attacks from supporters of the French Revolution.

Lamourette's influence is also reflected in both the plot and dialogic structure of Olavide's text, except that the storyline of *Les Délices de la religion* is not structured in the form of letters, but as a dialogue between the characters. Using the literary strategy of a found manuscript — and thanking Providence for providing him with such a discovery — the fictional author created by Olavide claims to have found in his cell letters exchanged between a philosopher and some of his friends.[41] The author acts as the editor of the letters that narrate the life of the philosopher, which happens to be a model of how religion creates better individuals and citizens. His adulthood was marked by irrational behaviour as a consequence of his defective religious education; only his embrace of Christianity turned him into an honourable and useful man. The motivation of the author to publish the letters is their potential usefulness for a Christian nation like Spain, 'donde el cristianismo tiene su mejor trono' [where Christianity has its best throne].[42]

In this way, *El Evangelio* becomes the story of the spiritual evolution of the philosopher, who, with the help of a wise priest, abandons his dissolute lifestyle to devote himself to the practice of the Gospel and to enjoying the cultivation of his land. Thus, *El Evangelio* covers the three stages in the evolution of the philosopher's existence: 1) the narration of his dissolute habits, which reaches a climax when he believes he has killed a man, escapes justice, and ends up in a convent where he is converted by an enlightened priest; 2) the actions performed by the philosopher to reform his life, which basically consist in devoting himself to agricultural work on his landed properties and in living an exemplary life that will give him the chance to learn that the man he thought he had killed was actually alive; and 3) the uniting of his Christian virtues with civic ones and the application of his rational spirit to the creation of advantageous conditions for society to flourish, a cause he remained committed to until his death.

Religion and agriculture are presented as the foundational elements of the philosopher's conversion to Christianity, which is developed in the first three volumes and part of the fourth volume of Olavide's work, in thirty-five letters from the philosopher to his friend Teodoro. The final six letters (XXXVI–XLI) of the fourth volume contain the description of the utopian town devised by the philosopher as a practical application of Christian and civic virtues.[43] In the letters, Mariano, a close friend and collaborator of the philosopher, informs his friend Antonio of the progress of the plan designed by the philosopher to reform the town (Antonio's replies are not part of the narration). Mariano and Antonio had arrived together in the nameless village of the philosopher, but Antonio abandoned it to spend five years in the New World. Mariano, then, recounts the improvements made to the village, a place that used to be miserable and unproductive, during Antonio's absence:

> Las novedades y mejoras que mi amigo ha hecho y hace todos los días en este lugar son tan rápidas como prodigiosas. [...] [L]a mutación de la escena es completa: lo que dejaste ruina, asco y miseria, lo hubieras visto convertido en hermosura, limpieza, abundancia y felicidad.[44]
>
> [The innovations and improvements that my friend has made and makes every day in this place are as speedy as they are prodigious. [...] [T]he change of scene is complete: you would have seen the ruin, disgust, and misery that you left turned into beauty, cleanliness, abundance, and happiness.]

To some extent, the place becomes the symbolic representation of a Spain that, like the philosopher, is intrinsically good and productive, but has been corrupted by the harmful ideology of the times. It was his acceptance of the Gospel that turned the philosopher into a model human being:

> [M]ientras fue incrédulo y se abandonó a sus pasiones, fue malo, despreciable y no solo infeliz, sino que hacía también infeliz a cuanto dependía de él o le rodeaba. Pero que desde que tomó por regla al Evangelio, se transformó en un filósofo justo, amable, útil en todo para todos; que no solo consiguió ser feliz él mismo, sino que hacía felices a cuantos estaban en la esfera de su influencia; y que se le vio tan buen ciudadano, tan buen padre y tan buen amo, como había sido malo cuando lo gobernaba la filosofía del siglo.[45]
>
> [While he was a non-believer and gave himself up to his passions, he was bad, despicable, and not only unhappy, but also made everything that depended on or surrounded him unhappy. But once he took the Gospel as his norm, he became a just, amiable philosopher, useful in everything for everyone. He not only succeeded in achieving personal happiness, but also made all those who were in his sphere of influence happy, and he was seen as such a good citizen, such a good father, and such a good master, as he had been bad when he was ruled by the philosophy of the era.]

The utopian character of *El Evangelio* lies in the assumption that the transfiguration of the philosopher into a leader is the first step towards guaranteeing the happiness of his community, which depends on the impact of his actions and decisions.[46] The dynamics of this interrelationship triggers a parallel between the spiritual conversion of the philosopher and the radical transformation of his village; both the town and the philosopher have been saved from their shortcomings by unconditionally accepting the precepts of the Gospel. As a result, the philosopher becomes the personification of the ideal ruler destined to favourably influence those under his protection. Olavide's concept of an ideal ruler ultimately refers to the leader as an incarnation of God, the governor par excellence, and this also applies to absolute monarchs. The philosopher thinks of himself as the universal father of all of the people living in his domains, entrusted with a divine mission based on his inherited privileged social and economic status. He is basically an intermediary for God's plan. There is certainly a contradiction between a wealthy leader and a Christian ideology that encourages frugality as a lifestyle, but the inconsistency is easily resolved by the argument that the most favoured citizens are supposed to help the less fortunate. As in other Spanish political-religious utopias, in *El Evangelio* austerity in all aspects of life is the key to maintaining a successful social order.

Not only is the concept of progress, in the sense of a socio-economic reform agenda, present in Olavide's work, but also other utopia-related discourses such as that of colonialism in terms of the desire to discover unknown territories.[47] Although the colonizing purpose of foreign farmers in Olavide's plan does not imply the actual act of exploration and colonial domination, it aims to establish an improved social order in an already occupied territory, one in which the philosopher plays a patriarchal role. The topic of colonialism, in turn, brings up the question of national identity, which in certain utopian contexts turns into a xenophobic hostility towards foreign realities. In the case of Olavide's programme, there is an evident interest in protecting Spanish identity from being undermined by the culture of immigrant colonists. Apart from these characteristics, it should be noted that Olavide's project is an example of what Ernst Bloch calls a 'concrete utopia' or Stelio Cro an 'empirical utopia' for the Spanish tradition, as previously explained in Chapter 2. Both terms refer to the implementation of utopia as opposed to the abstract representation of utopian worlds.

The Agrarian Utopia

The philosopher's socio-economic and spiritual plan can be seen as the utopian equivalent of the Sierra Morena colonization project.[48] However, such a re-elaboration requires a positive validation of the traditionally anti-utopian feature of private property. A key component of Olavide's repopulation plan is the division of land into autonomous parcels (*suertes*) on which the farmers settle. This feature of self-interest led Luis Perdices Blas to deny the label 'utopian' to Olavide's project and its corresponding fictionalization in the philosopher's plan. According to Perdices, the Peruvian thinker does not foresee the creation of an agrarian colony as an egalitarian republic because he does not attempt to modify the reality of the existing social structures. As a result, for Perdices, the concept of a utopian communal society is not applicable to Olavide's narrative. Nevertheless, as Gérard Dufour points out, an important utopian feature of Olavide's text is the fact that none of the land in the philosopher's town is owned by the Church.[49] Dufour also argues that the 'Cartas de Mariano a Antonio' were included by Olavide in *El Evangelio* as a way of pleasing the interest that the Prime Minister of Spain Manuel

Godoy — who claimed to have protected the publication of Olavide's work — had in achieving certain Enlightenment goals and as a way of helping him promote the *Semanario de Agricultura y Artes Dirigido a los Párrocos* [*Weekly of Agriculture and Arts Addressed to Parish Priests*] (1797–1808), the first Spanish periodical dedicated exclusively to agriculture and conceived by Godoy as an initiative to support his agrarian policy:

> Así entendemos por qué Olavide se empeñó en redactar las *Cartas de Mariano a Antonio*: no para expresar su adhesión a la Ilustración que no había abandonado a pesar de su conversión al cristianismo, [...] sino porque estaba al tanto de que el omnipotente Príncipe de la Paz [Manuel Godoy] deseaba al mismo tiempo difundir obras que estableciesen la verdad de la fe católica por el uso de la razón [...] y movilizar a los curas párrocos para fomentar la agricultura como intentaba hacerlo con la publicación de *El Semanario de Agricultura y Artes dirigido a los párrocos* cuyo primer número salió a luz pocos meses antes de que Luis Urbina [Godoy's nephew] se pusiera en contacto con el Consejo de Castilla respecto a la posibilidad de publicar *El Evangelio en triunfo*.[50]

> [Thus we understand why Olavide insisted on writing the *Letters from Mariano to Antonio*: not to express his adherence to the Enlightenment that he had not abandoned despite his conversion to Christianity, [...] but because he was aware that the all-powerful Prince of Peace [Manuel Godoy] wanted both to disseminate works that established the truth of the Catholic faith through the use of reason [...] and to mobilize parish priests to promote agriculture as he tried to do with the publication of *The Weekly of Agriculture and Arts Addressed to Parish Priests*, whose first issue was published a few months before Luis Urbina [Godoy's nephew] made contact with the Council of Castile about the possibility of publishing *The Triumph of the Gospel*.]

Perdices also regrets the fact that, having read More's *Utopia* — a book known to be in Olavide's private library[51] — Olavide did not follow the canonical utopian guidelines to create his model society, as was the case with the colonizing enterprise depicted in *Sinapia*, for example. Nonetheless, Perdices fails to identify the particular treatment of utopianism in *El Evangelio*, which consists of the depiction of the philosopher's village as an imaginary location where rural life makes all the inhabitants happy. In this respect, Dufour rightly observes that Antonio is a passive visitor or traveller who requests information from Mariano — virtually a native of the imaginary community — about the progress of the place where he used to live, which has now been radically transformed. Mariano, for his part, plays the role of the learned guide who lives in the utopian country. This narrative transposition in the elements of the utopian story does not influence or reduce the impact of its idealistic effect. Dufour identifies the geographical circumstances of the philosopher's town with Spain: 'Olavide arrive donc à faire une sorte d'île perdue dans l'océan de ces terres du Philosophe désabusé, terres qui par ailleurs rappellent étrangement l'intérieur de la Péninsule Ibérique' [Olavide thus manages to create a kind of island lost in the ocean of these lands of the disillusioned Philosopher, lands that also strangely resemble the interior of the Iberian Peninsula].[52] Although not literally an island, but rather an isolated place, the philosopher's land, like Sinapia, ironically represents an improved version of eighteenth-century Spain.

Another curious feature in Olavide's utopia is the reformism underlying the immigration process to repopulate the philosopher's town. Employing Bloch's view in *The Principle of Hope*, this process of voluntary displacement constitutes the paradoxical dimension of a utopian space that results from a mass exodus to 'the Promised Land', but 'promised by process'.[53] In other words, the utopian country in *El Evangelio* is not a pre-existing perfect world, but the result of calculated strategic planning. In the same vein, Ana Rueda argues for a nebulous utopian configuration of the philosopher's village due precisely to the migratory process from which it is born: '[E]sta utopía no es *u*-tópica, es decir, se instala en tierras que posee el Filósofo, y tampoco es *a*-histórica, puesto que presenciamos cómo se levanta' [This utopia is not *u*-topian, that is, it is set in lands owned by the Philosopher, and it is not *a*-historical either, since we witness how it is established].[54] However, despite the conceptual validity of this argument, it is possible to maintain that both the internal transformation of the philosopher and the external reproduction of that change by means of reforming actions in his community are the starting point for the development of a critical-utopian account that questions the existing socio-economic order.

Besides the study of religion, the training in agricultural techniques is conceived of as the most dignifying activity for the members of a society. What makes agriculture a formative experience is the possibility of learning by imitating the actions of knowledgeable landowners such as the philosopher. Echoing the mission of eighteenth-century Spanish economic societies, the philosopher persuades his neighbours to abandon their traditional farming methods by showing them how to cultivate their lands in a rational and more effective way.[55] This perspective, accepted as a norm by the economic societies, derives from the economic thought of the Spanish economist and politician Bernardo Ward, who, in the reign of Fernando VI, travelled across Europe and Spain collecting information to facilitate reform in the Spanish empire.[56] Olavide was influenced by the economic ideas for improvement of the period, but some of the alleged contradictions in his reformist proposals, attributed to his supposedly shallow theoretical analysis, are shared by other Spanish Enlightenment thinkers, with the notable exception of Jovellanos.[57] Perdices has identified the scholarly theorists that Olavide was aware of:

> Olavide estaba al tanto de lo que se había escrito de economía en España y en Europa. Conocía las obras de [Pedro] Fernández de Navarrete, Campomanes o Mirabeau, aunque desconocía las de [Adam] Smith. Recogió de los extranjeros lo que consideraba que se podía aplicar a España.[58]
>
> [Olavide was aware of what had been written about economics in Spain and Europe. He knew the works of [Pedro] Fernández de Navarrete, Campomanes, and Mirabeau, although he did not know the text of [Adam] Smith. He took from foreigners what he thought could be applied to Spain.]

In the description of the agricultural model in *El Evangelio*, it is remarkable to note the explicit reference to Spain as a case that contrasts with the economic reality of the philosopher's town, hence the advisability of emulating a foreign system that allows making the most of the abundance and fertility of Spain:

> [A]unque Dios ha dotado a nuestra España de las más excelentes tierras de Europa, y tan fecundas que se podría aumentar diez veces más el número de sus habitadores, se halla tantas veces angustiada y con los justos temores de no poder sustentar los pocos [habitantes] que tiene [...]. [E]sta miseria nace de la poca atención que se da a la agricultura; y, aunque se pudieran alegar otros defectos de ella, como son la mala distribución de las poblaciones, el mal ordenado repartimiento de las tierras y otros que es fácil numerar, es menester reconocer que todos estos males [...] se reúnen todos a producir este cultivo ligero, atropellado y superficial, que es la causa más inmediata y próxima de todos los daños.[59]

> [Although God has endowed our Spain with the most excellent lands in Europe, and so fertile that the number of their inhabitants could be increased ten times more, it is so often in trouble, with the justified fear of not being able to sustain the few [inhabitants] that it has [...]. This misery derives from the scant attention given to agriculture; and, although its other defects could be highlighted, such as the inadequate distribution of the population, the badly organized distribution of land, and others that are easy to list, it is necessary to recognize that all these evils [...] come together and result in this light, hasty, and superficial cultivation, which is the most immediate cause of all the damage.]

This passage contains the main arguments supporting the implementation of a socio-economic scheme based on an appropriate use of rural land. In that sense, the most urgent problem to be tackled is the depopulation of the countryside, the situation addressed in Olavide's *Plan de Nuevas Poblaciones*. In *El Evangelio*, the philosopher justifies the need to increase the rural population by claiming that, if a farmer were in sole charge of his land, the cultivation would be badly carried out and the final product unsatisfactory. More importantly, the philosopher's plan stipulates that the grant of land means more than a simple lease agreement: tenant farmers are entitled to have full authority over their plots as long as they respect the conditions imposed by the owner and his property rights. Even their descendants have the right to enjoy the benefits. The success of the experiment depends on appropriate and reasonable laws and conditions.

It is important to note that, although the notion of *colono* is certainly enunciated in *El Evangelio*, the idea of the process of colonization by foreign farmers is not explicitly mentioned in the description of the philosopher's project. The omission of such an essential aspect of the official reform plan for the *Nuevas Poblaciones* may be a result of the patriotic posture adopted by Olavide in his fictional recreation or of his belief that the importing of foreigners did not work. This attitude, bordering on nationalism, is reflected in the educational plan described in the 'Cartas de Mariano a Antonio', which provides the foundation for *El Evangelio*'s agricultural utopia.

The Educational Utopia

In order to set up his socio-economic programme and achieve public well-being, the philosopher creates an educational system in which religion and the study of nature have a vital role. The philosopher asks Mariano to take charge of the education of his children, Félix and Paulino, because he has to see to properties he owns elsewhere. The main reason Mariano qualifies as the perfect tutor for the philosopher's sons is that he has had a sound religious training and rejects the frivolous customs of city life. Because urban life is viewed as a source of vain pleasures, vices, and corruption, the philosopher wants Félix and Paulino to be educated in the pristine, natural environment of the countryside, where simplicity and innocence are the basis of happiness. However, he is aware that his children are free to choose to live in the city, the court, or join the army instead of restricting themselves to the limitations of a rustic existence. The utopian programme delineated in *El Evangelio* is a rural, egalitarian society based on a rational knowledge and practice of Christianity.

What problematizes this utopian social model is the image of the disenchanted philosopher who sees his project as at the crossroads of the spirituality of salvation and the secular concerns of civilization. Ana Rueda stresses the differing relationship between the Christian conversion of the philosopher and his secular utopian project to reform the village, a contradiction that she concludes to be a result of Olavide's division between his religious beliefs and utopian vision.[60] Noël Valis argues for the opposite view: the philosopher's utopian enterprise is a direct result of his religious conversion; that is to say, the existence of religious belief is affirmed through Enlightenment reform, an argument that is in agreement with the viewpoint of the present book.[61] This is a dilemma that, according to Rolando Carrasco, 'bien podría ser una inflexión problemática al momento de inscribir esta obra de Olavide en el marco histórico de una estrecha colaboración con los "ilustrados" ministros del rey Carlos III' [could well be a problematic turning point at the time of including this work by Olavide in the historical framework of a close collaboration with the 'enlightened' ministers of King Charles III].[62] Nevertheless, Mariano validates the efficiency of his friend's plan by explaining that a genuine education is universally applicable in any context of life, regardless of the kind of knowledge involved:

> La buena educación es buena para todo. La religión, la moral, los principios de las ciencias sólidas y los conocimientos de las artes útiles [...] sirven para todas las situaciones y destinos, y son tan propios a dirigir y hacer feliz al hombre del campo, como al cortesano, al militar o al ciudadano.[63]
>
> [Good education is good for everything. Religion, morality, the principles of sound science, and the knowledge of beneficial arts [...] are useful for all situations and aims, and are suitable for instructing and making country-dwellers happy, as well as courtiers, soldiers, or citizens.]

The constitutive elements of the educational plan proposed by the philosopher[64] are in many respects similar to the ones set down by Olavide in his reform plan for the University of Seville in 1768. In Javier Herrero's view, for Olavide, 'la clave para el cambio se encuentra en la educación y en reformas racionales' [the key to change lies in education and rational reform].[65] The objective of the philosopher's educational scheme is the development of a model man, capable of making others happy and of paying tribute to God for the benefits given and for the opportunity to do good to society by means of his privileged social position. Given that Olavide's earlier project was focused on meeting the needs of university reform in Spain, instead of being conceived as a comprehensive plan that would be inclusive of all levels of education, the politician suggested the implementation of new educational actions in 1798. Similar to his previous programme, the new one was addressed to the prosperous sectors of society, while children from the working class would receive compulsory education in the same way as the children of the farmers in the Sierra Morena. However, this time Olavide proposed a system of home education (*educación doméstica*) in which instruction was delivered by tutors or parents in the home. This type of education is intended to get children used to living on the land and to showing them how to achieve and maintain prosperity.[66] Since the Spanish state failed to create public educational institutions that would put into effect the planned reforms, the home-based educational system was seen as a solution to the shortcomings of the existing model. This alternative proposal is evidently exemplified in the role played by Mariano as tutor to Félix and Paulino, even though he does not feel prepared to carry out such a task due to his childlessness. The emphasis put on the early training of children by their parents, specifically the father, is also a remarkable feature in *Sinapia*, in which a paternalistic authoritarian system is the ideal form of government.

The preference for a moderate, religious lifestyle endorsed in *El Evangelio* is further underlined by the conviction that agriculture is the basis of national and personal growth, a viewpoint common to many eighteenth-century Spanish economists who adopted the physiocratic model introduced by French economic theorists, an attitude that for some cast doubt on the intellectual originality of Spanish thinkers.[67] However, although Olavide's ideas were initially influenced by Mirabeau's work, his attitude does not necessarily reflect an acceptance of physiocracy, an economic theory developed by a group of eighteenth-century French economists who firmly believed that agriculture was the only industry that produced the wealth of nations. Unlike the physiocrats, Olavide believed that agriculture was a major sector of the economy, but not the only one to generate wealth. His perception of the agricultural system differed from the physiocrats: 'Los fisiócratas defienden las grandes explotaciones arrendadas a *fermiers* porque permiten que el *produit net* aumente. [...] Olavide, en cambio, propone una agricultura basada en pequeñas explotaciones cultivadas por labradores que tienen al menos el dominio útil de la tierra' [Physiocrats defend large farms leased to farmers because they allow the net proceeds to increase. [...] Olavide, on the other hand, proposes an agriculture based on small farms cultivated by farmers who have at least the practical control of the land].[68] As previously stated, Olavide's thought was largely grounded in private ownership. In terms of the interdependent relationship between the concepts of population and subsistence, Olavide adopted an intermediate position between the theories of agrarianism and mercantilism. His vision would correspond to a group of theorists who subscribe to elements of both.[69]

Since the study of religion is the central component of *El Evangelio*'s educational model, the secular sciences must be subordinated to Catholic doctrine. In this respect, the importance of having a catechism or handbook on Christianity is a crucial concern in the socio-spiritual project developed by the philosopher and corroborated by the priest. The latter strongly condemns the fact that a book containing the basic principles of the Christian faith does not yet exist.[70] Such a book should be the cornerstone of any social order and must be written in a style accessible to anyone. In trying to underline the beneficial effects of organized religious practice in society, the philosopher points to the civil happiness and political stability following the cultivation of a communal religious consciousness. Religion prevents the interference of sophistry, and seditious thinking can lead to extreme and undesirable events like the French Revolution:

> ¿Quién puede dudar [...] que si [...] se propagara en la nación el estudio y la práctica de una religión santa, y que no predica más que virtudes que no tienen otro objeto que la felicidad de los hombres, no sólo esto sería el mejor preservativo para no dejarnos inficionar de esa filosofía devastadora, no sólo aseguraría esto la consistencia de la religión, la estabilidad del trono y la pública tranquilidad, sino sería el motivo más eficaz de mejorar las costumbres y hacernos tan felices como la condición humana puede alcanzar a serlo?[71]

> [Who can doubt [...] that if [...] the study and practice of a holy religion, which preaches only virtues that have no other objective but the happiness of men, were propagated across the nation, not only would this be the best protection against letting us become infected with that devastating philosophy, not only would this ensure the constancy of religion, the stability of the throne, and public tranquillity, but it would also be the most effective reason to improve behaviour and make us as happy as the human condition can allow?]

Similar arguments about the necessary preservation of religion are put forward in the author's prologue, which makes an explicit reference to the corruption of French culture: 'Si el pueblo francés hubiera estado más instruido de la verdad de su religión, la falsa filosofía no hubiera hecho tantos progresos' [If the French nation had been more educated in the truth of their religion, false philosophy would not have made so much progress].[72]

Through Mariano's explanation of the areas of knowledge to be covered by the subjects taught, Olavide reaffirms the idea that religion and modern secular knowledge are not incompatible, but complementary dimensions that promote progress and civilization:

> [N]o pienso que para ser cristiano, pueda conducir ser ignorante y bárbaro. Pero digo que la ciencia de la salud eterna debe ocupar la primera atención; que no se deben aprender las otras, sino cuando el espíritu, ya formado por la primera, está dispuesto a hacer buen uso de ellas.[73]

> [I do not think that to be a Christian, one must be ignorant and barbaric. But I would say that the science of eternal welfare must be the first focus of attention, that other sciences should not be learned until the spirit, once shaped by the science of eternal welfare, is ready to make good use of them.]

Thus, the study of 'la ciencia de la salud eterna' [the science of eternal welfare], that is, of religion, does not preclude the teaching of other disciplines, but they are all subordinated to the predominance of religion. Resembling *Sinapia*'s claim that all the arts and sciences taught are intended to reinforce the supremacy of religious dogma, the educational method of *El Evangelio* advocates the teaching of arts and sciences that help students develop the ability to reflect critically upon their own learning because the ultimate goal is to make them understand, when they reach the age of reasoning, why they should live according to the precepts of the Catholic faith. Dufour draws attention to the fact that the Inquisition overlooked Olavide's conviction that the intensive instruction of religion should be deferred until the pupil was eighteen or nineteen years old.[74]

Up to the age of seventeen, students are trained in grammar, Latin, geometry, and algebra. On this point, the philosopher's plan diverges from that of the *Nuevas Poblaciones* because the *Instrucción y fuero de población* does not consider the study of grammar or of any other field of knowledge as part of the education of a farmer's children: they are meant to learn mechanical arts because these contribute to the progress of the state.[75] They are allowed to learn foreign languages and other disciplines, but only after having acquired an excellent command of the Spanish language and succeeded in becoming good men, Christians, and Spaniards: '[E]s menester haber aprendido a ser hombre, cristiano y buen español antes de aprender a ser historiador, poeta o extranjero' [It is necessary to have learned to be a man, a Christian, and a good Spaniard before learning to be a historian, a poet, or a foreigner].[76] In this regard, *El Evangelio* coincides with the *Instrucción*, which prescribes the learning of Christian doctrine and of the Spanish language at the same time.[77] The idea of learning how to be a good Spaniard may be the reason behind Olavide's decision to omit the process of immigration as a functional mechanism for the recreation of the philosopher's town. The introduction of a foreign element is here perceived as a threat to Spanish identity, which was not considered as such in the Sierra Morena project.

Among the exact sciences, the study of mathematics is especially important because it helps children improve their powers of concentration and abstract reasoning; consequently, they develop the ability to instinctively access the truth of things.[78] In order to motivate the analysis and questioning of pre-existing truths, the study of sciences that stimulate critical thinking is preferred to those that encourage rote learning. However, the study of history — the representative discipline of the faculty of memory[79] — must not be regarded as a subjective source of knowledge as long as students have obtained the cognitive tools to distinguish fact from fiction. The acquisition of this intellective ability is particularly crucial for the study of sacred history. What is emphasized in the study of natural history is a better understanding of the greatness of nature. The contemplation of the natural world is a vehicle not only to refine the study of God's creation, but also to initiate the learning of agriculture-related aspects, a feature that connects the educational and agrarian dimensions of Olavide's utopia: 'El campo debe ser nuestra escuela, y divirtiéndonos aprenderemos el nombre, la realidad y las propiedades de cuantos objetos se nos presentan a los ojos' [The countryside must be our school, and by focusing our activity in this way, we will learn the names, the reality, and the characteristics of all the objects that are presented to our eyes].[80] The study of natural history becomes an ally of theology and will be supported by the study of physics, geography, and astronomy. This panegyric on nature reasserts the superiority of virtuous rural occupations and pleasures over futile urban ones, but, more importantly, it can be interpreted as a critique of some Enlightenment historians, and natural historians in particular, who practise their professions in the limited space of their studies instead of collecting data in situ.

Another characteristic of the educational programme that is relevant to the art of agriculture is the practice of gardening. Mariano recommends that Félix and Paulino should become gardeners at the age of seventeen in order to gain experience for cultivating their future territories.[81] He explains his method as follows:

> [Y]o daría a cada uno un corto terreno cerrado, y donde ninguno pudiera entrar sin su permiso. Permitiría el primer año que tu jardinero fuese a hacer el plantío y enseñarles; pero después debería correr por cuenta de los propios jóvenes el cultivo ulterior.[82]
>
> [I would give each one a small piece of enclosed land and where no one could enter without their permission. I would allow your gardener to do the planting and give instruction in the first year, but afterwards the subsequent cultivation should be carried out by the young people themselves.]

On this point, Defourneaux highlights the subtle connection between Rousseau's *Émile, ou de l'éducation* [*Emil; or, On Education*] (1762) and Olavide's *El Evangelio en triunfo*. Both texts are founded on the relationship between nature and education and foster training in manual labour: while the philosopher's sons are advised to work as gardeners, Émile is supposed to become a carpenter.[83]

As Dufour notes, another similarity between the works of Olavide and Rousseau is the importance given to the teaching of drawing because it is the language of art and enables landowners to deal with designers concerning the manufacture of tools or the repair of buildings.[84] Since it is an objective reflection of reality, drawing is an effective way of protecting truth from misinterpretation or falsehood, which is a fundamental maxim of Olavide's plan: 'El que sabe dibujar sabe ver porque se fija en el espíritu la idea de los objetos y de sus proporciones con exactitud, se los retrata con fidelidad y tales como son' [He who knows how to draw knows how to see because the idea of objects and their dimensions settle in his mind with accuracy; objects are thus portrayed with fidelity and as they really are].[85] The perception of reality as a mirror of nature is implied in the principles by which an agrarian society shapes the innate character of its inhabitants. Nonetheless, this social behaviour needs to be modelled on and adjusted to civilized standards, which is why the philosopher encourages the creation of an institution devoted to this specific task, as will be seen next.

The Civic Utopia

The educational and economic scope of Olavide's utopian programme is complemented by the presence of an organization involved in the consolidation of a functional agrarian society: a Committee for the Public Good (*Junta del Bien Público*), a patriotic group dedicated to eradicating poverty and encouraging good behaviour. The creation of institutional mechanisms through which citizens can have political participation in the running of their community is also a constituent of the administration system in the utopian country of the Ayparchontes in *El Censor*. In their society, the *Consejo Supremo de la Nación* [Supreme Council of the Nation] functions as a regulating body that judges all issues concerning the jurisdiction of the nobility.[86] In a similar way, the ecclesiastical organization of the Ayparchontes is divided into several boards that control the internal discipline of their Church, as has been seen in Chapter 5.

The *Junta del Bien Público* was established with clear goals: '[P]ara desterrar la ociosidad y la mendicidad, para excitar la industria, promover las artes y reformar las costumbres' [To banish idleness and begging, to foster industry, to promote the arts, and to reform behaviour].[87] Its members are organized into subcommittees with specific functions. Women are called upon to form a commission responsible for assisting the poor and the sick. In this respect, the *Junta* emphasizes that the poor and unemployed must be occupied in useful activities. In various respects, the activities of the *Junta* reflect those of the Spanish economic societies as originally set out in Campomanes's *Discurso sobre el fomento de la industria popular*.[88] The following passage sums up the objectives of the *Junta*, underlining the advantages of the philosopher's plan:

> El socorro de los pobres [...] será lo de menos, porque con él se debe esperar el estudio de la religión, la buena crianza de los muchachos, la honestidad pública, la decencia exterior, la urbanidad, la paz de las familias, la extinción de los pleitos y discordias, el destierro de los vicios vergonzosos, y en fin la extensión de las artes, el amor y aplicación al trabajo, la prosperidad de los Estados, y todos los bienes particulares de que resulta la felicidad pública.[89]
>
> [The relief of the poor [...] will be the least of it, because with it one should expect the study of religion, the good upbringing of boys, public honesty, external decency, politeness, peace within families, the ending of lawsuits and disagreements, the banishing of shameful vices, and, in short, the spread of the arts, love of and dedication to work, the prosperity of states, and all the particular goods from which public happiness arises.]

The *Junta* was created as a charitable institution to assist needy and underprivileged individuals and as an alternative to the simple action of giving alms to the poor, that is to say, as a job creation tool. The introduction of this institutional body is in accord with Olavide's earlier participation in the direction of the Hospice of San Fernando in Madrid, a position to which he was appointed in 1766.[90] It is worth mentioning that the *Instrucción y fuero de población* similarly included the running of hospices as a solution to the idleness and incapacity of the poor.[91] In her analysis of *El Evangelio*, Noël Valis defines the philosopher's programme as a 'philanthropic project' in which 'Olavide intended a thorough reform of society, from agricultural improvements to good manners, schoolrooms to spiritual reawakening'.[92] In almost the same vein, Leonardo Mattos-Cárdenas stresses the pursuit of public happiness that permeates the comprehensive socio-economic plan of *El Evangelio*.[93] Javier Herrero has also emphasized Olavide's utopian vision of how Spain could be a happy nation according to an optimistic Enlightenment project within the goals of the Bourbon reforms.[94]

Comparing the dynamics of the *Junta* with that of the utopian agricultural project, there is an analogous conception of success based on the degree of engagement of the citizens: the experiment will be successful if the participants become active agents. Making a commitment to something perceived as a possession is instinctive behaviour that must be used in favour of society. In the same way that farmers exert control over their lands because they see themselves as property owners, the members of the *Junta* must experience the project as their own and deservedly expect benefits in return:

> Tal es el corazón humano: él desea ser actor en todo; el papel de testigo le cansa, el de admirador le fastidia, el de instrumento le humilla, pero el de actor le sostiene, y cuando imagina que le alcanzará una parte del interés o de la gloria, con este estímulo se le lleva adonde se quiere.[95]

> [Such is the human heart: it wishes to be an actor in everything; the role of witness tires it, that of admirer annoys it, that of an instrument humiliates it, but that of an actor sustains it, and when it imagines that part of the interest or glory will be achieved, with such a stimulus one can direct it wherever one wishes.]

Mariano informs Antonio that, after observing the conditions in which the settlers and their families live, many other residents want to follow their example and enjoy the same benefits. According to Mariano, this state of happiness and self-fulfilment prevents the population from migrating to other countries, where it is unlikely that they will achieve a better existence. A perfect nation must ensure that its citizens do not feel like foreigners in their own country. This argument could be seen as conflicting with the process of immigration by which the philosopher's town has been built, but it could also be a way of demonstrating that the project was a radical enterprise for the sake of preserving the sense of homeland in the utopian space:

> Todos han tomado amor a su país, todos sienten las ventajas que logran, y han perdido este espíritu errante y vagabundo con que se abandona sin pena el país natal en que no se está bien, para buscar otro en que no se está mejor: espíritu de miseria que quita toda especie de aplicación, que hace al hombre extranjero en su país y que no le presenta una patria en ninguna parte.[96]

> [Everyone has grown fond of their country, they all feel the advantages that they achieve and have lost this roaming, wandering spirit that makes one abandon without regret one's native country, in which one is not at ease, in order to look for another in which one is no better: one possesses a wretched state of mind that eliminates any kind of dedication, which makes a man a foreigner in his own country and makes him feel at home nowhere.]

The contents of the next-to-last letter of the 'Cartas de Mariano a Antonio' are dedicated to refuting the rhetoric of the period that seeks to distort the truth of the Christian Gospel. Olavide's sharp criticism is especially addressed to Voltaire, whose ideas are condemned as outrageous and worthy of vituperation:

> Su encarnizado furor contra los principios de la moral y de la religión le han transformado en un monstruo maléfico, que ha cegado y corrompido todas las naciones. Jamás hombre ninguno hizo tanto mal a los hombres como Voltaire.

> Este señor es [...] la causa principal de los extravíos, impiedades y escándalos de nuestro siglo.⁹⁷
>
> [His fierce rage against the principles of morality and religion has turned him into a dangerous monster who has blinded and corrupted all nations. No man ever did so much harm to men as Voltaire. This man is [...] the main cause of the misconduct, impiety, and scandals of our age.]

In accord with the Spanish utopian tradition, Olavide's ideal society strives to reconcile the civic and religious realms in the process of modelling good citizens and Christians. The philosopher epitomizes the image of the perfect Christian who has overcome a series of setbacks to become the reformer and leader of an ideal community thanks to his religious re-education. This is the virtuous portrayal of the philosopher that the final letter contains in order to intensify the solemnity of the account of his decease. His sudden death suggests that his life was meant to end once his reform plan began to bear fruit:

> Dios le dio tiempo no sólo para emprender y acabar todas las empresas que imaginó útiles para la felicidad de esta población, sino para que pudiese ver los frutos, y gozar él mismo de los beneficios que había hecho. Este pueblo es hoy el trono de la paz, el centro de la abundancia y el modelo de lo que puede caber en la perfección humana.⁹⁸
>
> [God gave him time not only to undertake and finish all the tasks that he thought would be useful for the happiness of this people, but also to see the fruits and enjoy for himself the benefits that he had brought. This village is today the throne of peace, the centre of abundance, and the model of what is possible in the realm of human perfectibility.]

Thus, the philosopher's spiritual conversion was the instrument through which a comprehensive social transformation was correspondingly reproduced in his material world. In this sense, the narrative structure of the 'Cartas' can be interpreted as a symbolic correspondence between the personal reinvention of the philosopher and the salvation and restructuring of the society he belonged to.

The construction of a rural social system grounded in a rational Catholicism and in which all the inhabitants practise their spiritual and civic virtues is the utopian project depicted in the 'Cartas'. The utopian enterprise of the disenchanted philosopher — Olavide's alter ego to a certain extent — restates and transmits many basic features of Olavide's Sierra Morena reform plan in a critical and practical manner. Both the fictional creation and the Sierra Morena implementation reveal Olavide's dual condition as reformer and utopian thinker. Even though the earlier plan had an essentially utopian impulse, both ideological discourses are discernible as separate concepts: while reformism can be utopian in a general sense, utopia as a genre disguises its reformist or subversive spirit by presenting the new social order proposed in terms of a parallel or alternative reality. Destined to failure due to clerical opposition and the contemptuous attitude of Olavide's successors, the Sierra Morena project aspired to a reordering of rural society by applying the leading socio-economic theories of the time, and especially Olavide's extensive experience as an administrator. Having initially only identified the reformist nature of the actions intended to transform the philosopher's town into an ideal village,[99] Dufour questioned Olavide's originality in reusing projects that had already been put into practice and eventually failed, but, more importantly, Dufour inconsistently claims that, in doing so, the author's intention was to show the inefficiency of those reforms.[100]

In *El Evangelio en triunfo*, the religious conversion of the philosopher works as a device that simultaneously triggers his disillusionment with the existing world and his creative capacity to develop an enlightened socio-political system based on the formation of good Christian citizens and good Spaniards. In other words, the text is built on the premise that living in a corrupt society is a useless illusion that can be converted into an ideal social order. The utopian constitution of the society 'saved' by the philosopher can be understood as a direct projection of his religious reorientation, a central component of Olavide's vision. The dual composition of *El Evangelio*'s reformist model, in which the progress of the agricultural system depends on the correct implementation of the educational programme, ultimately entails a utopianism rooted in the conviction that human nature and the natural world have inherently positive attributes that can be wisely improved in order to mould skilful citizens and workers who are able to live happily as a consequence of the fruits of the land that they cultivate.

Notes to Chapter 7

1. The major source for Olavide's life in this chapter is Marcelin Defourneaux, *Pablo de Olavide ou l'afrancesado (1725–1803)* (Paris: Presses Universitaires de France, 1959).
2. Gonzalo Anes, *Informes en el expediente de ley agraria: Andalucía y La Mancha, 1768* (Madrid: Instituto de Cooperación Iberoamericana, Sociedad Estatal Quinto Centenario, Instituto de Estudios Fiscales, 1990), p. xvii.
3. Gérard Dufour, 'Utopie et *Ilustración*: El Evangelio en triunfo de Pablo de Olavide', in *Las utopías en el mundo hispánico*, pp. 73–78 (p. 76). See also Gérard Dufour, 'Elementos novelescos de El Evangelio en triunfo de Olavide', *Anales de Literatura Española*, 11 (1995), 107–15 (p. 109).
4. Gérard Dufour, ed., *Cartas de Mariano a Antonio: el programa ilustrado de 'El Evangelio en triunfo'* (Aix-en-Provence: Université de Provence, 1988). An unchanged reprint of Dufour's edition appeared in 1997. All quotations from this work in the present chapter correspond to the 1988 edition.
5. Maravall, *Utopía y reformismo en la España de los Austrias*, p. 4.
6. Denis Diderot, 'Don Pablo Olavidès: précis historique, rédigé sur des mémoires fournis par un espagnol', in *Œuvres de Denis Diderot: Mélanges de littérature et de philosophie*, ed. by Jacques André Naigeon, 26 vols (Paris: J. L. J. Brière, 1821–34), III (1821), pp. 384–93 (p. 384).
7. Defourneaux, p. 39. Enlightened intellectual circles throughout Europe were shocked at the later actions of the Inquisition against Olavide. Diderot was especially fascinated by Olavide's case and, in his account of the Peruvian thinker's life, asserts that Olavide was a victim of fanaticism (Diderot, 'Don Pablo Olavidès', p. 392).
8. In his study of the earthquake's aftermath, Charles Walker explains that Lima was seen by some as the target of God's wrath due to its apparent arrogance and ostentation (Charles F. Walker, *Shaky Colonialism: The 1746 Earthquake-Tsunami in Lima, Peru, and its Long Aftermath* (Durham, NC: Duke University Press, 2008), p. 79).
9. Juan Marchena Fernández, *Pablo de Olavide: el espacio de la Ilustración y la reforma universitaria. Vida y obra de un ilustrado americano y español* (Seville: Junta de Andalucía, Universidad Pablo de Olavide, 2000), p. 24.

10. For a detailed study of the reforms introduced by Olavide in Seville, see Francisco Aguilar Piñal, *La Sevilla de Olavide, 1767–1778* (Seville: Ayuntamiento de Sevilla, 1966).
11. Julio Caro Baroja, 'Las "nuevas poblaciones" de Sierra Morena y Andalucía: un experimento sociológico en tiempos de Carlos III', *Clavileño: Revista de la Asociación Internacional de Hispanismo*, 18 (1952), 52–64 (p. 58).
12. Gonzalo Anes, *El Siglo de las Luces* (Madrid: Alianza, 1994), p. 259.
13. In contrast with the attention given to his official reports for the Spanish Crown, Olavide's fictional narratives have not received substantial critical interest, particularly his moralistic ones, of which the Peruvian literary critic Estuardo Núñez found and edited (in 1971) six unknown short novels, written by Olavide under the pseudonym of 'el autor de *El Evangelio en triunfo*' [the author of *The Triumph of the Gospel*] and published in New York in 1828. Núñez, who found printed editions of the texts in several university libraries in the United States, stresses the fact that Olavide's novels were strongly influenced by the works of English writers such as Samuel Richardson, Henry Fielding, and Daniel Defoe. Despite his efforts to reconfigure the Spanish narrative of his time, Olavide's prose fiction seemed to have been ignored by editors in Spain (Estuardo Núñez, 'Biografía de un inquietador', in Pablo de Olavide y Jáuregui, *Obras selectas*, ed. by Estuardo Núñez (Lima: Banco de Crédito del Perú, 1987), pp. xi–xxxiv (p. xiv)).
14. For a discussion of the topic, see Francisco Larubia-Prado, '¿Una Ilustración *suficiente*? Mito, utopía y colonización interior en la España del siglo XVIII', *Bulletin of Hispanic Studies*, 76 (1999), 627–48 (pp. 640–44).
15. Francisco Aguilar Piñal, *Plan de estudios para la Universidad de Sevilla por Pablo de Olavide* (Barcelona: Ediciones de Cultura Popular, 1969), p. 21.
16. Olavide y Jáuregui, *Informe sobre la ley agraria*, pp. 495–96.
17. Fernando Ciaramitaro, 'Pablo de Olavide (1725–1803): A Spanish-Economist at the Service of the Institution', in *Economics and Institutions: Contributions from the History of Economic Thought*, ed. by Pier Francesco Asso and Luca Fiorito (Milan: Franco Angeli, 2007), pp. 368–88 (p. 379); Juan Marchena Fernández, *El tiempo ilustrado de Pablo de Olavide: vida, obra y sueños de un americano en la España del s. XVIII* (Seville: Alfar, 2001), pp. 60–61.
18. *Real Cédula de su Majestad y Señores del Consejo, que contiene la Instrucción y Fuero de Población, que se debe observar en las que se formen de nuevo en la Sierra Morena con naturales y extranjeros católicos* (Madrid: Antonio Sanz, 1767), pp. 1–5, 10.
19. Juan Marchena Fernández underlines the fact that repopulation projects were important lines of action according to the Enlightenment mentality (Marchena Fernández, *Pablo de Olavide*, pp. 67–68).
20. For the sake of creating a better social system, the concept of colonization acquires a different meaning in terms of processes of repopulation in already occupied territories. As Cipriano Juárez and Gregorio Canales argue, 'En los casos de planificación agraria, la legislación está dirigida sobre un medio ya ocupado [...]. [E]l concepto de colonización varía en el tiempo y consecuente con él las formas del establecimiento de la población y sus lugares de hábitat' [In cases of agrarian planning, the legislation applies to an already occupied space [...]. The concept of colonization varies over time and, in accordance with it, the types of settlement of the population and its places of habitation] (Cipriano Juárez Sánchez-Rubio and Gregorio Canales Martínez, 'Colonización agraria y modelos de hábitat (siglos XVIII–XX)', *Agricultura y Sociedad*, 49 (1988), 333–52 (p. 333)).
21. Defourneaux, p. 180.
22. Cayetano Alcázar Molina, *Las colonias alemanas de Sierra Morena* (Madrid: n. pub., 1930), p. 18.
23. After Olavide's administration, Miguel de Ondeano took over the government of the new settlements in 1774 and was successively followed in the role by Tomás González Carvajal, Hermenegildo Llanderal, and Pedro Polo de Alcocer, with whom the system of the *Nuevas Poblaciones* came to an end in 1835 (Alcázar Molina, pp. 94–96).
24. Alcázar Molina, pp. 57–58.
25. Anes, *Informes en el expediente de ley agraria*, pp. xxxii–xxxiii. Marchena Fernández remarks that the intellectual contact Olavide had with other cultural realities prompted his reformist spirit: 'La necesidad de reformar todo lo que veía, porque la distancia entre ambos mundos le pareció

abismal, nació sin duda de esta comparación entre lo visto y lo vivido a uno y otro lado de los Pirineos, aunque fuese una "ilustración" comprada en las librerías, vista en el teatro o aprendida en las tertulias' [The need to reform everything he saw, because the distance between both worlds seemed enormous to him, derived without a doubt from this comparison between the seen and the lived on both sides of the Pyrenees, even if it was an 'enlightenment' bought in bookshops, seen in theatres, or learned in social gatherings] (Marchena Fernández, *Pablo de Olavide*, pp. 33–34).

26. Estuardo Núñez, 'La reforma agraria', in Pablo de Olavide y Jáuregui, *Obras selectas*, ed. by Estuardo Núñez (Lima: Banco de Crédito del Perú, 1987), pp. xciv–xcvii (p. xcv).
27. Olavide y Jáuregui, *Informe sobre la ley agraria*, p. 489.
28. Ibid., p. 520.
29. From a philosophical perspective, Kant's theory of private property, postulated in *The Metaphysics of Morals* (1797), states that everyone has the innate right to acquire and own things as private property: '*a right to a thing* is a right to the private use of a thing of which I am in (original or instituted) possession in common with all others' (Immanuel Kant, *The Metaphysics of Morals*, ed. and trans. by Mary Gregor (Cambridge: Cambridge University Press, 1996), p. 49).
30. Jovellanos, *Informe de la sociedad económica de esta corte al real y supremo Consejo de Castilla en el expediente de ley agraria*, p. 65. In his *Elogio de Carlos III* [*In Praise of Charles III*] (1788), Jovellanos applauds the creation of the new settlements as a key achievement of the Bourbon reforms (Gaspar Melchor de Jovellanos, *Elogio de Carlos III*, in Gaspar Melchor de Jovellanos, *Obras completas*, ed. by Vicent Llombart i Rosa and Joaquín Ocampo Suárez-Valdés, 14 vols (Oviedo: Ayuntamiento de Gijón, Instituto Feijoo de Estudios del Siglo XVIII, KRK Ediciones, 1984–2010), X: *Escritos económicos* (2008), pp. 669–85 (p. 673)).
31. Liana Vardi, *The Physiocrats and the World of the Enlightenment* (New York: Cambridge University Press, 2012), pp. 128–30.
32. For an analysis of the commercial strategies used to promote the sale of *El Evangelio* in Spain and to turn it into a best-selling book, see Gérard Dufour, '*El Evangelio en triunfo* o la historia de la fabricación de un éxito editorial', *Cuadernos Dieciochistas*, 4 (2003), 67–77.
33. José Luis Gómez Urdáñez and Diego Téllez Alarcia give an account of Olavide's encounter with the Inquisition, which also pays attention to his early career and later utopian text (José Luis Gómez Urdáñez and Diego Téllez Alarcia, 'Pablo de Olavide y Jáuregui, un católico ilustrado', *Brocar: Cuadernos de Investigación Histórica*, 28 (2004), 7–30 (pp. 24–30)). For more details of Olavide's Inquisition experience, see Gérard Dufour, '*El Evangelio en triunfo* devant l'Inquisition', in *Hommage à Madame le Professeur Maryse Jeuland à l'occasion de son départ à la retraite* (Aix-en-Provence: Université de Provence; Marseille: Diffusion, J. Laffitte, 1983), pp. 225–31.
34. Pablo de Olavide y Jáuregui, 'Prólogo del autor', in Pablo de Olavide y Jáuregui, *El Evangelio en triunfo*, 4 vols (Valencia: Imprenta de los hermanos de Orga, 1797–98), I (1797), pp. iii–xvi (p. iii).
35. Estuardo Núñez, *El nuevo Olavide: una semblanza a través de sus textos ignorados* (Lima: P. L. Villanueva, 1970), pp. 35–36.
36. Sarrailh, p. 622.
37. Alfred Morel-Fatio, *Études sur l'Espagne*, 4 vols (Paris: Édouard Champion, 1888–1925), IV (1925), p. 161.
38. Miguel Benítez, '"El sueño de la razón produce monstruos": *El Evangelio en triunfo*, de Pablo de Olavide', in *Actas del Congreso Internacional sobre 'Carlos III y la Ilustración'*, 3 vols (Madrid: Ministerio de Cultura, 1989), III: *Educación y pensamiento*, pp. 199–225 (p. 224). See also Miguel Benítez, 'Trazas de pensamiento radical en el mundo hispánico en los tiempos modernos', in *La actitud ilustrada*, ed. by Eduardo Bello and Antonio Rivera (Valencia: Biblioteca Valenciana, 2002), pp. 195–231. Andrea Smidt indicates that the concept of a Catholic Enlightenment included the desire for a less hierarchical structure of the Catholic Church. This would imply a return to the spirit of early Christianity and an attempt to make the Christian faith more reasonable and useful to society (Smidt, 'Luces por la fe', p. 409). However, Smidt draws attention to the fact that Spanish Jansenism and regalist reform of the Church overshadowed the issues of religious reform because they did not correspond with the aims of the state (Smidt, pp. 437–39).

39. Amable Fernández Sanz, 'El último Olavide, ¿un ilustrado o un reaccionario?', in *Nuevos estudios sobre historia del pensamiento español: actas de las V Jornadas de Hispanismo Filosófico*, ed. by Antonio Jiménez García, Rafael V. Orden Jiménez, and Xavier Agenjo Bullón (Madrid: Fundación Ignacio Larramendi, Asociación de Hispanismo Filosófico, 2005), pp. 141–53 (p. 152).
40. Olavide y Jáuregui, 'Prólogo del autor', pp. xiii–xiv.
41. For a detailed narrative analysis of the epistolary structure of *El Evangelio*, see Enid M. Valle, 'La estructura narrativa de *El Evangelio en triunfo* de Pablo de Olavide y Jáuregui', in *Pen and Peruke: Spanish Literature of the Eighteenth Century*, ed. by Monroe Z. Hafter (Ann Arbor: University of Michigan, 1992), pp. 135–51.
42. Olavide y Jáuregui, 'Prólogo del autor', p. x.
43. Another Spanish utopian text that seems to share the same features as Olavide's utopia is the apparently unpublished work entitled *Viaje al país de los Panteocracios, su descubrimiento e historia de sus costumbres* [*A Voyage to the Country of the Panteocracios, their Discovery and a History of their Customs*], written by José Rasilla in 1796. A description of the story and the announcement of the forthcoming publication of the work in two volumes can be found in *Gaceta de Madrid*, No. 95, 25 November 1796, pp. 1006–08 (pp. 1007–08).
44. Olavide y Jáuregui, 'Cartas de Mariano a Antonio', p. 40.
45. Olavide y Jáuregui, 'Prólogo del autor', p. xiii.
46. The ideal of a philosophically trained ruler comes from Book v of Plato's *Republic*. In Kallipolis, Plato's utopian city-state, philosopher-kings are the only people entitled to become rulers. Everyone else is predestined to be a follower rather than a leader. In his dialogue with Glaucon, Socrates argues that philosopher-kings are the light in the darkness of the world: 'Until philosophers are kings, or the kings and princes of this world have the spirit and power of philosophy, and political greatness and wisdom meet in one, and those commoner natures who pursue either to the exclusion of the other are compelled to stand aside, cities will never have rest from their evils — nor the human race, as I believe — and then only will this our State have a possibility of life and behold the light of day' (Plato, p. 158).
47. Katarzyna Kwapisz-Williams claims that the relationship between the concepts of utopia and colonialism appears to be falsely problematic because, in her opinion, 'Colonialism, though based on far-fetched fantasies of distant lands, brings associations with aggressive politics, destruction and guilt rather than ideal political systems, social order and brotherhood, which is why it is easy to forget about the utopian ideals that often constituted its foundations' (Katarzyna Kwapisz-Williams, 'Utopia of the Southern Land in Colonial Literary Imagination', *A Quarterly Magazine of Australia, New Zealand and Oceania Research Association*, 3 (2010), 41–58 (p. 41)).
48. José Luis Abellán has drawn attention to the links between Olavide's activities overseeing the settlement at the Sierra Morena and the enlightened Catholicism of the utopian narrative in *El Evangelio*. However, Abellán believes that Olavide's utopianism began to develop thanks to his intellectual contact with Jovellanos and that utopian thinking is inherent in Enlightenment ideology (Abellán, III, pp. 603–06, 615–20). Another apparently relevant academic work on Olavide's utopian narrative is a doctoral thesis by Amable Fernández Sanz, which unfortunately remains unpublished, and hence it has not been possible to have access to it for the purpose of this chapter (Fernández Sanz, 'Utopía y realidad en la Ilustración española'). The potential importance of its contribution resides in its thought-provoking title, although the abstract of the thesis explains that Olavide's social utopia principally serves to prove that the realization of utopian ideals was the main basis of the Spanish Enlightenment.
49. Gérard Dufour, 'Le Rôle du curé dans l'utopie des lettres de Mariano à Antonio', in *L'Espagne du XVIIIe siècle: acte des journées d'étude sur 'Ville et campagne' et 'Cartas marruecas' des 5 et 6 décembre 1997*, ed. by Jacques Soubeyroux (Saint-Étienne: Publications de l'Université de Saint-Étienne, 1997), pp. 205–15 (p. 209).
50. Gérard Dufour, '*El Evangelio en triunfo* en el dispositivo político del Príncipe de la Paz', in *Ideas en sus paisajes: homenaje al profesor Russell P. Sebold*, ed. by Guillermo Carnero, Ignacio Javier López, and Enrique Rubio (Alicante: Universidad de Alicante, 1999), pp. 159–66 (p. 163).
51. In analysing the composition of Olavide's large library, Perdices suggests that the version of *Utopia* that Olavide read was a French translation of the text. See note 8 in Luis Perdices Blas,

'El desarrollo intelectual de Jovellanos en la Sevilla de Olavide (1768–1776)', *Dieciocho*, 36 (2013), 51–78 (p. 62).
52. Dufour, 'Utopie et *Ilustración*', p. 75.
53. Bloch, I, p. 205.
54. Ana Rueda, *Cartas sin lacrar: la novela epistolar y la España ilustrada, 1789–1840* (Madrid: Iberoamericana; Frankfurt am Main: Vervuert, 2001), p. 300.
55. In fact, the objectives of the Economic Societies of Friends of the Country reproduce those of utopian societies in seeking to stimulate the political, economic, and cultural development of an enlightened Spain (Enciso Recio, p. 9).
56. Sarrailh, p. 258.
57. Perdices Blas, *Pablo de Olavide*, p. 493.
58. Ibid., p. 492.
59. Olavide y Jáuregui, 'Cartas de Mariano a Antonio', pp. 78–79.
60. Rueda, pp. 297–300, 411–23.
61. Noël Valis, *Sacred Realism: Religion and the Imagination in Modern Spanish Narrative* (New Haven, CT: Yale University Press, 2010), pp. 74–75.
62. Rolando Carrasco M., 'Un mito en movimiento: Pablo de Olavide y su *Evangelio en triunfo* (1797)', *Revista Chilena de Literatura*, 71 (2007), 19–42 (p. 37).
63. Olavide y Jáuregui, 'Cartas de Mariano a Antonio', p. 51.
64. Rosa Calatayud Soler has traced the components of the educational system presented in the 'Cartas de Mariano a Antonio' from a purely descriptive perspective (Rosa Calatayud Soler, 'La utopía de un filósofo desengañado: Pablo de Olavide', in *Educación e Ilustración en España: III Coloquio de Historia de la Educación* (Barcelona: Universidad de Barcelona, 1984), pp. 33–40).
65. Javier Herrero, *Los orígenes del pensamiento reaccionario español* (Madrid: Cuadernos para el Diálogo, 1971), p. 137.
66. Perdices Blas, *Pablo de Olavide*, p. 482.
67. Ernest Lluch and Lluís Argemí i D'Abadal, *Agronomía y fisiocracia en España (1750–1820)* (Valencia: Alfons el Magnànim, 1985), p. 45.
68. Perdices Blas, *Pablo de Olavide*, p. 252.
69. Manuel Martín Rodríguez, *Pensamiento económico español sobre la población: de Soto a Matanegui* (Madrid: Pirámide, 1984), p. 201.
70. The basic truths and virtues of the Gospel are set out in Olavide's subsequent *Poemas cristianos, en que se exponen con sencillez las verdades más importantes de la religión* [Christian Poems, in Which the Most Important Truths of Religion Are Simply Explained] (1799).
71. Olavide y Jáuregui, 'Cartas de Mariano a Antonio', p. 188.
72. Olavide y Jáuregui, 'Prólogo del autor', p. vii.
73. Olavide y Jáuregui, 'Cartas de Mariano a Antonio', p. 55.
74. Dufour, 'Introducción', in *Cartas de Mariano a Antonio*, 1988, pp. 5–31 (p. 17).
75. *Real Cédula*, p. 10.
76. Olavide y Jáuregui, 'Cartas de Mariano a Antonio', p. 57.
77. *Real Cédula*, p. 10.
78. Elena Ausejo provides an informed overview of the Spanish promotion of mathematics during the reign of Carlos III (Elena Ausejo, 'Las matemáticas en la Ilustración hispana: estado de la cuestión', in *Ilustración, ilustraciones*, ed. by Jesús Astigarraga, María Victoria López-Cordón, and José María Urkia, 2 vols (Donostia-San Sebastian: Real Sociedad Bascongada de los Amigos del País; Madrid: Sociedad Estatal de Conmemoraciones Culturales, 2009), I, pp. 693–713 (pp. 698–710)).
79. Memory in the history of ideas is an extensive topic in the study of knowledge representation. What is interesting is the conception of history as the science of the unvarnished fact that utopian thinkers such as Francis Bacon and Tommaso Campanella endorsed: 'Campanella made history, divine and human, the fundamental science, since all knowledge comes from sensation; Hobbes made history, natural and civil, synonymous with knowledge of facts; and most influential of all, Bacon designated history as the representative discipline of the faculty of memory, just as philosophy served the faculty of reason, and the arts, imagination' (Lorraine J.

Daston, 'Classifications of Knowledge in the Age of Louis XIV', in *Sun King: The Ascendancy of French Culture During the Reign of Louis XIV*, ed. by David Lee Rubin (Cranbury, NJ: Associated University Presses, 1992), pp. 207–20 (p. 215)).
80. Olavide y Jáuregui, 'Cartas de Mariano a Antonio', p. 60. The observation of the natural world can also refer to the metaphorical concept of learning from the Book of Nature, a common feature of Enlightenment thought.
81. The garden motif could, of course, be seen as an allusion to the Garden of Eden.
82. Olavide y Jáuregui, 'Cartas de Mariano a Antonio', p. 61.
83. Defourneaux, p. 466.
84. Dufour, 'Introducción', p. 17.
85. Olavide y Jáuregui, 'Cartas de Mariano a Antonio', p. 62.
86. *El Censor*, III, 'Discurso LXI', p. 231.
87. Olavide y Jáuregui, 'Cartas de Mariano a Antonio', p. 105.
88. [Campomanes], *Discurso sobre el fomento de la industria popular*, pp. xxxi–xxxv.
89. Olavide y Jáuregui, 'Cartas de Mariano a Antonio', p. 137.
90. Defourneaux, p. 90.
91. *Real Cédula*, p. 5.
92. Valis, p. 74.
93. Leonardo Mattos-Cárdenas, 'Olavide y el urbanismo', in *Actas de las VII Jornadas de Andalucía y América*, 2 vols (Seville: Junta de Andalucía, 1990), I, pp. 109–34 (p. 127).
94. Herrero, p. 137.
95. Olavide y Jáuregui, 'Cartas de Mariano a Antonio', p. 115.
96. Ibid., p. 147.
97. Ibid., p. 166.
98. Ibid., p. 196.
99. Gérard Dufour, 'Le Village idéal au début du XIXe siècle selon *El Evangelio en triunfo* de Pablo de Olavide', in *L'Homme et l'espace dans la littérature, les arts et l'histoire en Espagne et en Amérique Latine au XIXe siècle*, ed. by Claude Dumas (Lille: Presses Universitaires du Septentrion, 1985), pp. 11–25. This article includes a more detailed description of the diverse Spanish editions and translations of *El Evangelio* than the one that appeared in Dufour's edition of the 'Cartas de Mariano a Antonio' (see Dufour, ed., *Cartas de Mariano a Antonio*, 1988, pp. 33–35). A censored excerpt from letter XXXIX of volume IV is also transcribed in the article.
100. Dufour, 'Utopie et *Ilustración*', pp. 77–78.

CONCLUSION

The overall aim of this book has been to amplify and enrich the current state of knowledge concerning utopian writings in eighteenth-century Spain, with special reference to the five major texts of the period. On the one hand, the analysis has focused on bringing out their subtle and imaginative relationship with classical works in the utopian tradition; on the other, it has shed new light on the role played by these narratives in relation to the social and cultural debates of Enlightenment Spain. Scholars of the past twenty years have not, for the most part, explored the subtlety with which the featured utopian authors understood and experimented with the inherited model to produce texts attractive to contemporary readers. In this regard, the present research has defined the specific characteristics of the Spanish utopian tradition within the body of Western utopian literature. Moreover, it has aimed to show that utopian fiction in eighteenth-century Spain displayed notable literary artistry.

The utopian model had a significant role in setting out comprehensive schemes to rethink Spanish society in the eighteenth century. Utopian plans involved the creation of an ideal society whose inhabitants and institutions provided a means of questioning the status quo in Spain. However, as shown in Chapter 2, the reformist mentality that reached its peak during the reign of Carlos III contributed to the development of a utopian spirit that aimed to expand the limits of reformism and offer an unofficial alternative vision. In this sense, Spanish utopian fiction emerged as a socio-political genre that built on the Morean model, but also shaped it to address the specific needs and circumstances of the existing situation. The fact that no earlier Spanish utopian texts have been found can thus be explained by the argument that they needed the impulse of a reformist environment in order to come into being. As Chapter 2 argues, there was also a tradition of Spanish American social experimentation following the discovery and colonization of the New World that inevitably shaped the pragmatic nature of Spanish utopianism. Alongside this empirical precedent, the reformist vision of Spanish pre-Enlightenment thinkers established the basis for the unfolding of a utopian consciousness in Spain.

As discussed in Chapter 1, Thomas More's 1516 founding text provided the starting point for rethinking and experimenting with society and its main areas of concern, such as political institutions, social structures, education, religion, property ownership, and individual morality. By creating a narrative involving an imaginary voyage to a foreign, distant territory, which evokes *Utopia* and its focal points, the five texts analysed identify themselves as explicitly belonging to the utopian tradition, in contrast with which they expect to be read. Some include allusive comments to More's text or specifically refer to it, like the *Suplemento de los viajes de Enrique Wanton al país de las monas*. Others also hint at aspects of the utopian works of Francis Bacon (*Sinapia*) or Tommaso Campanella (*Monarquía columbina*).

From a traditional generic point of view, utopia relates to the didactic model of the fable, a literary form that notably reappears in later eighteenth- and early nineteenth-century Spain. Of the five texts studied, the *Suplemento* and the *Monarquía columbina* are closely allied to the realm of fable in that both narratives depict an alternative world populated by animals, in one case monkeys and in the other birds. In both cases, the author makes human society an explicit point of contrast with that of the animals. In Gutierre Vaca de Guzmán's text, two European humans visit the monkey society on the other side of the world, while in Andrés Merino de Jesucristo's case, only at the end of the utopian story is contact made between birds and humans, with the authorial assertion that the dove kingdom is superior to the human one.

Generic frameworks are not fixed; in practice, they evolve over time. Attitudes of authors in relation to their audiences, such as authorial intentions concerning tone and narrative manner, bring about changes over the decades and even centuries. Thus, accounts of imaginary journeys that were written after More's foundational work diverted from the original utopian paradigm, while usually maintaining the basic starting point of a contrast between the society of the writer, which acts as his assumed major audience, and the encounters with the Other, the society used to provide a point of contrast. Thus, in many respects, utopian writings resemble historical accounts because the author sets out details of a particular society to present it to his readers much as a historian would. The tone of a utopian account is meant to be realistic, or verisimilitudinous to use the terminology of the sixteenth to eighteenth centuries, an objective that especially concerns the unknown authors of *Sinapia* and the *Monarquía de los Ayparchontes*.

However, many utopian writings are also comparable to earlier and even contemporary novels as the attitude of the narrator and the narrative techniques employed are often similar to those of a novelist. What is different is the intention guiding the work: whereas the label of novel indicates an intention of being entertaining and not excessively fanciful (that is to say, inverisimilitudinous), a utopian text starts by presenting a chimeric setting, while seeming to claim that the society portrayed really exists, though a convention of its literary model is that it does not since the utopian space is a no place or ideal place. The intention of a utopian text is, then, to oblige the reader to make constant comparisons between the society described and their own world. The utopian text always presupposes the contrapuntal effect of comparison with the reality that the reader knows. Whatever takes place in the utopian account, the specific aspect focused on is the contrast, and the reader is continuously required to judge and think for him- or herself concerning the merits of the two worlds and even imagine relative mixtures of the two.

A major aspect of literary expression that has a significant impact on utopian texts is the satirical tone adopted by some of them. This is especially the case with the *Suplemento* and the *Monarquía de los Ayparchontes*. In consequence, rather than representing a perfect or ideal society, as *Sinapia* and the 'Cartas de Mariano a Antonio' do, utopian writings can partially create non-ideal worlds, without getting to the point of becoming dystopias in which chaos and corruption subjugate the citizens of a fearful society. In other words, some utopian texts allow themselves to be satirical about the existing social system that needs to be changed, while others focus on the characterization of an idealized society. Moreover, satire can be used to provide variety in the usually serious tone of the work. Since the constant mental demand on the reader made by the author of a utopia is to make comparisons and judgements about political, social, religious, or economic structures, a text that alternates the ideal with the satirical can prove attractive, as Jonathan Swift's iconic travel account demonstrates.

In addition to these narrative functions, satire can provide an effective tool to mitigate social criticism and avoid censorship, which may be seen as the strategy of the *Monarquía de los Ayparchontes*, although part of it could not escape being banned by the Inquisition. Anonymity is another tactic used to evade censorship, a means also employed by the author of the utopian narrative of *El Censor*. In this respect, the apparent religious orthodoxy of the authors of *Sinapia* and the *Monarquía columbina* would not have brought problems with the governmental censorship system or that of the Inquisition. Nevertheless, *Sinapia* was not published at the time that it was written, and Merino's work was only published posthumously. As to the *Suplemento*, the author was careful not to explore religious features of society in detail and, therefore, not to provoke demands for textual changes from the government's censors.

The creative interaction between satire and utopia was most successfully demonstrated by Swift's *Gulliver's Travels*, a major innovative text in the utopian tradition. The full, original title of the work, *Travels into Several Remote Nations of the World. In Four Parts by Lemuel Gulliver*, emphasizes the imaginary journey aspect by dividing up the treatment of alternative societies between the work's different parts, including one in Part IV depicting an animal society (mainly Houyhnhnms, but also Yahoos). Swift is widely assumed to be satirizing British society, but he also makes the reader imagine a parallel society and different attitudes of individuals (whether human or not) towards living together. Swift's model has been most evident in the treatment of social customs and cultural traditions presented in Vaca de Guzmán's *Suplemento*, as seen in Chapter 4.

What the five texts analysed ultimately reveal is that the utopian framework can be treated in different ways. The content can be varied to a considerable degree, staying close to the idea of setting out the model of an ideal society or, at an opposite pole, appearing to satirize the organization and inhabitants of an existing one. In order to work, the Morean model needs only to be lightly alluded to and inventive new ideas put forward; alternatively, it can be followed fairly closely while producing the variation by means of detailed focus on features of the society to be described or satirized. The literary character of the text can be set out like a historical text (*Sinapia*), become a third-person narration close to that of the novelistic omniscient narrator (*Suplemento*, *Monarquía de los Ayparchontes*, *Monarquía columbina*), or take an epistolary form ('Cartas de Mariano a Antonio'). The text can be fundamentally descriptive with the impersonal narratorial voice apparently distant from what is described and can discuss societal structures in a seemingly objective, detached way, but it can also approach reality from a close perspective and even appear to reflect an individual person's character, conveying a sense of detailed examination of human behaviour in which individuals matter and are constantly seen in relationship with one another.

Sinapia is closest in form and style to More's *Utopia*. Many of the elements of the description of the geography, social composition, and political and economic systems evoke More's work. The anonymous author seems especially concerned with institutional structures and presents them in great detail. While spirituality and religious practices are the features most similar to Spain, much of the rest of the text portrays a unique and exemplary imaginary society, whose success and efficiency are unquestionable since the text lays claim to realistic credentials by supposedly being based on the notes of a historically verifiable figure, Abel Tasman. This aspect supports the conception of *Sinapia* as a text inspired by the organizational model of the Paraguayan Jesuit *reducciones*, a practical utopia in itself.

Vaca de Guzmán's *Suplemento de los viajes de Enrique Wanton al país de las monas* is by far the most elaborate and extensive of the five texts studied in this book. Its literary peculiarity lies in the way it is presented as a continuation of an existing imaginary journey, Zaccaria Seriman's *Viaggi di Enrico Wanton*, although the French addition to Swift's travel account provides an obvious recent precedent. However, Vaca de Guzmán's originality is evident in apparently seizing on the Swiftian mode of satire by showing both good and bad features of the kingdom of the apes over two new volumes of text. The author seems to take his cue for his narrative style from the Spanish periodical publications of the 1760s, describing and adopting a critical perspective on the varied experiences undergone in different locations of the exotic country where the work is situated. Vaca de Guzmán's moral standpoint is constantly present, and consequent moral judgements are expected to emerge in the mind of the reader. He also touches on important and even sensitive political issues such as the seigneurial system, but, more interestingly, he proposes the idea of a rural utopia as a way of counteracting the practice of having recourse to a cosmopolitanism that may threaten the nature of Spanish identity. The conception of a rural utopia emerges as a solution to the alienating effects that an eminently urban utopia can cause. Such an objective leads the reader to perceive a support for nationalism as a way of defending the importance of geographical and cultural uniqueness.

The account of the *Monarquía de los Ayparchontes* is one of the shorter texts, and perhaps for that reason, as well as for the need to fit the standard format of the periodical in which it is featured, the references to the imaginary journey tradition are brief. The text immediately centres on social organization and, in particular, the position of the nobility and the Church, which are evidently the main focus for critical comment and analysis. Few Spanish readers could have been unaware that the targets of the author's satirical pen were the privileges of these two institutions in Spain, both of which occupied the attention of contemporary reformist thinkers. The attack on the Church soon resulted in denunciation to the Inquisition of the Church-focused *Discurso 75*, which was followed by its prohibition shortly afterwards. In the three *discursos* of the text, the author is unashamedly satirical, and the features of the two institutions are sharply presented as in need of reform. The utopian model serves as a reminder that the existing state of society can be improved, with areas for that improvement clearly delineated.

The *Monarquía columbina*, also quite short, uses the fable aspect of the utopian tradition in a challenging way. Within a society of birds, the birds of prey are negatively contrasted with the peaceful, virtuous doves. Although the arrogant character of the birds of prey is meant to be seen as reflecting the attitude of proponents of Enlightenment thought, the arguments that would appear to present this criticism are not always easy to follow. The text, nevertheless, requires the reader to meditate on current society and to focus on its possible flaws, a stance that corresponds to the standard position adopted in utopian texts.

Pablo de Olavide y Jáuregui's 'Cartas de Mariano a Antonio' in *El Evangelio en triunfo* make use of a key aspect of many successful eighteenth-century novels, the epistolary format, but its formal features are only lightly exploited, since it is the social and ideological dimensions of utopianism that the author wishes to foreground. Although Olavide echoes More's original utopia in presenting an ideal society, the literary form yields to the description of the philosopher's town and the beliefs and practices of its inhabitants as the major characteristics most deserving of the attention of the reader. The treatment of people and their attitudes to organized religion reveals the author's engagement with the Catholic Church in Spain, while the arguments concerning beliefs and their social consequences show that Olavide is prepared to argue in favour of an enlightened Catholicism, one that progressive Spanish Catholics would have sympathized with. That is to say, this is a model designed to capture the sympathy of a potentially hostile reading public. Nothing included in the letters as published would have offended Catholics. Beliefs and attitudes are the central interest for the reader, and the ideas set out seem designed to be applicable to Spain, especially considering that Olavide's utopian proposal was based on his previous reform project for the Sierra Morena. This fictional, though refocused, recreation of a governmental programme not only reflects the intersection of utopianism and reformism, but also reaffirms the hypothesis of an experimental or practical utopia underlying the distinctive nature of Spanish utopian fiction. *Sinapia* and the 'Cartas de Mariano a Antonio' best exemplify such a condition.

In spite of addressing Spain's need for reorganization by prioritizing different societal issues of the period, the five Spanish utopias deal with fundamental thematic components of the utopian genre, such as the process of colonization that leads to the establishment of the utopian space (predominantly in *Sinapia* and the *Monarquía columbina*), the balance between a spiritual and a practical education, the abolition of private property, public happiness, and economic and scientific progress. They also imply the emergence of a potentially dangerous isolationism and a sense of xenophobia and authoritarianism as a result of the geographical and ideological insularity that belongs to the utopian mentality. This dogmatic and repressive side of utopia is more visible in *Sinapia* and the *Monarquía columbina*, possibly due to the strong religious basis of their ideal societies.

The five texts also portray the conceptual confrontation between civilization and barbarism. The image of the good savage as the ideal inhabitant of a utopian country brings up the debate about the risk to the innocent and pristine nature of the natives of the New World due to the corruption and oppression of the European colonizers. On the other side of the controversy, the superiority of Western civilization is praised in relation to the backwardness of the uncivilized indigenous peoples in the newly conquered lands. In this manner, Spanish imperialism seems to have found in the colonization process that precedes the creation of the utopian settlement a means of legitimizing its ethical vision of colonialism as a civilizing mission. The alleged progress and sophistication that result from the rise of civilization are particularly acclaimed in *Sinapia* through the description of a complex, state-controlled system of knowledge production.

As far as key aspects of society are concerned, the unjustified privileges of the nobility and the Church are recurring topics in these utopian narratives. The role and concept of nobility and its place in society are highly questioned, but some potential solutions to the problem that they pose are suggested: *Sinapia* and the 'Cartas de Mariano a Antonio' propose the elimination of the nobility as a class, but Antonio recommends the devotion of nobles to social usefulness instead. However, the treatment of an idle aristocracy is not as strong as that of religion, which produces a major polarization of attitudes. While the social function of a rational Christianity and a religion-oriented education are central in *Sinapia*, the *Monarquía columbina*, and the 'Cartas de Mariano a Antonio', the questionable material enrichment of the Church is attacked in the *Monarquía de los Ayparchontes*. The matter is overlooked in Vaca de Guzmán's *Suplemento*, perhaps following the example of More's *Utopia*, in which the discussion about religion is fundamentally philosophical and presented in terms of tolerance for different religious beliefs.

Thus, the five texts explored in this book stand out for their imaginative and creative approach to a pre-existing literary format or framework as their authors freely interpret and vary the existing tradition. Each one highlights specific features that the author wishes to emphasize. Their aim is always to provoke contrasts with the state of Spain as it existed at the points in time at which they were written and to lead the readership to imagine and believe that the dominant status quo might be changed for the better. Two of the texts (*Suplemento de los viajes de Enrique Wanton* and *Monarquía de los Ayparchontes*) are presented as satires of the Spain of their moment; two others (*Sinapia* and 'Cartas de Mariano a Antonio') describe idealized societies; and the last one (*Monarquía columbina*) comes across, in part, as a counter-utopia or dystopia, taking what some would consider progressive aspects of the Spain of Carlos III and presenting them in a negative light.

Much previous work on eighteenth-century Spanish utopias has been limited to a focus on more obvious surface features, and a substantial number of recent studies have tended to reiterate points made in earlier research. Somewhat surprisingly, few critics have tried to set the five texts in the utopian tradition. Most scholars have treated specific texts in isolation and have taken their relationship with the utopian model for granted. In that respect, the present book has contributed to a more probing analysis of the works in question in the light of their indebtedness to More's text and their ideological links with a well-established Spanish reformist tradition. What this book has also aimed to show is how the adoption and adaptation of the traditional utopian framework prioritize narrative elements that serve to portray and criticize the functioning of social institutions in Spain. This subject was central to Enlightenment debate at the time and a key constituent of the focus on progressive reform that occupied the attention of reformers from the era of the *novatores* to the period of fierce discussion at the end of the eighteenth century, when signs of political and cultural crisis were most evident. More importantly, the study has demonstrated the coexistence of utopianism and reformism in Enlightenment Spain and has revealed how both ideological discourses interacted and sought to bring about change during a time of questioning of political and social priorities, although they were both incapable of producing the comprehensive transformation that progressive minorities earnestly endeavoured to achieve.

BIBLIOGRAPHY

Texts Analysed

El Censor, 8 vols (Madrid: n. pub., 1781–87; facsimile edition by José Miguel Caso González, Oviedo: Universidad de Oviedo, Instituto Feijoo de Estudios del Siglo XVIII, 1989), III [1784]: 'Discurso LXI', pp. 225–39, 'Discurso LXIII', pp. 257–70; IV [1785]: 'Discurso LXXV', pp. 131–50

Descripción de la Sinapia, península en la tierra austral, in *'Sinapia': una utopía española del Siglo de las Luces*, ed. by Miguel Avilés Fernández (Madrid: Editora Nacional, 1976), pp. 67–134

[MERINO DE JESUCRISTO, ANDRÉS], *Monarquía columbina*, in *'Tratado sobre la monarquía columbina': una utopía antiilustrada del siglo XVIII*, ed. by Pedro Álvarez de Miranda (Madrid: El Archipiélago, 1980), pp. 1–29

OLAVIDE Y JÁUREGUI, PABLO DE, 'Cartas de Mariano a Antonio', in *Cartas de Mariano a Antonio: el programa ilustrado de 'El Evangelio en triunfo'*, ed. by Gérard Dufour (Aix-en-Provence: Université de Provence, 1988), pp. 37–229

[VACA] DE GUZMÁN Y MANRIQUE, [GUTIERRE] JOAQUÍN, *Suplemento, o sea tomo tercero [–cuarto y último] de los viajes de Enrique Wanton al país de las monas*, 2 vols (Madrid: Antonio de Sancha, 1778)

Other Primary Texts

ANDREAE, JOHANN VALENTIN, *Christianopolis: An Ideal State of the Seventeenth Century* (Oxford: Oxford University Press, 1916)

ARISTOPHANES, *'The Birds' and Other Plays*, trans. by David Barrett and Alan H. Sommerstein (London: Penguin, 2003)

ARISTOTLE, *Politics*, trans. by Ernest Barker, and rev. and ed. by R. F. Stalley (Oxford: Oxford University Press, 2009)

AVILÉS FERNÁNDEZ, MIGUEL, ed., *Descripción de la Sinapia, península en la tierra austral* (Madrid: Círculo de Bellas Artes, 2011)

BACON, FRANCIS, *New Atlantis*, in *Three Early Modern Utopias: Thomas More, 'Utopia'; Francis Bacon, 'New Atlantis'; Henry Neville, 'The Isle of Pines'*, ed. by Susan Bruce (Oxford: Oxford University Press, 1999), pp. 149–86

CADALSO, JOSÉ DE, *Cartas marruecas. Noches lúgubres*, ed. by Emilio Martínez Mata (Barcelona: Crítica, 2008)

—— *Escritos autobiográficos y epistolario*, ed. by Nigel Glendinning and Nicole Harrison (London: Tamesis, 1979)

CAMPANELLA, TOMMASO, *La Città del Sole: dialogo poetico / The City of the Sun: A Poetical Dialogue*, trans. by Daniel J. Donno (Berkeley: University of California Press, 1981)

—— *A Discourse Touching the Spanish Monarchy*, trans. by Edmund Chilmead (London: Philemon Stephens, 1654)

CAMPOMANES, PEDRO RODRÍGUEZ, CONDE DE, *Dictamen fiscal de expulsión de los jesuitas de España*, ed. by Jorge Cejudo and Teófanes Egido (Madrid: Fundación Universitaria Española, 1977)

[——] *Discurso sobre el fomento de la industria popular* (Madrid: Imprenta de Antonio de Sancha, 1774)

—— *Discurso sobre la educación popular de los artesanos y su fomento*, 5 vols (Madrid: Imprenta de Antonio de Sancha, 1775–77)

CASAS, BARTOLOMÉ DE LAS, *Obras escogidas*, 5 vols (Madrid: Atlas, 1957–58), IV: *Apologética historia*, ed. by Juan Pérez de Tudela Bueso (1958)

El Censor, 8 vols (Madrid: n. pub., 1781–87; facsimile edition by José Miguel Caso González, Oviedo: Universidad de Oviedo, Instituto Feijoo de Estudios del Siglo XVIII, 1989), I [1781]: 'Discurso I', pp. 17–28, III [1784]: 'Discurso LXV', pp. 289–306; IV [1786]: 'Discurso LXXXIX', pp. 155–84, 'Discurso XC', pp. 385–408; V [1786]: 'Discurso CVII', pp. 715–37; VIII [1787]: 'Discurso CLXI', pp. 565–79, 'Discurso CLXV', pp. 629–60

COLUMBUS, CHRISTOPHER, *Select Letters of Christopher Columbus, with Other Original Documents, Relating to his Four Voyages to the New World*, ed. and trans. by Richard Henry Major (London: Hakluyt Society, 1870)

Continuación del Memorial Literario, Instructivo y Curioso de la Corte de Madrid, February 1794, pp. 161–239

Correo de Madrid, No. 57, 9 May 1787, pp. 241–44; No. 58, 12 May 1787, pp. 245–48; No. 59, 16 May 1787, pp. 249–52; No. 60, 19 May 1787, pp. 253–56

CRO, STELIO, ed., *'Descripción de la Sinapia, península en la tierra austral': A Classical Utopia of Spain* (Hamilton, Ontario: McMaster University, 1975)

CYRANO DE BERGERAC, SAVINIEN, *Œuvres complètes*, 2 vols (Paris: Galic, 1962), I: *Histoire comique des états et empires de la lune et du soleil*

Diario de Madrid, No. 79, 20 March 1799, pp. 321–24

Diccionario de autoridades, 6 vols (Madrid: Real Academia Española, 1726–39; facsimile edition, Madrid: Gredos, 1969), I (1726), IV (1734)

Diccionario de la lengua española, 23rd edn (Madrid: Real Academia Española), <http://dle.rae.es> [accessed 7 July 2017]

DIDEROT, DENIS, 'Don Pablo Olavidès: précis historique, rédigé sur des mémoires fournis par un espagnol', in *Œuvres de Denis Diderot: Mélanges de littérature et de philosophie*, ed. by Jacques André Naigeon, 26 vols (Paris: J. L. J. Brière, 1821–34), III (1821), pp. 384–93

—— *Supplément au voyage de Bougainville* (Rosny-sous-Bois: Bréal, 2002)

FERNÁN NÚÑEZ, CARLOS GUTIÉRREZ DE LOS RÍOS, CONDE DE, *Vida de Carlos III*, ed. by Alfred Morel-Fatio and Antonio Paz y Meliá, 2 vols (Madrid: Fernando Fé, 1898; facsimile edition, Madrid: Fundación Universitaria Española, 1988)

FILÓSOFO INCÓGNITO, EL [ANDRÉS MERINO DE JESUCRISTO], *La mujer feliz, dependiente del mundo y de la fortuna*, 3 vols (Madrid: Imprenta Real, 1789), I, II

Gaceta de Madrid, No. 32, 8 August 1769, pp. 257–64; No. 44, 29 October 1771, pp. 371–82; No. 9, 3 March 1778, pp. 77–88; No. 35, 30 April 1779, pp. 293–300; No. 103, 24 December 1793, pp. 1353–68; No. 95, 25 November 1796, pp. 1006–08

GATELL I CARNICER, PEDRO, 'Aventura magna del Bachiller', No. 8, in *El Argonauta Español: Periódico Gaditano*, ed. by Marieta Cantos Casenave and María José Rodríguez Sánchez de León (Seville: Renacimiento, 2008), pp. 210–13

GIMENO PUYOL, MARÍA DOLORES, ed., *Tres utopías ilustradas: 'Viaje al país de los Ayparchontes', 'La isla', 'La utopía de Zenit'* (Nuremberg: Clásicos Hispánicos, 2014), ebook

HOBBES, THOMAS, *Leviathan; or, The Matter, Form and Power of a Commonwealth Ecclesiastical and Civil*, ed. by Michael Oakeshott (New York: Simon & Schuster, 1997)

Índice último de los libros prohibidos y mandados expurgar: para todos los reinos y señoríos del católico rey de las Españas, el señor Don Carlos IV (Madrid: Imprenta de Antonio de Sancha, 1790; facsimile edition, Valencia: Librerías París-Valencia, 1997)

JOVELLANOS, GASPAR MELCHOR DE, 'Discurso sobre la necesidad de unir al estudio de la legislación el de nuestra historia y antigüedades', in Gaspar Melchor de Jovellanos, *Obras publicadas e inéditas de Don Gaspar Melchor de Jovellanos*, ed. by Cándido Nocedal, 5 vols (Madrid: Atlas, 1952–63), I (1963), pp. 288–98

——*Elogio de Carlos III*, in Gaspar Melchor de Jovellanos, *Obras completas*, ed. by Vicent Llombart i Rosa and Joaquín Ocampo Suárez-Valdés, 14 vols (Oviedo: Ayuntamiento de Gijón, Instituto Feijoo de Estudios del Siglo XVIII, KRK Ediciones, 1984–2010), X: *Escritos económicos* (2008), pp. 669–85

——*Informe de la sociedad económica de esta corte al real y supremo Consejo de Castilla en el expediente de ley agraria* (Madrid: Imprenta de Sancha, 1795)

——*Memoria sobre las diversiones públicas*, in Gaspar Melchor de Jovellanos, *Obras completas*, ed. by Elena de Lorenzo Álvarez, 14 vols (Oviedo: Ayuntamiento de Gijón, Instituto Feijoo de Estudios del Siglo XVIII, KRK Ediciones, 1984–2010), XII: *Escritos sobre literatura* (2009), pp. 191–318

KANT, IMMANUEL, 'An Answer to the Question: What is Enlightenment?', in Immanuel Kant, *Political Writings*, ed. by Hans Reiss and trans. by H. B. Nisbet (Cambridge: Cambridge University Press, 1991), pp. 54–60

——*The Metaphysics of Morals*, ed. and trans. by Mary Gregor (Cambridge: Cambridge University Press, 1996)

LARRA, MARIANO JOSÉ DE, '"Panorama matritense". Cuadros de costumbres de la capital observados y descritos por un Curioso Parlante. Artículo segundo y último', in Mariano José de Larra, *Fígaro: colección de artículos dramáticos, literarios, políticos y de costumbres*, ed. by Alejandro Pérez Vidal (Barcelona: Crítica, 1997), pp. 544–48

MACANAZ, MELCHOR DE, *El deseado gobierno, buscado por el amor de Dios para el reino de España*, Huesca, Biblioteca Pública de Huesca, MS 141, Miscelánea, 1855, fols 57^v–94^r, <http://bibliotecavirtual.aragon.es/bva/i18n/catalogo_imagenes/grupo.cmd?posicion=122&aceptar=Aceptar&path=1000180&presentacion=pagina> [accessed 21 February 2016]

MARCHENA, JOSÉ, 'Discurso cuarto' [in *El Observador*], in José Marchena, *Obra española en prosa: historia, política, literatura*, ed. by Juan Francisco Fuentes (Madrid: Centro de Estudios Constitucionales, 1990), pp. 67–72

[MARQUÉS Y ESPEJO, ANTONIO], *Viaje de un filósofo a Selenópolis, corte desconocida de los habitantes de la tierra* (Madrid: Gómez Fuentenebro, 1804)

MASSON DE MORVILLIERS, NICOLAS, 'Espagne', in *Encyclopédie méthodique, ou par ordre de matières*, ed. by Denis Diderot and Jean le Rond d'Alembert, 203 vols (Paris: Panckoucke, 1782–1832), I: *Géographie moderne* (1782), pp. 554–68

[MERINO DE JESUCRISTO, ANDRÉS], *Tratado sobre la monarquía columbina*, in *Semanario Erudito, que comprende varias obras inéditas, críticas, morales, instructivas, políticas, históricas, satíricas y jocosas de nuestros mejores autores antiguos y modernos*, ed. by Antonio Valladares de Sotomayor, 34 vols (Madrid: Antonio Espinosa, 1787–91), XXX (1790), pp. 61–84

MESONERO ROMANOS, RAMÓN DE, 'Memorias de un setentón', in Ramón de Mesonero Romanos, *Obras de Ramón de Mesonero Romanos*, ed. by Carlos Seco Serrano, 5 vols (Madrid: Atlas, 1967), V, pp. 1–247

——*Panorama matritense. Cuadros de costumbres de la capital, observados y descritos por un Curioso Parlante*, 3 vols (Madrid: Imprenta de Repullés, 1835–38), I (1835)

MIRABEAU, VICTOR DE RIQUETI, MARQUIS DE, *L'Ami des hommes, ou traité de la population* (Avignon: n. pub., 1756)

MONTAIGNE, MICHEL DE, 'Des cannibales', in Michel de Montaigne, *Essais*, ed. by Albert Thibaudet (Paris: Gallimard, 1950), pp. 239–53

MONTENGÓN, PEDRO, *El Antenor*, 2 vols (Madrid: Antonio de Sancha, 1788)

——*Eusebio*, ed. by Fernando García Lara (Madrid: Cátedra, 1998)

——*El Mirtilo, o los pastores trashumantes* (Madrid: Imprenta de Sancha, 1795)

MONTESQUIEU, CHARLES-LOUIS DE SECONDAT, BARON DE, *De l'esprit des lois*, 6 vols (Paris: Lebigre Frères, 1834), I

—— *The Spirit of the Laws*, ed. and trans. by Anne M. Cohler, Basia Carolyn Miller, and Harold Samuel Stone (Cambridge: Cambridge University Press, 1989)
MORE, THOMAS, *Utopia*, ed. and trans. by Edward Surtz (New Haven, CT: Yale University Press, 1964)
——*Utopia*, ed. by George M. Logan and trans. by Robert M. Adams (Cambridge: Cambridge University Press, 2006)
——*La 'Utopía' de Tomás Moro, gran canciller de Inglaterra, vizconde y ciudadano de Londres*, trans. by Jerónimo Antonio de Medinilla y Porres (Cordova: Salvador de Cea, 1637)
——*La 'Utopía' de Tomás Moro, gran canciller de Inglaterra, vizconde y ciudadano de Londres*, trans. by Jerónimo Antonio de Medinilla y Porres, 2nd edn (Madrid: Imprenta de Pantaleón Aznar, 1790)
——*La 'Utopía' de Tomás Moro, gran canciller de Inglaterra, vizconde y ciudadano de Londres*, trans. by Jerónimo Antonio de Medinilla y Porres, 3rd edn (Madrid: Imprenta de Mateo Repullés, 1805)
MORELLY, ÉTIENNE-GABRIEL, *Naufrage des îles flottantes, ou Basiliade du célèbre Pilpai*, 2 vols (Messine: n. pub., 1753)
NEBRIJA, ANTONIO DE, *Gramática sobre la lengua castellana*, ed. by Carmen Lozano (Madrid: Real Academia Española, 2011)
Novísima recopilación de las leyes de España, 6 vols (Madrid: n. pub., 1805–07), III, IV (1805)
OLAVIDE Y JÁUREGUI, PABLO DE, *Informe sobre la ley agraria*, in Pablo de Olavide y Jáuregui, *Obras selectas*, ed. by Estuardo Núñez (Lima: Banco de Crédito del Perú, 1987), pp. 483–531
——'Prólogo del autor', in Pablo de Olavide y Jáuregui, *El Evangelio en triunfo*, 4 vols (Valencia: Imprenta de los hermanos de Orga, 1797–98), I (1797), pp. iii–xvi
PERAMÁS, JOSÉ MANUEL, *La 'República' de Platón y los guaraníes* (Buenos Aires: Emecé, 1946)
PLATO, *The Republic* (University Park: Pennsylvania State University Press, 1998)
QUIROGA, VASCO DE, *Información en derecho*, in Rafael Aguayo Spencer, *Don Vasco de Quiroga: pensamiento jurídico. Antología*, ed. by José Luis Soberanes (Mexico City: Porrúa, 1986), pp. 82–212
RAMIRO AVILÉS, MIGUEL ÁNGEL, ed., *Descripción de la Sinapia, península en la tierra austral* (Madrid: Dykinson, 2013)
Real Cédula de su Majestad y Señores del Consejo, que contiene la Instrucción y Fuero de Población, que se debe observar en las que se formen de nuevo en la Sierra Morena con naturales y extranjeros católicos (Madrid: Antonio Sanz, 1767)
REJÓN Y LUCAS, DIEGO VENTURA, *Aventuras de Juan Luis: historia divertida que puede ser útil* (Madrid: Joaquín Ibarra, 1781; facsimile edition, Murcia: Tres Fronteras, 2008)
ROUSSEAU, JEAN-JACQUES, *Émile, ou de l'éducation*, 4 vols (Paris: Duchesne, 1762), IV
RUBÍN DE CELIS, MANUEL, *El Corresponsal del Censor*, ed. by Klaus-Dieter Ertler, Renate Hodab, and Inmaculada Urzainqui (Madrid: Iberoamericana; Frankfurt am Main: Vervuert, 2009)
SAVATER, FERNANDO, *Vente a Sinapia: una reflexión española sobre la utopía*, in Fernando Savater, *Último desembarco; Vente a Sinapia* (Madrid: Espasa-Calpe, 1988), pp. 77–138
Semanario Pintoresco Español. Lectura de las familias. Enciclopedia popular, 22 vols (Madrid: Oficinas y Establecimiento Tipográfico del Semanario Pintoresco, 1836–57), XVIII (1853)
SEMPERE Y GUARINOS, JUAN, *Ensayo de una biblioteca española de los mejores escritores del reinado de Carlos III*, 6 vols (Madrid: Imprenta Real, 1785–89; facsimile edition, Madrid: Gredos, 1969), II (1785), IV (1787), V (1789)
SERIMAN, ZACCARIA, *Delli viaggi di Enrico Wanton alle terre australi*, 4 vols (London: Tommaso Brewman, 1772), I

―― *Viajes de Enrique Wanton al país de las monas*, trans. by [Gutierre] Joaquín [Vaca] de Guzmán y Manrique, 2 vols, I (Alcalá: Imprenta de María García Briones, 1769), II (Madrid: Imprenta de Pantaleón Aznar, 1771)
SHELLEY, MARY, *Lives of the Most Eminent French Writers*, 2 vols (Philadelphia, PA: Lea and Blanchard, 1840), I
SWIFT, JONATHAN, *Gulliver's Travels*, ed. by Claude Rawson (New York: Oxford University Press, 2005)
―― 'To Mr Pope', in Jonathan Swift, *Epistolary Correspondence. Letters from September 1725 to May 1732* (Edinburgh: Archibald Constable, 1824), pp. 3–6
UZCANGA MEINECKE, FRANCISCO, ed., *El Censor* (Barcelona: Crítica, 2005)

Secondary Sources

ABELLÁN, JOSÉ LUIS, *Historia crítica del pensamiento español*, 7 vols (Madrid: Espasa-Calpe, 1979–92), II: *La Edad de Oro* (1979), III: *Del Barroco a la Ilustración (siglos XVII y XVIII)* (1981)
AGUILAR PIÑAL, FRANCISCO, 'La anti-utopía dieciochesca de Trigueros', in *Las utopías en el mundo hispánico: actas del coloquio celebrado en la Casa de Velázquez*, ed. by Jean-Pierre Étienvre (Madrid: Casa de Velázquez, Universidad Complutense, 1990), pp. 65–72
―― *Bibliografía de autores españoles del siglo XVIII*, 10 vols (Madrid: Consejo Superior de Investigaciones Científicas, 1981–2001), VIII (1995)
―― *La España del absolutismo ilustrado* (Madrid: Espasa-Calpe, 2005)
―― *Plan de estudios para la Universidad de Sevilla por Pablo de Olavide* (Barcelona: Ediciones de Cultura Popular, 1969)
―― *La prensa española en el siglo XVIII: diarios, revistas y pronósticos* (Madrid: Consejo Superior de Investigaciones Científicas, 1978)
―― *La Sevilla de Olavide, 1767–1778* (Seville: Ayuntamiento de Sevilla, 1966)
ALCÁZAR MOLINA, CAYETANO, *Las colonias alemanas de Sierra Morena* (Madrid: n. pub., 1930)
ÁLVAREZ BARRIENTOS, JOAQUÍN, 'Los hombres de letras', in Joaquín Álvarez Barrientos, François Lopez, and Inmaculada Urzainqui, *La república de las letras en la España del siglo XVIII* (Madrid: Consejo Superior de Investigaciones Científicas, 1995), pp. 19–61
―― *Los hombres de letras en la España del siglo XVIII. Apóstoles y arribistas* (Madrid: Castalia, 2006)
―― *Ilustración y neoclasicismo en las letras españolas* (Madrid: Síntesis, 2005)
―― 'Sobre utopías y viajes imaginarios: Gutierre Joaquín Vaca de Guzmán', in *Historia de la literatura española*, ed. by Ricardo de la Fuente, 50 vols [incomplete] (Madrid: Júcar, 1991–97), XXVIII: *La novela del siglo XVIII* (1991), pp. 131–41
ÁLVAREZ DE MIRANDA, PEDRO, 'Las academias de los novatores', in *De las academias a la enciclopedia: el discurso del saber en la modernidad*, ed. by Evangelina Rodríguez Cuadros (Valencia: Alfons el Magnànim, 1993), pp. 263–300
―― 'Introducción', in *'Tratado sobre la monarquía columbina': una utopía antiilustrada del siglo XVIII*, ed. by Pedro Álvarez de Miranda (Madrid: El Archipiélago, 1980), pp. v–lviii
―― 'Los libros de viajes y las utopías en el XVIII español', in *Historia de la literatura española*, ed. by Víctor García de la Concha, 4 vols (Madrid: Espasa-Calpe, 1995–98), VII: *Siglo XVIII (II)*, ed. by Guillermo Carnero (1995), pp. 682–706
―― 'El Padre Andrés Merino, autor de la *Monarquía columbina*', in *Las utopías en el mundo hispánico: actas del coloquio celebrado en la Casa de Velázquez*, ed. by Jean-Pierre Étienvre (Madrid: Casa de Velázquez, Universidad Complutense, 1990), pp. 19–39
―― 'Proyectos y proyectistas en el siglo XVIII español', in *La Ilustración española: actas del Coloquio Internacional celebrado en Alicante, 1–4 octubre 1985*, ed. by A. Alberola and E. La

Parra (Alicante: Instituto Juan Gil-Albert, Diputación Provincial de Alicante, 1986), pp. 133–50

—— 'Un relato inédito e inacabado del P. Andrés Merino: la *Monarquía de los leones*', *Dieciocho*, 16 (1993), 13–23

—— 'Sobre utopías y viajes imaginarios en el siglo XVIII español', in *Homenaje a Gonzalo Torrente Ballester*, ed. by Víctor García de la Concha (Salamanca: Biblioteca de la Caja de Ahorros y Monte de Piedad de Salamanca, 1981), pp. 351–82

—— 'Vuelta a *Sinapia*', in *Littérature et politique en Espagne aux siècles d'or: colloque international*, ed. by Jean-Pierre Étienvre (Paris: Klincksieck, 1998), pp. 349–60

AMALRIC, JEAN-PIERRE, and LUCIENNE DOMERGUE, *La España de la Ilustración (1700–1833)* (Barcelona: Crítica, 2001)

ANES, GONZALO, *Informes en el expediente de ley agraria: Andalucía y La Mancha, 1768* (Madrid: Instituto de Cooperación Iberoamericana, Sociedad Estatal Quinto Centenario, Instituto de Estudios Fiscales, 1990)

—— *El Siglo de las Luces* (Madrid: Alianza, 1994)

ARTHUR, PAUL LONGLEY, *Virtual Voyages: Travel Writing and the Antipodes, 1605–1837* (London: Anthem, 2011)

ASTIGARRAGA, JESÚS, ed., *The Spanish Enlightenment Revisited* (Oxford: Voltaire Foundation, 2015)

AUSEJO, ELENA, 'Las matemáticas en la Ilustración hispana: estado de la cuestión', in *Ilustración, ilustraciones*, ed. by Jesús Astigarraga, María Victoria López-Cordón, and José María Urkia, 2 vols (Donostia-San Sebastian: Real Sociedad Bascongada de los Amigos del País; Madrid: Sociedad Estatal de Conmemoraciones Culturales, 2009), I, pp. 693–713

AVILÉS FERNÁNDEZ, MIGUEL, 'Introducción', in *'Sinapia': una utopía española del Siglo de las Luces*, ed. by Miguel Avilés Fernández (Madrid: Editora Nacional, 1976), pp. 13–65

—— 'Otros cuatro relatos utópicos en la España moderna: las utopías de J. Maldonado, *Omnibona* y *El Deseado Gobierno*', in *Las utopías en el mundo hispánico: actas del coloquio celebrado en la Casa de Velázquez*, ed. by Jean-Pierre Étienvre (Madrid: Casa de Velázquez, Universidad Complutense, 1990), pp. 109–28

BACZKO, BRONISŁAW, *Lumières de l'utopie* (Paris: Payot, 1978)

BAKER-SMITH, DOMINIC, *More's 'Utopia'* (London: HarperCollins Academic, 1991)

—— 'Reading *Utopia*', in *The Cambridge Companion to Thomas More*, ed. by George M. Logan (Cambridge: Cambridge University Press, 2011), pp. 141–67

BAQUERO, ANA L., 'El viaje y la ficción narrativa española en el s. XVIII', in *Libros de viaje: actas de las Jornadas sobre 'Los libros de viaje en el mundo románico', celebradas en Murcia del 27 al 30 de noviembre de 1995*, ed. by Fernando Carmona Fernández and Antonia Martínez Pérez (Murcia: Universidad de Murcia, 1996), pp. 21–29

BAQUERO GOYANES, MARIANO, 'Realismo y utopía en la literatura española', *Studi Ispanici*, 1 (1962), 7–28

BAREIRO SAGUIER, RUBÉN, and JEAN-PAUL DUVIOLS, eds, *Tentación de la utopía: la república de los jesuitas en el Paraguay* (Asuncion: Servilibro, 2012)

BARNADAS, JOSEP M., 'The Catholic Church in Colonial Spanish America', in *The Cambridge History of Latin America*, ed. by Leslie Bethell, 11 vols (Cambridge: Cambridge University Press, 1984–95), I (1984), pp. 509–40

BENÍTEZ, MIGUEL, '"El sueño de la razón produce monstruos": *El Evangelio en triunfo*, de Pablo de Olavide', in *Actas del Congreso Internacional sobre 'Carlos III y la Ilustración'*, 3 vols (Madrid: Ministerio de Cultura, 1989), III: *Educación y pensamiento*, pp. 199–225

—— 'Trazas de pensamiento radical en el mundo hispánico en los tiempos modernos', in *La actitud ilustrada*, ed. by Eduardo Bello and Antonio Rivera (Valencia: Biblioteca Valenciana, 2002), pp. 195–231

BERNABÉU ALBERT, SALVADOR, 'Las utopías y el reformismo borbónico', in *El reformismo borbónico: una visión interdisciplinar*, ed. by Agustín Guimerá (Madrid: Alianza, 1996), pp. 247–63

BERRY, CHRISTOPHER J., *The Idea of Luxury: A Conceptual and Historical Investigation* (Cambridge: Cambridge University Press, 1994)

The Blackwell Companion to the Enlightenment, ed. by John W. Yolton and others (Oxford and Cambridge, MA: Blackwell, 1995)

BLOCH, ERNST, *The Principle of Hope*, trans. by Neville Plaice, Stephen Plaice, and Paul Knight, 3 vols (Oxford: Blackwell, 1986), I

BLOOMFIELD, PAUL, *Imaginary Worlds; or, The Evolution of Utopia* (London: Hamish Hamilton, 1932)

BOWDEN, BRETT, *The Empire of Civilization: The Evolution of an Imperial Idea* (Chicago, IL, and London: University of Chicago Press, 2009)

BREWER, JOHN, *The Pleasures of the Imagination: English Culture in the Eighteenth Century* (London: HarperCollins, 1997)

CALATAYUD SOLER, ROSA, 'La utopía de un filósofo desengañado: Pablo de Olavide', in *Educación e Ilustración en España: III Coloquio de Historia de la Educación* (Barcelona: Universidad de Barcelona, 1984), pp. 33–40

CALLAHAN, WILLIAM J., *Church, Politics, and Society in Spain, 1750–1874* (Cambridge, MA, and London: Harvard University Press, 1984)

CALVO CARILLA, JOSÉ LUIS, 'Las fábulas de Iriarte: microutopías de la razón pragmática', in José Luis Calvo Carilla, *El sueño sostenible: estudios sobre la utopía literaria en España* (Madrid: Marcial Pons, 2008), pp. 63–104

CAÑAS MURILLO, JESÚS, 'Utopías y libros de viajes en el siglo XVIII español: un capítulo de historia literaria de la Ilustración', in *Aufklärung: estudios sobre la Ilustración española dedicados a Hans-Joachim Lope*, ed. by Jesús Cañas Murillo and José Roso Díaz (Cáceres: Universidad de Extremadura, 2007), pp. 71–88

CARO BAROJA, JULIO, 'Las "nuevas poblaciones" de Sierra Morena y Andalucía: un experimento sociológico en tiempos de Carlos III', *Clavileño: Revista de la Asociación Internacional de Hispanismo*, 18 (1952), 52–64

CARRASCO M., ROLANDO, 'Un mito en movimiento: Pablo de Olavide y su *Evangelio en triunfo* (1797)', *Revista Chilena de Literatura*, 71 (2007), 19–42

CASO GONZÁLEZ, JOSÉ MIGUEL, '*El Censor*, ¿periódico de Carlos III?', in *El Censor*, ed. by José Miguel Caso González (Oviedo: Universidad de Oviedo, Instituto Feijoo de Estudios del Siglo XVIII, 1989), pp. 776–99

—— 'La crítica religiosa de *El Censor* y el grupo ilustrado de la Condesa de Montijo', in *La Ilustración en España y Alemania*, ed. by Reyes Mate and Friedrich Niewöhner (Barcelona: Anthropos, 1989), pp. 175–88

—— 'Introducción', in José de Cadalso, *Cartas marruecas*, ed. by José Miguel Caso González (Madrid: Espasa-Calpe, 2007), pp. 11–28

CEJUDO LÓPEZ, JORGE, *Catálogo del Archivo del Conde de Campomanes (fondos Carmen Dorado y Rafael Gasset)* (Madrid: Fundación Universitaria Española, 1975)

CHORDAS, NINA, *Forms in Early Modern Utopia: The Ethnography of Perfection* (Farnham, UK, and Burlington, VT: Ashgate, 2010)

CIARAMITARO, FERNANDO, 'Pablo de Olavide (1725–1803): A Spanish-Economist at the Service of the Institution', in *Economics and Institutions: Contributions from the History of Economic Thought*, ed. by Pier Francesco Asso and Luca Fiorito (Milan: Franco Angeli, 2007), pp. 368–88

COLMEIRO, MANUEL, *Biblioteca de los economistas españoles de los siglos XVI, XVII y XVIII* (Madrid: Real Academia de Ciencias Morales y Políticas, [1954])

CORREA CALDERÓN, EVARISTO, *Registro de arbitristas, economistas y reformadores españoles (1500–1936): catálogo de impresos y manuscritos* (Madrid: Fundación Universitaria Española, 1981)
CRO, STELIO, *The American Foundations of the Hispanic Utopia, 1492–1793*, 2 vols (Tallahassee, FL: DeSoto Press, 1994), I: *The Literary Utopia. 'Sinapia', A Classical Utopia of Spain and the 'Discurso de la educación'*, II: *The Empirical Utopia*
—— *A Forerunner of the Enlightenment in Spain* (Hamilton, Ontario: McMaster University, 1976)
—— 'El mito de la ciudad ideal en España: *Sinapia*', in *Actas del VI Congreso de la Asociación Internacional de Hispanistas*, ed. by Evelyn Rugg and Alan M. Gordon (Toronto: University of Toronto, 1980), pp. 192–94
—— *Realidad y utopía en el descubrimiento y conquista de la América Hispana (1492–1682)* (Troy, MI: International Book Publishers, 1983)
—— 'Las reducciones jesuíticas en la encrucijada de dos utopías', in *Las utopías en el mundo hispánico: actas del coloquio celebrado en la Casa de Velázquez*, ed. by Jean-Pierre Étienvre (Madrid: Casa de Velázquez, Universidad Complutense, 1990), pp. 41–56
—— 'Sinapia, el Viejo Testamento y la teocracia cristiana', in *Actas del XII Congreso de la Asociación Internacional de Hispanistas*, ed. by Jules Whicker, 2 vols (Birmingham: University of Birmingham, 1998), II, pp. 130–36
—— 'La utopía de las dos orillas (1453–1793)', *Cuadernos para Investigación de la Literatura Hispánica*, 30 (2005), 15–268
—— 'La utopía en España: *Sinapia*', *Cuadernos para Investigación de la Literatura Hispánica*, 2–3 (1980), 27–40
CURTIUS, ERNST ROBERT, *European Literature and the Latin Middle Ages*, trans. by Willard R. Trask (New York: Pantheon Books, 1953)
DASTON, LORRAINE J., 'Classifications of Knowledge in the Age of Louis XIV', in *Sun King: The Ascendancy of French Culture During the Reign of Louis XIV*, ed. by David Lee Rubin (Cranbury, NJ: Associated University Presses, 1992), pp. 207–20
DAVIS, J. C., *Utopia and the Ideal Society: A Study of English Utopian Writing, 1516–1700* (Cambridge: Cambridge University Press, 1981)
DEACON, PHILIP, 'El autor esquivo en la cultura española del siglo XVIII: apuntes sobre decoro, estrategias y juegos', *Dieciocho*, 22 (1999), 213–36
—— '*El Censor* y la crisis de las Luces en España: el *Diálogo crítico-político* de Joaquín Medrano de Sandoval', *Estudios de Historia Social*, 52–53 (1990), 131–40
—— 'La novela inglesa en la España del siglo XVIII: fortuna y adversidades', in *Actas del I Congreso Internacional sobre novela del siglo XVIII*, ed. by Fernando García Lara (Almería: Universidad de Almería, 1998), pp. 123–39
—— 'La prensa dieciochesca española como agente de las Luces', in *Francisco Mariano Nipho: el nacimiento de la prensa y de la crítica literaria periodística en la España del siglo XVIII*, ed. by José María Maestre Maestre, Manuel Antonio Díaz Gito, and Alberto Romero Ferrer (Alcañiz: Instituto de Estudios Humanísticos; Madrid: Consejo Superior de Investigaciones Científicas, 2015), pp. 225–44
—— 'Señas de identidad de Juan Pablo Forner: una aproximación a las *Demostraciones palmarias*', in *Juan Pablo Forner y su época (1756–1797)*, ed. by Jesús Cañas Murillo and Miguel Ángel Lama (Mérida: Editora Regional de Extremadura, 1998), pp. 379–99
DEFOURNEAUX, MARCELIN, *Pablo de Olavide ou l'afrancesado (1725–1803)* (Paris: Presses Universitaires de France, 1959)
DOMERGUE, LUCIENNE, *La Censure des livres en Espagne à la fin de l'Ancien Régime* (Madrid: Casa de Velázquez, 1996)
DOMÍNGUEZ ORTIZ, ANTONIO, *Carlos III y la España de la Ilustración* (Madrid: Alianza, 1989)

——— *Las clases privilegiadas en la España del Antiguo Régimen* (Madrid: Istmo, 1973)
——— 'El ocaso del régimen señorial en la España del siglo XVIII', in Antonio Domínguez Ortiz, *Hechos y figuras del siglo XVIII español* (Madrid: Siglo Veintiuno de España, 1973), pp. 1–62
DONATO, CLORINDA, and RICARDO LÓPEZ, eds, *Enlightenment Spain and the Encyclopédie méthodique* (Oxford: Voltaire Foundation, 2015)
DONNO, DANIEL J., 'Introduction', in Tommaso Campanella, *La Città del Sole: dialogo poetico/ The City of the Sun: A Poetical Dialogue*, trans. by Daniel J. Donno (Berkeley: University of California Press, 1981), pp. 1–21
DUFOUR, GÉRARD, 'Elementos novelescos de *El Evangelio en triunfo* de Olavide', *Anales de Literatura Española*, 11 (1995), 107–15
——— '*El Evangelio en triunfo* devant l'Inquisition', in *Hommage à Madame le Professeur Maryse Jeuland à l'occasion de son départ à la retraite* (Aix-en-Provence: Université de Provence; Marseille: Diffusion, J. Laffitte, 1983), pp. 225–31
——— '*El Evangelio en triunfo* en el dispositivo político del Príncipe de la Paz', in *Ideas en sus paisajes: homenaje al profesor Russell P. Sebold*, ed. by Guillermo Carnero, Ignacio Javier López, and Enrique Rubio (Alicante: Universidad de Alicante, 1999), pp. 159–66
——— '*El Evangelio en triunfo* o la historia de la fabricación de un éxito editorial', *Cuadernos Dieciochistas*, 4 (2003), 67–77
——— 'Introducción', in *Cartas de Mariano a Antonio: el programa ilustrado de 'El Evangelio en triunfo'*, ed. by Gérard Dufour (Aix-en-Provence: Université de Provence, 1988), pp. 5–31
——— 'Le Rôle du curé dans l'utopie des lettres de Mariano à Antonio', in *L'Espagne du XVIIIe siècle: acte des journées d'étude sur 'Ville et campagne' et 'Cartas marruecas' des 5 et 6 décembre 1997*, ed. by Jacques Soubeyroux (Saint-Étienne: Publications de l'Université de Saint-Étienne, 1997), pp. 205–15
——— 'Utopie et *Ilustración*: *El Evangelio en triunfo* de Pablo de Olavide', in *Las utopías en el mundo hispánico: actas del coloquio celebrado en la Casa de Velázquez*, ed. by Jean-Pierre Étienvre (Madrid: Casa de Velázquez, Universidad Complutense, 1990), pp. 73–78
——— 'Le Village idéal au début du XIXe siècle selon *El Evangelio en triunfo* de Pablo de Olavide', in *L'Homme et l'espace dans la littérature, les arts et l'histoire en Espagne et en Amérique Latine au XIXe siècle*, ed. by Claude Dumas (Lille: Presses Universitaires du Septentrion, 1985), pp. 11–25
ECO, UMBERTO, 'Los mundos de la ciencia ficción', in Umberto Eco, *De los espejos y otros ensayos* (Barcelona: Lumen, 1988), pp. 185–92
EGIDO, TEÓFANES, 'Los anti-ilustrados españoles', in *La Ilustración en España y Alemania*, ed. by Reyes Mate and Friedrich Niewöhner (Barcelona: Anthropos, 1989), pp. 95–119
EGIDO, TEÓFANES, and ISIDORO PINEDO, *Las causas 'gravísimas' y secretas de la expulsión de los jesuitas por Carlos III* (Madrid: Fundación Universitaria Española, 1994)
ELLIOTT, ROBERT C., *The Shape of Utopia: Studies in a Literary Genre* (Chicago, IL, and London: University of Chicago Press, 1970)
ELORZA, ANTONIO, *El fourierismo en España* (Madrid: Ediciones de la Revista de Trabajo, 1975)
——— *La ideología liberal en la Ilustración española* (Madrid: Tecnos, 1970)
——— *La modernización política en España: ensayos de historia del pensamiento político* (Madrid: Endymion, 1990)
EMIEUX, ANNICK, 'Un roman qui cherche sa forme: le manuscrit de l'*Eudamonopeia* du Père Joaquín Traggia', in *Mélanges offerts à Paul Guinard*, 2 vols (Paris: Éditions Hispaniques, 1990–91), II: *Hommage des dix-huitièmistes français*, ed. by Jean René Aymes and Annick Emieux (1991), pp. 97–108

ENCISO RECIO, LUIS MIGUEL, *Las sociedades económicas en el Siglo de las Luces* (Madrid: Real Academia de la Historia, 2010)

EQUIPO MADRID DE ESTUDIOS HISTÓRICOS, *Carlos III, Madrid y la Ilustración: contradicciones de un proyecto reformista* (Madrid: Siglo Veintiuno de España, 1988)

ERNST, GERMANA, *Tommaso Campanella: The Book and the Body of Nature*, trans. by David L. Marshall (Dordrecht: Springer, 2010)

ESCOBAR, JOSÉ, 'Más sobre los orígenes de *civilizar* y *civilización* en la España del siglo XVIII', *Nueva Revista de Filología Hispánica*, 33 (1984), 88–114

ESCOBAR, JOSÉ, and ANTHONY PERCIVAL, 'An Italo-Spanish Imaginary Voyage: Zaccaria Seriman (1709–1784) and Joaquín Vaca de Guzmán (1733–1808)', in *The Enlightenment in a Western Mediterranean Context*, ed. by Frederick Gerson, Anthony Percival, and Domenico Pietropaolo (Toronto: Benben Publications for the Society for Mediterranean Studies, 1984), pp. 87–96

—— 'Viaje imaginario y sátira de costumbres en la España del siglo XVIII: los *Viajes de Enrique Wanton al país de las monas*', in *Aufstieg und Krise der Vernunft: Komparatistische Studien zur Literatur der Aufklärung und des Fin-de-Siècle*, ed. by Hans Hinterhäuser, Michael Rössner, and Birgit Wagner (Vienna: Hermann Böhlaus Nachfolger, 1984), pp. 79–94

FALLOWS, NOEL, *Satire and Invective in Enlightened Spain: 'Crotalogía, o ciencia de las castañuelas' by Juan Fernández de Rojas* (Newark, DL: Juan de la Cuesta, 2001)

FAUSETT, DAVID, *Images of the Antipodes in the Eighteenth Century: A Study in Stereotyping* (Amsterdam: Rodopi, 1994)

—— *Writing the New World: Imaginary Voyages and Utopias of the Great Southern Land* (Syracuse, NY: Syracuse University Press, 1993)

FERGUSON, GEORGE, *Signs and Symbols in Christian Art* (New York: Oxford University Press, 1961)

FERNÁNDEZ SANZ, AMABLE, 'El último Olavide, ¿un ilustrado o un reaccionario?', in *Nuevos estudios sobre historia del pensamiento español: actas de las V Jornadas de Hispanismo Filosófico*, ed. by Antonio Jiménez García, Rafael V. Orden Jiménez, and Xavier Agenjo Bullón (Madrid: Fundación Ignacio Larramendi, Asociación de Hispanismo Filosófico, 2005), pp. 141–53

—— 'La utopía solucionista de Jovellanos', *El Basilisco*, 21 (1996), 25–27

—— 'Utopía y realidad en la Ilustración española: Pablo de Olavide y las "nuevas poblaciones"' (unpublished doctoral thesis, Universidad Complutense de Madrid, 1990)

FERNS, CHRIS, *Narrating Utopia: Ideology, Gender, Form in Utopian Literature* (Liverpool: Liverpool University Press, 1999)

FOUST, REBECCA A., '*Sinapia*: An Enlightened Ideal' (unpublished master's thesis, University of North Carolina at Chapel Hill, 1988)

FUENTES QUINTANA, ENRIQUE, ed., *Economía y economistas españoles*, 9 vols (Barcelona: Galaxia Gutenberg, 1999–2004), III: *La Ilustración* (2000)

GARCÍA-PANDAVENES, ELSA, '*El Censor* (1781–1787): A Study of an Essay Periodical of the Spanish Enlightenment' (unpublished doctoral thesis, University of California, Berkeley, 1970)

GAY, PETER, *The Enlightenment: An Interpretation*, 2 vols (London and New York: W. W. Norton, 1966–69), II: *The Science of Freedom* (1977)

GERSON, FREDERICK, *L'Amitié au XVIIIe siècle* (Paris: La Pensée Universelle, 1974)

GIL NOVALES, ALBERTO, 'Para los amigos de Cañuelo', *Cuadernos Hispanoamericanos*, 229 (1969), 291–323

GIMENO PUYOL, MARÍA DOLORES, '*Viaje al país de los Ayparchontes*: The Limits of a Spanish Utopia in the Eighteenth Century', in *Trans/Forming Utopia: The 'Small Thin Story'*, ed. by Elizabeth Russell (Bern and Oxford: Peter Lang, 2009), pp. 175–86

GLENDINNING, NIGEL, 'New Light on the Circulation of Cadalso's *Cartas marruecas* before its First Printing', *Hispanic Review*, 28 (1960), 136–49
—— 'Tendencias liberales en la literatura española a fines del siglo XVIII', *Dieciocho*, 9 (1986), 138–52
—— *Vida y obra de Cadalso* (Madrid: Gredos, 1962)
GÓMEZ COUTOULY, ALEX-ALBAN, 'Spanish Literary Utopias: *Omnibona* and *The Desired Government*', in *Nowhere Somewhere: Writing Space and the Construction of Utopia*, ed. by José Eduardo Reis (Porto: Universidade do Porto, 2006), pp. 71–85
GÓMEZ-TABANERA, JOSÉ, 'La *Sinapia*, una España imposible en el mundo austral o la forja de una utopía hispana en el siglo XVII', in *España y el Pacífico*, ed. by Antonio F. García-Abásolo (Cordova: Asociación Española de Estudios del Pacífico, 1997), pp. 121–34
GÓMEZ URDÁÑEZ, JOSÉ LUIS, *Fernando VI* (Madrid: Arlanza, 2001)
GÓMEZ URDÁÑEZ, JOSÉ LUIS, and DIEGO TÉLLEZ ALARCIA, 'Pablo de Olavide y Jáuregui, un católico ilustrado', *Brocar: Cuadernos de Investigación Histórica*, 28 (2004), 7–30
GONZÁLEZ HERNÁNDEZ, ÁNGEL, and JUAN SAEZ CARRERAS, '*Sinapia* o la Ispania utópica de la Ilustración: claro-oscuro de una polémica', in *Educación e Ilustración en España: III Coloquio de Historia de la Educación* (Barcelona: Universidad de Barcelona, 1984), pp. 90–100
GOVE, PHILIP BABCOCK, *The Imaginary Voyage in Prose Fiction* (London: Holland Press, 1961)
GUINARD, PAUL-JACQUES, *La Presse espagnole de 1737 à 1791: formation et signification d'un genre* (Paris: Centre de Recherches Hispaniques, Institut d'Études Hispaniques, 1973)
—— 'Remarques sur une grande revue espagnole du XVIIIe siècle: *El Censor* (1781–1787)', *Les Langues Néo-Latines*, 212 (1975), 90–105
—— 'Les Utopies en Espagne au XVIIIe siècle', in *Recherches sur le roman historique en Europe, XVIIIe–XIXe siècles*, 2 vols (Paris: Les Belles Lettres, 1977–79), I, ed. by Michel Apel-Muller (1977), pp. 171–202
GUTIÉRREZ NIETO, JUAN IGNACIO, 'El pensamiento económico, político y social de los arbitristas', in *Historia de España*, ed. by Ramón Menéndez Pidal and José María Jover Zamora, 42 vols (Madrid: Espasa-Calpe, 1935–2003), XXVI: *El siglo del Quijote (1580–1680): religión, filosofía, ciencia* (1986), pp. 233–351
HAFTER, MONROE Z., 'Toward a History of Spanish Imaginary Voyages', *Eighteenth-Century Studies*, 8 (1975), 265–82
HAYBRON, DANIEL M., *Happiness: A Very Short Introduction* (Oxford: Oxford University Press, 2013)
HELMAN, EDITH, *Trasmundo de Goya* (Madrid: Alianza, 1983)
HERMOSILLA MOLINA, ANTONIO, *Cien años de medicina sevillana: la Regia Sociedad de Medicina y Demás Ciencias, de Sevilla, en el siglo XVIII* (Seville: Diputación Provincial de Sevilla, 1970)
HERR, RICHARD, *The Eighteenth-Century Revolution in Spain* (Princeton, NJ: Princeton University Press, 1958)
HERRERO, JAVIER, *Los orígenes del pensamiento reaccionario español* (Madrid: Cuadernos para el Diálogo, 1971)
HIATT, ALFRED, '*Terra Australis* and the Idea of the Antipodes', in *European Perceptions of Terra Australis*, ed. by Anne M. Scott and others (Farnham, UK, and Burlington, VT: Ashgate, 2011), pp. 9–44
JACOBS, HELMUT C., 'Aspectos de la imagen utópica de España en la literatura española del siglo XVIII', in *Una de las dos Españas: representaciones de un conflicto identitario en la historia y en las literaturas hispánicas. Estudios reunidos en homenaje a Manfred Tietz*, ed. by Gero Arnscheidt and Pere Joan i Tous (Madrid: Iberoamericana; Frankfurt am Main: Vervuert, 2007), pp. 619–33

JAMESON, FREDRIC, *Archaeologies of the Future: The Desire Called Utopia and Other Science Fictions* (New York: Verso, 2005)
—— 'Of Islands and Trenches: Naturalization and the Production of Utopian Discourse', *Diacritics*, 7 (1977), 2–21
JOHNSON, JULIE GREER, *Satire in Colonial Spanish America: Turning the New World Upside Down* (Austin: University of Texas Press, 1993)
JUÁREZ SÁNCHEZ-RUBIO, CIPRIANO, and GREGORIO CANALES MARTÍNEZ, 'Colonización agraria y modelos de hábitat (siglos XVIII–XX)', *Agricultura y Sociedad*, 49 (1988), 333–52
KAMEN, HENRY, *Spain, 1469–1714: A Society of Conflict* (London and New York: Longman, 1983)
—— *Spain in the Later Seventeenth Century, 1665–1700* (London and New York: Longman, 1980)
—— *Vocabulario básico de la historia moderna*, trans. by Montserrat Iniesta (Barcelona: Crítica, 1986)
—— *The War of Succession in Spain, 1700–15* (London: Weidenfeld and Nicolson, 1969)
KEEN, BENJAMIN, and KEITH HAYNES, *A History of Latin America*, 2 vols (Boston, MA: Wadsworth/Cengage Learning, 2013), I: *Ancient America to 1910*
KIERNAN, SUZANNE, 'The Exotic and the Normative in *Viaggi di Enrico Wanton alle Terre Australi Incognite* by Zaccaria Seriman', *Eighteenth-Century Life*, 26 (2002), 58–77
KRAUSS, WERNER, 'Algunos aspectos de las teorías economistas españolas durante el siglo XVIII', *Cuadernos Hispanoamericanos*, 246 (1970), 572–84
KUMAR, KRISHAN, *Utopia and Anti-Utopia in Modern Times* (Oxford: Basil Blackwell, 1987)
—— *Utopianism* (Minneapolis: University of Minnesota Press, 1991)
KWAPISZ-WILLIAMS, KATARZYNA, 'Utopia of the Southern Land in Colonial Literary Imagination', *A Quarterly Magazine of Australia, New Zealand and Oceania Research Association*, 3 (2010), 41–58
LAFFRANQUE, MARIE, 'La *Descripción de la Sinapia, Península en la Tierra Austral*', in *La Contestation de la société dans la littérature espagnole du Siècle d'Or: actes de colloque de la R. C. P.*, ed. by Centre National de la Recherche Scientifique (Toulouse: Université de Toulouse–Le Mirail, 1981), pp. 193–204
LARUBIA-PRADO, FRANCISCO, '¿Una Ilustración *suficiente*? Mito, utopía y colonización interior en la España del siglo XVIII', *Bulletin of Hispanic Studies*, 76 (1999), 627–48
LEVITAS, RUTH, *The Concept of Utopia* (London: Philip Allan, 1990)
LLOMBART, VICENT, *Campomanes, economista y político de Carlos III* (Madrid: Alianza, 1992)
LLUCH, ERNEST, and LLUÍS ARGEMÍ I D'ABADAL, *Agronomía y fisiocracia en España (1750–1820)* (Valencia: Alfons el Magnànim, 1985)
LOGAN, GEORGE M., and ROBERT M. ADAMS, 'Introduction', in Thomas More, *Utopia*, ed. by George M. Logan and trans. by Robert M. Adams (Cambridge: Cambridge University Press, 2006), pp. xi–xxix
LOPE, HANS-JOACHIM, '¿Mal moral o necesidad económica? La polémica acerca del lujo en la Ilustración española', in *La secularización de la cultura española en el Siglo de las Luces: actas del Congreso de Wolfenbüttel*, ed. by Manfred Tietz and Dietrich Briesemeister (Wiesbaden: Harrassowitz, 1992), pp. 129–50
LOPEZ, FRANÇOIS, 'Une autre approche de *Sinapia*', in *Las utopías en el mundo hispánico: actas del coloquio celebrado en la Casa de Velázquez*, ed. by Jean-Pierre Étienvre (Madrid: Casa de Velázquez, Universidad Complutense, 1990), pp. 9–18
—— 'Considérations sur *La Sinapia*', in *La Contestation de la société dans la littérature espagnole du Siècle d'Or: actes de colloque de la R. C. P.*, ed. by Centre National de la Recherche Scientifique (Toulouse: Université de Toulouse–Le Mirail, 1981), pp. 205–11
—— 'Los novatores en la Europa de los sabios', *Studia Historica. Historia Moderna*, 14 (1996), 95–111
—— 'El pensamiento tradicionalista', in *Historia de España*, ed. by Ramón Menéndez Pidal

and José María Jover Zamora, 42 vols (Madrid: Espasa-Calpe, 1935–2003), XXXI: *La época de la Ilustración: el Estado y la cultura (1759–1808)* (1987), pp. 813–51

—— 'La resistencia a la Ilustración: bases sociales y medios de acción', in *Historia de España*, ed. by Ramón Menéndez Pidal and José María Jover Zamora, 42 vols (Madrid: Espasa-Calpe, 1935–2003), XXXI: *La época de la Ilustración: el Estado y la cultura (1759–1808)* (1987), pp. 767–812

—— 'Un sociodrama bajo el antiguo régimen: nuevo enfoque de un suceso zaragozano. El caso Normante', in *Actas del I Symposium del Seminario de Ilustración aragonesa*, ed. by María-Dolores Albiac Blanco (Zaragoza: Diputación General de Aragón, 1987), pp. 103–16

—— 'Una utopía española en busca de autor: *Sinapia*. Historia de una equivocación. Indicios para un acierto', *Anales de la Universidad de Alicante. Historia Moderna*, 2 (1982), 211–21

—— 'La vida intelectual en la España de los novatores', *Anejos de Dieciocho*, 1 (1997), 79–90

LÓPEZ ESTRADA, FRANCISCO, 'Más noticias sobre la *Sinapia* o *Utopía* española', *Moreana*, 4 (1977), 23–33

—— 'La primera versión española de la *Utopía* de Moro, por Jerónimo Antonio de Medinilla (Córdoba, 1637)', in *Collected Studies in Honour of Américo Castro's Eightieth Year*, ed. by Marcel P. Hornik (Oxford: Lincombe Lodge Research Library, 1965), pp. 291–309

—— *Tomás Moro y España: sus relaciones hasta el siglo XVIII* (Madrid: Universidad Complutense, 1980)

LORENZO ÁLVAREZ, ELENA DE, 'Literatura de viajes y utopías', in *Literatura española del siglo XVIII*, ed. by Alberto Romero Ferrer and Joaquín Álvarez Barrientos (Madrid: Liceus, 2005), pp. 1–21, ebook

—— 'La polémica sobre el lujo y *el noble inútil*', in Elena de Lorenzo Álvarez, *Nuevos mundos poéticos: la poesía filosófica de la Ilustración* (Oviedo: Instituto Feijoo de Estudios del Siglo XVIII, 2002), pp. 289–368

MACÍAS DELGADO, JACINTA, 'Estudio preliminar', in Miguel Antonio de la Gándara, *Apuntes sobre el bien y el mal de España*, ed. by Jacinta Macías Delgado (Madrid: Instituto de Estudios Fiscales, 1988), pp. xiii–clv

MANNHEIM, KARL, *Ideology and Utopia: An Introduction to the Sociology of Knowledge* (London: Routledge and Kegan Paul, 1936)

MANUEL, FRANK E., and FRITZIE P. MANUEL, *Utopian Thought in the Western World* (Cambridge, MA: Harvard University Press, 1979)

MARAVALL, JOSÉ ANTONIO, 'Las tendencias de reforma política en el siglo XVIII español', in José Antonio Maravall, *Estudios de la historia del pensamiento español (siglo XVIII)*, ed. by María del Carmen Iglesias (Madrid: Mondadori España, 1991), pp. 61–81

—— *Utopía y contrautopía en 'El Quijote'* (Madrid: Visor Libros, 2006)

—— *Utopía y reformismo en la España de los Austrias* (Madrid: Siglo Veintiuno de España, 1982)

MARCHENA FERNÁNDEZ, JUAN, *Pablo de Olavide: el espacio de la Ilustración y la reforma universitaria. Vida y obra de un ilustrado americano y español* (Seville: Junta de Andalucía, Universidad Pablo de Olavide, 2000)

—— *El tiempo ilustrado de Pablo de Olavide: vida, obra y sueños de un americano en la España del s. XVIII* (Seville: Alfar, 2001)

MARILUZ URQUIJO, JOSÉ M., 'Una utopía jurídica española del siglo XVIII', *Revista de Historia del Derecho*, 9 (1981), 303–33

MAROTO CAMINO, MERCEDES, *Exploring the Explorers: Spaniards in Oceania, 1519–1794* (Manchester: Manchester University Press, 2008)

MARTÍN GAITE, CARMEN, *Usos amorosos del XVIII en España* (Madrid: Siglo Veintiuno de España, 1972)

Martín Rodríguez, Manuel, *Pensamiento económico español sobre la población: de Soto a Matanegui* (Madrid: Pirámide, 1984)

Martínez García, José Carlos, 'Un catálogo de utopías de la Ilustración española', *Cuadernos de Ilustración y Romanticismo*, 14 (2006), 257–69

—— 'Historia de la literatura utópica española: las utopías de la Ilustración' (unpublished licenciatura thesis, Universidad de Salamanca, 2004)

Mattos-Cárdenas, Leonardo, 'Olavide y el urbanismo', in *Actas de las VII Jornadas de Andalucía y América*, 2 vols (Seville: Junta de Andalucía, 1990), I, pp. 109–34

Menéndez Pelayo, Marcelino, *Historia de los heterodoxos españoles*, 8 vols (Buenos Aires: Emecé, 1945), VI

Mercier, Claire, 'De la alegoría de las aves en *Tratado sobre la monarquía columbina*, del padre Andrés Merino de Jesucristo', *Visitas al Patio*, 5 (2011), 103–19

Montesinos, José F., *Introducción a una historia de la novela en España en el siglo XIX* (Valencia: Castalia, 1972)

Morange, Claude, 'Variations sur un thème: le monde rural dans le *Suplemento [...] de los viages de Enrique Wanton* (1778)', in *Les Voies des Lumières: le monde ibérique au XVIIIe siècle*, ed. by Carlos Serrano, Jean-Paul Duviols, and Annie Molinié (Paris: Presses de l'Université de Paris-Sorbonne, 1998), pp. 79–111

Morel-Fatio, Alfred, *Études sur l'Espagne*, 4 vols (Paris: Édouard Champion, 1888–1925), IV (1925)

Moylan, Tom, *Demand the Impossible: Science Fiction and the Utopian Imagination* (London and New York: Methuen, 1986)

Mumford, Lewis, *The Story of Utopias: Ideal Commonwealths and Social Myths* (London: Harrap, 1923)

Muñoz Pérez, José, 'Los proyectos sobre España e Indias en el siglo XVIII: el proyectismo como género', *Revista de Estudios Políticos*, 81 (1955), 169–95

Navarro Domínguez, Eloy, 'Relaciones de viajes y ficción novelesca en la *Descripción de la Sinapia*', in *Utopía: los espacios imposibles*, ed. by Rosa García Gutiérrez, Valentín Núñez Rivera, and Eloy Navarro Domínguez (Frankfurt am Main: Peter Lang, 2003), pp. 131–46

Neal, Thomas Cassidy, *Writing the Americas in Enlightenment Spain: Literature, Modernity, and the New World, 1773–1812* (Lewisburg, PA: Bucknell University Press, 2017)

Nieva de la Paz, Pilar, 'El arte de cultivar la razón o descripción del establecimiento de la colonia de Ponthiamas: un texto utópico traducido del francés en el siglo XVIII', in *Las utopías en el mundo hispánico: actas del coloquio celebrado en la Casa de Velázquez*, ed. by Jean-Pierre Étienvre (Madrid: Casa de Velázquez, Universidad Complutense, 1990), pp. 79–94

Noel, Charles C., 'Clerics and Crown in Bourbon Spain, 1700–1808: Jesuits, Jansenists, and Enlightened Reformers', in *Religion and Politics in Enlightenment Europe*, ed. by James E. Bradley and Dale K. Van Kley (Notre Dame, IN: University of Notre Dame Press, 2001), pp. 119–53

Núñez, Estuardo, 'Biografía de un inquietador', in Pablo de Olavide y Jáuregui, *Obras selectas*, ed. by Estuardo Núñez (Lima: Banco de Crédito del Perú, 1987), pp. xi–xxxiv

—— '*El Evangelio en triunfo* y su texto censurado', in Pablo de Olavide y Jáuregui, *Obras selectas*, ed. by Estuardo Núñez (Lima: Banco de Crédito del Perú, 1987), pp. xcii–xciv

—— *El nuevo Olavide: una semblanza a través de sus textos ignorados* (Lima: P. L. Villanueva, 1970)

—— 'La reforma agraria', in Pablo de Olavide y Jáuregui, *Obras selectas*, ed. by Estuardo Núñez (Lima: Banco de Crédito del Perú, 1987), pp. xciv–xcvii

Ortega y Gasset, José, 'El siglo XVIII, educador', in José Ortega y Gasset, *Obras completas*, 12 vols (Madrid: Revista de Occidente, 1946–83), II: *El espectador (1916–1934)* (1946), pp. 599–601

―――, *El tema de nuestro tiempo* (Madrid: Tecnos, 2002)
PAGDEN, ANTHONY, *The Enlightenment: And Why It Still Matters* (Oxford: Oxford University Press, 2015)
PAJARES INFANTE, ETERIO, *La traducción de la novela inglesa del siglo XVIII* (Vitoria: Portal Education, 2010)
PALACIOS FERNÁNDEZ, EMILIO, 'El Padre Andrés Merino de Jesucristo y la cultura española del siglo XVIII', *Boletín de la Real Sociedad Bascongada de los Amigos del País*, 47 (1991), 3–42
PAQUETTE, GABRIEL B., *Enlightenment, Governance, and Reform in Spain and its Empire, 1759–1808* (Basingstoke: Palgrave Macmillan, 2008)
PASTOR, BEATRIZ, *Discurso narrativo de la conquista de América: ensayo* (Havana: Casa de las Américas, 1983)
PERDICES BLAS, LUIS, 'El desarrollo intelectual de Jovellanos en la Sevilla de Olavide (1768–1776)', *Dieciocho*, 36 (2013), 51–78
―――, *Pablo de Olavide (1725–1803), el ilustrado* (Madrid: Complutense, 1992)
PÉREZ MAGALLÓN, JESÚS, *Construyendo la modernidad: la cultura española en el 'tiempo de los novatores' (1675–1725)* (Madrid: Consejo Superior de Investigaciones Científicas, Instituto de la Lengua Española, 2002)
PÉREZ-REY, JORGE, 'Sinapia, una utopía en el mundo hispánico del siglo XVIII: la imagen especular invertida de la nación real', in *Communautés nationales et marginalité dans le monde ibérique et ibéro-américain* (Tours: Université de Tours, 1981), pp. 49–57
PIMENTEL, JUAN, *Testigos del mundo: ciencia, literatura y viajes en la Ilustración* (Madrid: Marcial Pons, 2003)
PIÑERA TARQUE, ISMAEL, 'Retórica de la ficción utópica: del género al texto en torno al siglo XVIII español', *Cuadernos de Estudios del Siglo XVIII*, 12–13 (2003), 137–65
POHL, NICOLE, 'Utopianism after More: The Renaissance and Enlightenment', in *The Cambridge Companion to Utopian Literature*, ed. by Gregory Claeys (Cambridge: Cambridge University Press, 2010), pp. 51–78
PORTILLO VALDÉS, JOSÉ M., 'Los límites de la monarquía: catecismo de Estado y constitución política en España a finales del siglo XVIII', *Quaderni Fiorentini*, 25 (1996), 183–263
RAMIRO AVILÉS, MIGUEL ÁNGEL, 'Sinapia, A Political Journey to the Antipodes of Spain', in *Utopian Moments: Reading Utopian Texts*, ed. by Miguel Ángel Ramiro Avilés and J. C. Davis (London: Bloomsbury Academic, 2012), pp. 80–85
REES, CHRISTINE, *Utopian Imagination and Eighteenth-Century Fiction* (London and New York: Longman, 1996)
REY PEREIRA, CARLOS, 'El Paraíso en el Nuevo Mundo. Entre el ejemplo y la excepción', *Cuadernos para Investigación de la Literatura Hispánica*, 29 (2004), 141–59
RICŒUR, PAUL, 'Civilisation universelle et cultures nationales', in Paul Ricœur, *Histoire et vérité* (Paris: Seuil, 1964), pp. 274–88
RODRÍGUEZ CASADO, VICENTE, 'El intento español de "Ilustración Cristiana"', *Estudios Americanos*, 9 (1955), 141–69
ROURA I AULINAS, LLUÍS, 'Expectativas y frustración bajo el reformismo borbónico', in *Historia de España, siglo XVIII: la España de los Borbones*, ed. by Ricardo García Cárcel (Madrid: Cátedra, 2002), pp. 167–221
RUEDA, ANA, *Cartas sin lacrar: la novela epistolar y la España ilustrada, 1789–1840* (Madrid: Iberoamericana; Frankfurt am Main: Vervuert, 2001)
RUS RUFINO, SALVADOR, 'Evolución de la noción de derecho natural en la Ilustración española', *Cuadernos Dieciochistas*, 2 (2001), 229–59
RUYER, RAYMOND, *L'Utopie et les utopies* (Paris: Presses Universitaires de France, 1950)
SAMBRICIO, CARLOS, 'Sinapia: utopía, territorio y ciudad a finales del siglo XVIII', *Scripta Nova: Revista Electrónica de Geografía y Ciencias Sociales*, 18 (2014), <http://www.ub.es/geocrit/sn/sn-475.htm> [accessed 12 August 2015]

——'*Sinapia*: Utopia, Territory, and City at the End of the Eighteenth Century', in *Views on Eighteenth-Century Culture: Design, Books and Ideas*, ed. by Leonor Ferrão and Luís Manuel A. V. Bernardo (Newcastle-upon-Tyne: Cambridge Scholars Publishing, 2015), pp. 44–77

SÁNCHEZ AGESTA, LUIS, *El pensamiento político del despotismo ilustrado* (Madrid: Instituto de Estudios Políticos, 1953)

SÁNCHEZ-BLANCO, FRANCISCO, *El absolutismo y las Luces en el reinado de Carlos III* (Madrid: Marcial Pons, 2002)

——'*El Censor*': un periódico contra el Antiguo Régimen (Seville: Alfar, 2016)

——*La Ilustración en España* (Madrid: Akal, 1997)

——*La mentalidad ilustrada* (Madrid: Taurus, 1999)

SANTOS PUERTO, JOSÉ, *Martín Sarmiento: Ilustración, educación y utopía en la España del siglo XVIII*, 2 vols (La Coruña: Fundación Pedro Barrié de la Maza, 2002), II

——'La *Sinapia*: luces para buscar la utopía de la Ilustración', *Bulletin Hispanique*, 103 (2001), 481–510

SARGENT, LYMAN TOWER, 'Colonial and Postcolonial Utopias', in *The Cambridge Companion to Utopian Literature*, ed. by Gregory Claeys (Cambridge: Cambridge University Press, 2010), pp. 200–22

——*Utopianism: A Very Short Introduction* (Oxford: Oxford University Press, 2010)

SARRAILH, JEAN, *L'Espagne éclairée de la seconde moitié du XVIIIe siècle* (Paris: Imprimerie Nationale, 1954)

SCHMIDT-NOWARA, CHRISTOPHER, *The Conquest of History: Spanish Colonialism and National Histories in the Nineteenth Century* (Pittsburgh, PA: University of Pittsburgh Press, 2008)

SHAFER, ROBERT JONES, *The Economic Societies in the Spanish World (1763–1821)* (Syracuse, NY: Syracuse University Press, 1958)

SHKLAR, JUDITH, 'The Political Theory of Utopia: From Melancholy to Nostalgia', in *Utopias and Utopian Thought*, ed. by Frank E. Manuel (London: Souvenir Press, 1973), pp. 101–15

SKINNER, QUENTIN, *Visions of Politics*, 3 vols (Cambridge: Cambridge University Press, 2002), II: *Renaissance Virtues*

SMIDT, ANDREA J., 'Luces por la fe: The Cause of Catholic Enlightenment in 18th-Century Spain', in *A Companion to the Catholic Enlightenment in Europe*, ed. by Ulrich L. Lehner and Michael Printy (Leiden: Brill, 2010), pp. 403–52

STIFFONI, GIOVANNI, 'Considerazioni su di una possibile storia dell'utopia nella Spagna del Sei-Settecento', in *Un 'hombre de bien': saggi di lingue e letterature iberiche in onore di Rinaldo Froldi*, ed. by Patrizia Garelli and Giovanni Marchetti, 2 vols (Alessandria: Edizioni dell'Orso, 2004), II, pp. 577–87

SUVIN, DARKO, *Defined by a Hollow: Essays on Utopia, Science Fiction and Political Epistemology* (Bern and Oxford: Peter Lang, 2010)

TOMSICH, MARÍA GIOVANNA, *El jansenismo en España: estudio sobre ideas religiosas en la segunda mitad del siglo XVIII* (Madrid: Siglo Veintiuno de España, 1972)

TORRECILLA, JESÚS, 'El tiempo y los márgenes: utopía y conciencia de atraso', in Jesús Torrecilla, *El tiempo y los márgenes: Europa como utopía y como amenaza en la literatura española* (Chapel Hill: University of North Carolina, Department of Romance Languages, 1996), pp. 19–52

TROUSSON, RAYMOND, *Voyages aux pays de nulle part: histoire littéraire de la pensée utopique* (Brussels: Éditions de l'Université de Bruxelles, 1999)

URZAINQUI, INMACULADA, 'Diálogo entre periodistas (1737–1770)', in *Francisco Mariano Nipho: el nacimiento de la prensa y de la crítica literaria periodística en la España del siglo XVIII*, ed. by José María Maestre Maestre, Manuel Antonio Díaz Gito, and Alberto Romero

Ferrer (Alcañiz: Instituto de Estudios Humanísticos; Madrid: Consejo Superior de Investigaciones Científicas, 2015), pp. 375–418

—— 'Un nuevo instrumento cultural: la prensa periódica', in Joaquín Álvarez Barrientos, François Lopez, and Inmaculada Urzainqui, *La república de las letras en la España del siglo XVIII* (Madrid: Consejo Superior de Investigaciones Científicas, 1995), pp. 125–216

VALDEZ, MARÍA LASTENIA, 'Fernando Savater y el género utópico en España: de *Sinapia* (siglo XVII) a *Vente a Sinapia* (siglo XX)', in *Actas del XV Congreso de la Asociación Internacional de Hispanistas 'Las dos orillas'*, ed. by Beatriz Mariscal and María Teresa Miaja de la Peña, 4 vols (Mexico City: Fondo de Cultura Económica, 2007), III, pp. 417–25

VALIS, NOËL, *Sacred Realism: Religion and the Imagination in Modern Spanish Narrative* (New Haven, CT: Yale University Press, 2010)

VALLE, ENID M., 'La estructura narrativa de *El Evangelio en triunfo* de Pablo de Olavide y Jáuregui', in *Pen and Peruke: Spanish Literature of the Eighteenth Century*, ed. by Monroe Z. Hafter (Ann Arbor: University of Michigan, 1992), pp. 135–51

VARDI, LIANA, *The Physiocrats and the World of the Enlightenment* (New York: Cambridge University Press, 2012)

VARELA SEPÚLVEDA, CAROLINA, 'La Ilustración europea: el racionalismo de las letras en el siglo XVIII. Utopías en la España del siglo XVIII: *Sinapia* y el expansionismo holandés' (unpublished *licenciatura* thesis, Universidad de Chile, 2007), <http://www.repositorio.uchile.cl/tesis/uchile/2007/varela_c/html/index-frames.html> [accessed 3 November 2015]

VENTURI, FRANCO, *Utopia and Reform in the Enlightenment* (London: Cambridge University Press, 1971)

VIEIRA, FÁTIMA, 'The Concept of Utopia', in *The Cambridge Companion to Utopian Literature*, ed. by Gregory Claeys (Cambridge: Cambridge University Press, 2010), pp. 3–27

VILAR, JEAN, *Literatura y economía: la figura satírica del arbitrista en el Siglo de Oro* (Madrid: Revista de Occidente, 1973)

VILLASEÑOR, RAÚL, 'Luciano, Moro y el utopismo de Vasco de Quiroga', *Cuadernos Americanos*, 68 (1953), 155–75

WALKER, CHARLES F., *Shaky Colonialism: The 1746 Earthquake-Tsunami in Lima, Peru, and its Long Aftermath* (Durham, NC: Duke University Press, 2008)

WHITE, DONALD MAXWELL, *Zaccaria Seriman (1709–1784) and the 'Viaggi di Enrico Wanton': A Contribution to the Study of the Enlightenment in Italy* (Manchester: Manchester University Press, 1961)

WYNTER, SYLVIA, 'A Utopia from the Semi-Periphery: Spain, Modernization, and the Enlightenment', review of Stelio Cro, ed., *'Descripción de la Sinapia, península en la tierra austral': A Classical Utopia of Spain* (1975), *Science Fiction Studies*, 6 (1979), 100–07

ZAVALA, IRIS M., 'Utopía y astrología en la literatura popular del setecientos: los almanaques de Torres Villarroel', *Nueva Revista de Filología Hispánica*, 33 (1984), 196–212

ZAVALA, SILVIO, *Recuerdo de Vasco de Quiroga* (Mexico City: Porrúa, 1987)

—— *Sir Thomas More in New Spain: A Utopian Adventure of the Renaissance* (London: Hispanic and Luso-Brazilian Councils, 1955)

INDEX

Abellán, José Luis 5–6, 29, 38, 83 n. 9, 186 n. 48
Aguilar Piñal, Francisco 6, 103, 143
Alcázar Molina, Cayetano 166
Alembert, Jean le Rond d' 137
Almeida, Teodoro de 152
Álvarez Barrientos, Joaquín 96–97
Álvarez de Miranda, Pedro 2, 5–6, 61–62, 103, 143–44,
    151–52, 154–55, 157, 161 n. 4, 162 n. 49
Andreae, Johann Valentin:
    Christianopolis 23, 82
Aristophanes 16, 158
Aristotle 11 n. 29, 87, 137
Arroyal, León de 40–41, 161 n. 3
Arthur, Paul Longley 26 n. 12
Augustine, St:
    The City of God 24, 85 n. 51
Avilés Fernández, Miguel 12 n. 43, 59–61, 80–81,
    83 nn. 5, 7, 8 & 9, 85 nn. 28 & 34

Bacon, Francis 24, 32, 59, 64, 66, 77, 80, 187 n. 79, 190
    New Atlantis 22, 47, 63, 65, 76, 79, 86 n. 74, 152, 154
Baczko, Bronisław 24
Baker-Smith, Dominic 17
Baquero, Ana L. 148
Baquero Goyanes, Mariano 36
Benítez, Miguel 168
Bernabéu Albert, Salvador 6
Bloch, Ernst 34, 171, 173
Bowden, Brett 96
Buffon, Georges-Louis Leclerc, Count of 30, 115 n. 13,
    162 n. 44

Cabriada, Juan de 39
Cadalso, José de 1, 6–7, 11 n. 35, 48, 88, 104, 136,
    140 n. 22, 141 n. 67
Calatayud Soler, Rosa 187 n. 64
Calvo Carilla, José Luis 4
Campanella, Tommaso 24, 59, 64–65, 68, 148, 159,
    187 n. 79, 190
    La Città del Sole 23, 63, 77, 146, 161 n. 11, 162 n. 40
    Monarchia di Spagna 148
Campillo, José del 40, 42
Campomanes, Pedro Rodríguez, Count of 40–45, 48,
    54 n. 76, 59–61, 164–66, 173, 180
Cañas Murillo, Jesús 7
Carlos II 41, 45, 61–62

Carlos III 5, 39–40, 42, 44, 46, 113, 125–26, 131, 152,
    160, 163, 165, 175, 187 n. 78, 189, 194
Caro Baroja, Julio 164
Carrasco M., Rolando 175
Casas, Bartolomé de las 31–32
Caso González, José Miguel 10 n. 7, 120, 131, 136,
    139 n. 16
Cejudo López, Jorge 59
censorship 28, 45, 151
    authorial anonymity 2, 7–8, 31, 59–61, 63, 65, 68,
        70, 104, 119–23, 131, 135, 143, 168, 191–92
    Council of Castile 41, 119, 122, 141 n. 67, 172
    pseudonymity 11 n. 25, 47, 105, 120, 152, 184 n. 13
    Spanish Inquisition 5, 8, 37, 41, 44, 48, 53 n. 54, 78,
        129, 131, 133, 148, 178, 191, 193
Chateaubriand, François-René de 169
Cioranescu, Alexandre 26 n. 29
Clavijo y Fajardo, José 46, 162 n. 44
Colmeiro, Manuel 34
Columbus, Christopher 16, 20, 29, 148
Correa Calderón, Evaristo 36
Cro, Stelio 4, 8, 30–31, 59–62, 65, 71–72, 83 nn. 4, 8
    & 9, 85 nn. 28 & 51, 171
Curtius, Ernst Robert 25 n. 4
Cyrano de Bergerac, Savinien 3, 88, 158, 162 n. 46

Davis, J. C. 25
Defourneaux, Marcelin 165–66, 179, 183 n. 1
Descartes, René 80
Diderot, Denis 117 n. 72, 137, 183 n. 7
Don Quixote 31, 51 n. 13, 62
Dryden, John 51 n. 32
Dufour, Gérard 163, 171–72, 178–79, 183, 183 n. 4,
    188 n. 99

Elliott, Robert C. 16
Elorza, Antonio 55 n. 110, 127
Emieux, Annick 5, 11 n. 27
Enlightenment, the:
    anti-Enlightenment 5, 9, 44, 143, 152, 160
    Bourbon reformism 41–45, 49–50, 180, 185 n. 30
    Catholic Enlightenment 48–49, 185 n. 38
    Encyclopédie méthodique 44, 137
    and the French *philosophes* 33
Escobar, José 88, 95, 97–98, 103, 108, 111–12, 117 n. 68

fable 4, 9, 98, 144, 160, 190, 193
Feijoo, Benito Jerónimo 61, 88, 141 n. 55
Felipe III 148
Felipe V 41, 81
Fénelon, François 11 n. 36
Fernández de Rojas, Juan 11 n. 25
Fernández Sanz, Amable 36, 168, 186 n. 48
Fernando VI 40, 43, 54 n. 86, 173
Ferns, Chris 20–21
Foigny, Gabriel de 91
Forner, Juan Pablo 138, 142 n. 75
French Revolution 22, 48, 168–69, 177

Gándara, Miguel Antonio de la 40
García del Cañuelo, Luis 46, 120–21, 131–32
Gatell i Carnicer, Pedro 3
Gay, Peter 45
Gil Novales, Alberto 120
Gimeno Puyol, María Dolores 133, 139 n. 16
Glendinning, Nigel 161 n. 3
Godoy, Manuel 172
Goldsmith, Oliver 115 n. 32
Gómez-Tabanera, José 84 n. 20
Gómez Urdáñez, José Luis 40, 42, 185 n. 33
good savage, myth of the 9, 33–34, 51 n. 32, 123, 147, 194
  see also Montaigne, Michel de; Rousseau, Jean-Jacques
Gove, Philip Babcock 97, 103
Goya, Francisco de 139 n. 15
Guinard, Paul-Jacques 4–6, 47, 132–33
Gutiérrez Nieto, Juan Ignacio 35–36

Hafter, Monroe Z. 4–6
Harrington, James 22
Herr, Richard 46–47, 131
Herrero, Javier 175, 180
Hobbes, Thomas 159

Iriarte, Tomás de 4

Jacobs, Helmut C. 7
Jameson, Fredric 21, 52 n. 36, 73
Jansenism 49, 131–32, 185 n. 38
Jesuit *reducciones* 8–9, 31, 33, 71–72, 192
Jovellanos, Gaspar Melchor de 5, 36, 40, 45, 48, 86 n. 63, 111, 120, 156, 162 n. 36, 167, 173, 185 n. 30, 186 n. 48

Kamen, Henry 35, 41
Kant, Immanuel 115 n. 11, 133, 185 n. 29
Kiernan, Suzanne 98
Kumar, Krishan 24, 27 n. 55
Kwapisz-Williams, Katarzyna 186 n. 47

Laffranque, Marie 64

La Fontaine, Jean de 125, 140 n. 24
Lamourette, Antoine-Adrien 169
Larra, Mariano José de 114 n. 5
León Pinelo, Antonio de 29–31
Levitas, Ruth 22, 25, 27 n. 47
Lopez, François 38, 60–62, 83 n. 9
López Estrada, Francisco 3–4, 83 n. 9
Lorenzo Álvarez, Elena de 6, 97
Lucian 32

Macanaz, Melchor de 7, 41, 54 n. 83, 73
Magallón, Jesús Pérez 38
Mannheim, Karl 23
Maravall, José Antonio 28, 36, 51 n. 13, 163
Marchena, José 5, 120
Marchena Fernández, Juan 184 nn. 19 & 25
Marqués y Espejo, Antonio 3
Martí, Manuel 61
Martínez García, José Carlos 6
Masson de Morvilliers, Nicolas 44, 137–38
Mattos-Cárdenas, Leonardo 180
Mayans y Siscar, Gregorio 60–61
Medinilla y Porres, Jerónimo Antonio de 36–37
Medrano de Sandoval, Joaquín 121
Mercier, Claire 147, 158
Merino de Jesucristo, Andrés:
  Monarquía de los leones 159
  La mujer feliz, dependiente del mundo y de la fortuna 7, 152–53, 159
Mesonero Romanos, Ramón de 114 n. 5
Mirabeau, Victor de Riqueti, Marquis of 93, 97, 167, 173, 176
Montaigne, Michel de 115 n. 21
  Essais:
    'Des cannibales' 16, 33, 92
Montengón, Pedro 2
Montesinos, José F. 103
Montesquieu, Charles-Louis de Secondat, Baron of 136–37, 140 n. 23
Morange, Claude 104, 111
More, Thomas:
  Utopia, see Spanish utopianism; utopia
Morel-Fatio, Alfred 168
Morelly, Étienne-Gabriel 16
Moylan, Tom 24
Mumford, Lewis 22
Muñoz, Juan Bautista 30
Muñoz Pérez, José 39

Navarro Domínguez, Eloy 84 n. 24, 85 n. 31
Nebrija, Antonio de 81
Nieva de la Paz, Pilar 12 n. 43
Núñez, Estuardo 184 n. 13

Olavide y Jáuregui, Pablo de:
  and the Lima earthquake 164

and physiocracy 167, 176
  prosecuted by the Spanish Inquisition 168, 183 n. 7, 185 n. 33
  and the Sierra Morena settlement project 3, 6, 9, 43, 45, 163–66, 171, 176, 178, 182, 186 n. 48, 193
Omnibona 7, 12 n. 43
Ortega y Gasset, José 52 n. 49, 54 n. 97

Palanco, Francisco 38
Peramás, José Manuel 33
Percival, Anthony 88, 95, 98, 103, 108, 111–12, 117 n. 68
Perdices Blas, Luis 171–73, 186 n. 51
Pereira, Luis Marcelino 46, 120, 132
Pérez-Rey, Jorge 75
Piñera Tarque, Ismael 4, 127
Plato 22–23, 31, 65
  allegory of the cave 148, 161 n. 16
  Republic 15, 33, 68, 186 n. 46
Pohl, Nicole 20
Pope, Alexander 90, 113
Portillo Valdés, José 134

Quevedo, Francisco de 36, 105, 115 n. 21
Quiroga, Vasco de 31–32, 51 n. 18

Ramiro Avilés, Miguel Ángel 61, 73
Rasilla, José 186 n. 43
readership 24, 37, 47, 52 n. 36, 59, 64–65, 73, 95–96, 103, 105–07, 114, 115 n. 7, 116 n. 66, 122–23, 128, 130, 139, 145, 156, 160, 189–94
regalism 41, 49, 132
Rejón y Lucas, Diego Ventura 2
Ricœur, Paul 94
Rousseau, Jean-Jacques 34, 51 n. 32, 179
Rubín de Celis, Manuel 47, 120, 135
Rueda, Ana 173, 175
Ruyer, Raymond 23

Sánchez-Blanco, Francisco 131, 133–34
Santos Puerto, José 61
Sargent, Lyman Tower 21
Sarmiento, Martín 61
Sarrailh, Jean 168
Savater, Fernando 61
Sempere y Guarinos, Juan 46–47, 120
Seriman, Zaccaria 4, 8, 87–88, 97–98, 100, 103–07, 109–10, 113, 114 nn. 3 & 7, 116 n. 63, 119, 144, 192
Skinner, Quentin 18
Smidt, Andrea 49, 185 n. 38
Spanish apologists 44, 137–38
Spanish Black Legend 30, 50 n. 10
Spanish Church 5, 9, 40–44, 46–50, 122, 129–32, 134, 138, 141 n. 38, 156, 167, 185 n. 38, 192–94
Spanish economic societies 39, 43–48, 50, 60, 173, 180, 187 n. 55

Spanish nobility 9, 40–44, 46, 48, 50, 74, 132–33, 136, 138, 140 nn. 20, 22 & 29, 155, 192, 194
Spanish periodical press 1, 3, 5–6, 46–47, 102, 135, 137, 143, 192
  El Apologista Universal 120
  El Censor:
    governmental suspensions 119–22
    influenced by *The Spectator* 119
    see also García del Cañuelo, Luis; Pereira, Luis Marcelino
  Correo de Madrid 2, 140 n. 22, 143
  El Corresponsal del Censor 5, 47, 120, 135–36, 143
    see also Rubín de Celis, Manuel
  Diario de Madrid 116 n. 66
  Gaceta de Madrid 114 n. 7, 116 n. 59, 186 n. 43
  El Observador 5, 120
    see also Marchena, José
  and pamphlets 47, 139 n. 11
  El Pensador 46–47, 88, 120
    see also Clavijo y Fajardo, José
  Semanario Erudito 2, 143, 160 n. 1, 161 n. 4
    see also Valladares de Sotomayor, Antonio
Spanish utopianism:
  Catholic/Christian utopia 8, 50, 60, 66, 72
  empirical/experimental/practical utopia 1, 4, 21–23, 28, 30–32, 34, 37, 164, 171, 189, 193
  pre-utopian thinkers:
    arbitristas 8, 34–42, 52 n. 36
    novatores 8, 9 n. 1, 38–39, 43, 59, 61–62, 195
    proyectistas 8, 39–40, 42, 50, 155
    see also Arroyal, León de; Cabriada, Juan de; Campillo, José del; Gándara, Miguel Antonio de la; Ward, Bernardo
Suvin, Darko 23–24
Swift, Jonathan 16, 105, 192
  Gulliver's Travels 87–91, 97, 99, 111, 113–14, 114 n. 7, 162 n. 46, 191

Tasman, Abel 62–65, 87, 192
Téllez Alarcia, Diego 185 n. 33
tertulia 39, 45, 107, 185 n. 25
Thürriegel, Johann Kaspar von 165
Torrecilla, Jesús 4
Torres Villarroel, Diego de 52 n. 36, 60
Traggia, Joaquín:
  Eudamonopeia 5, 11 n. 27
  see also Emieux, Annick
Trigueros, Cándido María 6
Trousson, Raymond 21, 23, 25 n. 2

Urquijo, José Mariluz 136
Urzainqui, Imaculada 46
utopia:
  categories:
    abstract utopia 6, 23, 51 n. 33, 171
    astrological utopia 52 n. 36

concrete utopia 3, 6, 34, 36, 51 n. 33, 171
critical utopia 24, 173
literary utopia 1, 4, 6, 9, 15–16, 20, 25, 27 n. 47,
    31, 36, 73, 85 n. 51, 164, 189–90, 194
micro-utopias 4
utopia of escape 22
utopia of reconstruction 22
related concepts:
    authoritarianism 21, 81, 144, 150, 160, 176, 194
    civilization versus barbarism 9, 21, 90, 102, 111,
        138, 147, 177, 194
    colonialism 8, 20–22, 171, 186 n. 47, 194
    reformism 1, 7, 9, 25, 28, 31, 35–45, 48–49, 60,
        113, 119, 121, 126, 133, 136, 139, 160, 163,
        173, 182–83, 184 n. 25, 189, 193, 195
    satire 4, 8, 11 n. 25, 16, 32, 87–89, 94–99, 101–05,
        107–09, 113–14, 119, 126, 128, 140 n. 22,
        158, 160, 161 n. 3, 190–94
    science fiction 15
    utopian socialism 22, 27 n. 43
    utopianism 1–2, 7–9, 20, 22, 25, 26 n. 29, 28, 31,
        33–36, 50, 83, 85 n. 51, 163, 169, 172, 183,
        186 n. 48, 189, 193, 195
    xenophobia 21, 154, 171, 194
utopian traditions:
    Arcadia 15–16, 157, 164

earthly paradise 2, 15–16, 25 n. 4, 29–30, 164
Golden Age 15–17, 32–33, 157
New World [America] 8, 16, 20, 28–32, 37, 64,
    92, 146, 148, 170, 189, 194
Terra Australis Incognita 16, 62, 87, 89, 98,
    114 nn. 1 & 4, 119
Uzcanga Meinecke, Francisco 10 n. 6, 133

Vaca de Guzmán, Gutierre Joaquín:
    and *costumbrismo* 88, 97, 114 n. 5
    see also Seriman, Zaccaria; Swift, Jonathan
Valis, Noël 175, 180
Valladares de Sotomayor, Antonio 143, 151
Varela Sepúlveda, Carolina 84 n. 10
Venturi, Franco 55 n. 102
Vespucci, Amerigo 20
Vieira, Fátima 20, 23
Vilar, Jean 34
Voltaire [François-Marie Arouet] 72, 136, 181

Walker, Charles F. 183 n. 8
Ward, Bernardo 40–41, 173
White, Donald Maxwell 103

Zavala, Iris M. 52 n. 36
Zavala, Silvio 32

www.ingramcontent.com/pod-product-compliance
Lightning Source LLC
LaVergne TN
LVHW061250060426
835507LV00017B/2001